IPL BO
TRAINCA

Colin Taylor was born of missionary parents in Nigeria in 1928 and grew up in Yorkshire. He has been a lifelong rail enthusiast and spends as much time as he can travelling on trains. Since migrating to Australia he has travelled over 200,000 km on its railway systems. He has produced numerous articles and spoken at seminars and on radio on the fascination of railways. He is the author of the books *Great Rail Non-Journeys of Australia* (QUP, 1986), *Australia by Rail* (Bradt, 1988, 1992) and *Steel Roads of Australia* (IPL, 1991).

A chartered Town Planner until retirement, Colin Taylor is a Fellow of the Royal Australian Town Planning Institute, The Royal Town Planning Institute and the Chartered Institute of Transport.

This book is dedicated to all those railway workers of whatever grade who are dedicated to their job and have tried to maintain a service in spite of the sometimes total lack of support of their bosses and the abuse of their users including travellers like me.

TRAIN CATCHER

ADVENTURES OF A RAIL TRAVELLER

COLIN TAYLOR
FOREWORD BY IAN McNAMARA

First published in 1996
in Australia and New Zealand by:

IPL Books
9 Cooper Street
Smithfield, NSW 2164
Australia

and

P.O. Box 10-215
Wellington
New Zealand

All Rights Reserved

Copyright © 1996 Colin Taylor

ISBN 0-908876-94-7

Pre-press production by IPL Publishing Services, Wellington, NZ
Printed by HarperCollins Publishers, Hong Kong

Cover photo: The author prepares for the experience of the *Gulflander* between Normanton and Croydon in Queensland.
Back cover photo: A slight contrast – Sweden's X-2000. (Statens Järnvägar)

Frontispiece: The launch of *Great Rail Non-Journeys of Australia* in 1986.
Title page: The *Alice* stops for the author at The Gorge.

Contents

Foreword		8
Introduction		9
Chapter 1 —	Eurail Odyssey	13
Chapter 2 —	A Happy Wanderer	41
Chapter 3 —	Finding the Station	63
Chapter 4 —	Going Troppo	86
Chapter 5 —	Passenger Fare	96
Chapter 6 —	Great Rail Non-Connections	117
Chapter 7 —	The Train that Died of Shame	131
Chapter 8 —	Legendary Journeys	143
Chapter 9 —	Slow Train to Biloela	169
Chapter 10 —	Through Irish Eyes	179
Chapter 11 —	Britrail Revisited	193
Chapter 12 —	Food for Thought	211
Chapter 13 —	The Long Straight	234
Chapter 14 —	Great Circle Routes	254
Chapter 15 —	The Far Outback	269
Chapter 16 —	The Sunshine Route	286
Chapter 17 —	Suburban Shuffle	299
Chapter 18 —	Through the Veil	311
Chapter 19 —	A Cook's Tour	330
Chapter 20 —	Against the Trend	365
Chapter 21 —	The Last Ride	397
Appendix I		429
Appendix II		436
Maps		438
Bibliography		443
Acknowledgements		444
Index		445

Place names

Place names in this book are given in the form used in the country concerned where this can be done in Roman typeface, with or without accents. Where other alphabets are in use, e.g. Cyrillic, Arabic, or Chinese, the anglicised spellings as used in *Thomas Cook European and Overseas Timetables* are adopted. The following are the currently accepted local and (former) English versions of places referred to in the text:

Basel	Basle	Milano	Milan
Beijing	Peking	Moskva	Moscow
Beograd	Belgrade	München	Munich
Braunschweig	Brunswick	Napoli	Naples
Firenze	Florence	Oostende	Ostend
Genève	Geneva	Plzeň	Pilsen
Genova	Genoa	Porto	Oporto
Göteborg	Gothenburg	Roma (Italy)	Rome
Hameln	Hamelin	Sevilla	Seville
København	Copenhagen	Swinoujscie	Swinemünde
Köln	Cologne	Szczecin	Stettin
Kraków	Cracow	Torino	Turin
Lisboa	Lisbon	Venezia	Venice
Luzern	Lucerne	Warszawa	Warsaw
Wien	Vienna		

Train times

With a few exceptions, where the context made it appropriate to spell out train departure or arrival times in words, or where a timetable is set out in column format, all train times in this book are given according to the 24-hour clock, with the leading zero omitted for hours under 10 and with a period separating hours from minutes. This follows the practice used in the timetables of Italy, France, Sweden, Denmark, Belgium, Finland, Poland, and doubtless some other countries. While not my own preferred format it combines the advantages of being easy to understand, unambiguous and compatible with the obscure spelling checker principles adopted by word processing software!

Foreword

Recently I did one of my Sunday morning programs at the town of Junee, in of all places, the Railway Refreshment Rooms. The RRRs are still there, but the local baker now runs the rooms, not to service the trains, but for the people of Junee.

I was reminded of the glory of the age of steam, and the days of rail. Families came to town on Saturday night to watch the trains come and go – *The Albury Mail, The Riverina Express* and many others. You could stay at the Hotel, upstairs from the refreshment rooms.

Yes, Junee was a Railway Town, and apart from the station it had the 'Roundhouse' where up to 350 men and apprentices – fitters, boiler makers – worked repairing the rolling stock.

While we were there (on the Saturday actually) an XPT whose brakes had jammed was pulled into a siding at Junee. The engine had a 'flat tyre' as it's called, a flat spot caused by the brakes jamming.

In the old days, that is up until 1993 when the 'Roundhouse' closed, that engine could have been repaired right there. Now all repairs, even the most basic like changing a fuse, have to go to Sydney. That XPT was towed at 20 km/h to Sydney. And that's progress? No, that's stupidity.

Colin Taylor should be Commissioner for Railways. People who love railways and the place they hold in Australia's heart, should be charged with their care. Instead we get... well you see what we get and what we've got.

But we've still got Colin Taylor, his love of trains, and his boundless enthusiasm.

Most of us won't be able to make these journeys, some have disappeared. But *Traincatcher* is a great place to make contact with Colin Taylor – the real Colin Taylor is on a train somewhere and can't be contacted.

Ian McNamara
ABC *Australia All Over*

Introduction

*"My heart is warm with the friends I make
And better friends I'll not be knowing
Yet there isn't a train I wouldn't take
No matter where it's going."*

— Edna St Vincent Millay: *Collected poems*

But knowing where it's going can be rather important, especially if you're in a hurry to keep an appointment. Finding out where it's going is not always easy. "It's fun finding out," wrote Bernard Wicksteed but with rail travel that may not always be true. The destination may be an anticlimax.

Robert Louis Stevenson maintained that to "travel hopefully" was "a better thing than to arrive." (*Virginibus Puerisque 1,i-El Dorado*)

That would sum up most of my earliest experiences of travel – by train or any other mode. Getting there was most of the fun. Stevenson's assertion has since been disrespectfully and wrongly attributed to Dr Richard Beeching, architect of the first of several serious attempts to dismantle the rail system of Britain under the guise of 'rationalisation'. That term has subsequently been applied to numerous similar exercises elsewhere in the world, exercises motivated ostensibly by economic considerations but in fact frequently influenced by powerful vested interest lobbies.

When these people get their way there is no question of travelling hopefully or otherwise, let alone ever arriving. There is no way to go.

Most rail travellers and all rail workers could tell tales as long as your arm, stranger than fiction, stranger than any in this book. There is something about rail travel, more so than any other kind, which invariably weaves a tale.

As for my own tales, in the words of the late bard Robert Service (of *The Shooting of Dan McGrew* fame):

"Though names I've changed from time to time,
A stickler for correctness I'm.
To write God-honest truth I strive
And here, to best of memory, I've."

— R.W. Service: *Ploughman of the Moon.*

But unlike Service's book quoted above, this book is not really an autobiography: it is not chronologically arranged; neither is it just a collection of tales, true or apocryphal, nor an authoritative treatise on world railways. It is a bit of all these and more. It examines railway systems and philosophises about them and the people who run them. It looks at railway operation and management practice and blows away the myths that still infest official propaganda to reveal the naked truth.

As railway passengers soon learn, railways are no longer run for people. They are stress-relief toys for management to play games with. The only 'traffic' they want is profit-producing, uncomplaining, and preferably inert, that can be manipulated at their pleasure. My own and other experiences recounted here will have the ring of familiarity and should strike a chord with anyone who has ever travelled any distance on almost any railway, evoking the likely response of 'Been there — done that!'

From my earliest days I must have been fascinated by trains. Recently my brother unearthed from my late mother's archives the first unassisted letter I wrote, at the age of four and a half:

"DADDY   I MADE A BOOK FOR ELMIRA. IT HAD TRAINS IN IT. COLIN."

Elmira was my cousin. So *Great Rail Non-Journeys of Australia* was

INTRODUCTION

not my first book on trains.

This one, not I hope my last, began as an update and revision of *Great Rail Non-Journeys*. It has since changed, drawing on much wider travel experiences over a longer period. Nevertheless, the reader should be warned that some episodes from the previous book have been repeated and some other material has also been published elsewhere. Good stories are often worth re-telling.

Some people may refer to me as a 'train buff'. I sympathise with journalist Jim Nicholls, whose articles about rail journeys enlivened recent issues of Queensland's *Valley Times*, when he says, "I dislike the terms 'train buff' or 'enthusiast' but don't quite know how else to describe myself".

'Buff' is a colloquial term of US origin derived from the colour of volunteer firemen's uniforms, first applied in 1955 to people interested in railways. It has since been applied to enthusiasts for everything from disarmament to wine tasting. It has the connotation of self-styled 'expert'. The same touch of derogatoriness is often attached to the word 'academic'. Call me neither. I like travelling. I like trains. Little old traincatcher me.

> DADDY I MADE A
> BOOK FOR ELMIRA
> IT HAD TRAINS IN IT.
> COLIN·

Early evidence of compulsive obsessive behaviour? The author's first unassisted letter, 1933.

TRAINCATCHER

A New South Wales Court accepted me as an 'expert' witness on the subject. Is that a qualification or does it prove the law is an ass?

Although on occasion I travel on steam train excursions I am not quite that kind of enthusiast. I have no objection to a diesel railcar or even an EMU (electric multiple unit). Even a tram is a railway vehicle not without its own romance.

Form and motive power may change. In place of steam (or earlier still, horse or slave-power), nowadays...

"We draw our power from the harnessed shower,
The lightning without the thunder
But a train is a train and will so remain
While the rails glide glistening under
Oh some like trips in luxury ships
And some in gasoline wagons
And others swear by the upper air
And the wings of flying dragons
Let each make haste to indulge his taste
Be it beer, champagne or cider;
My private joy, both man and boy,
Is being a railroad rider."

– from Ogden Nash: *Riding on a Railroad Train*

Or, as Thomas Southerland Jr and William McCleery put it in their book of this title, it is "The Way to Go".

Colin Taylor
Brisbane
November 1995

Chapter 1
Eurail Odyssey — From Piræus to Porto

"Many cities did he visit, and many were the nations with whose manners and customs he was acquainted." — Homer: *The Odyssey Bk.1*

Hissing around the curve and on through Olten in Switzerland, the Trans-Europ Express *Rheingold* accelerated into the mini-blizzard of its own making. The track was two dark grooves in the carpeting snow. On the platform, passengers waiting for lesser trains stamped their feet and huddled into their furry wrappings against the bitter edge of the January cold spell.

In the warm air-conditioned comfort, reclining in a luxuriously upholstered seat, I relaxed in contentment. There is satisfaction in speed. In an express train the passenger is conscious of it as the landscape flashes by, and senses the envy of those less fortunate, who wait on platforms or sit imprisoned in automobiles at level crossing gates or in snowdrifts.

The passenger becomes aware of the railwaymen, to whom the job is no mere wage-packet but a way of life, a calling with its own pride and mystery, something too often forgotten by management and by those reactionary governments who wish to 'rationalise' the railway systems. Redundancy packages, however generous, can never compensate the deeper losses suffered by the workers affected.

There was half a metre of snow, and the skies were heavy and grey. Soon the blizzard became thicker, no longer of the train's making. The black ribbons of rail became faint, obscure; fresh white overprinting them with the opacity of the surroundings. A slackening pace testified to the driver's acknowledgement of adverse conditions as, still without noise or fuss, the train forged on into its own private world. Outside through the driving whiteness could be seen the snow ploughs bravely battling to reopen the less effective highway.

Slight jerks of acceleration came as something of a surprise when all around the blizzard seemed to rage. But ahead in the distance shone a patch of blue, and sunshine. Toward it we raced as the driver again piled on speed – 100, 120, 140 km/h: *Rheingold* would arrive at Genève on time. You can check your watch by the Swiss Federal Railways.

This early afternoon run after a delightful bacon and egg breakfast in a German train while speeding alongside the Rhine was a satisfying climax to a day that began oddly and to a journey that in fact had begun at Genova in Italy a couple of days before.

It was probably the fault of the weather or my lack of understanding of Italian but whatever the reason, it had become abundantly clear that I could not that day go from Genova through France to Spain – to the sunshine I craved. Genova was wet, windy and cold so I hopped on a train and ventured west. Alas, at Ventimiglia it was 'all change'. There had been a landslide and the line was blocked. They offered me an 'auto-pullman'. This sounded suspiciously like a bus, and it was. I had not bought a Eurailpass to travel on some old bus, 'auto-pullman' or otherwise. No, another rail route to Spain had to be found. Thus I proceeded in the opposite direction to Venezia, from where a possible route via Wien though Germany, perhaps Holland, and maybe the west of France sounded as good a way as any. A tad devious, perhaps, but the beauty of a Eurailpass is that you can go far out of your way without paying for it. None of those sickening experiences of proffering an economy or second class ticket for the wrong journey to a humourless ticket collector, and the embarrassment of having him slowly and laboriously write out the inevitable excess fare docket while the other passengers smirk silently to themselves and pretend not to notice.

The Eurailpass works like a charm; language difficulties disappear. You are allowed or even ushered into the super first class, anywhere you like, and you rarely have to book in advance. But on some European trains and without such a pass, prior booking is essential.

EURAIL ODYSSEY

Continuing north from Venezia after my aborted trip along the Riviera, I realised the train from Italy was going to be late. It is said Mussolini made Italian trains run on time, but he was no longer around and his influence had waned. This lack of punctuality was not therefore unusual nor, in view of the weather, something one could reasonably complain about, but why do trains the world over, once they start late, seem to become progressively later all the way? Their schedules allow what railways call 'recovery time' – an admission (though not publicly) that lateness is expected – but the recovery time is soon used up. In Japan you get part of your fare back if an express train is more than two hours overdue. If applied world-wide that would make some systems bankrupt in no time!

Riding on the 12.20 ex-Domodossola, 12 January 1977. (Colin Taylor)

TRAINCATCHER

The *Romulus* express (Roma–Venezia–Wien) was an hour overdue at Tarvisio and not making up time. A midnight arrival in Wien, in a metre or so of snow, with no guide book and little money to spare was not appealing, so the best thing was to change and head north. Diligent and close study of the *Thomas Cook European Timetable*, that essential companion of every serious Eurail traveller, showed a possible connection with a northbound train at Leoben, a previously unheard-of outpost. This was provided the connecting train was equally late. It came, I noticed, from Yugoslavia, where heavy snows had been experienced during the past week.

The on-board railway inspectors were doubtful, but at Leoben the station-master reacted instantly. *"Der Zug für Hamburg?"* asked I, in imitation German.

"Ja," he replied, gesturing for me to descend forthwith. The indicator panel on the next platform lit up. The train was due shortly. So far, so good. With luck, the train would be half empty. I could stretch out the way one can only do in European overnight trains. I could awake at leisure and dismount somewhere in Germany. There would be plenty of warm, fast trains to speed me through France to sunny Spain and Portugal.

But it was not to be that kind of night. *"Der Zug für Hamburg"* was *ein Zug aus Jugoslawien*, and I ought to have known better. I had experienced such trains before...

My European rail tour had begun in Greece on a Christmas Day. Having spent a week in December attending an international conference about pedestrians in "sunny Palestine" as Masefield called it, I had boarded the car ferry (sad substitute for a quinquireme but possibly just as amply provisioned, especially with the sweet white wine). From the port of Haifa this set sail (or rather started its engines) for Piræus, which marked the beginning of a railway kaleidoscope of people and places from there to Paris, to Port Bou, to Vigo in Spain and Lisboa in Portugal.

Israel had not seemed a happy country to stay long in. The Israelis always seemed to be remembering a war or getting ready for the next one – hardly surprising in view of their history. Highlights of that brief visit after the conference ended were a quick tour of historic sites like Bethlehem, the Sea of Galilee (excellent fish), and the Dead Sea. No flotation problems there but not having a 'cossie', I wore my trousers. These stiffened up with caked salt when they dried so that I felt like a walking Lot's wife. Then there was the wine at Cana of Galilee, good but rather better, I understand, in a distant time before the producer of it was assassinated. There was a wonderful richness of architecture and decoration in many buildings – even modern ones were architecturally superb – and I found the food varied and good, sampling such delights as felafel, hummous and sharma – the last not unlike Greek souvlaki but with its own special spicy flavour.

Leaving Jerusalem – by train of course – I was struck by a fairly scenic rocky gorge in which we travelled down from the heights, and which was spoiled half way down by a stinking sewage outfall which polluted the stream at the valley bottom. I was so incensed by this that I wrote a letter to the English language *Jerusalem Times* suggesting that the engineer responsible should be condemned to live the rest of his life beside it. To my amazement, they published it but I got out of Israel before he caught up with me. He could well have been at the conference, which was attended by engineers and medical people all professedly concerned about pedestrian safety. And many of them were: some very good material was presented but it is easy to remember the bad bits. I can never forget the South African delegate who said the main hazard faced by drivers there was the number of black pedestrians getting in the way of their motor cars: I wondered how he would have felt had he been a pedestrian and the black fellow the motorist.

A pleasant surprise was the sight of a stand of gum trees near the station at Beer-Sheba, making me feel almost homesick. I was told they were brought by some Australians during a war, but which war I did not find out – there had been so many.

Visiting the Gaza strip – a daring expedition organised by our driver from the hotel – I was interested to note a railway paralleling the road route. It looked well constructed but not visibly in use. I was given to understand it was for military use only but in fact it used to connect right through to Egypt via a bridge crossing of the Suez Canal. One might hope that with greater rapport these days between Egyptians and Israelis, this route might again be linked up, perhaps with the long mooted yet never completed Cape to Cairo railway, so that in future one could go from London, or Moskva, or Hong Kong to Capetown by train. What a trip to look forward to!

In Europe I saw the sun rise above Mount Olympus, home of the Gods. I saw the snow-clad Alps and Dolomites, the Costa Brava and the Riviera; all from the warm comfort of a moving train. I was able to cruise the canals of Venezia one day, have breakfast beside the Rhine the next and wander among the dockland cafes of Bilbao, Northern Spain a day later. There was amontillado in Montilla, spaghetti Bolognaise in Bologna and fried sardines on the Ligurian coast opposite Sardinia. In less than five weeks, in mid-winter, I was whisked in style for 29,000 km across more than 20 frontiers, with a pocketful of lire, Deutschmarks, escudos, francs and pesetas while, only dimly aware of frontiers, muttering *mi scusa* in France, *merci* in Spain, and *gracias* in Switzerland.

This was my first visit to Europe – 'the Continent' as it is called in Britain. My last train journey in the northern hemisphere had been from Dingwall on the shores of the Cromarty Firth. There, after a sad yet convivial farewell to my friends and home at Strathpeffer 'neath the majestic slopes of Ben Wyvis, we took the train to Inverness where we watched our 14 items of luggage labelled 'Australia' being loaded into the van of the *Royal Highlander* to London and thence to Southampton Docks where we boarded the vessel for Down Under.

In Athens I stayed at a rather sleazy hotel recommended by a fellow passenger on the boat from Haifa. I was not impressed with it, nor was I by the way the authorities in that city allowed motorists to park their cars on every footpath. But against this, there were narrow streets where pedestrians still held sway. More interesting, and colourful, were the cats of Athens. "Cats on the rooftops, cats on the tiles" goes the song: Athens must have been its inspiration. Dozens of moggies, all colours and sizes, cuddled up together in the warm sun, seemingly all friendly.

But I always went for the smaller places. From Athens I took the train down to Piræus again to look for a restaurant mentioned in the guide book at which you could eat and drink as much as you liked for a handful of drachmas. Alas, I think the book's author was not up-to-date. First of all, the place was closed, which being between Christmas and New Year was perhaps not unexpected. But then I saw it: on the door was an American Express sign – a sure indication the place had been 'discovered' and no doubt the prices upwardly adjusted accordingly!

The train north from Piræus was almost like being in the UK again except for the language. It was like trains I had known there, crowded, friendly, comfortable, sometimes fast, but late if there was any good excuse.

Soon a conversation developed. It is surprising how few words of another's language are necessary to communicate. I found myself sharing the food of people I had never met before and whose names I still do not know. In the buffet car, delightful skewered lamb was available for only a few drachmas. It was warm and comfortable, while outside the snow began to fall.

Seeing the morning sun touch the snow-clad crest of Mount Olympus was an experience I will never forget. Nor will I forget the woman in the booking office queue at Thessaloniki, who stridently demanded to be served first. "I have to catch a train" she said. What did she think the rest of us were doing – waiting for takeaways? It would have been understandable if the train she wanted was just about to leave, but it was not. The *Akropolis Express* was overdue. It had not arrived from Athens and the woman who found it imperative to catch it was herself 20 minutes late!

Thus at Thessaloniki I boarded the *Akropolis* for Skopje in Yugoslavia, which seemed a convenient place for a nightstop. Let me say at once that I have nothing really against trains in Yugoslavia. Some are quite excellent. The people, too, I found extremely friendly to foreigners, though events have brought out differences in their attitudes to each other. At any rate, they were helpful to me. Indeed, on this first entry to their country a compartment full of total strangers not only rescued me from the police; they got me back my passport too.

I had not actually lost my passport; I'd just not seen it for some considerable time. We had not long left Thessaloniki before my compartment-mates had managed to convey, in that mixture of English, French, Greek and signs and symbols which people of different races use when thrust together in railway trains, that they were Yugoslavians who had been on a brief visit to Greece. Apparently some things like hi-fi radios were a little cheaper there than where they lived.

Especially helpful was an attractive young woman of about 20 who had better English than the others. She and they pointed out quite reasonably that the luggage of a respectable looking Australian 'professor' (anyone who teaches is regarded as a professor in Europe) would never be glanced at, much less examined and searched. We were approaching the border post at Gevgeli. It was put to me that I might like to indicate to the Customs that about a quarter of their luggage, especially the hi-fi equipment and accessories, in fact belonged to me.

The girl asked this so nicely on their behalf. She was going to Skopje herself and I fondly imagined ways she might show her gratitude if I obliged. I was anxious to appear helpful but could not risk arrest for smuggling. I therefore informed them that "my government" had "forbidden me" to do this sort of thing, making it sound almost a personal injunction from the Prime Minister rather than mere commonsense advice from the guide book. This they accepted and thanked me profusely. Whereupon they proceeded to unpack their purchases and stow the several components in different parts of their baggage, at the bottom of bags of oranges, under the seat, in overcoats, and anywhere else they could think of. By the time the Customs men came there was no sign of the newly acquired illicit goods.

All went well. I smiled with relief. The young lady smiled too. They thanked me again, presumably for keeping quiet. Considering I hardly knew a word of the language it would have been difficult for me to do otherwise. They told me the man would come back with my passport after he had stamped it.

But I became increasingly concerned as time went by and no passport appeared. As we pulled out of the station, in panic I urged my companions through the girl to enquire for me. After a shouted exchange across the platform I was assured that "the man had it on the train" and that I would get it back in due course.

"She'll be right, mate" would be the rough Australasian translation.

They reassembled the hi-fi and defiantly turned it up full volume as we moved on into the Yugoslavian night. Just then the door opened again. The music and the radio disappeared in an instant. But it was the ticket collector, not the Customs. Horrors! In the confusion I had neglected to re-book at the border, the guide book having advised this course as a way of saving money, because railways the world over have a pernicious habit of surcharging trips across a border – international or, as in Australia, merely interstate. Not only that, I had not changed any travellers cheques for Yugoslavian dinars and had only Greek drachmas. I explained my predicament to the charming English-speaking member of the group, mentioned already. I was told not to worry about it – they would all sort it out for me in good time.

A fierce altercation then developed. The whole carriage was arguing with the collector. Another official appeared. Tempers rose, the argument flowed into the corridor. There were gesticulations and muttered references to the "*Australien*". I fumbled with my wallet and showed Greek notes with a helpless gesture, hoping the officials would understand. Strangely, their anger did not seem directed at me but at their fellow countrymen. I sighed with relief as the officials went away.

I then found out the reason for the argument. None of the group had tickets!

Still apprehensive about my passport, I was beginning to congratulate myself on obtaining a free rail journey when the door again opened and the police came in, light blue uniformed and conspicuously armed. Further argument ensued. It went on for some time, first one, then another. Eventually it died down, cigarettes were exchanged, and the police went away.

Then the Inspector returned, there was more discussion, but he sat down and friendship appeared to prevail. Apparently he was apologising for doing his duty in calling the railway police. Shortly after that my passport was handed back and we reached Skopje without further incident. Luggage was handed out through the opened carriage window (the simplest way) and the girl helpfully showed me to a nearby hotel, and fixed up a room for me. It was then two-thirty in the morning and very cold when she left me to go, alas, to her own home.

The two days after that which I spent travelling through Yugoslavia were almost equally eventful. There was the train on which everybody filled the reserved seats except the people who had reservations, provoking bitter arguments but fortunately without resort to weapons. There was the overnight train where the first class had no heating and I left my luggage in one compartment when I was shown another one to sleep in. It was still there next morning though I had some anxious moments locating the actual compartment. Then at Kosovo Polje I was nearly arrested for trying to photograph a steam engine. *"Tito, dobra!"* I cried, while hastily putting my camera away. This seemed to be the accepted greeting. Strange how united the Yugoslavian people were under Marshal Tito's communist government. They were rough, they were argumentative, but they had a sense of humour and were friendly. I would have trusted them any time.

Their sense of bizarre humour is well illustrated by their railway timetables of that time, an excerpt from which is reproduced here. Yugoslavia was very near to earning a place in the *Railway Gazette International*'s roll of honour, the World Speed League of trains that achieved 120 km/h or more between stops, when their internal distrust of each other flared into the bitter ethnic conflict that has shattered so many of their historic cities and so many lives. In 1991, three *rapide* trains were advertised as running between Zagreb, Slavonski Brod and Vinkovci at 118.2 km/h but, as the gazette's editor commented in an editorial addition to the speed review of that year: "in the present political climate it is unlikely that these timings are being achieved". This surely was the understatement of the year.

Dubrovnik, on the shores of the Adriatic, was one place I had always wanted to visit. There is, or at least was, a rail link there, but by the time I manage to get there, if I ever do, I wonder what will remain either of the line or of the old city.

Arriving at the now Croatian capital of Zagreb around dawn, I found the station buffet packed. Snow was lying on the platform and the temperature was around zero so it was surprising to see people consuming pint pots of beer. I wanted a coffee but none came; the only alternative to beer was slivoviça, which seemed to accompany it. I asked about the train to Rijeka, and whether it had a buffet. The answer was yes but the train was late.

When it finally arrived, it simply could not decide whether to go or not. Thinking back on it, I am not sure if it was really the right train. I had sought a 6.50 to Rijeka. The booking office said it left at 7.08. In fact I think it was really the 6.20 because that was the one with a buffet.

It came into the platform at 7.30 and at 8.04 it was still there. The buffet was open but there was no heating on the train, and no hot food. I asked for an omelette, which was on the menu, but the best the buffet could offer was pepperoni and three kinds of hard liquor – brandy, viniak, and slivoviça. I settled for the viniak which sounded the least corrosive.

Finally at 8.57 the train moved – all of 10 metres, and stopped.

At 9.03, reluctantly, it edged forward again, a significant movement extending almost to 100 metres and actually going beyond the end of the platform.

Then it went back again. This must have been a mistake, for yet again it moved forward. No, that too was a mistake! Again it reversed and

TRAINCATCHER

15 SEVNICA–

		6079 2, ✗	6071 2, ✗	26081 2, †	6073 2	6075 2	6077 2	Tar. km		
		4 10	5 10	7 06	12 42	15 18	19 53	0	p	SEVN
		4 13	5 13	7 09	12 45	15 21	19 56	2	♥	Bošt
		4 19	5 19	7 16	12 51	15 28	20 02	8		Jelov
		4 32	5 27	7 24	12 59	15 36	20 10	15		Trži
	...	4 35	5 30	7 27	13 03	15 40	20 13	17		Pijav
	...	4 41	5 36	7 33	13 09	15 46	20 19	22		Mok
	...,	4 45	5 40	7 38	13 13	15 41	20 24	25		Šent
	... ...	4 49	5 44	7 42	13 18	15 55	20 28	28		Mirr
	... ...	4 54	5 49	7 46	13 23	16 00	20 33	30	↓	Gorr
	... ...	5 03	5 58	7 55	13 34	16 09	20 42	37	d	TREB

A = Saobraća subotom ⑥, nedeljom ⑦ i praznikom (†).
B = Ne saobraća subotom ⑥, nedeljom ⑦ i praznikom (†).

18 ZAB(

Tar. km	Stanice	3170 2	3172 2,B	6350 2,✗	3140 2,A	3350 2	31 2
0	ZABOK ♀ ...... p	...	...	4 45	...	7 00	
4	Štrucljevo ...... ♥	...	...	4 53	...	7 06	
7	Začretje	...	...	4 58	...	7 11	
12	Velika Ves	...	...	5 07	...	7 18	
17	Krapina ♀ 🚌 ...	...	...	5 17	...	7 26	
19	Žutnica	...	...	5 23	...	7 32	
21	Đurmanec	...	...	5 28	...	7 36	
25	Hromec	...	...	...	...	7 42	
29	Lupinjak	...	5 00	...	...	7 50	
31	Dobovec	...	5 03	...	...	7 54	
37	Rogatec	4 20	5 13	...	...	8 16	
45	**ROGAŠKA SLATINA** 🚌 .	4 31	5 24	...	...	8 29	
52	Podplat	4 42	5 35	...	...	8 41	
53	Mestinje	4 45	5 38	...	...	8 45	
56	Stranje	4 51	5 44	...	6 05	8 50	9
61	Šmarje	4 58	5 51	...	6 12	...	9
65	Šentvid	5 08	6 00	...	6 21	...	9
69	Grobelno 🚌 ...	5 12	6 04	...	6 25	...	9
74	Šentjur	5 17	6 08	...	6 30	...	9
81	Štore ...... ↓	5 24	6 15	...	6 36	...	9
86	CELJE ✗ 🚌 .... d	5 29	6 20	...	6 41	...	9
102	Ljubljana 2 ..... d	7 20	8 06	...	8 17	...	11
76	Maribor 19 ..... d	6 38	...	...	...	...	

A = Ne saobraća subotom⑥, nedeljom⑦ i praznikom (†).
B = Lupinjak — Rogatec ne saobraća nedeljom⑦ i praznikom

do planina i do mora
samo željeznicom

Unusual embellishments in the Yugoslavian train timetables (1977).

EURAIL ODYSSEY

JE NA DOLENJSKEM

e		6072 2, ✕	6074 2	6076 2	6084 2, ✕	6078 2	6082 2,A	6086 2,B			
....	d	4 54	9 06	15 01	...	18 24	21 56	23 01	...		
....		4 51	9 03	14 58	...	18 21	21 53	22 58	...		
....		4 45	8 57	14 52	...	18 15	21 47	22 52	...		
....		4 38	8 50	14 45	15 30	18 08	21 40	22 45	...		
....		4 27	8 46	14 41	15 27	18 04	21 36	22 41	...		
....		4 22	8 42	14 37	15 22	18 00	21 32	22 37	...		
....		4 18	8 38	14 33	15 17	17 56	21 28	22 33	...		
....		4 14	8 34	14 29	15 13	17 52	21 24	22 29	...		
....		4 10	8 29	14 24	15 09	17 48	21 19	22 24	...		
IJSKEM	p	4 01	8 20	14 15	15 00	17 39	21 10	22 15	...	...	...

🚗 = Šinobus — ručni prtljag ograničen.

OBELNO—CELJE

(Vidi i polje 19)

174 2	6354 2	6356 2	6114 2,B	3144 2	3356 2	3178 2	3358 2	3146 2			
...	12 37	14 25	...	...	15 45	16 45	20 03	...	...	...	...
...	12 43	14 31	...	...	15 53	16 51	20 11	...	...	...	...
...	12 48	14 37	...	...	15 59	16 57	20 16	...	...	...	...
...	12 55	14 44	...	...	16 08	17 04	20 25	...	...	...	...
1 20	13 03	14 53	...	...	16 19	17 40	20 35	...	...	...	...
1 25	13 09	14 59	...	...	16 26	17 45	...	...	...	...	...
1 29	13 13	15 03	...	...	16 31	17 49	...	...	...	...	...
1 34	...	...	...	...	16 38	17 55	...	...	...	...	...
1 42	...	...	16 01	...	16 47	18 03	...	...	...	...	...
1 45	...	...	16 04	...	16 52	18 06	...	...	...	...	...
1 58	...	...	16 50	...	17 02	18 25	...	...	...	...	...
2 09	...	...	17 02	...	...	18 36	...	...	...	...	...
2 20	...	...	17 14	...	...	18 47	...	...	...	...	...
2 23	...	...	17 17	...	...	18 50	...	...	...	...	...
2 49	...	...	17 22	17 31	...	18 56	...	20 29	...		
2 56	...	...	...	17 38	...	19 03	...	20 36	...		
3 05	...	...	...	17 47	...	19 12	...	20 45	...		
3 10	...	...	...	17 52	...	19 17	...	20 50	...		
3 15	...	...	...	17 56	...	19 22	...	20 54	...		
3 22	...	...	...	...	...	19 29	...	21 01	...		
3 27	...	...	...	...	...	19 34	...	21 06	...		
5 16	...	...	...	18 08	...						
...	...	...	...	20 27	...	...	...	...	...	...	...
...	...	...	...		20 25	...					

🚗° = Motorni voz — ručni prtljag nije ograničen.

at 9.17 was standing once more in the station, as far as I could see at the same platform and in the same place at which it had first arrived.

At this point, and I made a special note to this effect in my travel diary, I came to a decision that I would make my way as fast as possible to the sunny south, to Italy, just as soon as I was safely in Eurailpass territory, and that while gallivanting around Central Europe in the depths of winter was all right for healthy young students and cuddly warm Yugoslavian girls, it was not for forty-odd year old grandfathers softened by Australia's indulgent ways and sun.

By 9.37, still in Zagreb station, I managed to establish friendly relations with fellow sufferers in the buffet car by asking in Serbo-Croatian (after careful study of the phrase book) how long it took to get to Rijeka. The question provoked unseemly laughter. Encouraged or stung by my remarks the train lurched into motion again at 9.45 only to grind to another halt in less than 100 metres.

My impression is that it repeated this oscillatory performance several more times, although by then it seemed that I and the whole train population were tending to oscillate in rhythmic harmony with the growing array of empty viniak and slivoviça bottles. I distinctly recall a great cheer when at 10.48, a mere 3 hours 40 minutes late (or was it four and a half hours?) the train finally, and creating the distinct impression of determination, left Zagreb station on its journey to the Adriatic.

At Rijeka, or Fiume as it used to be called when I was a stamp collector, I changed to a local train not advertised in the Cook's timetable. A special, perhaps? No, the other passengers told me it was a *"Putnik"*.

Sputnik 1 had 20 years earlier been launched by the Russians, but the Yugoslavian *putnik* did not go round the world nor did it reach the speed of an orbiting satellite. More than three hours it took to cover the uphill crawl away from the coast to inland Ljubliana. It was night-time when we reached there but the crowd on the train were friendly and it was not long before we were sharing slivoviça and brandy. I remember explaining where I was from (they thought at first I meant Austria) by showing them an Australian dollar note and leaping about with my hands bent in front of my waist to explain how the kangaroo it pictured got around.

Among the useful tips they gave me was to avoid the police at all costs.

Somehow later that day I managed to time my crossing of the Austrian border at Jesenice to a few minutes past midnight, so as to extract the maximum hours of benefit from my Eurailpass. But the only hot food I could get was a huge bowl of bean soup at Ljubljiana station and it took me two further days to recover from my Yugoslavian initiation!

I should therefore have been cautious when I alighted from the *Romulus* express at Leoben in Austria. The train for Hamburg was expected, yes, but the train for Hamburg was the *Beograd Express* from Yugoslavia. It was not replete with empty compartments: it was full. Aware then of what to expect I sought a first class non-smoker, and settled for one with four other passengers, only three of them smoking.

I was allowed the middle seat facing the engine. This may sound unremarkable but to be allowed any space at all in a compartment occupied by one or more grown Yugoslavs is something not readily forgotten. There is no unwillingness to make room. It is just that even one Yugoslav, if he puts his mind to it, can occupy an entire six-seat railway compartment without difficulty. Sprawling back over the middle seat with legs out diagonally onto the opposite corners and arms over the adjacent spaces, he will leave only the seat opposite unused, and even this will prove a convenient repository for small baggage.

Take four such passengers, with their heavy luggage, a few large radios, and a litre or two of slivoviça...

The warm tobacco fug enveloped me as I squeezed into the tiny space on the middle seat not occupied by the legs of the gentleman opposite, who was almost asleep. His companions were in a party

TRAINCATCHER

mood. Accepting a proffered cigarette as inevitable in spite of giving them up a year before – after all, if you have to suffer passive smoking you may as well share the enjoyment – I politely but firmly declined the proffered slivoviça in favour of my own flask of brandy, carried for emergencies, of which this was clearly one.

The train sped on through the night, the radio blared, and the bottles were passed around. They were returning to work abroad after a Christmas holiday at home, and were leaving the train at different points en route. This information I gleaned largely from snippets of conversation when the ticket collector came and wrote out the inevitable excess fare dockets. It is useless attempting to travel anywhere on the railways of Europe without a ticket, so why do people do it? One man was going to Linz, another to Wels, which was further along the line. The Linz passenger had been drinking beer and was soon asleep. In time, the radio was hushed and all were a-snore, with mouths gaping, legs and arms spread and intertwined. Eventually I too dozed off.

Something made me open my eyes. Probably the lack of movement. We were stationary. Through the window shone the bluish white lights of a station platform, its surface blanketed in snow – Linz.

Linz! But the man in the corner was supposed to be leaving us there! He lay sprawled in oblivion. Just then his friend in the opposite corner opened an eye and groped for the slivoviça. Glancing towards the window he took in the sign and its significance.

Linz! Leaping forward he shook his slumbering fellow traveller. There was a sluggish acknowledgement. He shook him again, urgently. The train began to move, slowly but purposefully. The traveller leapt to his feet, grabbed his hand luggage and rushed out along the corridor.

Noticing that he had neglected to take his heavy luggage, the friend reached it down from the rack, hesitated, then went to the window to pass it through in the approved European fashion.

There was no sign of life on the platform, now rushing past as the train gathered speed in the way only electrically-hauled trains can do. It seemed like an age but it must have been only a few minutes.

The window was opened, the case suspended uncertainly a moment or two, then dropped into the darkness as the train continued to accelerate. If the man had not already jumped, I thought, he would kill himself. Perhaps he was even then lying in the snow, soon to be buried by the silently descending mantle. The other man closed the window, sat down, and wiped his brow.

At that moment the corridor door slid open.

It was possible without understanding a word of Serbo-Croatian to follow the ensuing conversation exactly. Open mouths, enquiring glances, gesticulations in the direction of the luggage rack and window, the pulling out of a wallet and its brushing aside told more than any words. 'With friends like you, who needs enemies?' seemed the predominant theme.

I felt sorry for the big man next to me; he had tried to help. It was hardly his fault that his friend was now speeding on towards Germany while his baggage lay broken and bruised in the snow of Linz railway station.

Eventually they shook hands. Another traveller had woken in time to witness the altercation and a drop of slivoviça all round seemed to soothe. The train was now approaching Wels, where the two would have to leave, one presumably to find his way back to Linz to retrieve whatever remnants of his baggage still existed.

But before then, voices approached down the corridor, official-sounding voices, speaking German in a no-nonsense way, speaking with authority. The door opened once more to reveal what might best be termed a posse of railway officials. They were enquiring, I gathered, about a piece of luggage that had been reported thrown from the train at Linz. Documents were called for, tickets produced, and the last I saw of my two travelling companions was their being led away, no doubt to 'assist the police in their enquiries'.

I found that the man remaining opposite me had a sense of humour. A good Slav sense of humour. A rocking, bone-shaking sense of humour. For the rest of the journey we had only to look at each other and point to the window or the luggage rack for the tears to roll from our eyes in helpless mirth.

The incident highlights one of the problems of travelling overnight on international and other long distance express trains – falling asleep. The other is not being able to sleep. The non-availability of food and drink, particularly water, is also a problem (especially in Europe where water costs the earth) but one which can be overcome with a little foresight. Not all trains suffer from these defects. The Trans-Europ Express trains (now replaced by the rather less distinguished 'Euro-City' group) were first class in nearly every way – indeed on the best of the European trains the only real lack, to an Australian, was a shower cubicle. Very few, even now, have showers except in the newest and most expensive sleeping cars. It is difficult to keep clean when on some trains the only water source is a broken tap in a tiny cupboard compartment. Sometimes there are hot taps, more often than not producing only spurts of superheated steam and labelled *caldo* to make the unsuspecting English-speaker think it means cold.

On the credit side, European trains are by international standards (not forgetting the Japanese) incredibly fast and both the trains and the stations they serve are well provided with facilities and staffed. Even where the trains have no buffet you can usually obtain a snack at some station en route or from a trolley on the platform.

That is, provided you have money of a negotiable kind. I recommend every Eurail traveller to carry half a dozen wallets (useful when thieves relieve you of one of them), each filled with a different currency, plus a wad of small denomination travellers cheques in either English pounds, US dollars, Swiss francs or Deutschmarks. Don't try to change escudos in France or lire in Spain.

I once successfully changed Austrian schillings at a French railway station bar at three o'clock on a Sunday morning, and coins at that, which are very rarely accepted even in reputable banks. I had spent a fruitless 10 minutes at Genève main station trying to fit a French franc into a Swiss slot machine in an attempt to rid my pockets of their weight of surplus coinage. When travelling across so many borders you can easily forget where you are. Arriving fortuitously at Metz some hours later, having slept through my intended disembarkation point of Strasbourg on the Calais portion of the 'I've been everywhere, man' *Arlberg Express* I found the platform cold and deserted with no other train in sight or heralded.

Why do I so describe the *Arlberg Express*? Simply because bits and pieces of this train can be found at different times in so many different places. Probably no other train in the world combines so many different portions in one – a nightmare if you get in the wrong carriage!

The practice of splitting up passenger trains between several origins and destinations is still common in Europe, though probably its days, like the days of the old slip coach, are numbered. The route of the *Arlberg Express* was crossed at Basel by that of the Holland-Italy Express and the scene at the station around midnight and again in the early morning when the trains in each direction were split up and re-marshalled was something which had to be seen to be believed. The way the little Swiss electric shunting engines fussed around backwards and forwards with one, two or three carriages at a time and then put them all back in their proper places was testimony to the ingenuity of the European railway planners and the operating skill of their staff.

In the winter of 1977 the *Arlberg Express* proper would leave Wien at 9.45 for Paris, arriving there the following morning. First and second class sitting cars went all the way. Not counting bits and pieces from other places which became attached or detached at intermediate stations like Linz, Salzburg and Zurich, by the time it reached Basel it would include sleepers, couchettes, and sitting cars from Chur and Innsbruck for Basel, for Paris and for Calais. And that was only the main part of the train!

By the time we left Basel, I was actually in train 398 for Calais, rather than the *Arlberg Express* proper (train 498 for Paris). When I woke up at Metz, clearly some form of sustenance was required. To my surprise and delight – it then being three-thirty on a Sunday morning at which time in some parts of the world everything would have been closed – I found the station buffet open. Not only open, but doing a roaring trade; warm, crowded and swinging. Upwards of 100 customers were engaged in noisy revelry. There was an overall party spirit, evidenced by the pint mugs of beer, glasses of wine, coffee, and general noisy hilarity punctuated by the occasional punch-up.

The strange thing about European travel, at least by rail, is that people you meet are helpful and where you are or where you think you are doesn't seem to matter to them. Metz, I thought, was in Germany or sounded like it. As I had no Deutschmarks I considered Schillings gleaned in Austria the week before the next best thing - especially as I was anxious to unload coins which the money changing people will not take back. I tried.

The reception at first was cool. The management were not over-keen to accept schillings but a friendly local reveller at the bar who appeared to know them and spoke the lingo came to my rescue, seeing, no doubt, the chance of a 'shout'. He spoke the right word and to my surprise the change was given, from his drink and mine, in French francs. I had a wallet full of francs but only by later reference to a map did I discover my error.

A cancelled train is more frustrating than a late one. Arriving in Genova one night, hoping to catch the sleeper to Roma, I found the departure indicator made no mention of its running. I checked the timetable. Yes, there should be one, but where was it? Cancelled, the officials told me – something to do with the sea. I caught the word *mare*. Walking round the streets near the station I found little comfort: there were no pleasant cafés where I could while away the time until some other train could be found; only a few females lurking in doorways who said things in Italian I didn't understand but could guess at.

Returning to the Porto Princippe station I found to my relief a new notice had gone up, announcing a *treno straordinario* to Roma at 2.02. What a time! Why are railways so fond of odd departure times – the five-nineteen, the eight-twenty-seven? Only in recent years, it seems, has there been a move to regular, interval, on-the-hour or other straightforward departure times. Whoever heard of a Board meeting starting at nine-fifty-one or ten-seventeen?

I was kept busy while waiting for that train. An elderly female began pursuing me round the pillars of the station foyer, muttering *"sette mille lire"* which I assumed must have been something to do with an offer of accommodation.

As I was not looking for accommodation in Genova I hid in the men's toilet until the train came in. Then it was packed and I was squeezed into the corridor, rather close to a younger, more attractive Italian girl. Everyone should have at least one Italian love affair, they say, but though she conversed well in English her Italian boyfriend appeared most disinclined to join in the conversation. I found out later why the earlier train was cancelled, when we went a roundabout way through Parma and Aulla. The coastal track had been washed away by storms at Chiavari.

Marine invasion of the track at Lavagna near Chiavari, Italy. (Colin Taylor)

TRAINCATCHER

On another Italian train I was thrust together with a young woman in a different way. I had decided it was one of the occasions to use a sleeper – the cheaper kind called a 'couchette' which in first class comprises four bunks in a compartment, with sheet, pillow and blanket. You are supposed to be able to lie down, but not undress, and there was no effort to segregate the sexes. On the overnight *Roma Express* to Calais – yes, Signore! – there was a vacant couchette berth. Seeing my Australian passport, the Italian conductor's face lit up. He could put me in with a fellow Australian. How pleased I would be. It was in fact a very pleasant surprise. She was 23 and came from Melbourne. Just the two of us all the way to Paris.

In Australia, of course, such things would never be permitted, yet they will put two strangers together in a sleeper if both are male or, I must assume, if both are female. Nothing queer about that, they reckon.

Returning from France another day, also on the *Roma Express*, I had comfortably ensconced myself in a first class compartment when another passenger entered. He was English – I could tell from his clothes. Who but Englishmen and waiters wear waistcoats nowadays? He was also grumbling about the foreigners – in this case the French and with this attitude he was undoubtedly the worst example of a tourist being a bad advertisement for his country that I have ever met. He was abusive of the Conductor because he did not speak English and he explained to me that he should have had a sleeper.

It turned out that he was bound for northern Italy, where his wife was to meet the train. She was evidently already on holiday somewhere in the Italian Alps and he had been detained by business.

Then our compartment door opened and a dark Italian with wife and children came in. Were there seats vacant? Of course there were but the Englishman was not in the mood for European détente. "This is first class," he proclaimed, in a tone which suggested that such ordinarily dressed, quiet 'foreigners' could not possibly be travelling first class.

"*Si, Signore, Grazie,*" said the Italian with a condescending smile, as if complimenting the Englishman on a remarkable discovery.

I moved over to make way for one of the children, a young lad who soon fell asleep with his head on my knee.

In the early hours of the morning, amid the snow clad Alps of the Franco-Italian border, the train stopped at, I think, Bardonecchia, and the Englishman got out, no doubt expecting his wife to be meeting him. The sky was dark but clear; it was bitterly cold, and the station was deserted. As the train left I saw him pacing fretfully up and down the platform. But it dawned on me when I checked the timetable later it was obvious he had been on the wrong portion of the train: the sleeping car section for stations up to Torino on which he had presumably been booked ran as a later train. The different portions of the train actually left Paris together and separated at Chambéry.

If he had adopted his superior and offensive attitude with all the railway staff he met, it was not surprising he had ended up as he did. He would now have a couple of hours to wait if his wife came to meet the right train. Poetic justice, I thought. Perhaps she was even then snuggled up with some dark, handsome Italian lover she had met at the resort. I rather hoped so.

Of all the trains in Europe, those in Spain had the reputation of being the slowest – that is, until Spain leapt onto the 200 km/h World Speed League with a vengeance in 1993 when its AVE services were introduced. In terms of overall average the former reputation may or may not have been deserved, but what I found most irksome was Spanish trains' incredible ability to crawl for endless kilometres at a pace only slightly above walking speed. It seems the trains had a specially low gear. They had another habit of standing still for long periods, as if waiting for something that never came. Spanish station clocks were rarely correct; although this helped in that you didn't know how late the train was, assuming you could read the timetable in the first place. Though beautifully printed, this was artfully arranged to confuse the passenger. The trains on a particular line would not all be on the one table and the tables did not always have the trains arranged in chronological order of departure.

Thus it was not so bad when you found you had missed a train you didn't know existed – it would be running late anyway. An incessant mournful blowing of horns heralded the approach of these unexpected and long forgotten trains.

Slow trains and long waits feed the tobacco habit. Attempting to give up a former 60-a-day addiction around that time I was frustrated by long periods of restless waiting, in motionless trains or at junction stations. In some countries of Europe it was difficult to find a non-smoking compartment that was not filled with smokers. This was particularly noticeable in Yugoslavia, Greece and Italy, and the officials seemed to care little.

The Spaniards were more practical: they simply did not provide any non-smoking seats – or if they did I could not find one in 1977. Perhaps they just knew it would be hopeless to expect obedience. When trains crawl along at 5 km/h for an hour on end, people simply have to smoke or do something desperate to relieve their frustration.

It is said that Spanish trains were slow because the track had so many right-angle bends. Certainly it had some curious sudden kinks as though someone with giant pincers had reached from above and twisted it, but the reality is probably that the Spaniards are not in a hurry. It is a sun-drenched leisurely country where nobody likes to waste energy rushing about, especially in the sensible afternoon siesta.

In fact the finest train of my first Eurail tour was Spanish, although the TEE *Rheingold* and the Italian *Settebello* with its nose-cone observation lounge were close runners-up. The Spanish *Catalan Talgo*, still running, is unique. Low, wide bodied and articulated together like a caterpillar with 17 short little carriages flush with the platform for easy entry, it is a train of top luxury class. The incredible thing is its ability to change wheels at Cerbère on the French border, without the passengers being aware of more than a few curious noises as it slowly moves off the end of the broad gauge (1676 mm) Spanish RENFE system onto standard gauge (1435 mm) SNCF track.

Because of the air conditioning you cannot open the windows and lean out to see what actually happens. You are instead enjoying pre-lunch sherry in the gourmet dining car, and before you realise anything unusual has occurred the train is speeding effortlessly once more along the Mediterranean coast.

My first experience of a *Talgo* was not altogether plain sailing. I had arrived at Irun from France and had determined to visit Bilbao and possibly explore the northern Spanish coast. The first attractive-sounding train was the 15.45 *Talgo* (train 354) to Miranda de Ebro where I would connect for Bilbao.

Passes were needed to board Spanish express trains. I sought one at the booking office. The attendant was unhelpful. I showed him my Eurailpass and wrote down the train number and departure time.

"*Hora tres*" he said and made to shut the window. Not understanding more than a word or two of Spanish at that stage I said so (as well as I could) and looked helpless.

"*Hora tres*" he repeated, this time pointing at the booking hall clock.

Perhaps I was a bit dim. I worked out he must be referring to the time of the train. Perhaps he meant it had left, but no, aha!, *tre* was Italian for three and Spanish was somewhat similar for many words – did he mean the train left at three? In fact, as I realised later, he was explaining that tickets would not be available until three o'clock. I should have realised – this was siesta time.

I was impressed by the *Talgo* at first sight. Not so was a well dressed lady in first class who stood next to me in the bar of the buffet car. The *Talgo* is designed to speed quickly round the sharp curves of some of the Spanish rail lines, but even the *Talgo*s cannot cope with the sudden kinks you find in the track. As the train lurched, some red wine from my glass flew out and spotted the lady's neat grey suit. I made apologetic noises and waved my arms vaguely to indicate the train itself as the culprit, and offered a handkerchief to wipe away the stains. This overture was rejected. I have since found that Spanish is one of the best languages to swear in: looking back on it I think I could have learned a lot of choice words that day!

It was in Spain that perhaps my most memorable journey of the entire European tour took place. The TER (diesel luxury air-conditioned train) *Ruta de la Plata* consisted of two coaches, of which the buffet occupied half of one. There were some two dozen passengers in all, and I faced a long and probably slow journey to where I wanted to be.

I sought the bar to sample its offerings. There did not seem to be much in the food line but I tried a ham sandwich. It was about the worst and most expensive (for what it was) I have ever experienced. Buffet and restaurant cars through most of Europe are operated by a consortium, but this does not mean identical facilities and service. Each country seems to have its own standards and there are tremendous variations. Spain, which is generally cheap, produced a sandwich consisting of one wafer-thin slice of smoky ham between two dry slices of cut bread, with no butter, for the then (1977) equivalent of about 70 cents Australian. By contrast France, which is on the whole expensive, produced on the luxury first class Trans Europ Express *L'Arbalete* half a French bread roll at least a quarter of a metre long, crisp, loaded with butter, and filled with rolls of juicy ham, all for less than a dollar. Nevertheless, the Spanish car attendant was friendly and the serveza (beer) was cold and sharp.

Returning later from my seat I found several men in the buffet. One I recognised as the travelling ticket collector, another was the guard. They all had the appearance of railwaymen and were spooning into a large plate of fresh and extremely tasty tossed salad. I know it was tasty because I was welcomed like an old friend and offered a spoon. Then the buffet attendant Manuel appeared with a plate of meat and some rolls of bread, hot and crisp from the oven. I asked "how much?" but was told: "No, not for public. Help yourself."

Manuel then produced a wicker basket containing a large glass jar of the local fresh rosé wine of the north. Very refreshing. He filled my glass. It was quite a party. Wishing to reciprocate I sought in my baggage and came up with a bottle of Spanish brandy and an Alto Duoro port. They chose the port.

"What a pity," I said after several more glasses all round, "that the driver has to miss out", showing off my few words of Spanish and trying to be jocular.

"Oh no," said the Conductor, whose English made up for the deficiencies in my Spanish, "this is the driver", and he introduced the man on my left.

"Then what, who, how ..." I began, starting to panic. They were able to calm me down before I ran screaming for the escape hatch by explaining that there were two drivers, in fact two whole train crews, because of the length of the journey, Gijon to Sevilla, a 15 hour trip. The other driver joined us later in the buffet.

It was a memorable journey because I spent an hour or so later in the driver's compartment, watching the track unfurl before us, the dream-come-true of every schoolboy of my day. Like all kids of my age group and time, I once wanted to be an engine driver.

The *Ruta de la Plata* (the 'Silver Way' in English equivalent) no longer runs. In fact, much of that ever so memorable journey was on lines that have been closed or if still open are no longer served by passenger trains. The *Ruta de la Plata* itself ran right across Spain from Gijon in the north to Sevilla, though Astorga, Salamanca, and Merida, a total trip of 964 km, of which over 300 km south from Astorga no longer carry passenger trains. I joined the train at Salamanca after a trip up the Duoro valley from Porto to Barca d'Alva on the frontier, and then across the mountains – another route since closed. In fact it could almost be said that now the trains in Spain go mainly on the plain.

If anything, I found some of the trains in Portugal even slower than the Spanish. Certainly the one I took from Vigo in Spain south across the frontier to Porto far from merited its label *rapido* at an overall 39.6 km/h! The main station in Porto is Campagna, on the north-south route and terminus for the expresses to Lisboa. There are convenient eating places nearby of the English transport café type, but of course always having wine as well, usually on draught. Here I had a most English meal of fish, and some potato soup, served by a delightful young lady of about thirteen. At the conclusion of the meal she brought a clove of garlic, which tasted so much sweeter than garlic I had been used to that on re-visiting Europe on a later occasion I tried to bring some back with me. I also re-visited the same little café and I am sure the attractive 20-year-old who was serving was the same little girl grown up.

There is another quite large station at Porto more in the centre of town, Porto Sao Bento, and here I had yet another reminder of childhood pleasures. Outside the station portico was a street vendor. From a cart with a brazier he was selling roasted chestnuts, just like we used to have round the kitchen fire in England when I was a boy.

Chapter 2
A Happy Wanderer

"A-wandering, a-wandering, until the day I die"

– Robert Service: *The Rolling Stone*

I have admitted that I once wanted to be an engine driver. That was when I began travelling on trains by myself. Before that I wanted to be an ice-cream man, as most kids did. At the age of six I was too young to be allowed on a train by myself, but I had a tricycle. Wandering off one day from my home in Acklam, Middlesbrough, I reached with difficulty the mining town of Eston, railhead of a branch line that even then had been the victim of early achievements by the 'unremunerative branch line closure' advocates. There was little road traffic then on what later became part of the main road to Whitby, but enough for a policeman to nearly have a fit as he encountered little me on my tricycle among the traffic at the relatively busy Marton Hall crossroads on the outskirts of town.

The escapade probably earned me a thrashing when I faced my worried parents back at home but I have no recollection of it so their relief must have outweighed their anger.

Eston was also on the 'country' route to the coast at Redcar and Saltburn. Some buses went that way but most used the coast road skirting the Tees-side steelworks area, through which the railway ran even more directly. Twelve minutes was all it took a Redcar express but most trains stopped at Cargo Fleet, South Bank and Grangetown and some also at Warrenby, a works Halt since renamed as British Steel (Redcar). The buses travelled through housing estates: the trains through the heavy industrial area; the glue works (which gave Middlesbrough its famous 'dead cat' smell when the wind was right), Dorman Long Engineering, Cargo Fleet Ironworks, more ironworks, and yet more ironworks.

Indeed, a whole district of Middlesbrough is marked on the map as the Ironmasters' District. With no permanent residents it is just a mass of industrial buildings and railway sidings – or was in my younger days. Powerful little 0-4-0 saddle tank locos and sometimes crane tanks chuffed backwards and forwards with long trains of wagons carrying pig iron or rolled steel. The bright glow of the opening furnaces would light up the evening sky, and when the shifts ended the steelworkers would make for the nearest pub. There were plenty in the old part of town, St Hilda's Ward, known locally as 'over the border'. The border was the main railway line between the northern perimeter of the town and the River Tees, separating the main business centre and town proper from the Ironmasters' District on the west and the docks on the east.

St Hilda's residential area was regarded as a 'no go' zone for most people at night. You could get a woman for a packet of Woodbines and a beating up for nothing without asking. Seamen from Scandinavian countries mingled with local steelworkers, consuming pint after pint of the strongest beer in Britain. It was said that even policemen went over the border only in pairs. The beer was brewed specially strong for the steelworkers – but I was too young to know any of this. I was taught to keep away from such places.

"All around the town" was a "ring of iron", as a Tees-side folk group, The Fettlers, put it in song years later:

"Coal mines to the north, steelworks to the south,
Nowt else but muck and grime right to the river mouth.
It's all around the town, the ring of iron"

Naturally Tees-side became a prime target for German bombers in World War II and I well remember the day when out of a cloudless sky a Junkers dive bomber suddenly appeared and scored a direct hit on

A HAPPY WANDERER

Middlesbrough station, destroying the magnificent arched iron roof and cutting the 12.20 Newcastle express in two.

One of my earliest recollections of songs my mother used to sing started something like "Here we are for the Redcar train". The chorus, obviously from steam train days, went "Ringety, ringety puff puff puff". As I remember them, the trains were usually hauled by 2-6-4 tank locomotives and the Redcar line was one of the first on which the LNER introduced articulated carriages, with one bogie serving the middle of two conjoined coaches. The SNCF of France now uses the same principle for the TGV and it is not unlike the wheel arrangement Patentes Talgo adopted for RENFE's *Talgo* pendular cars.

After about the age of nine there was more freedom for a youngster infected with the wanderlust, and a little more pocket money. The LNER encouraged rail travel with their offer of weekly runabout tickets – half price for under-14s – which would let you take any train for a whole week within a defined area. Of several such tickets which included Middlesbrough, the most attractive was one covering the North York moors, most of which is now a National Park.

The ticket encompassed the lines from Darlington on the East Coast Main Line, inland to Catterick Camp and Richmond, then through Stockton to West Hartlepool on the north-east coast, down the south side of the River Tees through Middlesbrough to Redcar and Saltburn, and by inland as well as coastal routes to Whitby and Scarborough. In total, some 400 km of railway. One would think nothing of hopping on to a train at, say, Saltburn, leaving the old folks sitting on the sands with their parasols (forerunner of beach umbrellas) and taking an afternoon trip through North Skelton and Brotton some 30 km down the coast to Whitby and back. Actually, that would have been rather unusual. There were very few trains that used the Saltburn–North Skelton line. Saltburn was a dead end and almost all the Whitby trains followed the main Scarborough line up Ormesby Bank to Nunthorpe at gradients steeper than 1 in 40, round the back of the Eston Hills to Guisborough, a market town where there was an old ruined priory and near it, in the former priory grounds, a very old and magnificent spreading Chestnut tree, whose massive branches touched the ground and grew up again as secondary trunks causing the whole tree to cover an acre or more.

The railway then went round the back of Saltburn to become the Whitby coast route. It was joined to the Redcar line by the little used link which branched inland just west of Saltburn station.

It was at the junction of these routes east of North Skelton where I first began to question the way railways were operated. The train had stopped – for no reason that appeared at all obvious. This irritated me, as it does most passengers who are not busy reading newspapers or otherwise taking no notice of a train's progress. Looking out of the window I could see no adverse signal, yet there we were, just stopped. Then an inspector was seen walking alongside the track towards the guard's van. Leaning out of the window I asked him why we were halted. He stared up with a frown at this callow youth who dared to question railway operation and sought to penetrate its secrets. This was not to be! Passengers were not supposed to concern themselves with such matters – good heavens! Passengers would be wanting to run the railways themselves next!

Naturally I got no reply. It was probably this incident, the first of many similar, which set me wondering what was really behind all the baffling inconsistencies and peculiarities of train working, and led eventually to its becoming the subject of a major research undertaking at university much later in life. It also served as a primer to my penchant for writing to people for explanations rather than just verbally uttering displeasure at the time. It would not have been long after this when travelling on the local bus in Middlesbrough I observed the Chief Inspector of the Corporation Transport undertaking stepping off a moving bus – a practice which passengers were warned against and prohibited from. I was so incensed that I wrote my first ever letter to the newspaper. It was not published – criticism of authority was not encouraged. The age of the whistle-blower (except at railway stations) had yet to dawn.

A HAPPY WANDERER

The inland or 'country' route to Whitby diverged from the Scarborough line after Nunthorpe, passing under the face of Roseberry Topping, Tees-side's near-mountain landmark which is just short of 1000 feet (305 metres), then through Great Ayton (where Captain James Cook spent his schooldays) and round the back of the hill on which Cook's monument still stands, to continue down the valley of the Esk to Whitby. This line still exists but almost the entire scenically dramatic coastal route is long gone.

With the runabout ticket you could easily notch up as much as 1200 km in a week. So frequently did we cover some routes that the place names were indelibly printed on the mind: Ormesby, Nunthorpe, Pinchinthorpe, Hutton Gate, Boosbeck, Brotton; then round the edge of mighty Hunt Cliff to Skinningrove, Loftus and though Grinkle tunnel to Staithes. The coast line is now truncated just short of Staithes near Boulby cliff, England's highest, and remains open only to serve Skinningrove Ironworks and Boulby potash works. At Staithes there was an iron bridge with a wind-gauge on it, and every time the northeast wind blew too strongly, which it certainly could, a bell rang and the train was not allowed over. After Staithes came Hinderwell for Runswick Bay, Kettleness – where once again the line skirted the edge of the cliff, Sandsend – where the sand began – and Whitby, with its picturesque harbour from which Captain Cook made his first voyage, and where the *Endeavour*, in which he sailed to New Zealand and Australia, was built. Whitby then had two stations: West Cliff, and the Town station down by the harbour and close to the cafés and souvenir shops where you can still buy carved ornaments of the lovely black jet once extensively mined in the area.

A railcar shuttle service linked the two stations. The 'country' trains, not only from Middlesbrough but from Malton and York and even, at times, with a through coach from London, came in to Town station while the Scarborough trains on the coast line called at West Cliff before proceeding over the tall Esk viaduct, once as prominent a Whitby landmark as the Abbey but now gone.

South of the Esk the next station was Hawsker, to where Robin Hood allegedly shot an arrow from Whitby Abbey. Although Robin Hood is commemorated in the locality by the next place after Hawsker – Robin Hood's Bay – the story of the arrow is hard to authenticate. Most of that benevolent bandit's exploits are believed to have happened far to the south in Sherwood Forest near Nottingham. To shoot an arrow a distance more than three times the known world record sounds unlikely.

After Robin Hood's Bay the railway swung inland past Fyling Hall, then back to the high clifftop at Ravenscar, down through Stainton Dale to Hayburn Wyke on the coast again before finally swinging inland through Cloughton and Scalby to plunge into a tunnel under the western suburbs of Scarborough, where it joined the Malton line before reversing back into the station. Much of Scarborough was on a headland between two bays. At Peasholm Park there was a popular miniature railway which ran around a lake and under a tunnel out to the beach at North Bay, ending up at Scalby Mills. The trains always ran 'express' through the beach station by the sands where as a youngster I was keen to get off. When I asked why the train couldn't stop at Beach the staff told me it would need an Act of Parliament to authorise it. Although I thought this to be just a put down I am not now so sure. The government could well have been daft enough to have some bureaucratic rule under the Railway Act that wouldn't let Peasholm Park management (probably Scarborough Corporation) run a railway in competition with the LNER. Probably passengers were not allowed off at Scalby Mills either, but I did not put this to the test.

There was also a country route between Middlesbrough and Scarborough but no through trains went that way. It would have meant twice reversing direction, at Battersby and again at Grosmont in the Esk Valley. That should not really have bothered them since the coast route itself meant reversing at Gallows Close junction west of Scarborough tunnel, and sometimes earlier on if the trains called at Guisborough which was on a dead end spur. To go via the country route you changed

A HAPPY WANDERER

at Grosmont for a Whitby–Malton train, then changed again at Pickering to a railcar. I only once travelled this latter part of the route when the family had been holidaying near Kirby Moorside and I think it was one of the first branches to be closed during or probably even before the mad Beeching days.

But there was yet another route we hadn't dreamed about. Some time round about the end of World War II the railways introduced a non-stop express between Middlesbrough and Scarborough – at least so the timetable said. It was not in fact non-stop: that would have been impossible operationally unless the train took the East Coast Main Line south to York, circled round west of the goods yard and came back to Scarborough through Malton – a rather lengthy trip of almost 93 miles (150 km) compared to the 58½ mile (94 km) direct coast route. The train did have to reverse at one point, (and to do so of course it could thus not technically be called 'non-stop') but it did not otherwise change direction. It also did traverse part of the East Coast Main Line, leaving Middlesbrough on the Darlington line through Thornaby and Eaglescliffe, then down over the Yarm viaduct to join the main line at Northallerton. It continued south through Thirsk to a three-way junction at Pilmoor, where it turned sharp left along a line which skirted the southern slopes of the North York Moors. Branching right at Gilling junction, the train went on to cross over the York–Scarborough line just east of Malton on the now abandoned link to Driffield. There it reversed into Malton station, pausing only until the board was 'off' for a clear run into Scarborough. This Scarborough express service continued, if I recall correctly, for quite some time after the coast and the country routes had been closed, though by then the trains would have had to follow the longer route and reverse in York itself.

It was on the main line between Darlington and York that some of us used to go, by bicycle, to a little station where a road crossed the line at a level crossing, and we used to place pennies on the track when a train was coming. This was at Cowton, just south of Croft junction, where the expresses would be really getting up speed, and when a train had passed over we would retrieve our pennies – sometimes after a lengthy search as they were thrown clear under the train's blast and would land yards away – all flattened out and enlarged in circumference, almost paper thin. It was no doubt a practice the railways would have frowned upon but it was hardly likely to lead to a derailment, the impact being less noticeable to the locomotive and driver than the expansion joints in the track.

About this time 'train spotting' was a popular habit among young folk, encouraged (and profitably so) by the firm of Ian Allen, which published excellent booklets listing all the engine numbers by different sheds and regions. I once had one of these books but never seriously indulged in the practice. At Darlington on the main line there would be dozens of kids standing at the platform end with their Ian Allen books carefully marking off the different locos that passed, and sometimes venturing forward to the driver with the request: "Can I come on the footplate?" Some let you for a moment, others merely scowled.

I was more fascinated by the different carriages and their liveries than by the locomotives, but even more so by where the trains went and where they came from and what happened when they followed an unusual route and why. On one occasion a train returning from Kildale on the Whitby country line, instead of reversing at Battersby junction as these trains always did to go down the bank from Great Ayton into Middlesbrough, suddenly shot away in the forward direction and roared through Ingleby, Stokesley, Sexhow, Potto, and Trenholm Bar to Picton, where it paused respectfully to join the Leeds-Stockton line before continuing non-stop into Middlesbrough through Eaglescliffe and Thornaby. I never found out why. That particular line was comparatively little used and has now long been closed and lifted.

I remember once seeing a brown and yellow railcar at Pinchinthorpe on the Middlesbrough–Scarborough line. Those were Great Western colours but I was not close enough to read any identifying letters. What on earth a Great Western railcar would be doing in the north-east Yorkshire moors I could not then imagine but I have since discovered that such a railcar was on temporary loan to the LNER in 1944 for trials in the Newcastle area so the one I saw could have been it. Guesswork about railway mysteries can be a fascinating hobby. There always must be a explanation but trying to discover it from official sources at the time can be like extracting wisdom teeth.

Railway timetables became my most avidly sought reading matter in those days and I must have spouted so much about them that I became known for a time by the nickname "Timetables".

Of course all trains in those days were steam-hauled. Even the railcars were steam-powered. These were very popular because if you were lucky and the thing was going the right way, you could get a seat behind the driver and look ahead along the line, something which always gives a train journey that little extra thrill.

The green and yellow "Sentinel" steam railcars could be operated either from the front end or a tiny driving compartment at the rear, separated by a window from the passenger seats. Here you could watch the driver slide his brass knobbed handle up or down the control panel, like on a motor boat or tram.

Steam trains, though making a nice healthy chuffing sound, had one disadvantage: when you looked out of the window you risked getting a cinder in your eye. The sash windows had great leather straps by which to raise or lower them. Early railway vandals would cut these off, stealing them for use as razor strops.

In high school music classes we roared out songs from the *Scottish Students Song Book*. A favourite was a song about a train journey, Riding down from Bangor, with its thumping tune and slightly suggestive verses. The words of the song highlighted the steam train hazard of eye damage, but we young travellers were not usually so lucky as to have a sympathetic village maiden to minister to our injuries.

Talking of village maidens, there was a club down in the village of Marske-by-the-Sea on the Saltburn line where in my early teens my friends and I would go, usually by bike, to meet the local girls. Occasionally we would go by train and one day the girl I particularly fancied had to go home early but a couple of others saw me and my friend to the station. To my surprise one of them, a brunette called Dot, kissed goodbye in a more passionate way than any kiss I had known before. Wow! I thought, but like a fool never followed it up. Some years later I saw this girl again, then 18 years old and engaged, a beautiful young woman in full flower. What had I missed, just through catching a train! But I had been crazy about the other girl, also called Dot (a popular name at the time). She was a long haired blonde with a somewhat sulky pouting look, but not nearly so responsive to male attention.

In those days our infatuation with the pretty girls of Marske, Skelton and Brotton meant no more than innocent flirting with little budding females whose bodies we hardly dared touch. Kissing consisted of a few pecks, albeit on lips rather than cheeks but not the open mouth drawn-out tongue-searching ritual being made so fashionable by American movies. We talked more than acted when it came to serious sex, our knowledge being rudimentary and experience non-existent.

Our interests were rather in lemonade, newspaper-wrapped fish and chips, folk songs, going places and being seen. Television had not then invaded homes and changed the mores of society the way it has since; amusements were what you made them and self-devised.

At school some of us played a home-made paper and pencil game called Travel. Nowadays it would be called a 'problem solving exercise'. Two players each had a map of an imaginary country on which would be marked towns and railway routes, and each had a set of railway timetables, made up by himself. The first player would name two of the opponent's towns and nominate a departure time and day. The other would then calculate how long the journey would take. I'm not sure how or at what stage anyone was said to have won: perhaps it wasn't that kind of game. A bit like real travel in fact. Sometimes the operator 'wins'; sometimes the traveller.

After high school it was off to university, the nearest being at Newcastle on Tyne, a branch of the University of Durham, formerly called Armstrong College and noted for its courses in Naval Architecture, Tyneside being a major shipbuilding centre at that time. The fact that it was the only university to offer an undergraduate course in Town Planning – my chosen career path – had something to do with my going there. For about the first year I lived in digs but this became expensive and when I found that a season ticket between Middlesbrough and Newcastle would cost less I opted for home comforts and long distance commuting.

Between Middlesbrough and Newcastle there were two principal passenger train routes. A season ticket would normally cover one only, but could cover two if one was restricted to 'through' journeys only.

The railway meaning of 'through journey' is something one learns only by experience and I will comment on it further anon. My season ticket was for the coast route, Middlesbrough, West Hartlepool, Sunderland, Newcastle; places which the wooden corridor coaches displayed on nameboards on the side of the roof. This was the way the regular through trains went; they were express or rather semi-fast in that they omitted most intermediate stations, especially north of Tees-side. Loco-hauled, and usually including a buffet car, they took just over an hour and a half on the journey, leaving Middlesbrough at twenty past the hour and returning from Newcastle at a quarter past. Mostly these trains were full, and by getting in the same compartment most days you got to know the same people. Like a club, one made friends and sometimes useful contacts. It is interesting that there has long been some affinity between train and boat travel in the terminology used. Just as on a ship one talks of getting your 'sea legs', on a long distance or corridor train when you start walking about you talk of getting your 'train legs', and individual trains, like ships, have in the past often been referred to as 'she'.

Getting your 'train legs' has nothing to do with unsteady walk from other possible causes. Trains with buffet cars did not suffer from Britain's strange liquor licensing restrictions which in those days allowed drinking only between eleven and two in the middle of the day and from five to ten in the evening, although these times varied from place to place and where two towns straddled a border, say between counties, there would be a rush of traffic, sometimes by car but often merely on foot, between the pubs then closing and those still open on the other side. But the laws applied to 'premises' and a moving train was not included in the definition. The buffet car on the train could therefore remain open for the sale of alcoholic drinks (in any case its main revenue source) for as long as the management thought appropriate and the stewards were willing or able to work.

I say 'able to' because I well remember one occasion when the buffet crew of the Newcastle–Middlesbrough train had been over-indulging in Newcastle Brown Ale during their lunch break and they were exceedingly merry on the way down to Tees-side. One would hear from the kitchen the occasional crash of crockery followed by maniacal laughter. However, service was still given and I had no problems. I was therefore a little saddened when at Middlesbrough, the end of that particular run, an inspector boarded the train. There had been some complaint and on leaving the buffet I was asked if I had noticed anything unusual about the service. "No," I said, "it was very good. Those two are always good helpful friendly stewards" – as they in fact were, but I do not think my words would have impressed the Inspector when he saw the piles of unwashed dishes and talked to the fellows who were, in Geordie terms, more or less 'palatic'.

Some of the trains did not have a buffet. One time we were going from university on a geography excursion which involved taking the train to, I think, West Hartlepool. I recall protesting when I found the lecturer had booked for the three-fifteen. "That's the worst train," I said, but when pressed for a reason realised that it was only the lack of a buffet that distinguished it from most of the others. The five-eighteen was another bad one. I forget whether it had a buffet but it was always crowded and had extra stops which made for a very late arrival on Tees-side.

The coast line between Tyne and Tees was not without its scenic attractions, with glimpses of the coast between Sunderland and Hartlepool, even though the sand was often black from coal dust. Most fascinating were the aerial ropeways that carried buckets of colliery waste out to be tipped in the sea – awful pollution but it was certainly eye-catching. There was a film made entitled *Get Carter* starring Michael Caine which ended up with the bad guy being shot and dumped into one of these buckets and taken out to sea in it.

Approaching Tees-side one could glimpse the two striking bridges, the Transporter and the Newport lifting bridge. In fact the train went under the approach span of the latter. Both are unusual though not quite unique. On one occasion the Newcastle train had to be diverted north of Stockton and took the freight line over the Thorpe Thewles viaduct, one of several magnificent brick arch structures which were monuments to the early railway builders. There was another where the Newcastle-Ferryhill relief route, still used when trains are diverted at weekends for engineering work on the main line, crossed the River Wear south of Washington, but the Thorpe Thewles viaduct, like the Esk viaduct at Whitby, is long gone. It is a great pity that industrial archeology is not more carefully preserved. Even without the railway, these viaducts could serve a useful purpose as pedestrian ways.

Although the north-east coast line had basically a regular interval service, the timetable had some irregularities, particularly at peak and at off-peak (as distinct from normal or regular) times. For example there was no 7.20 morning express from Middlesbrough. To reach Newcastle by nine in the morning you had to catch the seven o'clock which was the same as all the others except that it stopped at a lot of intermediate stations and took longer.

If you wanted to reach Tyneside earlier still, there was the 5.20 workmen's train which would get you there about eight o'clock, but this was not my cup of tea.

There was often a quicker connection by going inland to Darlington on the London–Newcastle main line. I therefore soon changed my ticket to cover this mainline route, although the officials marked it "for through journeys only". Since there were no through trains between Middlesbrough and Newcastle via Darlington this always meant a change of train and here I first learned the true meaning of connectivity, something which railways almost the world over have yet to understand.

Mind you, I tried to cheat. Expecting a connection to be made when it is advertised as such is one thing. Expecting a clearly timetabled 'non-connection' to become effective is quite another. But this is where a knowledge of timetables coupled with experience of train running can be valuable.

There was a London to Scotland night express that came through Darlington around 5.40 in the morning. The first train from Middlesbrough at 5.29 missed it – if the express was on time. But often it was not, and I found it useful on occasion to risk the early rising necessary to catch the first of the local trains so that I might reach Newcastle before seven in the warm comfort of an overnight express which was never crowded. I would stand there with my fingers crossed as the main line train came into Darlington from the south. Either it would be the one I hoped for, or it would be "Number One Parcels" which followed it. They both looked about the same from the front, but the parcels train had no passenger accommodation, and my heart would sink when this was what it turned out to be. But I never asked: just waited in hope. "Better to travel hopefully" always. If I missed my secret non-connection it was not a totally abortive journey, because there was a Darlington–Newcastle workmen's passenger train via Bishop Auckland which still reached Newcastle before the first train on the coast route would have done. This went through Shildon, where the first steam-hauled passenger train started from on 27 September 1825 and which was the scene of a mass railway parade 150 years later for which many old locos were brought out from the museums.

Darlington was always a good place to stop to change trains: it bustled with railway activity and at the end of platform three sat *Locomotion No. 1*, the engine which hauled that first train down to Stockton-on-Tees, where the original ticket office is still to be seen in

Bridge Road. The locomotive itself has since been moved to Darlington North Road railway museum where, unfortunately, it is seen by far fewer people than would have been the case if it had stayed where it was.

Streamlined Scottish expresses thundered past on the main line outside the main station at Darlington Bank Top. From the point of view of a Tees–Tyne commuter, Darlington station also boasted a refreshment room, and nearly all the main line trains carried a buffet or restaurant car, which few did on the coastal line after steam trains had been superseded by diesel multiple units.

Since as a university student one gets to travelling at all sorts of hours, depending on the varying lecture times, I had the opportunity to sample many of the crack expresses such as the *North Briton*, the *Fair Maid* and the *Queen of Scots* Pullman. I did not experience the *Flying Scotsman*, which never recognised Darlington, or the *Aberdonian*, which only ran in the middle of the night, but I frequently travelled one way or the other on the *Heart of Midlothian* Kings Cross–Edinburgh express and it was here I met Charlie, the first of a number of British Rail restaurant car staff to whom I soon became a familiar face.

The occasion was a journey up to Edinburgh for a student function. Student finances do not usually extend to dining car indulgences but afternoon tea (pot of tea, bread and butter, jam and a slice of cake) at one shilling and fivepence seemed a reasonable deal. I had my tea. I paid the bill, with a shilling and a sixpence.

The table was cleared. Other passengers left. I remained seated.

The steward came along. "Was there anything else, sir?"

"Just my change," I said.

"Oh, of course, sir," he said through clenched teeth, turning quickly back to the kitchen, then reappearing. "Your penny change, sir," he said, with as much politeness as he could muster and hiding his feelings behind a forced smile. No-one ever asked for a penny change in his dining car before, I am sure, but possibly not many students considered a restaurant car meal to be within the reasonable scope of their meagre budget.

Charlie and I met many times after that and became great friends. Years afterwards when I worked in the Scottish Highlands and happened be in Edinburgh Waverley station just as the old *Heart of Midlothian* arrived from London I sought the restaurant car and there was Charlie, close to retirement but the same as ever. He took me to the Railway Club for a drink and we had a great laugh about old times and the penny change episode.

Another railway staffer I got to know was Danny, on the Liverpool–Newcastle train and later on the fairly short-lived *Tees-Thames* express which ran from Saltburn to Kings Cross. By then I was living in Redcar and liked to break my homeward journey from Darlington, where I then worked, at Eaglescliffe. There the Northallerton–Stockton and Darlington–Saltburn lines crossed, and by changing from the local train I could hop on the ex-London *Tees–Thames* and have a drink. Sometimes I even caught the same train as far as Eaglescliffe on my morning journey to work, and once or twice was treated to a free breakfast in the dining car kitchen.

An even quicker rail journey was possible between Tees-side and Newcastle avoiding both Hartlepool and Darlington by using the direct Stockton–Ferryhill line through Sedgefield. There were few connections this way and it was not strictly allowed by my ticket. Or so the black-coated, humourless, bowler-hatted ticket collectors of the day maintained when they wrote out an excess fare docket every time I tried to travel by this shortest route. The Stockton–Ferryhill line is still there and if through trains between Middlesbrough and Newcastle used it the journey time could be cut almost in half. Ever tried to make useful constructive suggestions to railway management?

A season ticket even on a straightforward point-to-point route is still a bonus and gives the traveller a feeling of superiority over even the most awkward ticket collector. And so it should! A season ticket 'cheats' on the proper fare, but it does so unquestionably legally. It is an arrangement whereby the normal repetitive daily fare is 'commuted' into something more agreeable to the traveller. This is the origin of the term 'commuter' which signifies not a daily traveller to work, as many think, but one who has a season ticket on public transport. Rail travel gave us the word, yet ironically we nowadays talk of a car commuter who travels daily to work but may never have seen a train in his life, much less travelled on one. I have even heard it applied to airline passengers on thousand mile journeys. Like so many English language terms, usage can blur distinctions in meaning and nowadays the word 'commuter' is nearly synonymous with 'traveller'.

Talking of words and their meanings, on Tees-side you will hear some curious expressions. By and large the area is not noted for a distinct regional accent. It is even said that some Professor of English once asserted that Tees-side accent was the purest – English as it ought to be spoken – but I have heard the same thing said about the way they talk in Inverness. You may have difficulty with Geordie talk if you go to Tyneside and they say "Howway then, hinnie, how ya gannin, then? That's a bonnie ganzie yer wearin'", but it can be roughly understood once you know what a 'ganzie' is.

In Middlesbrough a classic is "Ee aye, eh!" which stands for "How surprising. Yes, that's true. Isn't it remarkable?"

An economy of words, you might say. Beware, all you affirmative action and politically correct speech advocates! On Tees-side people will call you 'love' whatever your sex, although never if both speaker and hearer are male. If they are being really affectionate or just more than usually friendly and helpful they may call you 'pet' instead. If you get offended and start spouting about gender neutral language they won't know what you are talking about and you might end up, like Florrie or Andy Capp, getting 'thumped'.

Andy Capp's creator, cartoonist Reg Smythe, was from Hartlepool and his brother Bob was a steward on the *Tees–Thames* train.

Andy Capp cartoons are typical of England's Tees-side. The one in which Andy 'thumps' his wife Florrie and a policeman comes up and thumps Andy – then Florrie thumps the policeman, is absolutely true to life. I've seen it happen, though not actually with a policeman. Even on Tees-side you don't thump policemen with impunity. And if you visit Hartlepools don't ask them who hung the monkey until you have established a genuine friendship.

It always pays, if you want to get on with the 'natives', to learn a few words in the local idiom.

After university my first paid job was in the London area. I stayed with a friend of my father's at Ilford in Essex and worked some four miles (6.4 km) closer to the City at West Ham. I had a choice of transport modes for my daily home-to-work trip: my faithful bicycle, the Central Line 'tube' from Gants Hill to Stratford, or the surface electric train from Ilford to Stratford or Maryland station, the latter being a shade nearer to work.

It was not long before I found that by double booking return tickets between Ilford, Stratford and a place in between I could save a penny on the daily fare through one of the fare anomalies typical of railways the world over. That is, until the Inspector found out (damn these Inspectors!) and caught me with an outward half from Stratford to Forest Gate and a return half from there to Ilford, while travelling on a non-stop Stratford–Ilford train. At peak times the best trains on the Liverpool Street–Shenfield line stopped only at the main stations of Stratford, Ilford and Romford. I think I got away with it, pointing out to the inspector that both tickets had been validly purchased and together they covered the journey, so how could I be charged excess? But it was a bit too much of a hassle to have to break the journey midway every other day and possibly argue the toss with inspectors and I soon gave up this practice.

The idea of covering one journey with different tickets for different parts was something I developed in my university days when I tried to do a lot of travelling with limited financial resources. Possibly the extreme was one day in 1949 when I travelled with my friend Walter from Middlesbrough to Carlisle. Although my season ticket covered half the journey, my friend faced having to pay normal fare. I worked out a plan to reduce this by 'double booking' – or rather quintuple booking. Before seven in the morning it was possible for anyone to obtain a workman's return to selected places. Walter purchased a workman's to Sunderland (76.2 km) for 2/4½d. There he left the express, walked round to the booking office and took a 'cheap day return' to Newcastle (19.6 km at 2/7d – note the vast difference in fare per unit distance!) while I continued to Newcastle where I had time to buy two 'springtime cheap day' tickets to Hexham, another 35.9 km, at 3/- each. The normal return fare would have been over 6/-. Walter reached Newcastle at 9.30 and together we boarded the 9.45 stopping train. At Hexham we rested awhile outside the station, then booked cheap day returns on the 10.50 Carlisle express as far as Haltwhistle (3/4d each for the next 26.2 km). Another express was due 10 minutes later, allowing just time to go over the bridge to the booking office for 4/11d cheap day returns the remaining 37.1 km to Carlisle.

In all this came to 16/2½d for a round trip of 390 km – a fraction of the normal return fare and perfectly legal! The homeward trip involved only one train change at Newcastle and was accomplished rather quicker. No officious ticket collector harassed us and the only snag was arriving in Stockton on the last train of the day, the London night express, and having to walk the last 4 km home.

When I lived in London I went out with a young woman who lived in the same house, daughter of the owner who kept a fruit shop. We had friends over at Crouch End on London's north side, and since neither of us had a car we went there by train. We would take the electric from Ilford and then go by a comparatively little known and used cross-town line through Tottenham, home of the then famous 'Spurs' football team, to Crouch Hill. This was easier for us than to go to Crouch End via Liverpool Street, Kings Cross and Finsbury Park.

The Crouch End line has now long gone but the line we used remains as the Gospel Oak to Barking line with, I think, a rather more frequent service than I remember in the early 'fifties when we travelled on it between Crouch Hill and Wanstead Park, next door to Forest Gate on the Shenfield line.

TRAINCATCHER

Coming back to Ilford one evening from a night out at Crouch End we experienced the wrath that only passengers smoking in non-smoking compartments can show when caught at it. In the seat opposite a well dressed and made-up woman looked up at the non-smoking sign, calmly picked a packet of cigarettes from her handbag, and lit up. At that time I was a non-smoker and so was my companion. Politely I drew attention to the lady's error. She was indignant, but she extinguished the cigarette and muttered to her companion, another female, until we came to Ilford, our station. As we rose to depart she turned to face us, eyes blazing. "My husband's the Chief Constable of Ilford. You're a swine, that's what you are!" she said.

We rather doubted that she was old enough to have a husband in such a position, and if indeed she was, and he was, then we reckoned she ought to have known better. We somehow didn't think the Chief Constable would take kindly to his wife (or more possibly daughter or niece) being fined for contravening railway by-laws!

Nowadays in this sort of situation I quietly go off and find another carriage. As you meet all sorts when travelling by train you soon learn how best to cope with the awkward ones, when you can. I was nearly sick once travelling in the dining car of a London–Newcastle train. Opposite me sat a large American gentleman with a huge ring on his finger. It was a Bishop's ring.

"I am the Bishop of Birmingham, Alabama," he told me, but he spoiled our friendly little verbal exchange when he took out a huge cigar and lit up, making me just about puke over the remains of my meal. A cigar is a meal in itself and the regulations at that time, while allowing cigarettes in the dining car, certainly prohibited cigars and pipes.

I first encountered on a train another kind of person I soon learned to avoid, those people we would now refer to as 'alternatively sexually preferred' or something equally contorted.

Sitting alone in a compartment quietly reading a book I was joined by a respectable looking middle-aged gentleman who took the seat opposite. Breaking the unwritten English rule of not attempting conversation with strangers on a train, he quickly broke the ice by first asking about the book I was reading. In fact I think it was the Bible – which should have warned me about people like him. He went on to ask all sorts of things about my home and family, and by the time he got to asking what colour pyjamas I wore, I noticed his eyes had taken on a sort of glazed look and that he was edging across closer to me. I kept my knees close together and held the Good Book in a protective position.

I was only 16 years old at the time and this kind of encounter was something my parents had not told me about. In fact they had told me nothing about sex – my brother and I were even shooed out of the room when the cat had kittens and it was not until at school I had to draw the male and female genitals for biology homework that my mother, gasping with horror, said, "Oh, so they teach that at school now do they? So we needn't tell you about it, then" – and anything I had not been told then I had to find out for myself.

It can of course be fun finding out, but not about everything. I had heard of people then called 'queers' but it looked like I was now finding out about them the hard way.

Some lineside feature attracted my attention to the window and I gratefully took the opportunity to leap to my feet and rush into the corridor with a cry of, "Ah, the brickworks!" or something equally irrelevant and normally uninteresting. My compartment mate was not going to let things go as easily as that. He followed. I stood trembling in the corridor displaying as much interest as possible in nothing very startling outside. Then he suddenly took hold and kissed me on the cheek.

I thought of excusing myself to go to the toilet, but felt that might be more dangerous. Ah! The buffet! I remembered how that passenger on the Liverpool train had escaped the man with the cheeses in Jerome K. Jerome's *Three Men in a Boat*. "I'm going for a cup of tea," I said, tearing free and hurrying along the corridor. Of course he followed and insisted on paying. So while he was settling the bill I sneaked off and got into another carriage, which he no doubt though rather mean.

I still prefer a compartment to myself and have sought it ever since, but going in with other passengers in this case meant safety in numbers. What I do avoid is being in with just one other passenger, unless it is someone I know or, perhaps, someone I think I would like to know.

Chapter 3

Finding the Station

C'est magnifique, mais ce n'est pas la gare! (with apologies to Maréchal Bosquet)

Most people will have heard the one about the stranger in town who grumbled about the distance to the station: "Why didn't they put it nearer the town?" he asked. The reply: "Well, they thought it would be better near the railway."

A railway station in the heart of a city is always one of the things you expect and which makes touring Europe cheaply with a Eurailpass so attractive. Historically, however, stations were built mostly on the edges of city centres or, in smaller towns without neglected areas available for redevelopment, on the edge of the town itself. As Karlhans Müller observes in *The Architecture of Transport in the Federal Republic of Germany* the widespread occurrence of Bahnhofstrasse (Station Road) in German street names testifies to the urban development phenomenon of towns extending toward their already existing railway stations, just as 'Dock Street' would be a road leading to the docks and in recent years 'Airport Drive' its counterpart.

Railway stations became a meeting place and focus both for social interaction and for urban development, especially if they were close to the existing urban centres. Attempts to direct the course of urban growth by building stations miles from existing towns were usually doomed to failure. Wyalong Central in New South Wales was one such. Built in 1903 half way between the small town of Wyalong and a crossroads settlement 4 km away called West Wyalong, they hit on the 'Central' name in hopes for the future. But West Wyalong grew as a staging post on the Newell Highway linking Queensland to Victoria and Wyalong Central never became anything much more than a railway station, with no connecting transport, until it died in the 1970s during a rail closure frenzy by the NSW government. One cannot help thinking that rail systems may be cutting their own collective throats when they close stations in central locations in favour of some isolated spot in the sticks dependent entirely on private transport for access.

In most of the world's older cities the stations – often buildings of much grandeur – would be convenient for food shops, comfortable budget priced hotels, perhaps the post office and a bank. There would be local transport, too, although often not really needed because the station is in the middle of everything.

One of the advantages of rail has long been this facility of city centre to city centre travel. None of that tiresome journeying to an airport on the edge of the urban area. Hence rail has proved more than a match for air travel for distances up to about 300 km, where the time gained by the aircraft's faster speed is lost on the terminal to city sector.

The Australian National and the State Transport Authority of South Australia planners did not get their act together very well when the standard gauge railway was brought to Adelaide and they built a new long distance terminal at Keswick, 3 km from the city centre. Would it have been so difficult to take the new line into the old station in combination with the broad gauge as had been done in Melbourne years before? South Australian railway people had more experience of multiple gauge railways than anybody else in the world and the costs could have easily been swallowed up in the cost of the commercial redevelopment of the old city centre station. Instead, passengers now find themselves stuck out in the suburbs, with a minimum eight minute walk to the local platforms – at which most of the city-bound suburban trains do not even stop! Long distance passengers on the *Indian Pacific*, who once could enjoy an hour's stroll through the interesting streets of the historic city of Port Pirie (where the train was formerly turned) now spend that hour in inner suburban Adelaide with nowhere to go except a private enterprise refreshment room with limited bar and seating, and into which they cannot even take their luggage.

The two main railway stations in Brisbane – Central and Roma Street – are better examples of what can be done by intelligent redevelopment and co-operation between Government and developers. Three quarters of a kilometre apart and on the very edge of the central business district, both are served by all suburban trains. Brand-new hotels adjoin or stand above each station. At Central there are escalators, pedestrian walkways and overpasses, bars, bookstalls, and even the railway offices are conveniently adjacent. But even so, there is room for improvement. There are no banks, no post office (only a letter box) and, more surprisingly, no left luggage facilities. These can be found at Roma Street, the long distance interchange where the different gauges now meet and which is also the terminal for intrastate and city to airport buses. Further redevelopment is planned at both stations which may remedy the present minor defects, most obvious of which is the lack of an airport rail link.

In many cities, especially on the continent of Europe, new lines have been laid to link the airports to the city centre, or new stations have been built on existing lines to serve the airport. British examples of the former are Manchester and of the latter Birmingham International and Tees-side, northeast England. But in many places existing railways go right past an airport with no station serving it. Napier in New Zealand, Cairns and Proserpine in Queensland, and even Sydney are 'Down Under' examples.

At Gisborne in New Zealand the railway actually crosses the airport runway, but passenger trains did not stop there unless, one presumes, an aircraft was about to land or take off. During World War II a similar situation arose at Ballykelly in Northern Ireland where a necessary runway extension produced one of the world's most unusual level crossings, and air traffic controllers had to be linked into the electric block signalling system of the Belfast–Derry railway.

Level crossings have always been something of a nuisance to railway operation, as well as an inconvenience to highway traffic.

However, they are points of contact between transport modes and many have become the site of passenger stations, allowing potentially effective staff deployment by combining duties of ticket issue and gate control. There was something safe about the solid old gates that used to swing across the railway in the days when a 'level crossing keeper' was regarded as an honourable job. Why did they have to go? They were there more to benefit the road users than to benefit the railway, so should have been a responsibility of the highway authority. A beautiful crossing still remains at Ballarat, Victoria and deserves to be listed for preservation as part of Australian industrial heritage together with the magnificent gantry of semaphore signals and the station itself. Absence of gates, as in many such crossings, invites collisions.

Ballarat Station in Victoria, Australia – a monument to history. (Colin Taylor)

In the old days where the seaports were the points of entry to a country, the railways went right down to and along the quayside. Airports now

FINDING THE STATION

fulfil that entry function and equally need rail links, but preferably with the track underground and not along the runway. Migrants to Australia used to come by sea to Port Melbourne. The first thing they saw was the train lined up ready for them on the quay at the terminus of the oldest passenger line in the country. But people will be a long time waiting for a train at Melbourne's Tullamarine or Brisbane's new domestic and international terminals – in spite of plans and politicians' promises!

However, the announcement of Sydney as host city for the 2000 Olympics may yet see action on a long-mooted airport rail link there.

It is also sensible to have effective linkage between rail and other transport modes: buses, taxis, trams and ferries, and to provide car parking and setting down places for the 'kiss and ride' commuter. Brisbane's suburban system does this very effectively, and Queensland Rail planners have made sure also that the major stations in the city area have facilities close at hand, sometimes in air space above the station.

Yet in several other Queensland cities, recent changes have seen railway stations taken way out of town, accessible only by dedicated buses or taxi, with few if any facilities for passengers. In Western Australia, new stations on the Perth suburban system have been built in the centre of a freeway. One wonders how accessible such a location can ever be.

In Western Australia the Railways introduced a new fast train from Perth to Bunbury down the southern coastal belt, but at about the same time they closed the station and built a shopping centre over the line, so that some of the time saved by the new service is lost in waiting for and travelling the last 3 km on the connecting bus.

On my most recent visit to Britain I was dismayed to find how some once thriving stations had been sold off to developers with little or no thought for the passengers still wanting to use them. No left luggage office, no shelter, no toilets: how much longer does British Rail (BR) still expect to have passengers? Selling off railway land and buildings alone is no way to make the railways pay, any more than selling other government services is a valid way out of financial difficulty. Once the land and the buildings are lost, it will cost much more to replace them.

A city railway station is a 'central area' type of land use in town planning terms. They should be at places of maximum pedestrian circulation and activity. Apart from the obvious things like ticket office and timetable information, their facilities should include adequate shelter, seating, toilets, luggage lockers, telephones, baths/showers, tourist and public transport information and police presence or other emergency facilities, and, where any appreciable waiting or train changing is involved, shops, banks, post offices, dry cleaning, shoe cleaning, hairdressers, laundries and restaurants.

There is a fascination about any railway station, shared perhaps by modern airports and to a lesser extent by bus stations. They are places to get to somewhere from.

Even if the services are few and far between, at a railway station you see the lines going off into the distance and know they lead somewhere. What romantic spots lie beyond the point where the tracks disappear round that farthest bend, drop down over the distant obtuse summit, or converge to that disappearing point of perspective on the horizon?

Perhaps the station notice boards will tell you; or perhaps not. At Warragul in Victoria in 1980 the station nameboard proclaimed it to be the junction for Walhalla, far away up in the mountains on a long abandoned branch. And then there are the stations or unnamed junctions where you see lines going off somewhere, you know not where, and you wonder, do trains still go there and where is it they go? The timetable may give no indication and if there is not a named station where the tracks diverge you may not know exactly where you are anyway so even the map may be little help.

You cannot always carry maps with you, certainly not at a detailed scale covering a long journey. I have found it fascinating to look up a map afterwards, when I see some branch line disappearing off into the bush or into the hills or merely out of sight behind trees or buildings. It may be only a factory siding, a harbour branch, or leading to a mine. It could be long disused, or even a proposed railway to somewhere that

FINDING THE STATION

was never completed and has since been abandoned, like the Unanderra to Maldon coal line south of Sydney which was started by one government and scrapped by the next. In central Sydney there are still unused platforms at St James, built in 1926, and the long abandoned Eastern Suburbs branch of the City Railway lay uncompleted for more than 60 years until the government decided it made sense to finish it.

Elsewhere there are stations to which trains have never run. I remember seeing the name Bloomsbury on a London Underground station in a pre-war film. No station of that name existed. The scenes were shot in the disused British Museum station in the part of Holborn WC1 known by that name.

Many cities have more than one station, and some smaller places do too – or used to. Crianlarich in the Highlands of Scotland – population negligible – is at the crossing of the Stirling-Oban and the Glasgow–Fort William lines, one being the former Caledonian Railway at the low level and the other the North British with its station at Crianlarich (Upper). A short spur linked the two and allowed trains from Glasgow to drop down to the Oban line. This is now the only way to Oban since the scenic route from Dunblane Junction on the Perth line through the Pass of Leny and past lovely Lochearnhead (junction of another long abandoned link from Perth via Crieff) was closed.

Long ago I made the trip from Glasgow's former Buchanan Street station, down along Clydeside past Dumbarton to Helensborough, past Garelochhead to Loch Long, then over the pass to the bonnie banks of Loch Lomond opposite the steep, steep side of Ben Lomond itself. From there to Crianlarich (Upper) where, if I remember correctly, I changed and caught another train at Crianlarich (Lower). The track then continues westward to awesome Loch Awe and through the Pass of Brander to Connel Ferry, former junction for the branch to the slate quarries and Fort William ferry at Ballachulish, and then to Oban.

Oban is a typical west Scotland fishing port and resort about which I have three particular memories: there was a building looking like a Greek temple on a hill east of the town, I tasted for the first time fresh cockles and in a newsagent's I bought a copy of *Johnson's Road Atlas of Great Britain* which at a scale of 3 miles to an inch was tremendously detailed and, importantly to me, showed the railways. Now long without its covers, loosely held together by its remnant binding and frayed at the edges, it is still a well-used and treasured part of my library.

This was a sentimental journey in part, since my mother came from Port Glasgow and my great grandfather from Crieff.

Despite the closure of many railways, in urban as well as rural areas like the Scottish Highlands, many places still boast more than one railway station. In contrast to the distressing tendency of some systems to capitalise on the real estate value of inner city locations and make the train traveller go out of town it is interesting to see how some of the changes made under the banner of rationalisation – in the cases where it is correctly so called – have led to better use of city and railway infrastructure.

Rationalisation does not necessarily imply closure – it means making the best use of what you have. Sometimes rationalisation has meant the construction of new rail links at considerable expense – as when the Japanese National Railways linked its Tokyo Ueno and Central *Shinkansen* stations and Oslo acquired a new tunnel through the city's heart linking east and west main lines at Sentral. But much is owed to the multiplicity of early railway builders who criss-crossed urban areas as well as the countryside with a maze of lines, duplicating and overlapping each other and clearly ripe for genuine rationalisation.

British Rail sensibly redeveloped Liverpool Street in London (and in 1994 received a Vision Award for an outstanding example of area improvement in so doing) by combining with the terminus of the Great Eastern lines the cross-London branch of the London and North Western Railway which terminated immediately next door at the former Broad Street station, once served by morning breakfast car expresses from Manchester, taking businessmen close to the financial heart of the City.

Although these services no longer operate it is still possible, though

FINDING THE STATION

not done, to run trains from Liverpool Street to possibly more stations in Britain than from any other London terminus and even to run them to several other London termini without venturing onto the tube system, of which only the former Metropolitan and District lines have a loading gauge suitable for BR standard vehicles. In the past it was possible to connect to every other London mainline terminal in this way, even to Kings Cross, next door St Pancras, and Fenchurch Street. Even now there are lines within the Greater London area which would make it possible for a train to go 'direct' (i.e. without reversing direction) from Liverpool Street to Kings Cross Thameslink, to Waterloo, Victoria, London Bridge, Cannon Street and even Charing Cross. But you would not be able to traverse most of these links by passenger train and even if you could it would be a very long way round indeed.

At peak hour you can take a train direct from Liverpool Street to Willesden junction on the Euston–Glasgow main line, via Dalston and Primrose Hill but at other times you would need to change at Stratford. From Willesden the trains from Stratford continue on to Richmond, there linking with direct trains to and from Waterloo or, with a change usually at Clapham junction, Victoria.

With time on your hands and armed with a Britrail or similar Pass, it is therefore possible to nicely avoid paying a separate fare on the Underground on a trip between two of a number of London's mainline stations – and see more of the city on the way into the bargain.

It was in such a situation I decided once to travel from Kings Cross to Euston by train. There are frequent buses or taxis and they are only one station apart on the 'tube' but to get to and from the Underground platforms you have to walk nearly as far along tunnels and up and down escalators as if you simply hoofed it half a mile (800 metres) along Euston Road NW1. But it was a cold day and I chose to do it by train.

This attempt at circumnavigating central London (and circumventing London Transport fares) began by taking a train from Kings Cross Thameslink station. This has replaced the old Kings Cross Midland City station and is linked to surface lines and the original metropolitan network. The latter, incidentally, is quite different from the 'tube' or underground of which the Metropolitan now forms part. It was originally only partly covered over and was operated with steam locomotives with special smoke arresting equipment. I left the train I took – which to my surprise included a small first class section, something you certainly would not find on the 'tube' – at West Hampstead Thameslink at 19.25 one evening, from where a short walk brought me to West Hampstead on the BR North London line. From there it was my intention to go west to Willesden Junction, where I would descend from High Level to Low Level stations and catch a London Midland Region local back to Euston in time for the overnight sleeper to Scotland. Alas, the best laid schemes, as that country's famed bard so aptly put it, "gang aft a-gley".

I had it all neatly worked out: catch the North London Line 19.39 West Hampstead to Willesden, arrive 19.46 in good time for the 19.54 into Euston at 20.10. But there had been a derailment. All North London line trains were subject to long delays, the notice said. I could not risk cutting it too fine for the Scottish express leaving Euston just after nine. There was nothing for it but to retrace my steps to the Thameslink station for Kings Cross and the ubiquitous tube.

Surprisingly, the sleeper for Scotland – apart from being among the best of all BR services in its facilities for passengers and its convenient timing – ran to Inverness via Edinburgh (or so they told me) although it took the West Coast main line through Rugby and Crewe. I assume it must have been routed via Carstairs south and east junctions and Midcalder, and then either changed direction at Edinburgh or circled round the back of Arthur's seat on the freight lines, but I was fast asleep at this stage so never found out.

In Britain the established knowledge is, or was, that for Scotland and the north you went to Kings Cross station, if you wanted Edinburgh and the east coast route, and to Euston if you preferred the west coast route via Carlisle to Glasgow, although there were connecting lines to Edinburgh from Carlisle and Carstairs. For the West Country you used

FINDING THE STATION

Paddington, for the southwest Waterloo; Victoria for the south coast and Liverpool Street for the east. (This omits a few stations which served a more limited range of destinations.) The former Southern Railway probably had more London terminal stations than had any other system, serving as it did the highly populated southern hinterland of the capital where people commuted daily from Kent, Surrey and even Sussex and Hampshire, and where regular and frequent expresses came in from Brighton, Guildford, Horsham, Eastbourne and Tunbridge Wells as well as from numerous closer suburban centres.

But what few people knew was that there was nothing (other than bureaucracy, tradition, inter-system rivalry, stubbornness, lack of imagination and, to some extent, operational convenience and commercial common sense) to prevent a northeast of England train starting from Victoria or Waterloo, a Dover train (or maybe even the *Night Ferry* to Paris if the loading gauge was not too wide for the platforms) starting from St Pancras, or the *Cornish Riviera* starting from Liverpool Street.

But it did not happen, though it is interesting to note that in the last few years, BR has rediscovered the versatility the London rail network, with some trains to Cardiff starting from Waterloo, and a train from Edinburgh coming into Paddington and, since the advent of the 'Chunnel', some East Coast mainline trains terminating at Waterloo! Even not long after nationalisation one would sometimes find rolling stock from one region inexplicably forming a train in another. When the Eastern Region of BR introduced a through train from Kings Cross to Tees-side I remember once seeing in Middlesbrough station a complete rake of corridor Southern Region coaches, which must somehow have got shunted around London until they found themselves assembled to form the *Tees–Thames* that day.

Euston was among the least connected of London main line termini yet it has always been one of the most important: the former LMS served more destinations throughout Britain than did any of the other systems.

One wonders why, then, in the game of *Monopoly*, through which place names like Piccadilly, Leicester Square, and Oxford Street became familiar to people who never visited London, are all the railway stations former LNER ones? Granted that Kings Cross is one of the most famous railway stations anywhere, but surely Euston or St Pancreas could have represented the LMS, Victoria or Waterloo the Southern, and Paddington the Great Western? And why not Charing Cross – slap bang in the middle of the real localities denoted by the Pink, Orange and Red properties on the *Monopoly* board? There is a saying that if you stand long enough at Charing Cross station in London all the world will pass by (who said the English were masters of understatement?). Something similar has been claimed for Sydney Central in Australia – certainly it is surprising how many people one meets there from other states as well as New South Wales. But surely on such a basis Charing Cross would have deserved a place on the *Monopoly* board?

The LMS, GWR, SR and LNER became the 'Big Four' after the railway grouping of 1923 and they so remained until railway nationalisation in 1948. One wonders how long it will be now before the old company names reappear as the system is systematically dismembered under the privatisation mania of the current Conservative government.

But for *Monopoly* its makers chose just the four stations of the LNER. Apart from Kings Cross, geographically adjacent to Euston Road, Pentonville Road and the Angel, none of the other stations on the *Monopoly* board are close to the streets and districts among which they are set. Fenchurch Street, little known and used except by commuters from the Southend and Tilbury lines, and one of the few London termini not on the Underground, is a good mile beyond the eastern end of Strand and even further from Fleet Street, Trafalgar Square, Coventry Street or Leicester Square which surround it on the board, while Liverpool Street is about as far away as you can get in central London from Park Lane and Mayfair. But it's a good game anyway. Its creator must have been fond of railways – why else would he include four stations and have a miniature steam engine as one of the original tokens? In the

FINDING THE STATION

game the stations were good value too. The percentage return from any one station if you owned all four, was higher than from any other single unimproved property at 25% of the cost of your investment. Even the much vaunted Mayfair (site only) produced only half that return, which you could get from even one station alone. They were therefore especially valuable early in the game and always a welcome haven hopping around the board.

Geographically, the journey round the *Monopoly* board was exceedingly devious. Particularly because of the stations, you would be zooming diagonally across central London in several directions if you tried to follow the route on the ground. But if you wanted to go from Liverpool Street to Kings Cross (as you could in the game by shaking a '10' and ignoring Park Lane, Mayfair, Old Kent Road and Whitechapel) you could do it in reality even today by the Metropolitan and District Underground lines. On the way you would pass 'Go' in the game and it is interesting, as a trivial pursuit, to speculate on the location of this mythical and generous place: about midway between Liverpool Street and Kings Cross is Farringdon, oddly enough the City terminus of the world's first underground passenger railway, the Metropolitan, in January 1863. A good place for 'Go'? Well, where better to start on a great journey!

But the creator of that ever popular board game, Charles Darrow (an American) would have known nothing of this. The original *Monopoly* was based on Atlantic City, New Jersey. It was not until 1935, when Waddington's acquired the rights to produce a British version, that the London place names were selected. The *Illustrated London News* of December 1985 said a secretary of one of Waddington's directors picked them, and she was obviously more fond of the LNER than the LMS, the Southern or the Great Western. An LNER commuter, perhaps? More likely she had a relative who worked for that company.

As a further trivial pursuit I wondered how one might travel by rail nowadays between Liverpool Street and Kings Cross, or vice versa, without using the underground – since the *Monopoly* stations were mainline ones after all.

Can it be done? Starting from Farringdon (Go!) and shaking a '5' on the dice for Kings Cross you need a BR Thameslink train. These run about every five minutes and the journey takes three (you can go first class if you want). Now you have to get to Marylebone and that's the big problem. Even back before 1923, the first station out of Marylebone with any connection with another line (apart from the Metropolitan) was South Ruislip and this only with the Great Western into and out of Paddington. It is still the same today. The only passenger train connections Marylebone has with BR lines are northwards at Kings Sutton near Banbury (again with the Great Western), then Leamington Spa and Coventry.

Places like that ought to be well connected and indeed they are. There are links from Coventry through Nuneaton to St Pancreas or via Leicester and Peterborough to Kings Cross, but that sounds a very long way round. There must be a better way.

There is, or at least was in 1992 when I worked it out. From Kings Cross to Marylebone is a distance of roughly 4 km on the ground. Instead of battling with all that central London traffic you could take the 9.11 from Thameslink station to Tulse Hill, arriving 9.35, depart there 9.55 for Streatham Hill, arriving 9.58, depart 10.05 to Clapham Junction arriving 10.13. Then you could take the *Sussex Scot* InterCity at 10.25 northwards to Banbury, arriving 12.19. From there you would go south on the local Chiltern line service at 12.30 to reach Marylebone at a minute before two in the afternoon, a total of 169 miles (272 km) requiring just four and three quarter hours. And with a Britrail Pass you would have saved at least a 50p fare on the Underground!

Still want to play? Well, getting from Marylebone to the next station, Fenchurch Street, by BR is even worse. I leave it to the reader to work out how long it would take. I offer clues so that if you are really keen all you need are the timetables. There is a choice of routes. You could go back to Kings Cross the way you came and thence via Cambridge, but this would be cheating because in the game you cannot move your

FINDING THE STATION

piece backwards, nor could you go from Marylebone to Kings Cross in one turn because it would take three successive double fives and you would then have to go to jail (which, incidentally, is very appropriately placed at Pentonville) and not be able to collect your £200.

So instead you would need to retrace the former route as far as Banbury, then continue north to Coventry before coming back south to Willesden Junction and the North London line to Stratford. From there, if you are lucky you may catch a train to Barking to come into Fenchurch Street from the east (the only way), but as there seems to be only one train a day from Stratford to Barking, you would be better to change from the North London Line at Gospel Oak and go to Barking the slightly longer way via Crouch Hill and Blackhorse Road. You will have a great view of the Metropolitan Waterworks on the way. I hope you have fun.

Fenchurch Street to Liverpool Street is easy by comparison but from there round to King's Cross again is another matter. It can be done but the tube must be a tempting alternative, especially if you want to pass 'Go'.

Anyone foolhardy enough to try this journey would deserve a place in the *Guinness Book of Records* but it does highlight the fact that Marylebone is not a readily accessible station.

In *Monopoly* a 'chance' card gives you the pleasure of taking "a trip to Marylebone station" – not to mention collecting £200 as you pass 'Go', or collecting £200 anyway if someone else takes the trip and you own Marylebone along with the other three stations! Yet I do not think that apart from in a *Monopoly* game I have ever visited this station. It was the last of the London mainline termini to be established: it is also as I have shown, among the least accessible and always has been. You can of course take a red London bus there, or walk, or use the Underground (Bakerloo line only) but from most places outside the capital it is not easy to reach. Once terminus of the famous Great Central, Marylebone in its heyday hosted express trains from Leicester, Sheffield, Bradford and Manchester, but the routes they used have been severed. From 10 miles (16 km) north of Aylesbury, famous for its tender ducklings, the GC line through Rugby, Leicester, Nottingham (Victoria) and Chesterfield is no more. All that remains are some of the lines in Yorkshire and a six mile (10 km) off-cut of the main line through Quorn to Loughborough, operated privately as the Great Central Railway.

In my younger days I regularly travelled from north-east England to my cousin's home in Quorn and so was familiar with this line. This part of the Great Central route was regularly used in World War II by an advertised through train from Newcastle upon Tyne to the south of England via Sheffield, Leicester, Banbury, Oxford and Reading. Its route by-passed Chesterfield, a city whose crooked cathedral spire was always clearly visible from the train. I recall with wry amusement a travelling collector haranguing a passenger whose ticket was for Chesterfield.

"You should have changed," he snarled at the unfortunate fellow. "You're on your way to Ashford in Kent!" This made it sound miles away (which it was) but the ticket collector omitted to mention the several intervening stations where the passenger could easily have got off to return to Chesterfield. Ashford was the ultimate destination of the train, a major military barracks town at that time.

Railway staff can sometimes be like that: quite rude, making a mountain out of a molehill, causing consternation when often a problem is of no great importance. Scottish National activist Ian Hamilton QC found occasion to remark on this in his enthralling account of how the Stone of Destiny was taken from Westminster Abbey back to Scotland where it rightfully belonged.

"There are no baths at Charing Cross," he records, "so we took a tube across to Waterloo. It was magnificent. We lay and steeped until the attendant came and thumped on the doors and abused us." He added, "British Rail seem to pick out their minor officials for their rudeness...".

Since the introduction of through trains via Kensington Olympia on the west of London and the construction of the Thameslink line

FINDING THE STATION

following part of the old and long disused Farringdon–Holborn route through Smithfield Market just east of the city proper, cross-London travel has been made far easier and a Newcastle to Ashford train would no longer have to wander through the by-ways of Berkshire.

The early rivalry between competing companies had some benefits to the traveller which were carried over well into the nationalised British Railways era. For example, one could purchase a ticket to Middlesbrough in north-east England on the former North Eastern and later London and North Eastern Railway not just from Kings Cross but from St Pancras, the former LMS company obviously wanting to attract traffic to their own network which went as far north-east as Leeds.

There was also a provision that "passengers between Stockport and the south thereof and Stalybridge and the north thereof may travel via Manchester". This came, I presume, from a volume called the "Book of Routes", which I never saw but which was quoted on many tickets when the normal route 'via someplace' was specified.

"For alternatives, see Book of Routes", the ticket would say.

It so happened that when I lived in the London area my best friend lived in Manchester. What was more natural then, when heading for my parents' home on Tees-side, to take the opportunity of including Manchester in a round trip? Almost like having a runabout ticket for the price of an ordinary return.

Some London stations, and many in other cities and countries, are noted for their architectural merit if not grandeur. St Pancras has been cited as a magnificent, if ostentatious, monument to the Victorian Gothic style. Designed by engineer W.H. Barlow and famous architect Giles Gilbert Scott (who was also responsible for Liverpool Cathedral) the building combines a railway terminus and a hotel now converted to offices.

When I was a university student there was a controversy expressed in letters to the student newspaper about the architecture of Kings Cross station. No-one seemed to find much good to say about it. One student letter summed it up beautifully: "There are only two good things about

Kings Cross station. You can take a train to Newcastle and, only then, obtain a decent glass of beer."

I am glad to say you can still do both.

At a magnificent station like München Hauptbahnhof in Bavaria you can also get a decent glass of beer, and once the Channel Tunnel's benefits are fully integrated into the rail networks of Britain as well as Europe, you may even be able to take a train to Newcastle from there!

For a small place, Vila Vicosa in Portugal has one of the most magnificent station buildings I have ever seen. Amid a wonderful pattern of mosaic tiling, the station name itself was picked out in white tiles against a black tiled background. The steps, the plinth, the architraves and the lintels of the doors were all marble, as was even the platform edging.

A feature of many of the great railway stations of the world is the vast steel arched roof covering platforms and tracks. Apart from their mundane function of protecting passengers from rain or snow these identify the station as a building of importance. Fortunately, few have been used for outdoor advertising. However, misguided efforts to 'make the railways pay' have resulted in the demolition rather than the maintenance of these magnificent structures. It is debatable whether this is preferable to plastering them with commercial advertisements as happens to many bus stations and even buses themselves.

Advertising within a building is another matter: it is quite traditional and even exempted from control under the very stringent Town and Country Planning (Control of Advertisements) Regulations imposed in Britain in 1948. Within the great archway of Köln Hauptbahnhof is a huge sign advertising '4711', as the famous 'Eau de Cologne'. Germany has retained most of these station roofs – Britain seems to have gone in for systematic demolition. I looked in vain on my last visit for the Stockton station roof, but there was still one at Darlington.

Other less imposing but still well built stations have lost most of their superstructure. In one of my first jobs I worked at the County Hall of Yorkshire's North Riding which adjoined Northallerton station. To the

FINDING THE STATION

station buffet we used to go in our lunch break. There was found shelter, food and drink and pretty girls to serve it. As far as I can recall there were at least six platforms and of course a booking hall, waiting rooms, and 'the usual offices' as politically correct speakers in those days called the lavatories. Now there is next to nothing. Trains still call, but gone are the covered platforms. What the passengers do in rain or sleet I would not like to think. On my last visit some sort of transparent plastic cubicle posed as a shelter of sorts but I found it locked, like the toilets on so many stations which management in its drive for economy has decreed to become unstaffed.

Stranraer Harbour station had nothing except a platform and a roof; not even any left luggage facilities, but the reason for that may have been the same as the reason some stations in northern Spain and all in Israel lacked this convenience – the fear of terrorist bombs.

At Euston on the other hand there was a special pullman lounge for passengers with first class tickets (note my very correct wording there – had I written 'first class passengers' it might imply others were inferior). There were telephones, fax machines, and a buffet service of drinks and snacks. Kings Cross has a similar though much smaller buffet. The Euston chairs were uncomfortable, however. They had a modern design, probably given a design award but not by people who could have sat in them. The curiously angled back-rest caught you just below the ribs. Perhaps it was to encourage you not to stay too long.

Although Waterloo's new International Terminal has won Europe's prestigious RIBA 'Building of the Year' award, Waterloo has been a station more famed for its trains than for its architecture. As terminus of the London & South Western routes to Exeter, Plymouth, Weymouth, Bournemouth and Southampton it was the starting point for boat trains connecting with steamers of the Union Castle, White Star, Cunard, and many other companies to destinations as far apart as New York, Capetown and Fremantle, as well as the company's own steamers to Jersey and the French ports of Le Havre, Cherbourg and St Malo. Added to this were suburban lines to Chiswick, Richmond, Kingston,

TRAINCATCHER

Hampton Court, Staines, Shepperton and Epsom – highly populated commuter suburbs from very early days to the present time. Even before its extension to accommodate *Eurostar* trains Waterloo had 23 platforms, more than any other station on the BR system, and with boat trains tending to irregularity, it is not surprising that sometimes there were platform mix-ups. At least that was my experience back in about 1950 or earlier when I remember hurling abuse at railway staff because the train my parents and I were seeking was switched from one platform to another, then back again and left just before all the passengers, hurrying along with their luggage, managed to reach it. A marvellously humorous depiction of a similar occurrence in northern France was featured in the Jacques Tatti silent film, *Monsieur Hulot's Holiday*.

The story is told of a young couple who were discussing their forbears and what they did.

"My grandfather was killed at Waterloo," said one.

"Oh," said the other, "Which platform?" A woman overhearing the conversation related it to her husband, scorning the stupidity and ignorance of the youngsters.

"I should think so!" said her husband, "As if it mattered which platform!"

It matters when travelling by rail, not only to start at the right station, but the right platform too.

However well signposted the platforms, however clear the announcements, however plentiful the amenities and however imposing the buildings, a railway station must above all have railway tracks and it must have trains. Much is being done in some countries to re-furbish the station buildings, adopt new logos and install emergency telephones for use when there are no station staff and you are about to be gang-raped. Platform barriers are coming down – there is no-one to check tickets or even sell them. Some rail systems in Australia have even gone to the extent of closing the ticket window at the stations of quite substantial towns, even when the office is manned, making passengers buy their rail tickets at travel agencies elsewhere in the town. Obviously

FINDING THE STATION

they are forgetting, to their ultimate loss, that the agency offices typically follow normal shop hours and may not be open when the trains are around, and that such agencies also obtain income by promoting and selling travel and tours by rival modes and by accepting and forwarding road freight.

St Louis Union station is one of the great non-stations of the United States. It is said you can spend a whole day there without seeing it all, but unlike Grand Central Terminal in New York, the world's largest railway station with (in 1993) its 44 platforms and 550 trains a day, you are lucky to find a railway track or platform anywhere in Union and you will look in vain for a train. It is just a great big shopping centre, a fate which has befallen far too many stations world-wide when declining train patronage and falling revenues are mistakenly met by short-term (that is, short-sighted) solutions to make the books balance by 'selling off the farm'.

I could find only one train at a single siding at St Louis Union, a sparkling black 2-8-8-2 Norfolk & Western loco with some carriages from the former *West Wind*, privately owned by some millionaire. At one time there were 27 tracks (American-speak for platforms) here, a convergence of lines belonging to a dozen or more companies including the Illinois Central, Norfolk and Western, Southern, Burlington Northern, Missouri Pacific, Rock Island, and the 'Katy' (the local name for the Missouri Kansas Texas railroad). Operated by the Terminal Railroad Association of St Louis, all that remains of the former maze of tracks as far as today's passengers are concerned are a few through lines running past what looks like a downtown bus shelter in a back street under a freeway.

There are no local services. Only the *Texas Eagle* (Chicago, St Louis, Dallas, Houston and Los Angeles) out of the eight trains which called daily at the new St Louis South 16th Street station could really be called a long distance train, although until 1994 the *River Cities* (Kansas City–St Louis–Carbondale) carried through cars for the *City of New Orleans* service to the 'Crescent City'. This connection has been replaced by a bus. Other trains using St Louis station were regional intercity services linking St Louis with Kansas City (*The Mule*), Chicago (*The State House*) and with both, the *Ann Rutledge*. The last-named, with the *Texas Eagle*, was one of only two trains still serving this city in 1995.

The station is in a fairly run-down area where you would not want to be alone at night. It is possible, and preferable, to join the train at one of the two suburban or outer urban stations which remain – Kirkwood, Mo, 23 km west, and Alton, Ill, 43 km north at which, fortunately for the would-be passenger, all(!) trains stop.

It struck me as strange that no passenger platforms had been constructed in the railway cutting on the Alton line where it passes practically underneath St Louis' famous monument – Eero Saarinen's Memorial Arch, the Gateway to the West. The world's tallest building of its kind, the arch has its own little internal train, or 'tram' service from the base to the viewing gallery 190 metres above.

Which is worse – a railway in the right place with no station or a station in the right place with no trains? Unfortunately, the railway planners and the town planners rarely get their act together or if they do, it is by accident rather than design. In one of the early 'New Town' planning exercises after World War II, the planners of Aycliffe New Town in County Durham proposed a new station for the soon to be expanded village, not where the existing station was, on the East Coast Main Line, but on the west side of the site where two lines converged. One was the line from Shildon connecting with the main line at Darlington while the other was a freight line running direct to the Teesside conurbation of Stockton–Thornaby–Middlesbrough and thus offering potentially quick access to the beach resorts of Redcar, Saltburn and Seaton Carew. Good thinking; town planning in a regional context! But the railways did not take a blind bit of notice.

Newton Aycliffe, as it is now called, now has no station at all, yet other 'planned' new towns have become more important in the railway network than the older towns they were near. Milton Keynes in

FINDING THE STATION

Buckinghamshire, for example, is better served by trains than nearby Bletchley, its new Central station being a stopping place for Liverpool and Scottish expresses. It is refreshing to see town planning and transport planning work together but it is unfortunately the exception rather than the rule.

Chapter 4
Going Troppo

"When shall I see my native land: I'll never forget my home" – from *Home Again*: alleged Nigerian song popular among expatriates

After my early working days in London I had the urge to wander further afield. A position was advertised in West-Africa – not a missionary position as my father had held but one in the then 'Colonial Service' as a town planner.

It was in Nigeria, the land of my birth. What could be more romantic? – to see the place where I was born, to meet people who had known me as a little child, and to see with adult eyes something of the world outside the British Isles.

So to Nigeria I went.

On arrival at Lagos I was to take the train to Zaria in the Northern Region. Having seen my trunks and cases unloaded from the ship's hold, the next thing was to make sure they were transferred to the baggage car of the train. The Public Works Department (PWD) had its own porters and a thin wizened old man with a PWD badge appeared to take care of my needs. My largest trunk was an old tin one weighing, in colloquial terms, a ton. I think it was actually about 150 lbs (68 kg); certainly it was impossible for me to lift more than one edge of it. How would this undernourished-looking near-geriatric cope? I need not have worried. A colleague and a couple of small boys helped lift the thing up, while he bent down for them to place it on his grizzled head, on which rested a curled up piece of cloth as padding. Getting it balanced right, he then staggered along to the baggage car with it, while I found my sleeping berth and took the smaller luggage items with me.

It was a pleasant and leisurely train ride and of course all new to me. Nigeria is a land of brilliant colour and full of contrasts – poverty on one hand, opulence on the other. The deep green of the jungle and the bright orange of the laterite earth; the shiny dark brown skins and the white teeth; the brightly coloured cloths the women wound round their bodies and the colourful robes the better-off men wore, and the often dirty white garments like cheap nightgowns worn by the beggars. Here, I think for the first time, I saw a naked female in public; a shapely teenager. Bare breasts were common enough, though most women wore some sort of wrap from the waist down.

In the yellow and green liveried train, the stewards were not long in coming through with bowls of tasty local fruit salad, or "jungle juice" as it was known. Pawpaw I had never previously tasted. It is delicious mixed with pineapple, banana, orange and mango.

Meals were served in the dining car, plain but adequate. A typical meat dish was "hump", not of camel but of the humped cattle typical of tropical climes. At every station we stopped at, colourful crowds of people would throng the platform and the tracks so it was a wonder nobody got killed. Traders carrying loads that in European countries would require a small truck, women with calabashes on their heads and babes on their backs and breasts, held only by the folds of the "mammy cloth" they wore, and beggars on crutches. Some of the beggars were just on stumps of deformed or amputated limbs, yet moved about on all fours with astounding speed and agility. In these days of 'politically correct' language they would be referred to as 'alternatively abled' and able they certainly were. Here you could buy local fruits, palm wine and some unrecognisably edible savouries wrapped in leaves. It was all too new to me so I stuck to the restaurant care fare. I was introduced to a new word I first took to be in the local Yoruba language but soon found to be in much wider use. "*Dash*" was pidgin English, a request for a tip, not necessarily in appreciation of any service rendered. 'Alms for the love of Allah' would be its Middle Eastern equivalent. Indeed, Allah and His Prophet Mohammed were very much in evidence. Northern

Nigeria is basically Moslem though the south is nominally Christian. Throughout the country Ramadan was added to the traditional British holidays.

At dawn the next day we crossed the long single bridge shared by road and rail at Jebba which geographically marked the entrance to the real northern Nigeria, when you cross the Niger itself from Ilorin Province. As one travels north, the vegetation thins out, the deep green of the 'bush' or jungle being replaced by savannah country and further north giving way to desert with the hot dust-laden harmattan wind bringing a haze to the horizon. The Jebba crossing is matched on the east of the country by a similar bridge carrying the line north from Port Harcourt over the Benue, the main tributary of the Niger which it joins at Lokoja. Near Lokoja the Niger was crossed by a 'car ferry' consisting of a rather small boat with two planks on the deck, onto which a driver had to negotiate his vehicle. Having only just acquired a car and being a newly qualified driver you can imagine how I felt when approaching this deterrent to reckless driving. The London driving instructor had not prepared me for anything of such a nature.

Reckless driving was a constant threat to Nigerian road users, and so were the roads themselves. On my first car journey in Nigeria, when my boss took me up by his car from Zaria to Kano I quickly learned that on the corrugated laterite unsealed roads the only way to keep from being shaken to pieces and losing control of steering was to drive at a steady 50 miles an hour (80 km/h) or more. This was all very well, but something of a strain for a novice driver accustomed to the regulation 30 miles an hour (48 km/h) on smooth London tarmac. You might suddenly meet another vehicle round a blind corner or find yourself heading down to a narrow bridge with a heavy passenger lorry approaching at breakneck speed from the other side. These single lane bridges, constructed of two long running planks over transverse wooden sleepers laid over longitudinal baulks of strong timber, had no side rails.

Large vehicles known as "mammy wagons" – road trucks partly

covered over at the rear and fitted with wooden seating for passengers – would hurtle towards each other down the opposing slopes either to meet head on or, more likely, swerve into the bush at the roadside which was marked by the scattered remains of vehicles that had failed to make it. On each would be displayed the transport company name and motto. Captions like "Trust in God", "God's time is best" offered encouragement to prospective passengers and possible comfort to the relatives of the deceased.

As it was, I had only just taken my driving test (and miraculously been granted a Nigerian licence in spite of reversing almost into the ditch through trying to steer backwards using only the inside mirror) and a powerful Opel Kapitan on a loose surface was asking too much. The car was overloaded with all my heavy luggage, not to mention my newly acquired cook, Daniel. They towed me back to Jos from the place where I had left the road and had ended up just short of a deep ravine, and after an enforced nightstop while the car was being fixed I took it more gently down from the plateau to the river crossing the next day.

Travel was undoubtedly safer by rail, yet even the railways were not immune from dangerous driving and the risk of 'going for bush'. It could have been in Nigeria the tale was first made up about the passenger on the rocking, rolling, swaying, rattling train who noticed suddenly it had all become smooth. He remarked on the welcome change.

"Yes, that's all right," said a seasoned fellow passenger. "We're off the track now". North of the Jebba bridge near Zungeru we were diverted from the track onto a shaky and hastily constructed temporary by-pass loop to avoid a derailed goods train.

Trains were not immune from collision with road vehicles either. I very nearly came to grief with a train and my own car shortly after acquiring it in Kano. Motoring slowly round town in the evening getting used to the gears I suddenly became aware of a loud klaxon horn noise. Immediately ahead on the left some large railway wagons were about to cross in front of the car. It was a railway level crossing but without gates, boom, or warning lights. Possibly I would have seen a warning notice if I had been looking in the right direction.

But that was after I had reached Kano. It was a wonder I got there in the first place, at least with all my gear.

The train for Zaria was locally known as the *Plateau Limited*, at least to those expatriates who used it to travel to the hill station at Jos much favoured by the self-styled elite of the colonial service, the administration, as a place to spend local leave. I doubt if the PWD had ever heard of local leave – if they had they failed to mention it to me.

But the expatriates were wrong, as they were in so many things, like 'how to treat the natives – kick them in the backside'. The train I was on was in fact the *Up Kano Limited*, number 15 Up from Lagos.

Nigerian Railways, like some other systems (Queensland Rail among them) do not follow the usual convention that 'up' means towards the main station or capital city and 'down' means away from it. In Britain it was always 'up' to London unless you were brought up in north-east England where we looked down on London. Instead, the Nigerian Railways adopted geographical criteria for its train identification system, in which 'up' meant north and 'down' meant south. The same applies in Queensland with the added qualification that when the line runs east and west 'up' means uphill, away from the coast, and 'down' the opposite, though I doubt if such criteria were really in the minds of the railway builders.

Once weekly on Thursdays number 15 Up and its return working number 6 Down were correctly called the *Plateau Limited* and the main part of the train went to Jos.

On Wednesdays number 15 *Up Limited* was bound only for Kano and carried no first class accommodation or restaurant car, but on Mondays and Saturdays it carried both, as well as through carriages to Jos. From Kaduna onwards these became the *Jos Limited*, returning as the *Kaduna Junction Limited*. There was also an *Eastern Limited* (Kaduna to Port Harcourt and v.v.), an *Up Limited* (Kaduna to Kano connection), and a *Down Limited* (Kano to Kaduna connection).

Kaduna was the place where all these trains met, being the up country junction of the northern main lines from Lagos on the west and from Port Harcourt on the east. The branch to Jos actually took off from the eastern line at Kafanchan 178 km from Kaduna but trains were not re-marshalled there other than to attach or detach Jos coaches to or from the *Eastern Limited*.

Not surprisingly, if there were to be a bad case of snafu, it would occur at Kaduna Junction. A typical platform scenario at Kaduna Junction in the evening would be as set out below. This was in 1954. The *Limited* still runs but the scheduling is now somewhat different. Tuesday is taken as the example:

20.10   Arrival of *Kano Limited* from Lagos
20.46   Arrival of *Eastern Limited* from Port Harcourt
21.36   Arrival of *Kaduna Junction Limited* from Jos
21.55   Arrival of *Kano Limited* from Kano
22.10   Departure of *Kano Limited* for Kano
22.40   Departure of *Jos Limited* to Jos
23.37   Departure of *Kano Limited* for Lagos
23.50   Departure of *Eastern Limited* for Port Harcourt

The ritual performance of splitting and re-marshalling these trains at Kaduna Junction rivalled anything seen at Basel or Frankfurt in Europe – except that it only applied to one basic service and it took a good while longer to work out. On arrival at Kaduna the *Up Kano Limited* – the train I was on – comprised, from Lagos, four third class cars, one second class car, a canteen car, baggage van and brake van for Kano and Nguru (beyond Kano), a first class and a second class car and baggage van for Port Harcourt, a baggage van for Jos, and the restaurant car, staff coach and a composite first class/second class car for Kano only.

On leaving Kaduna Junction for Kano the train would have, in addition to those vehicles coming from Lagos, a baggage van and a combined first class/second class car from Port Harcourt.

TRAINCATCHER

It was a balmy evening and I left my compartment for a stroll along the platform while all the shuffling and shunting was going on. Then I saw my luggage. At that stage I had no idea where the van was that my loads had been put in or whether they were to stay in that van all the way to Kano. But now I saw my large trunk standing on the platform, its bold red shipping labels clearly still showing its original destination – Lagos! There had been no time to affix new labels at the terminal.

Realising that all my worldly goods – at least those that were in the baggage van – were about to be transferred to the *Down Limited* and lost to me for ever in the labyrinths of the Nigerian Railways parcels headquarters, I immediately approached the porters engaged on this mistaken but well-meaning activity and explained the error. Being accustomed, in those days, to display grudging respect, at least on the surface, for the 'white man' as Massa they very quickly rectified the matter. I wonder how railwaymen in Britain would have reacted – no doubt a lengthy argument would precede any grudging compliance. The Nigerian porters probably expressed their feelings in a language they knew I would not understand, and who could blame them? They were only doing their job and doing it efficiently. Checking the correctness of labelling was not part of their duty.

It did not take me long to find out that in Nigeria a friendly smile and a few words in the local lingo were far more rewarding than threats and abuse when dealing with Africans on their home ground.

I did not stay long in Zaria. It was only a preliminary posting and after meeting my boss and being briefed on my duties I was soon transferred to Kabba Province at Okéné, a place with few Europeans and probably the better for that. It was never quite clear what I was really expected to do in Okéné. They had asked for a town planning officer but there was no map worthy of the name except on too small a scale to show buildings or even streets in towns. It was first necessary to produce a town map and this I did by tracing from aerial photographs, then using a crude form of plane tabling as a ground control to fix the relationship of key locations. Photogrammetry as such was then only in its infancy.

By the time the map was done they must have forgotten what I was sent there for. I was posted again, this time to the larger government station at Ilorin – and Ilorin was on the railway. Food in Nigeria, and many other things besides, had to be obtained, if not from local markets then from company-operated stores whose supplies were irregular in the extreme. There were no cold stores in Ilorin at that time, i.e. shops with refrigerated store rooms, so commodities like fresh meat were unobtainable unless ordered in advance from Lagos or unless someone was known locally to be killing a pig and one's cook was present for the occasion. Otherwise fowls were the standard protein source.

Items ordered from Lagos cold stores would come up by train, and we would troop down to the railway station when the supply train came in.

One day we learned that a new expatriate engineer was to arrive on the *Kano Limited*, due in Ilorin at some ghastly hour in the early morning. We were having a bit of a party at the Club that day (like most other days) and some bright spark, probably the Provincial Engineer who would have been responsible for the newcomer, suggested we troop down to the station to meet the new arrival. After all, the poor fellow could not just be left there in the middle of the night not knowing where to go or how to get there even if he had the address. Taxis and even telephones were not easily found.

So, loaded up with a crate of cold beer and with the club steward carrying the club gramophone off we all trooped to the railway station. Cecil, the engineer newly arrived from Fife in Scotland, was greeted as the train rolled in with a crowd of revellers, the gramophone carried on the steward's head with a record loudly and tinnily rendering *Truly Fair* (or it might have been *Mocking Bird Hill* – the club had two records). Cecil must have thought he was back home at a Scottish Ne'earday party as we carried him bodily to the cars and then to the Rest House he was to stay at. There the party continued until some sober resident quite rightly complained that this was not a club and it was four o'clock in the morning.

TRAINCATCHER

It was at Ilorin I met Dick Williams, an inspector with the Nigerian Railways. Dick had his own coach which he could arrange to have attached to almost any train. What a way to travel! I remember as a kid I used to dream of something like that. The LNER in Britain had a number of "camping coaches" at various stations in scenic or holiday locations and I always hankered after the family to hire one. I was under the mistaken impression that they could be hitched to a train and taken anywhere – perhaps this is a tourist idea some enterprising railway somewhere should pursue?

Dick could not attach his carriage to the 'Limited' without special approval from the Chief Superintendent but there were other passenger and mixed trains to choose from and on one occasion I travelled with him the 45 km from Ilorin to Offa, where I then lived. The inspection coach had a stove, a fridge, bed, cupboards, and easy chairs, a railway version of a well equipped caravan. It was accessible to the rest of the train by a lockable corridor connection and I wandered along the train with Dick one day when he chose to inspect tickets. This was among his optional duties when there was no travelling ticket collector on board. It could be a major undertaking getting through some of the carriages as I went along with him trying to look like a railway official. In those days of course almost any white man, or *oyinbo* as the Yorubas called us, would be taken as an official of some sort unless they were obviously missionaries. These, however, were distinguishable not by virtue of any position they took in the privacy of their own quarters, but by the ancient style of sun helmets they persisted in wearing.

The corridor was cluttered with people and their belongings. I remember Dick being particularly disgusted to find a pile of human faeces in the vestibule at the end of one carriage. And in the second class at that! Presumably in third class it was more acceptable or at least common and passengers as likely as not would have their goats or other livestock with them.

Talking of livestock, Dick always had fresh meat on the train. This he kept not in the fridge (which was reserved for cold Heineken beer, or Énikéni beer as the Yorubas called it – *énikéni* being Yoruba for 'everybody') but in a private chicken pen which was outside at the back of the carriage above the buffers – part of the amenities provided by a thoughtful management for its staff!

It is to Dick that I am indebted for my copy of the *Nigerian Working Timetable* of that time which I still have, so any figures of train times and other statistics in this chapter are of guaranteed accuracy. You didn't think I could actually remember such detail after all this time, did you? *Hab-ba*! (an oft-heard expression in Northern Nigeria roughly meaning 'that's too much!').

Chapter 5
Passenger Fare

"If it breathes, we don't want it" – attributed to an anonymous railway chief traffic manager, based on the equally anonymous Australian standard motto: *"If it moves, shoot it; if it doesn't, chop it down."*

It is popularly believed that railway managements simply do not like transporting passengers. For one thing people can complain. For another thing they expect to be able to go to the toilet, to eat and drink, to sleep, and even to breathe.

David Jenkinson, in *Encyclopedia of Railways*, explains how passenger carriages very slowly evolved from the open trucks used for coal and iron ore, and how anything like a toilet, or worse, a corridor giving access to one, which took up space without bringing direct revenue, was only reluctantly accepted by railway companies as a necessity for passengers. I can recall some of the local trains in north-east England in which there might be, say, three or four toilets only, each having corridor access to a couple of adjoining compartments, so that you had to know when you got on the train whether or not you were likely to want to go to the toilet before the journey ended, in which case you had to make sure you got in the right kind of compartment!

"Be prepared" – that used to be the motto of the Boy Scout movement, and still is. I was never a boy scout – I found Girl Guides a lot more appealing and perhaps the same motto would apply – but the rail traveller really needs to be prepared for the unexpected, the bizarre, or the thing 'out of the blue'.

Long distance trains take on many of the characteristics of an ocean cruise, a similarity that is very evident crossing the Nullarbor, or on any long distance Australian journey, especially in the outback. Even in

PASSENGER FARE

Britain or Europe almost anything can happen and sometimes does on a night train.

Experienced rail travellers bemoan the trend away from compartment trains where the traveller can be alone or with company selected in advance or met by chance, in which people can pass the time according to their choosing, instead of having to sit in serried ranks bolt upright or uneasily curled into a foetal cocoon to the discomfort of the person on the next seat. This is the way so many of our rail managements now prefer us to travel, so they can keep an eye on us. The real reason of course is that open saloon carriages are cheaper to construct and maintain.

In some of these open-style carriages you may not be allowed a drink even on long journeys. This is understandable, as over-indulgence can distress other passengers, but in sleeping compartments the passenger is untroubled by such rules. An individual sleeping compartment, which is the normal first class accommodation style, becomes your own private world, with freedom to do pretty much as you would in your own home but enjoying an unfolding view of the changing world outside, while safely insulated from its harsh realities.

Australia has no couchette cars of the type so popular in Europe. Managements have opined they would not be acceptable to Australian travellers, naturally without their asking anyone and their ignoring the fact that a high proportion of the mainly migrant Australian population is of European origin.

One reason appears to be that Australian governments are somewhat patronising. Consequently rail managements like to keep close tabs on the behaviour of passengers. They are aware that in European style couchettes the different sexes are in very close proximity. During a long hot night immorality might rear its ugly head! With a sophisticated computer booking system, even for a seat they carefully ask the sex of each passenger so as not to appear to be facilitating any male-female shenanigans in government-run environments if they can possibly avoid it.

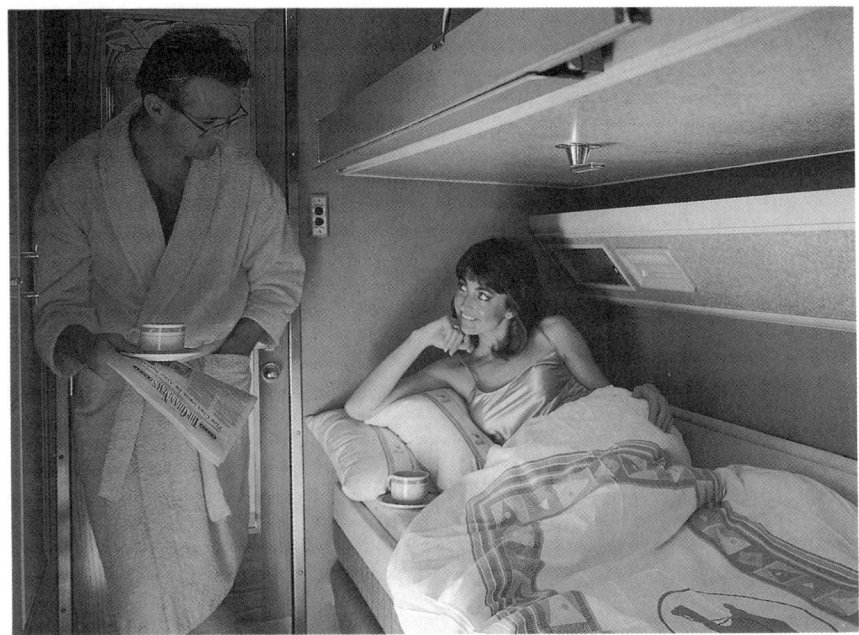

"Hello, so you're my couchette companion?"
"Yes. My, what a pleasant surprise — won't you come on in?"
(Australian National publicity photo for *The Ghan*)

This is one of the manifestations of the puritan or 'wowser' element in Australian society which some believe stems from the convict versus warder heritage of early days when 'transportation' had nothing to do with train travel. There is a leaning towards prohibition, applying to anything resembling good clean fun, be it flirting, drinking or singing and dancing. Restrictions like "no alcohol without a meal" are still to be found in some restaurants as well as on trains. You cannot even circumvent them in the time-honoured British way by "hiring a sandwich" because they will not classify a sandwich as a meal. Seeking a glass of wine with a meal on the overnight *Murwillumbah XPT*, I was refused on the grounds that wine had to be with a meal and they had no meals available. This was at barely ten at night and the train was less than an hour into its 13 hour journey. They only had potato crisps.

Would three packets count as a meal, asked the hungry and thirsty traveller. No way!

Not much chance for fun or pleasure in travel there, it seemed. Yet friendly conversation, and even romance, is possible in chance encounters on a train, even in a sitting car, more so than on any other mode of land transport.

Travelling overnight from Germany to Genova I was unable to secure a couchette but shared a first class compartment with a woman and her teenage daughter. They were Swiss, and bound for the Riviera. The daughter went to sleep on one side of the compartment and the mother and I chatted in adjoining seats for a while before dozing off. During the night not long after we had been awakened for the Italian border crossing I woke to find her lying sideways, her back to me, the tight jeans she wore stretched over shapely buttocks which encroached slightly on my seat. In fact our bodies just touched each other. This was naturally rather stimulating and as her body moved very slightly I wondered if she was asleep, or just pretending to be like the lady in Coventry Passmore's clever little poem *The Kiss*: "He thought me asleep: at least, I knew, He thought I thought he thought I slept". Well, I was not asleep but pretending to be raised interesting possibilities. I was wondering about the reaction if I just curled my arm over her shoulder in a natural half-asleep reaction to this close proximity... but just at that point I became conscious of a slight change in the sound of the train. It was a little louder, with a sort of rushing noise like a breeze, and a slight draught with it. I realised the door had opened.

I was fully awake in a flash. The Swiss lady gave a start and sat up quickly. There was a hand groping in my bag, which was on the seat opposite. A dark figure leaned through the doorway. At my challenge the hand withdrew and the man muttered "*Mi scusa*" as though he had made a careless mistake. He certainly had, and he very quickly slipped back out of our compartment.

Shortly afterwards there was a cry of distress from somewhere down the corridor: "My wallet has been stolen!" The thief, before trying our compartment unsuccessfully, had obviously been at work further along the train. Talking with the Swiss lady we agreed that this was one of the hazards of overnight train travel when you were not in a sleeper that could be locked and particularly when crossing a border into Italy. Apparently the 'banditos' regularly went up to Chiasso on the border. No doubt they would go to other borders too but this popular route was a favourite, being within convenient distance of Milano. It is a fair bet that some railway officials were in on the action. At least they seemed little concerned to do anything about it.

Thieves in the night. It was not the first time with me that something similar happened. In fact right at the end of my first visit to Europe I had myself been robbed of an attache case on a night train from Bologna to Napoli – almost certainly when the train stopped in Roma and I was asleep. The major loss was my camera – or rather my University's camera. Apart from that and my airline ticket, which Al Italia very generously and promptly replaced, the thief must have been somewhat disappointed at his haul, since the rest comprised only a well-used *Thomas Cook European Timetable*, a can of Heineken beer, a packet of Texta colour pens and a very heavy and dirty slab of Italian white marble which I had found discarded at a building site near Carrara and planned to take home for my wife to use as a pastry rolling board. This my insurance company replaced with a clean and genuine piece of similar size obtained in Australia at no small expense to the company. The theft brought one benefit – I did not have to lug the heavy thing back myself and possibly pay excess baggage because of its weight.

I am always uneasy when people stand right outside other people's compartments when there are plenty of seats free, as they seem to do in Italian and some Spanish trains. If it is just to look out of the window, then why not outside their own compartment? It makes me uneasy, not just because I have experienced or witnessed robberies: it is the way little dark men slide quietly into your compartment without a word and as quietly disappear. Even if you said *Buona sera* they would not reply.

What were they there for? The suspicion it arouses, especially at night, may be quite unfounded but it militates against untroubled sleep. It usually happened when the train was half empty – when I had been the only one in a first class compartment – the 'vacant possession' which all passengers brought up in Britain seek out automatically. I kept deciding that next time I was alone in such a compartment in the evening or at night, when fortuitous slumber was more than likely, I would first drag a heavy case across the door, or tie a string with a couple of empty cans to the door handle to warn me of intruders, but I never got properly organised for this.

Better on a night train to seek out some company or get a sleeper and have the conductor lock the door. But even that may pose a problem.

I remember reading of a woman travelling alone at night who woke up to find the Italian conductor groping between her legs, breathing heavily and murmuring *amore* and similar words of endearment. While the conductor obviously believed that every woman should have at least one Italian love affair that seems hardly the way that Ferrovie della Stato management would wish it to happen.

If I am alone in any compartment train at night, or even during the day, and I drop off to sleep while someone is outside or has crept in without saying a word, I always check my wallet when I wake up. A better idea still, as I learned, is to wear a money belt.

Passenger security, particularly on night trains, is something which perhaps needs to be more addressed. With a sleeping compartment the passenger can usually lock the door from inside, but then if he leaves it for any reason it may be necessary to call the conductor to lock it externally.

And sometimes conductors, keen to enjoy a little sleep of their own, are not overjoyed to be summoned by the call button merely to lock a compartment door because a passenger wants to visit the toilet or bathroom or to go along to the buffet. This of course would only apply on trains which have no toilet in the sleeping compartment or have all night catering service. On a train in New South Wales I encountered a very surly conductor who, when asked politely if he would lock the door for me, said, "Got the crown jewels with you, then?" All very well, but there had been systematic thefts on that line just the week before and I was not into taking chances.

Queensland Rail (QR) have a good innovation on their flagship the *Queenslander*. Sleeping compartments have their own individual key, so that passengers on leaving them at any time of day or night can lock up. Only the conductor has a duplicate so that access is possible in an emergency. Security cuts both ways. There was a tragic case in Britain some years ago where passengers were locked in a sleeping car which caught fire.

Locking the outside doors on moving trains can be important but again only if there is an emergency override. I have seen accidents and near accidents on several occasions when outer doors have been left open — exceedingly dangerous when trains are speeding along. Then there have been cases of trains moving away from stations with people caught in half open doors. Normally rail travel is noted for safety but this is an area where sound design must be supplemented by mechanical or electronic safeguards as well as staff vigilance.

The failsafe arrangements that come into operation should a driver have a sudden heart attack or stroke or simply fall asleep are not yet generally matched by arrangements to deal with doors not closing properly or being stuck when they have to be opened. This can prove not only life-threatening but very expensive for the railway concerned if successful litigation results from injury. I once enjoyed an all-expenses-paid trip to Sydney to give evidence in such a case. It was not particularly enjoyable — a man had been caught by a closing door and fell heavily onto the platform. Who was to blame? I could only say that in my experience guards always checked that doors had safely closed before the driver was given the "right away". Either this had not happened, or there was no warning light telling the driver one of the doors was not closed — I was not sure whether such devices were fitted. But I can remember seeing some irresponsible youths forcibly preventing the automatic doors from closing properly on a Melbourne suburban train. It is a little tough on the railways if they always get the blame when some people are totally careless and others are deliberately destructive.

In the early days of railway signalling, the semaphore arm would extend horizontally to indicate stop, giving rise to the railwaymen's expression "the board is on". When the line was clear the signal would drop to a 45 degree downward slope: the board was then "off". After a few accidents had shown that a faulty fixture could result in the semaphore arm dropping from the horizontal when not intended they changed it around and made the arm go upward to indicate "line clear". Failsafe became the name of the game.

At night, colour signals are used. I have long thought it strange that red and green should so long have survived when it is known that red-green confusion is the commonest form of colour blindness. No doubt train drivers are subject to colour blindness tests yet we use the same colours for our traffic lights and I certainly cannot recall ever doing a colour blindness test when applying for a driver's licence.

One safety feature that seems to be disappearing, at least in its traditional form, is the communication cord. 'To stop the train, pull the chain' – the butt of lavatory jokes but something which probably saved many lives. On many modern trains you look in vain for such a safety feature. It is possibly not so important in air conditioned trains with automatic doors and windows that a person cannot fall out of, climb out of, or be pushed out of, but some safety feature is almost always needed in vestibule areas and wherever there are doors or connections between coaches.

Often these concertina connections have gaps in the side or in the flooring where the unwary could get into difficulty. On the Lenk–Zweisimmen train in Switzerland I found there was an open gap between coaches where a child or elderly passenger could possibly fall. Safety handrails were provided on one side only. To me it looked dangerous, but open connections between coaches are fairly common in 'heritage' and similar rolling stock used on tourist railways and one supposes the risks have been carefully assessed. On such trains (and on the one I travelled on in Switzerland) speeds are not great and perhaps the danger is more apparent than real – that is, provided people act sensibly and keep children under control. One sees pictures of trains in India with passengers hanging out of the windows, on the carriage sides and even on the roof. This is not confined to India – it is common on the tourist trains of 'Puffing Billy' in Australia and 'Molli' in Germany.

Despite the apprehension of possible danger on the Lenk–Zweisimmen train I felt safe on the railways in Switzerland. At a few minutes past midnight on a fairly minor Swiss station (Zug) I found lights, facilities, plenty of railway people about, together giving a feeling of security. I was impressed by their efficiency, timekeeping, the comfort of the seats in quite ordinary trains and the friendliness of conductors and other railway staff. Altogether one could feel safe and comfortable on trains and stations in Switzerland. My recollection is that platforms were usually well above the rails, as they are in Britain. In the USA and at many small European stations, climbing down to platforms almost at track level involves potential danger to older passengers.

Provided passengers keep off the actual track when trains are around, train/pedestrian collisions are rare since, unlike motor vehicles, rail vehicles tend to stick to their defined path.

But strange things can happen even at a railway station. A 1992 newspaper report told of an incident at Bondi Junction underground station in the inner suburbs of Sydney where the assistant stationmaster, hearing a loud crash near his ticket office, looked up to see a white two-door Renault car looming over the top of the stairs. Unbelievingly he watched as the driver continued down the wide stairway from the street entrance and started driving around the concourse. He went over and asked the driver why.

"I wanted to get to the other side," replied the driver. Fortunately no-one was injured and when the police arrived it was found the wayward motorist registered zero on the breathalyser. "I was dazzled by the station lights," she said. Blame the Railways of course!

It is not, of course, unusual to find railway vehicles driving along platforms and luggage trains are often seen gingerly threading their way through waiting passengers when loading baggage to or from long distance trains. One of the advantages of long distance rail travel is that, as on an airline, luggage can be checked in to be collected at the final destination.

Many trains have luggage space at one or the other end of the car, where you can keep an eye on it at intermediate stops and have access if required during the journey. That is, so long as you do not have the unfortunate experience of some travellers one night on the southbound XPT from Murwillumbah.

A fellow in one carriage had been making something of a nuisance of himself to other passengers, especially females. Frustrated in his attempts at fraternisation, he had got up and started going through the carriage talking loudly and abusing passengers in general. Ignoring calls to 'shut up', he was threatened with being thrown off the train. Eventually the conductor was called. In spite of his admonition the disturbance still continued, but at Coffs Harbour around two in the morning they had the police waiting for him. Far from meekly surrendering he ran through the train, pausing only to throw people's luggage out onto the platform! He was eventually arrested and subdued and the train continued on its way south.

Sometimes, for reasons of their own, the railways forget that lugging heavy cases for long distances or through awkward passages causes passengers distress – it slows down their progress and makes them anxious about whether they will catch connections.

Economic rationalists at British Rail (BR) had been at work in 1985 when I essayed to go from Charing Cross to West Wickham at a weekend. All Hayes line trains at weekends started from London Bridge which meant that passengers had to break their journey and go up and down flights of stairs. Passenger inconvenience resulted from railway operating convenience.

The older sleeper cars in New South Wales, before XPT days, were non-air-conditioned but had showers at each end of the coach – one end for ladies and one end for gents, presumably in case they met half-dressed in the doorway. I travelled in one from Orange to Sydney which was once the pride of the NSW fleet. The gents' toilet had a urinal stall – one of only two I have ever seen on a train (the other was on the former Sydney–Melbourne *Spirit of Progress*). Such a facility reduces the risk of missing the target but the time I travelled, the train had run out of water for flushing. Perhaps they needed a plumber as well?

I wonder how long it will be before some mean-minded railway accountant decides that access to train toilets should be surcharged?

If you think it bad having to pay for a shower or bath in European hotels or for water to drink (as I do), what of having to pay for the loo? The old public loos in Britain were a penny in the slot for ladies but free for the gents – which would nowadays never pass the vigilant eyes of the sex discrimination police. At some railway stations in Britain they have resolved this by the invention of the 'Superloo'. Now everyone has to pay. "In for a penny" becomes "in for a pound". It is a disgraceful imposition. Toilets should be free, and washing facilities too. If they start charging for the loos on the train, as well they might, this could end up as a real health problem.

"What's that in the corner of the corridor?"

"Sorry, Inspector, I just couldn't wait."

It always amazed me to find, in Germany in particular but also in Austria and Switzerland, that passengers (and not just blind people) could take dogs with them on express trains – and even have them sitting calmly on a first class seat. Did they have to show a first class ticket? And what if they needed to do a poo (the dogs, that is) – did the owners take them to the loo or what?

Dogs or not, there was usually plenty of room in first class on European trains, both within the seats themselves and in the 'pitch' or distance apart, to provide leg room. In the space between groups of facing seats you could place a mountain of luggage – room almost for a cabin trunk.

In Switzerland the InterCity cars, besides having ample luggage space, have a rubbish receptacle under the window tables, and there are shades on the window to kill glare. Most Swiss trains have a mini-bar trolley service even when there is a restaurant car as well. They nearly always have a first class section, in contrast to railways in Britain which tend now to have them only on InterCity services and on some trains in the Greater London area.

I was impressed by some of the facilities in the standard Amtrak coaches in USA. Seats have tables in front and large luggage racks above. There is a rubbish receptacle and drinking water at the end of each carriage and a dressing room next to the toilet (but no showers). Yet otherwise the American obsession with cleanliness was exemplified by the conductor coming through every so often with a large plastic bag. "Amtrash" they announced, when collecting the rubbish. As well, they came through with vacuum cleaners during the longer trips.

Conductors and ticket collectors were both friendly and helpful. The trains are smooth, comfortable and generally quite fast, a pleasure to ride on apart from the often dirty windows which appear to be made of perspex.

They have single sleeping compartments rather similar in facilities to the roomettes of Australian National, except that the toilet and washbasin could not be used without putting the bed up. Under the table in the sleeper was a chessboard, but without a partner and some chessmen this was of doubtful utility.

There were pillows available to add to the comfort of non-sleeper passengers. They had these in New Zealand as well, but charged 50 cents for them.

This raises the question of what people actually expect – or what the railways intend them to have – when they pay first class fare. On the airlines if you travelled 'first' you got free use of headphones, while in 'economy' you paid for them. First class also meant free drinks, and most international flights have offered the same in 'economy' but over the last 20 years or more they have made so many changes that you hardly know now what to expect.

In the United States 'first class' on trains usually means a sleeper. On most other railways there are sleepers or couchettes available as an extra in either first or second class, and sometimes third. In Queensland there is no first class seating but you need a first class ticket to have a first class sleeper.

In Philip McCutchan's fiction novel *Cameron's Chase* a character who had been an ocean liner steward talks of "some passengers travelling first class, a nice distinction from first class passengers". How do you identify a first class passenger – do they look or act differently?

In Vietnam there are some second class sleeping cars which according to *Thomas Cook Overseas Timetable* consist of nine-berth compartments with three passengers assigned to each berth. It must be something of a mix-up sorting out who goes where.

I think I would try for first class if I go to Vietnam. Perhaps I would only have to share a berth with one other.

The provision of different classes of accommodation in trains is a proper response to market demands. People are simply not all one class, or at least do not consider themselves so. Sensibly managed railway systems cash in on this, providing extra comfort and amenities and service where they think people will be willing to pay and the bare minimum where they wish to attract the 'backpacker' element or the tourist who wants to see as much as possible as cheaply as possible. It is a mistake if they take this too far. The idea that fares should be set at 'the highest level the market will bear' is wrong. People will not bear for long what they consider unjustified. Almost everybody wants to get the best bargain they can and value for their money.

The price of travel is a matter of striking an effective balance between what the passenger is charged and what it costs the railways to provide it. The latter is something the economists will tell you about

PASSENGER FARE

" I seem to see an awful lot of third-class faces in here this morning ! "
[*The Star.*

if you are disposed to listen but it will probably be untrue because they leave a lot of things out of their sums that should be there and put in a lot that should not. These are the people who practice the 'dismal science' – who would close all our passenger railways and most of the freight, would charge by the minute for local telephone calls, and would close down all our country roads, schools, postal services, hospitals, public parks and beaches if they got the chance. They tell you it would be cheaper to provide all the pensioners with free motor cars than to subsidise the trains but do they ever do it? Oh no! The people have no trains: they can take a taxi: a modern variant of Marie Antoinette's reputed cynical solution when the peasants of France had no bread – "Let them eat cake!"

The first thing you may notice about train fares is their eccentricity. In some aspects they follow the long established business principle that the buyer in bulk gets things cheaper. Thus regular travellers enjoy reduced fare bulk package deals of weekly, monthly or season tickets. The same principle is applied to international, national and regional runabout passes like Eurailpass, Japan Rail Pass, Britrailpass, and the many others listed in the little booklet put out by Thomas Cook.

But when it comes to mere distance travelled on a single journey, a contrary principle may be applied, especially if you cross a border.

Some systems have adopted the pernicious European practice of surcharging international trips. Knowledgeable travellers in Europe are aware that breaking a journey at a border and re-booking can save money. Indeed, several guide books, especially those written for the backpacker, give specific advice on this.

Of course the railways don't like you doing that, and positively threaten you if you attempt to re-board the same train. In New South Wales a by-law effectively made it the passenger's responsibility to pay the highest rate – imagine a supermarket trying to force customers to buy a large packet of cornflakes if two smaller ones could be bought cheaper (as they often can!).

The reason for such anomalies is that within each country or state, the fares are generally set on a sensible and gradually reducing distance scale, which encourages people to travel to and from the capital city. But intersystem services are another matter. Costs and revenue have to

PASSENGER FARE

be apportioned between operators, adding administrative chores. Travellers are tempted to sample the attractions of rival cities. To counter this, specially reduced fares over long distances within one state are offered in the 'loss-leader' tradition of the market place – and the full-fare-paying intersystem traveller covers the subsidy. Parochial interest overrides public well-being.

Bureaux of Transport Economics and similar bodies have a lot to do with such nonsense, but to many observers of the transport scene it reeks of unfairness, if not deception.

By contrast, some railways are increasingly looking at their fares more from a genuine marketing than an accounting point of view, taking a leaf from the airlines and introducing 'standby' and other discounted incentives to travel, hoping to fill up empty seats with 'eleventh hour' acceptances.

Australia, for example, has introduced CAPER (Customer Advance Purchase Excursion Rail) fares. BR allow first class travel at weekends to economy class passengers on payment of only a small supplement. It might be noted in passing that passengers who have paid the full fare are not too happy about this. But for a long time, BR used to offer cheap day tickets in first class as well as economy. The Australian caper fares offer reductions in first class too.

On some trains special first class fares include meals as well. These vary from the very ordinary to the bordering on luxury and are probably priced accordingly. The danger sometimes with inclusive fares is that the extras, if you work them out, are really exorbitantly priced.

I do not know of any railway that has yet followed the airline practice of giving free drinks in first class, although first class passengers on the *Queenslander* are offered a second drink free during the Train Manager's 'Happy Hour' and first class sleeper passengers on Amtrak get a little cheese basket including a quarter bottle of Californian wine for supper in their cabin. In some countries politicians, especially government ministers on 'gold passes' get away with free drinks all the way. I remember a steward on the *Indian Pacific* telling me how disgusted he was at the squandering of public money when some politician, using this freedom to 'dip into the trough' at public expense was shouting rounds for everyone in the bar, hoping to impress them.

The occasion for the telling of the story was the one time when I was fortunate enough to enjoy a similar facility myself. I had written something a little critical of some aspects of the rail service and after an exchange of correspondence, at first somewhat vitriolic, I had made my peace with management. As a goodwill gesture – and in the knowledge that I would entertain passengers on the piano during the trip – they told the steward to open a bar account for me and send them the bill. Unlike the politician, I felt a little guilty when I saw the amount at the end of the trip: in three days across a continent one can go through quite a lot of grog without noticing, especially if music and other enjoyment accompanies it.

Australian National and now QR provide live music in the lounge bar in the knowledge that passengers will be more likely to frequent it and stay there. For the same reason they put little bowls of salty nuts on the counter, as is done in the most sophisticated lounge bars in hotels the world over.

Queensland Rail have even introduced a disco bar for economy passengers on their *Spirit of the Tropics* services to the north, taking a leaf from the European holiday cruise trains which introduced such a feature in a vehicle called a *Gesellschaftwagen*. QR copied the idea but not the name!

For a while the *Ghan* had an entertainment car with 'fruit machines' or 'pokies' and video games. Cinema cars are not unknown on the American continent.

I once travelled on the *Overland* from Melbourne to Adelaide when ABC television had arranged for one of its popular youth programmes, *Countdown*, to be videoed on the train. As the picture shows, the lounge was pretty well done out as a television studio. When the programme came to air it included shots of the passengers engaged in a singsong. The Seekers' *Morningtown Ride* featured prominently – "Train whistle

blowing..." for as long as any of us could remember the words. They also had a crazy shot of one of the troop stuck in a folding berth.

There are some good railway songs, including *The Wreck of the Old 97*, *Midnight Special* and *Rock Island Line*. Someone should compile an anthology of them. *Chattanooga Choo Choo* was my first introduction to 'swing' and through it, jazz. It was to see Glenn Miller that I first went to the cinema, more than frowned upon as the devil's invention by my parents. Unfortunately I lost our wartime ration book that day and when it arrived in the post, compliments of the manager of the Odeon my father was quick to see it as fulfilment of Moses' warning to the Israelites. "Be sure your sin will find you out" was the theme of the admonition I received.

But music is a stronger force than any lecture, as armies have found and advertisers well know. QR had a very catchy little song *Take it Easy, Take a Train* for a while.

Perhaps the New York Subway management should have used the

TRAINCATCHER

Ellington number *Take the 'A' Train* as a logotype.

On the other hand canned music is a mixed blessing on trains. Some find it soothing, others detest it. My feeling is that if it cannot be individually controlled (as it can in a single sleeper compartment) then it should be limited in time, perhaps to waiting periods prior to departure or when the train is held up by signals. It is at such times that passengers like some diversion.

Music in a lounge car, whether canned or live is acceptable. Some of my happiest train memories are of the lounge of the *Indian Pacific* when it had a proper piano and a singsong or just a recital would be enjoyed by the passengers there while the train rocked and rolled its way around the curves out west of Lithgow. But passengers bringing their own music in the form of hi-fi sets are another matter and to my mind should be prohibited unless they use only personal earphones. Perhaps on some systems there are by-laws about this. I found it particularly irritating having to listen to pop music blaring out from massive loudspeakers on trains in Sydney suburban area, on an Italian train along the shores of beautiful Lago di Como and on the Napier to Wellington train in New Zealand. Perhaps much depends on the train conductors or guards, if any.

On Amtrak trains the conductors check the seat position and put the destination of each passenger up on the side of the luggage rack above the seat, to identify them and make sure they get off at the right station. They also keep a watch on passenger behaviour to ensure that other passengers are not unreasonably disturbed. If passengers are really drunk and disorderly they are simply put off the train and may spend a night in jail until relatives come to pick them up next day. This is a sensible idea, but practices vary. Refusing further service is a simple remedy but muscle may be needed to enforce it and if passengers carry their own liquor supplies it serves no purpose. On the other hand, provided passengers are quiet and keep to themselves there is no reason why they should not carry a flask of something to keep them going. The silliest reaction to trouble on a train I ever experienced was when a bar

PASSENGER FARE

Passenger fare at its best – the author enjoys seafood on the *Queenslander*.

steward on a train in Gippsland, Victoria, closed the entire buffet because of an alleged insult by a merry passenger to the waitress. No-one else in the buffet had heard or noticed anything!

Smoking in trains is another problem where it is difficult to strike the right balance between individual freedom and pleasure on the one hand and annoyance or distress on the other. If railways ban all smoking they are turning away many potential passengers. On some trains in Britain it was hard to find any first class non-smoking seats that were genuinely smoke-free. Mere division by seat marking is no good. Non-smokers need at least either separate compartments or a full coach if of the open vestibule type. On the 17.00 Euston to Manchester InterCity there were 2½ coaches marked "1st class smoking" and only half a coach non-smoking with the reek of cigar smoke from the forward section penetrating the whole coach very quickly.

With compartment coaches it was easier to separate smokers and non-smokers and air conditioning now makes the problem more intractable. An amusing though highly anti-social attitude was displayed by one traveller I met on the Gisborne train in New Zealand: he said he preferred a seat in a non-smoking compartment so he could enjoy his smoke without breathing in the stale tobacco atmosphere created by other smokers!

Chapter 6
Great Rail Non-Connections

"Whom God would destroy, He first makes mad." – James Duport

The Spanish guitarist Segovia recalls in his autobiography a journey from Madrid to Granada over half a century ago. At Baeza it was necessary to change from the *Sevilla Express* to a train operated by another railway company. When the express was late they would deliberately hold back the 'connection' until it was seen approaching. Then at the last minute, as the express was drawing into the platform, the other train would be sent off from the other end before the passengers had a chance to catch it. At the time there was fierce rivalry between the two companies. One wanted to discredit the other in the fight for passenger custom and did so by this deliberate ploy.

Segovia's experience in Spain could be matched in more recent times, when the morning FEVE service along the north coast from Ferroll reached Oviedo just minutes after the departure of the RENFE (Spanish State Railways) afternoon *Talgo* express to Madrid. Before the *Talgo* was introduced in 1982 the FEVE train missed the express by an hour but after 1987 things improved and a connection became possible. To the experienced traveller it seems characteristic of railway systems that one train will miss another by a few minutes, or leave such short time for a connection as to cause the passenger to be anxiously chewing nails as the transfer point is approached.

In 1985 I sought to make the afternoon *Talgo* connection from Oveiedo. The 13.53 RENFE train from Aviles appeared to connect but the man in the ticket office said there was no way I would catch it at Oviedo with only nine minutes to spare. The proper connection, he said, would have been the 11.56 – allowing two hours! Waiting for the local

I enjoyed excellent bar snacks (gratis) in the station *cantina* with a drink. We started late and crawled along as though the station-master had spoken to the driver to make sure I missed my connection. He had said I would. Honour was at stake! But we made it, and the beautiful *Talgo* with its gourmet dining car meal would have been worth waiting two hours for anyway!

The lack of a connection, or an ineffective or missed connection, can do much to put people off travelling by train (or any public transport, because poor connectivity is not confined to the rail mode). Cynics have suggested that careful scheduling to achieve non-connections may be among the methods used by those transport bureaucrats who for one reason or another wish to reduce public transport usage. By discouraging passengers they can point to declining 'demand' which they then use to justify closure.

Many examples, past and present, of non-connections in rail services can be given.

They were certainly common in Britain before and for quite a long time after railway nationalisation. One could arrive at Leeds City Station from north-east England to find the Lancashire 'connection' just gone – that being on the former LMS and therefore a rival organisation. As recently as 1984 a study of connections at Crewe, England (of all places!) reported in *Modern Railways* showed that most trains from Manchester and Liverpool under a then new timetable missed a Cardiff train by five minutes or less, condemning passengers to a wait of an hour or more for the next one! Rail magazines constantly report such phenomena.

In 1985 I travelled through mid-Wales on a Shrewsbury to Swansea diesel multiple unit. I noted that its arrival there was carefully scheduled to miss the hourly HST London service by seven minutes. Over on the other side of the country I saw the 12.25 Pickering train of the North Yorkshire Moors Railway (NYMR) leaving the junction station of Grosmont. It left late at 12.35 just three minutes before the Whitby – Middlesbrough train of British Rail (BR) was due in. Whose fault would this be? Admittedly the NYMR ran an hourly service at that time between 10.25 and 16.25 but BR had fewer trains and for every one that made a reasonable connection another would miss just by several minutes.

Even on the East Coast Main Line, entirely under BR management, the 17.55 Scarborough to York train was timed to arrive there at 18.48, the exact time of departure of the *Cleveland Executive* InterCity to Middlesbrough with the next 'connection' train taking two hours longer including a 50 minute wait at Darlington.

Across the sea in Ireland connections could be equally bad. The 11.30 Cork to Dublin express missed the 13.57 Westport train (one of only three a day) at Portarlington junction by precisely four and a half minutes. That was remedied in 1992 but neither of the other two trains had a viable connection then or in 1995.

Even ÖBB, the Austrian State Railways – generally considered one of the most efficient systems in Europe – managed in the 1983 summer timetable to bring the *Romulus* express from Italy into Wien Südbahnhof just five minutes after the departure of the *Chopin* service to Poland and Russia.

To be fair to ÖBB, this was the nearest thing to a connection that had been seen for years between those particular trains, neither of which was entirely under Austrian railway control, and by 1989 they managed to create a regular 45 minute gap between arrival and departure which has been maintained ever since.

In Austria in general, punctuality is almost as legendary as it is in Switzerland and all train connections shown in the timetables are guaranteed. There are clear rules. Express trains and semi-fast trains normally wait 5 minutes; all other passenger trains 10 minutes. A special timetable symbol is used to indicate trains which do not wait for connections at particular stations.

In Australia any non-connection is particularly bad because the long distance trains are so few and far between.

Veteran train traveller and timetable watcher John Price, retired

Editor of the *Thomas Cook Continental Timetable*, told me that in early days when the rail route to Alice Springs was via Quorn, there was a lack of synchronisation between services that would make Segovia's experiences pale into nothingness.

More recently, Australia boasted one 5-day wait between 'connecting' trains. In the 1980s passenger trains served Chillagoe and Forsayth in north Queensland, the former noted for its old smelter chimneys, caves and marble deposits and the latter for goldfields. The lines to these places met at a junction called Almaden.

In transportation network jargon a junction is called a relay node. On any railway system there are both operative and non-operative relay nodes – an operative node being where physical transfer is possible between a train on one route and one on another. The transfer may be immediate, as where two trains simultaneously occupy adjacent platforms, which is the basis for the German InterCity system, or it may involve waiting time which detracts from its effectiveness. How much more then ought weight be given to effective connectivity in countries like Australia or Canada which operate far less intensive services!

Almaden was far from a fully operative node. A passenger wishing to travel from Chillagoe to Forsayth and back could catch a train from Chillagoe which reached Almaden at 9.00. The Forsayth train, if on time, would have been conveniently waiting at the opposite platform, scheduled to depart at 9.15.

But the return journey was a different matter. The once-weekly train back to Chillagoe left Almaden at 16.20 on Wednesdays, but one of only two weekly trains from Forsayth arrived there over two hours later. To avoid missing the connection by a week you would have done better to take the Friday train instead. This left Forsayth at nine in the morning and reached Almaden at eight the same evening, allowing you to spend five whole days in beautiful downtown Almaden (one pub, one shop and cafe, one post office).

This surely took the crown for great rail non-connections but it is no longer possible as trains have been withdrawn from the Chillagoe

GREAT RAIL NON-CONNECTIONS

branch and, since this chapter was written, from Almaden itself.
Australia had and still has many other great non-connections. For years, the southbound *Brisbane Limited* arrived in Sydney at the exact time of departure of the one train to Canberra – about which I shall have more to say. Also in New South Wales, and entirely under that State's control and management, the former *Central West Express* on its 'up' journey missed connecting with the Melbourne-bound overnight train *Spirit of Progress* by 15 minutes. A later Melbourne night train was advertised non-stop so passengers for the many intermediate provincial stations in southern New South Wales and north-east Victoria had to wait overnight in Sydney for the day train.

Before electrification between Sydney and Newcastle, the *Southern Aurora* sleeping car express from Melbourne reached Sydney just in time to miss the morning *Newcastle Express*, enforcing a four hour wait upon ongoing passengers.

All these could have been rectified by the mere introduction of brief stops at the junction of Strathfield in Sydney's western suburbs.

More recently the *Grafton Express* made non-connections at Maitland with trains to and from the Tablelands and Moree in northwest New South Wales. In the 1995 timetable it arrived at 14.06, half an hour after the *Tablelands Xplorer* departed and it left for the north coast at 14.01 only a quarter of an hour before the latter came back to Maitland.

Connectivity is potentially worse when different systems are involved. For several years the northbound *Brisbane Limited* arrived at Roma Street too late to catch Queensland's *Sunlander* to Cairns. During 1989 Queensland Rail (QR) re-timed the latter to make connection possible. The State Rail Authority of NSW (SRA) withdrew the *Limited* and substituted the XPT, enforcing a further change in the QR timetables. All this happened without any prior consultation.

One outstanding Australian exception (which highlights the 'rule') was a good daily connection in the Melbourne area between the *Intercapital Daylight* and the *Overland*, long maintained as part of the Sydney–Melbourne–Adelaide–Perth link. From time to time even

Brisbane was included in this linkup, at least in one direction, though this appeared to be more by accident than design. QR timetables rather overstated the matter when in their 1971 edition they used the heading "Through service – Cairns to Perth" for a series of journeys involving five train changes, one of which involved an overnight stop!

But the SRA, or V/Line (Victorian Railways), or both together, put an end to even this degree of connectivity in 1992 with complete withdrawal of the Sydney–Melbourne daylight express, thereby adding 11 hours to the normal Sydney to Adelaide journey. Only since the end of 1994 has a day link been reintroduced.

Even good connections are features to be avoided if they occur in the middle of the night.

The SRA, in their zeal to make every journey connect with the much-vaunted (and in many ways excellent) XPT services have, by replacing overnight sleeper trains and their local daytime rail connections by bus connections, condemned travellers to and from many country towns to the horror of middle of the night transfers between bus and rail. Sometimes these coincide with a meal stop and when one's internal clock has to adjust to having a main meal at such an hour the effect is similar to jet lag.

Among the worst examples, as in 1994, were buses leaving the *Riverina XPT* at Cootamundra for Griffith to arrive at 23.50, Hay at 1.40 (for a late supper?) and Balranald at 3.40. The return connection left Balranald at 1.30 with a nice early breakfast for the day at Hay at 2.55 and left the major town of Griffith (which used to have both day train and direct sleeper services to Sydney) at the comparatively civilised hour of 5.21. Yet other Riverina towns, formerly served by the same through trains, enjoyed a bus connection leaving Wagga Wagga at 3.40 for Narrandera and Leeton, from whence it returned for the morning train at 5.08 and 5.33 respectively. Replacement of the *Riverina* train by a Melbourne daylight XPT, the *Olympic Spirit,* in 1995 has restored some sanity to these schedules.

But in far west New South Wales the mining town of Broken Hill

GREAT RAIL NON-CONNECTIONS

was still linked to the XPT at Dubbo by a bus leaving at 3.30 in the morning local time. This may hold the record for the longest railway feeder bus service in the world, the bus connection taking nine hours for a six and a half hour train trip!

Further north, passengers on the night train from Sydney in 1995 could reach Byron Bay and Queensland's Gold Coast by changing from the train in Casino at 3.30 in the morning.

Curiously, despite the obvious attraction of a train like the XPT compared to a bus, passengers from southern New South Wales journeying to Canberra were turfed out of the XPT at Cootamundra at 13.51 for a two and a half hour bus ride, yet the train called at Yass 83 minutes later, from where the same bus had just over an hour's run to the National Capital.

In the reverse direction it was much the same in the 1995 timetable. To reach Cootamundra in time for the southbound XPT at 13.18 the passenger had to leave Canberra station at 10.05. From there a bus went – via Yass – to Cootamundra. The XPT called at Yass junction station at 11.57 while the bus (run by or on behalf of the same mob, Countrylink) called at Yass Town, some 4 km away, at 11.21, but only to take on extra passengers. No-one was dropped at Yass station to join the much vaunted XPT; they had to go all the way on the bus to Cootamundra. And worse! If their destination happened to be anywhere in the Riverina beyond Griffith they did not even get the chance to travel by rail between Cootamundra and anywhere further: they had to change at Cootamundra from one bus to another and use that one all the way - because the bus that connected for Griffith with the train at Wagga did not get into Griffith in time to catch the bus going further west!

"They're a weird mob," as Nino Culotta might well have said about the SRA, more than about Australians in general.

Scheduling faults like this could very easily be rectified if anyone thought about it even for a minute. It seems that almost the world over, when considering timetable changes the main consideration of the railways has often been operating convenience. Little thought seems to be given to the convenience of passengers and the need for sensible connections. This has certainly been a failing of British and Australian railways for years.

It is strange that no-one seems to have undertaken any behavioural research to find out what passengers regard as a reasonable wait between the arrival of one service and the departure of a connecting one – or if they have, why railway managements have taken little notice of it. Not that such a survey should be necessary. Common sense should tell anyone that nobody in their right mind wants to hang around for hours at some place they don't care to be at with nothing to do except wait for a train or bus that in all probability will be late anyway.

Successful rail travel involves not only finding the station but also a knowledge of the timetables, so that you join the right train at the right time – if it is on time – and avoid the worst of the non-connections.

In the Brisbane *Sunday Mail* in February 1993 columnist Don Busmer advised Queenslanders not to worry about the Brisbane railway service – there were worse things.

"A woman commuter in Sydney," he reported, had "told an inspector that she hadn't been able to buy a ticket before boarding because the train had arrived ON TIME". Her excuse was accepted.

Even experienced travellers tend to cling to a childish faith in railway timetables, despite evidence suggesting they are more in the nature of fiction.

"What's the use of this timetable?" asked the irate traveller in wartime England, when his train was reported fifty minutes late.

"Look at it this way, sir," said the patient station-master: "if it wasn't for the timetable you wouldn't know how late the train was."

Timetables tend to frighten some people. Few travel agencies will readily confess to having a railway timetable, and fewer still profess to understand or offer to interpret them. Thomas Cook are the notable exception and often appear to know more about railway timetables than the railways themselves.

The fact is that railway timetables are not among the easiest things to read. They fail to distinguish the important from the trivial. Even in a country as sparsely rail-provided as Australia (area-wise), railway timetables tend to give a wealth of information the railway administrations think you should know but which is of little concern to the ordinary traveller.

Timetables sometimes try to say too much. There is not enough room to contain it all. The traveller is not really concerned to know that the 5.17 calls at some obscure location "one minute later on Saturdays" as he knows it will be very lucky to call there on time anyway. Nor are many people except the student of geography or transportation, or the rail enthusiast, really concerned about mileages, altitude of stations, or railway history.

Some railway timetables seem to be designed to confuse the traveller. Complex and complicated, they have evolved a language of abbreviations and hieroglyphics all their own.

In common English language usage 'a.m.' and 'p.m.' are understood to signify morning and afternoon respectively, and abbreviations such as 'arr' and 'dep' for arrive and depart are equally familiar. Some timetables use light and heavy type to distinguish morning from evening; more expensive ones use different colours. The 'continental' twenty-four hour clock used by airlines and the military avoids the a.m/p.m. confusion but can mislead travellers unfamiliar with it. They may read 17.15 as 7.15 at night.

Queensland Rail, in some of their suburban timetable leaflets made the mistake of further abbreviating 'arr' and 'dep' to 'a' and 'd'. Unfortunately for them (and more so for their erstwhile passengers) this conflicted with the letter symbols the timetable people used to indicate stopping and boarding information. For example, the footnote 'a' was used to signify:

"Train stops if required to set down passengers, and by signal from station staff if required to pick up passengers. Passengers wishing to alight at that station should give due notice to Guard". Quite a mouthful — and the explanation of footnote 'd' was even more complicated!

When 'a' and 'd' could also mean 'arr.' and 'dep.' it is not difficult to see how confusion could arise.

One university colleague came to me indignantly brandishing a QR timetable leaflet. "Do I really have to tell the guard I want to get off at Brisbane Central?" he asked. I said no.

The Railways should realise that timetables are not as familiar to occasional travellers as they are to station and train staff – and sometimes these people are in confusion too!

The use of letters and symbols to augment the information in timetables is necessary and desirable but the user must be clear on what is intended. A legend or key should be given either below or adjacent to each table, or in a known place at the beginning of the book, with a reference to that place from every table in which the standard symbols are used. Difficulties of interpretation can arise where this rule is not followed, and a person who derives wrong information from a timetable and misses a train or stop in consequence will be a potential lost customer.

Thomas Cook, publishers of *Continental and Overseas Timetables* for years, have developed timetable symbolism almost into an art form (as have most European railway systems in their own publications). Symbols of four-poster beds for sleeping cars, couches for couchettes, knife and fork for meals, and wine glass for buffet service (ironically this symbol was used for Australia's *Albury Express* which was 'dry'), are easily understood by the reader, but crossed hammers for 'weekdays', a dagger sign for 'Sundays only' (perhaps it's meant to be a symbol of a cross?) and some of the other symbols are less obvious. The use of numerals 1 to 7 for days of the week Monday to Sunday follows the practice used in airline guides and is a sensible abbreviation so long as it is explained.

Queensland Rail, the most prolific among Australian timetable publishers, consider it important for travellers to be aware of by-laws. One of Australia's weirdest pastimes is litigation, and perhaps therefore QR felt the passengers should be fully aware of their rights.

GREAT RAIL NON-CONNECTIONS

Certainly there are some things every traveller should know, but it is doubtful whether 11 pages dealing with conditions of travel in one of QR's former timetables were really necessary – even though some of them covered by-laws which incurred penalties.

Nevertheless, they made fascinating reading, especially on a long train journey. It was good to know that loaded firearms and shooting were not allowed in railway carriages (Agatha Christie obviously never travelled in Queensland) and that missiles were not to be thrown or propelled (Go home, Saddam Hussein), but I wonder how often the offence of being in charge of a tramcar and failing to slacken speed to 10 miles an hour when approaching a level crossing occurred in Queensland, especially as the warning was printed long after the last trams had vanished from Brisbane streets!

It was also a punishable offence to empty nightsoil on railway premises, and, of course, (the ultimate horror!) to "consume alcohol other than that supplied by the Commissioner", generous though that Worthy undoubtedly must have been.

Careful study of railway timetables reveals two curious practices which, although not unique to railways, have never been developed to anything like the same degree on other modes of public transport.

These are the 'restricted stop' and 'conditional stop' phenomena. The former is where the train stops but the passenger is not allowed to get on, or get off, or possibly both: the latter is a game of chance on whether the train will stop at all.

Both stem from a problem railways faced from earliest times. The railways (and the passengers) wanted the trains to be fast. In this at least they were in agreement; speed of travel being a selling point. But this raised a problem: one way of having faster trains was to omit intermediate stops and this could result in fewer passengers. Still today the railways face this dilemma. The long distance traveller wants an express: the short distance traveller wants the train to stop at his station.

This means two trains are needed at the same time, one fast and one slow, which means building more lines and having more trains. One slightly unsatisfactory compromise was the 'semi-fast' train. Conditional and restricted stops are other attempts to resolve the problem.

It has never been very clear what dire fate awaits those intrepid travellers who dare to transgress the restricted stop rules. Fifty years ago a cartoonist-journalist lambasted this restrictive practice by the following tale:

"A passenger waiting on St. Albans platform for a London train was astonished to find a fast express, which usually dashed straight through, coming to a stop.

He made a dash for the door and jumped in. 'Hi!' shouted a porter, 'you can't do that. This train doesn't stop here'.

'That's all right, porter', retorted the man, 'I haven't got on!'"

According to Brian Hollingsworth's delightful book *The Pleasures of Railways* the late Professor Joad of England's BBC Brains Trust fame really did this one day at Reading when the *Cornish Riviera Express* made an unscheduled stop to detach a 'slip coach' which, because of the weather, could not be slipped in the usual way. But like so many railway stories, you hear the same thing about different places and different trains and different times. Somewhere, sometime, it must have happened.

More infuriating for a passenger is the train which is regularly scheduled to stop at stations where he is not allowed to get on or off. Australian railways have featured this to a degree found in few other countries.

If a town is well served by rail it is reasonable for some trains not to stop, or to stop only to take up or set down long distance passengers. Restrictions on short distance commuters crowding the aisles of country and inter-city trains are reasonable but should be imposed with discrimination. Allowing disembarkation at outer suburban stations from long distance trains makes sense. It is a convenience for passengers in that they do not have to go right into the city and out again. Such restricted stops give people access to express trains they would not otherwise have.

GREAT RAIL NON-CONNECTIONS

Of course the old slip coach idea was really the foolproof way of allowing passengers to alight but not board. It was widely used in Britain before World War II, especially on the Great Western. There was no point in a local passenger getting on: the slip coach had completed its journey once in the platform. This practice has not been revived since the demise of the last surviving slip coach in Britain on the 17.10 Paddington–Wolverhampton train in 1960.

When a capital-bound express calls somewhere to set down only and there are plenty of other trains for locals to use, no one can complain. For example, in England on a Sunday afternoon, London-bound expresses used to call at Rugby, 80 minutes from London by fast train, to "set down only". These trains were not intended for Rugby–London passengers, but there were more than twice as many other trains in a given period which took only 13 minutes longer to reach the capital.

No such options existed in the 1970s and 1980s for the visitor to Melbourne from Albury on the NSW border hoping for a late evening return. The former *Southern Aurora* at 20.00 hours, with buffet and dining car, could have provided a very pleasant conveyance home after a busy day's shopping or business in the city, but you were not allowed to travel on it the 317 km to Albury. Its call there was "definitely to take up only". There was no other Albury train from Melbourne until the next day.

It would seem much simpler for both management and passengers if trains were scheduled either to stop or not, and when stopped, to allow passengers on or off at will – especially when there are not many trains.

The 'conditional' stop differs from the restricted stop in that whereas the latter is one at which passengers are denied certain options, the former is one at which the train itself (like a bus at a request stop) will stop only if required to do so by a passenger.

It is therefore both a convenience and a nuisance. It is clumsy in that drivers have to be prepared to stop, guards have to be alerted, and the schedule has to be that of a stopping train even when the train runs express. Against that, it is undeniably a boon to would-be passengers to or from minor stations.

Some timetables abound in complicated variations of conditional stops, and conditional-restricted combination stops. These add much to their complexity, to the frustration of the traveller and, it seems to me, the detriment of efficient railway operation.

One can even find unadvertised conditional stops, where passengers may board, or presumably alight from, a train which stops unexpectedly. Whole trains are sometimes unadvertised yet scheduled to run regularly. So you can board a train you didn't know existed at a place you didn't know it stopped at! But how do you tell whether it is one you are allowed to board or one that has merely stopped by mistake, or because of a signal check?

The classic historic example of a conditional stop based on the exclusionist principle was of course Badminton in the Cotswolds of western England. For many years prior to railway nationalisation (and for over a decade afterwards) crack Great Western expresses had to stop at this tiny station because the member of Royalty who owned the land had made it a condition on the line's construction through his estate. In BR timetables there is no longer any trace of this little place of less than 500 souls, yet even as late as 1961, in the last issue of Bradshaw, Badminton featured as prominently in the heading of the main line timetable as Swindon, Bristol and Newport. It was significant as one of the few intermediate stops made by trains such as the *Capitals United Express* (Paddington–Fishguard Harbour) and the *Red Dragon* (Paddington–Cardiff–Carmarthen). I travelled on the latter's modern counterpart – *The Royal Duchy* – in 1992, which now goes only to Cardiff and Swansea. There was no mention of a stop at Badminton but the first stop at Reading was definitely 'to take up only'. That is where I got out from the restaurant car – along with a number of obviously regular business commuters!

Chapter 7

The Train that Died of Shame

"Thou art weighed in the balances and art found wanting."

– Daniel 5:27

The writing on the wall for the Sydney–Brisbane sleeping car express was worded slightly differently but effectively amounted to the same verdict:

"Consideration has been given to the running of N2 the Brisbane Limited and it has been decided that Interstate trains which lost their path between 6.0 a.m. and 9.0 a.m. and 4.0 p.m. and 6.0 p.m. Monday to Friday were to be held until another path becomes available."

So proclaimed the Working Timetable of the State Rail Authority of NSW (SRA) in 1980 in language as sloppy as the timekeeping of the train. Less than 10 years later the train was no more.

For some years the Up *Brisbane Limited* had struggled to maintain its 15½ hour schedule over the 987 km from South Brisbane to Sydney. It had been known to arrive on time on occasion. More often it did not and hence the warning. It was not exactly the kind of train you could rely on and SRA knew it.

A journey on this train was among my first Australian interstate trips. During a two-year sojourn in Melbourne I had learned that to travel to Sydney by first class sleeper on the *Southern Aurora* was not only a more pleasant but a cheaper way of travelling than by air. You had dinner on the train and arrived breakfasted and refreshed in the heart of the city at the start of business. The fare and meal together cost less than a night's hotel in Sydney. I therefore naturally looked first to similar rail travel when I was in Brisbane and wished to revisit Melbourne.

This was in 1972. The train from Brisbane was scheduled to reach Sydney at 8.33, missing the day train to Melbourne by nearly an hour but as I had business in Sydney this was of no consequence at the time. I booked on the overnight *Southern Aurora* for the Sydney–Melbourne leg of the journey, making only a mental note that the non-connection by day might be a future inconvenience.

This intelligence lay dormant in my memory cells until late the following year when a small news item in a national newspaper caught my eye: the southern States were going on to Summer Time. The interstate trains from Brisbane were to be re-timed: the Commissioner said that earlier departures were necessary "to maintain normal connections with interstate trains leaving Sydney for the other States".

This caused me to check the timetable. Rail travellers would be indeed gratified to learn that the *Brisbane Limited* would still land them in Sydney 11½ hours before the departure of the next train to Melbourne, or 6½ hours before the departure of the *Indian Pacific* for Perth. They would still be able to miss the Melbourne daylight train by 48 minutes. Into the bargain, they could still miss the *Canberra Monaro Express* by just over an hour. And they would also be in time to miss the *Riverina Express* for Albury and Griffith by a mere 28 minutes, but they might see it passing if they looked out of the window after leaving Strathfield, the last stop before Sydney.

There was, admittedly, an earlier Brisbane–Sydney train in those days which reputedly made a connection with the daylight service to Melbourne, and thence via the *Overland* to Adelaide, but this Brisbane–Sydney train was an unattractive service, running only 'semi-fast', and with no dining car or air conditioned sleepers.

It was a clear case for a 'Letter to the Editor'. For good measure I sent a copy to the Commissioner with a covering note containing some amateur suggestions. The response was friendly but the Commissioner was prompt in pointing out that Queensland Rail was "not responsible for the operation of services in New South Wales and Victoria". Obligingly, he passed my letter on to his southern colleagues.

After eight months' gestation this brought forth a response. There had been discussions and other developments – the other train, the old *Brisbane "Express"* (so-called) had been withdrawn, and SRA had re-timed the *Limited* to leave an hour or so earlier so as to connect at Strathfield, 12 km west of Sydney, with the Melbourne train. Connections to the *Canberra Monaro Express* and *Riverina Express* now also became possible.

The latter innovation was deemed sufficiently dramatic for Queensland Rail to include a new table in its public timetables, advertising (wrongly) a Brisbane–Sydney–Canberra "through" service. At least it was a service which connected and a footnote made it clear that passengers for Canberra had to change at Strathfield.

But the Strathfield stop was short-lived, being deleted in 1976 for no reason I was ever able to discover. It was simply abolished. Yet two years later the Queensland timetable still stated that the Brisbane Limited took passengers for Strathfield. Stranger still, a so-called "through" service to Canberra continued to be advertised. The *Brisbane Limited* was given as arriving in Sydney at 7.30, the exact time of departure of the *Canberra Monaro Express*. The so-called "through" service involved a 24-hour wait in Sydney, whether the passenger liked it or not. With both trains on the same route between Sydney and Strathfield the Canberra-bound passenger from the north would have the dubious pleasure of seeing the 'connection' departing as he arrived.

Questioned about this enforced stay in the New South Wales capital, a Railway spokesman expressed the view that it was a boon and blessing to travellers – a sort of bonus. But supposing one wished to go straight through to Canberra?

Ah! "There's not much demand for Brisbane–Canberra rail travel," was the response. Did they ever wonder why? Only one daily train from

Brisbane to Sydney and only one from Sydney to Canberra, missing each other by a whisker – the supreme example of a great rail non-connection, much less a "through" train!

Yet with luck and knowledge of the geography of Sydney and of the intricacies of the suburban timetables, it was perfectly possible to make a connection and be in Canberra, by train, the day of your arrival in Sydney, provided the *Limited* was not more than about 25 minutes late. It involved two quick changes of train in the Sydney suburbs, first at Hornsby (arrive 6.51, change to a local leaving at 6.57), or at Gosford if running late, and then again at Strathfield. There you had to hurry under the subway to the Canberra platform, with up to 13 minutes to do it in.

Attempting to make a booking on this basis, I found the railway clerk horrified. "It's not a connection," he exclaimed. "It can't be guaranteed [as if connections ever could]; they won't hold the *Monaro* for you". He must have been blissfully unaware of the non-connection advertised in the published Queensland timetable. I assured him I was quite content to take the chance. He was still uneasy, so I let it rest. In the event, it didn't connect. The *Limited* had "lost its path".

In late 1983 the *Limited* was allowed 15 hours 42 minutes southbound and almost 16 hours northbound. This generous schedule always included "recovery" time totalling up to 40 minutes on the southbound journey, spread among various sections of the route between Coffs Harbour and Gosford. In spite of this the train persistently suffered from late running, especially on the journey south. Yet there were exceptions. On one occasion, for reasons known only to the District Control, the Up *Mid North Coast XPT*, which was then SRA's newest and fastest train, was held eight minutes at Telegraph Point to allow the already late northbound *Limited* to cross. A member of the train staff remarked that the *Limited* had in fact been on time, he thought "one day about three weeks ago". A bit like an English summer: I can remember one a few years before I left; I think it was on a Thursday.

One of my last trips on the Up *Brisbane Limited* to Sydney was in

THE TRAIN THAT DIED OF SHAME

November 1983, just before a major re-scheduling took place, ensuring that never again would passengers or railway staff have to worry about this train making connections: it would no longer even try.

Setting off from South Brisbane dead on time the train comprised 15 vehicles hauled by two Class 44 diesels – stalwarts of the NSW fleet and withdrawn only in 1994 – and made good speed through Brisbane's outer suburbs as far as Greenbank. There it made a brief unscheduled stop as it nearly always did, in both directions, perhaps to exchange the time of day with the station-master. It was always a friendly train.

Bromelton, a conditional stop which served nearby Beaudesert, claimed our attention for barely a minute to allow passengers to board. In the dining car preparations were well under way for the evening meal and the girls were relaxing over a card game.

A colleague recently retired from university wandered through in search of a cuppa. "On through to the buffet," he was told. He smiled at me in recognition. "I love travelling by train," he said, as if in justification or as a fellow-conspirator, and ambled off happily down the corridor.

The countryside towards the border on both sides is scenically most attractive; mountains, rainforest and waterfalls interspersed with grassy meadows, traversed by little winding roads, and hidden now and then by clouds and mist. The line wends its way southward, climbing at gradients of up to 1 in 50, until it reaches the tunnels and spiral of Border Loop, when you look down on what appears to be another railway on the right. The cloudy and darkish sky made the scene especially dramatic on this trip. As we burst out of the tunnel there was a rushing stream to the right with the railway we had just traversed visible on the viaduct to our left.

It is a pity that no leaflet is provided giving details of this scenic route. There is no announcement made either, nor was there one about the need to adjust watches. The train runs on New South Wales time, which was then an hour ahead of Queensland. Perhaps they are reticent about this since the occasion when an airline pilot flying over the

Queensland border said: "We are now crossing into Queensland. Will passengers please put their watches back 20 years."

The old *Brisbane Limited* struck its first trouble at Grafton in northern New South Wales. It had been going great guns up to then and arrived in the platform dead on time; if anything half a minute early. At exactly 20.03, as scheduled, it moved forward again. I was booked to join the *Central West XPT* leaving Sydney at 8.08 the following morning. This allowed half an hour's grace to the *Limited* so things were going well.

It stopped.

A couple of minutes later we moved again – backwards. Backwards we continued, right out over the bridge towards the old station on the north side of the river. Half way across, at 20.10, we stopped again.

Curious heads poked out of doors (you can't open the windows on air-conditioned trains). What was it all about? Ahead lay the reason: the Down *North Coast Daylight Express*, running about 40 minutes late, was now in the station's single platform. We could not proceed further south on the single track without letting the *Daylight* into Grafton City first, but I wondered why it should have been thought necessary for the *Limited*, in theory at least the Number One passenger train of the line, to reverse and take the passing loop for a lesser train to attain the platform. Could not the *Daylight* have moved past us through the loop and reversed after we had cleared the points at the south end of the platform? Was the philosophy that if one train was late, another might as well be made late too? – especially if it was that old dragon, the *Brisbane Limited*!

At 20.15 we left the bridge and went on into the night with 15 minutes of our precious recovery time already debited. By next morning another five minutes had been lost, probably around Taree where, as I learned later, we had overtaken the *North Coast Overnight Express* (which had then replaced the *Limited* as the fastest service). This had broken down and had been delayed for more than an hour.

Just after breakfast we drew into a platform and stopped. Hawkesbury

THE TRAIN THAT DIED OF SHAME

River, said the sign: this was not a scheduled stop. At 6.44 we were now 23 minutes behind time, and the reason for the stop soon became clear: an inter-urban double-deck train sped through on another line. Giving it a generous four minutes to get clear we moved forward again, and from there on crawled miserably around the curves towards Cowan. The heavy *Brisbane Limited* was allowed 16 minutes to cover this steeply graded section: all other express trains had only nine minutes, even including the old *North Mail*, a train which was never noted for honours in the speed league!

The Conductor chose this moment to enquire solicitously about people wishing to make connections with other trains, like the *Intercapital Daylight* to Melbourne which the schedules then theoretically made possible. I told him I was booked on the XPT to the west. He nodded sagely and made a note of it.

Later, I wondered what he made the notes for. Cynically, I concluded it was so a message could be sent to the driver: 'Slow down, mate! Some folks here are thinking they will catch connections!' and that the driver, after doubling up in a paroxysm of mirth, would say to his mate: 'We'll soon fix that', and slide the regulator back a notch or two.

One thing is certain. They made sure no-one caught any connections that day. But I wondered why they asked. It would have been a simple matter, knowing the train was late and would not be able to make up time, to have informed passengers that they could catch connecting trains to Melbourne or the West by changing trains at Gosford, or even further down the track (as I did) at Hornsby which at that time was the last stop before Sydney.

I asked the conductor whether the SRA would hold any other trains for our arrival.

"They will hold the Melbourne *Daylight* for up to an hour," he said, "but not the XPT".

"They could stop us at Strathfield," I suggested, helpfully (or so I thought).

"Not a chance," he replied, "except in emergency".

I wondered what would constitute an emergency in the view of the SRA. It was beginning to look as though it would be touch and go whether we reached Sydney before even the departure of the XPT. If we kept going at our prevailing low speed we should just do it, but another stop was inevitable. Having allowed one local inter-urban to pass, they could soon find another.

"We'll probably stop in the loop at Cowan," volunteered the conductor. Was this meant to be a helpful comment? I wondered about getting off there to catch a fast local.

"No, we won't be stopping at a platform," he said, dashing my hopes.

In the event we passed through Cowan picking up speed. A timetable check was clearly indicated. I needed to get to Blayney junction west of the Great Dividing Range by early evening. This was to join the last train to Cowra – and I mean exactly that! Not the last train of the day but the very last for all time, as far as the intentions of SRA were known. The service – one of the few non-mainline cross-country links then remaining in Australia – was to be replaced by a bus that weekend.

I could not afford to miss the westbound XPT, since the next train after it was due in Blayney too late.

The stop at Hornsby had perforce to be my disembarkation point. We were unlikely to reach it by 7.18 in time to catch a local stopping train to Strathfield, but another inter-urban fast service, N 122, could only be about eight minutes behind and gaining on us. Provided we kept going we should just make it to Hornsby, since N 122 had intermediate stops to make at Cowan and Berowra.

Failing that, there was another local from Hornsby at 7.30 and another interurban less than 10 minutes later.

Approaching Hornsby we slowed almost to a standstill. Behind us, clearly visible, was the blunt blue and grey snout of double deck inter-urban 122, impatiently nudging our rear end as we crept into the platform.

I was ready and out in a flash. The time: 7.23. N 122 was due out at 7.25 and was ready to come into its usual platform as soon as the *Limited* left. There was nearly an hour to go before the XPT would leave

THE TRAIN THAT DIED OF SHAME

Strathfield – ample time in which I could cover the remaining distance.

At 7.26 the *Limited* set off once more, minus at least one passenger, and I boarded the interurban a minute later.

Down the track we went – and then I saw it. Hiding in a siding – I think it was called the "Up refuge" track – just south of Thornleigh, was unmistakably the *Brisbane Limited*. It rested motionless as we swished smoothly past at 7.33 – towards a Strathfield arrival just three minutes late at 7.51.

Why would they keep stopping a heavy express that took time to build up speed? Surely once it was moving, especially on a downhill run like that between Hornsby and Strathfield, it was capable of keeping ahead of the local trains? But no, the book decreed that once it lost its path...

At Strathfield's Platform 3 the next departure was announced as the *Intercapital Daylight*. So they were not holding it "up to an hour" at Sydney for the passengers from the north. Why then so carefully enquire about destinations?

I was not the only passenger hoping to catch the XPT that day, but I think I was the only one who made it and I am sure none of the passengers could have caught the *Daylight* to Melbourne because at 8.01 it left Strathfield for the south. It had barely disappeared round the bend when there! – skulking in the shadows, creeping apologetically into platform one, was the train that died of shame, N2, the *Brisbane Limited*.

It almost stopped, then caught a clear signal and accelerated (life in the old dog yet!), carrying at least some frustrated passengers the further 13 km to Sydney Terminal – that monument to faded Victorian grandeur; the poor man's Waterloo. There they could spend all day congratulating the SRA before catching the night sitter to Melbourne.

But could not the *Daylight*, on which some ex-Brisbane passengers probably had reservations to the south, have waited just two minutes at Strathfield, and the *Limited* have paused there momentarily before its final mad dash for the unattainable winning post? Would this really have so disrupted the morning rush hour traffic that the SRA would have been inundated with complaints from inconvenienced commuters? I doubted it.

When they re-timed the *Limited*, setting it back several hours, there was no possibility of any connection with any other train in any direction but the revised timing had its compensations. People from places in northern New South Wales could go for a day's shopping in Brisbane. Going south you had time for breakfast amid delightful scenery. I remember one trip when, running only 31 minutes late out of Gosford, I was enjoying breakfast in the diner. A passenger from overseas remarked, "Must be one of the top breakfasts in the world", as we wound our steady way along the shores of Brisbane Water, and on through the lovely scenery of the National Park of that name, past the lineside cottage on Mullet Creek where a white haired old lady who has lived there for years waved to us, and the driver hooted a greeting as they always did.

The catering staff on that train were wonderful and the food was generous. A young apprentice chef who was travelling from Brisbane to Eastwood, an outer Sydney suburb, came along to the diner for a light breakfast just before the station where he would have to change. He had only a few minutes to spare but they still made him a cup of tea and some toasted sandwiches. He was late because the night before he couldn't get to sleep (in a sitting car); the passenger next to him was leaning over him and was offensive. To get some rest, he saw the Conductor and changed to first class.

In another carriage there was one passenger who was muttering to himself, or to anyone who passed, throughout the evening and again the following morning: "Bastards, filthy swine!" he kept repeating. I heard he was English, had had his passport stolen, and couldn't wait to get out of Australia. But he needn't have blamed the people on the train! The fellow in the seat behind him must have got fed up listening. A magazine rack stuffed full of empty beer cans testified to his method of obtaining relief.

THE TRAIN THAT DIED OF SHAME

My return journey a few days later was the last in the extended schedule of rail journeys and non-journeys I had undertaken for the purpose of my first book.

It was fitting I should make it on the *Brisbane Limited*, which was so much responsible for the idea of writing about train journeys in the first place.

That day we left Sydney on schedule at ten to nine, the new evening departure time and I had a good dinner of lamb chops. The *Limited*'s menu was in its prime, the next best to the then top Australian trains, the *Southern Aurora* and the *Indian Pacific*.

The next morning, as we sped down from the Border Ranges into the "Sunshine State", I found they were serving early lunch, but decided to indulge instead in a pre-lunch snack: champagne (Great Western), cheese and biscuits – and it was good quality cheese, too. Bowling along at up to 115 km/h the old *Brisbane Limited* really felt like an express for once, and as it glided smoothly into South Brisbane, I checked my watch. The train that died of shame was 'dead' on time. Was this its resurrection?

If so, recovery was short-lived. Author Ian Fleming has James Bond being told: "You only live twice". The advent of the XPT marked the second and final death of the *Brisbane Limited*.

The writing on the wall appeared again when in 1986 the standard gauge line was extended across the Brisbane River to a new terminal dubbed the Brisbane Transit Centre. To mark the occasion and offer a glimpse of things to come the *Holiday Coast XPT* (Sydney–Grafton) overnighted in Grafton and became the first NSW train to cross the new Merivale Bridge into the Roma Street Transit Centre. By arrangement I was allowed to join this special train at Grafton.

A curious insensitivity to the plight of *Brisbane Limited* passengers rather marred this event. To allow the XPT special right-of-way the *Limited* was terminated at Casino, over 180 km and hours away from Brisbane. There the sleepy passengers were disgorged bleary eyed onto buses, carrying their own luggage, while the XPT slid past.

TRAINCATCHER

Any excitement the appearance of the XPT caused in Queensland may have been counterbalanced by the loss of goodwill this entailed, especially for those sleeping car passengers turfed out of their warm berths in the early morning. It was never explained why the *Limited* could not simply have followed the XPT to arrive half an hour or so later complete with passengers. Insult was added to injury when the Railways declined to transfer pre-booked luggage to the buses and those waiting for it had to wait until the now empty *Limited* finally crawled into Brisbane some hours later.

Chapter 8

Legendary Journeys

"If you want to see the land, ride the Ghan."

– Australian proverb

No longer does the *Orient Express* slink through the European night with its human cargo of potentates, manipulators and secret agents, but it is still possible to find glamour and excitement on the railways of Europe, by night or day.

And not only in Europe; all over the world there are fantastic journeys, trains weird and wonderful, trains with romantic names, trains with no names at all but full of surprises. Past glories are replaced by new excitements. Legends live on in names and places and some, like the phoenix, rise again from the ashes.

Britain's *Flying Scotsman* was arguably the most famous, and one of the oldest named trains in the world. Often confused with LNER A3 steam locomotive No. 4472 which took on the same name and which is still preserved in working order, the *Flying Scotsman* train still runs but has little now to distinguish it from other InterCity expresses on Britain's East Coast Main Line. Even the age-old traditional departure time of 10 o'clock from Kings Cross and 10 o'clock from Edinburgh Waverley has been varied in recent years. The northbound train now terminates in Glasgow and the southbound departure from Edinburgh Waverley has fluctuated between 10.00 and 10.35, with at one stage a quite ordinary InterCity replacing it in the 10 o'clock slot. Even its headboard and carriage name panels have gone: only a few stickers on the door windows and an acknowledgment on the station departure indicator remind the passengers of its former glory. It does remain one of the fastest trains on the line. One acknowledgment I noticed when last travelling on it was the announcement made on the train intercom that "we are just reaching 125 miles an hour" (201 km/h). We had already overtaken two other trains, one an HST standing near Durham and the other a diesel multiple unit which we overtook at speed near Thirsk on the four-line 'racetrack' section of the British East Coast Main Line between Darlington and York.

I once travelled on the Scotsman's unromantic night counterpart during wartime, when air raids, coal shortages, and general mayhem played havoc with train punctuality, but it was years before I travelled on the *Scotsman* proper. It mostly ran non-stop between London and Edinburgh – then the longest non-stop run in the world – and I lived half way between the two. My first trip on it was around the end of World War II. It had then lost most of its glory, like the *Direct Orient Express* in its latter days. The pre-war *Scotsman* had a special dining car done out in a charming old-world style, which the crew dubbed the 'Chinese Lantern'. After the war this car was frequently seen on another Scottish express, the mid-day Kings Cross – Edinburgh later to be named *The Heart of Midlothian*. By then the *Scotsman* had the newest electric kitchen and dining car with moveable seats and modern lighting.

The oldest named train in the world still exists. This is the *Irish Mail* from London to Holyhead on the Island of Anglesey across the Menai Strait past the Welsh place with the long name which, according to the *Guinness Book of Records* has a concocted extension to 58 letters and translated means "St Mary's church in a hollow by the white hazel, close to the rapid whirlpool, by the red cave of St. Tysillo". Locally just known as Llanfair, its official name is Llanfairpwyllgwyngyll.

Some of the most romantic train names originated with nicknames and it is doubtful if railway managements really should be credited as often as they might like. The nickname 'Flying Scotsman' sounded so much better than its official title of the *Special Scotch Express*. Indeed, as everyone knows, Scotch is something you drink and if that's what they meant they should have named it 'Whisky Galore'. Britain's *Royal Highlander* could earn such a name. While travelling on it in 1992 I hoped for some red wine with my supper. They were out of stock – yet we had barely left Euston! "This is a whisky train," explained the bonnie Highland lassie in the buffet.

For breakfast they offered smoked salmon with scrambled egg – something I suspect was intended more for the American than the Scots palate. Amid the snow-capped Cairngorms I had to leave the train at Kingussie to return south on an HST named the *Highland Chieftain*. Just as well I had breakfasted. This one was unfortunately short of staff that day and had nothing to offer the would-be breakfaster.

I therefore relaxed to enjoy the scenery which is so comfortably viewed from train windows on highland lines – the Pass of Killiecrankie with its deep gorge and the famous lovers' leap; Perth, Highland and former Scottish capital; then Gleneagles, famed for its golf course; past Dunblane, Stirling and historic Bannockburn where the English armies suffered their most ignominious defeat at the hands of the Scots under Bruce. The *Chieftain* follows the East Coast route to Kings Cross via Edinburgh and in earlier days an Edinburgh-bound train would have taken the old North British route south from Perth past Loch Leven and then over the Forth Bridge, but wherever the trains go in Scotland (barring some of the Lowland industrial belt) the scenery makes the trip memorable.

After a short morning break in Edinburgh to see friends I continued south to York that day on the *Aberdonian*, a name dating from 1927 but a different train in 1992. The old *Aberdonian* was a train you only saw in the north of England if you got up in the middle of the night. Northbound it left London at 19.30 with a restaurant car to York and sleepers to Aberdeen, which it reached around a quarter past seven in the morning. In the 1960s a later night express was introduced on this route and the name was transferred to it. In 1971 this new train became the *Night Aberdonian*, and the original name *Aberdonian* has since 1972 been attached to a mid-day service.

TRAINCATCHER

Trains like the *Irish Mail* kept the same name for years, but other names have been changed, such as when the LNER Leeds-Glasgow became the *North Briton*. In Australia the *Sydney Limited* became the *Spirit of Progress* and the name *Cooma Mail* was attached to a poor substitute, in timing as well as inspiration, for the former *Koskiusko Express*. Changing the name of a train may be a bad omen: none of the three above remain, and even the Up *Irish Mail* has vanished from British Rail (BR) timetables except for a Saturday morning working.

Some names just happen. In Australia you may hear about the "Fish and Chips". This signifies two trains, beginning with a nickname. Rail historian Robin Bromby in *Australian Name Trains of the '70s* recounts that in the 1860s there was a driver on the Sydney–Penrith inter-urban run with the name of John Heron, nicknamed 'The Big Fish'. This name was applied to the train he drove. Subsequently, the early morning commuter express from Mount Victoria, over a thousand metres above sea level at the top of the range, acquired this name and became officially known as *The Fish*. For a time it even carried a headboard.

Following *The Fish* another express picked up passengers from stations lower down the ranges. What more natural than to call this companion commuter train *The Chips*! And so it was. *The Fish* and *The Chips* still leave the Blue Mountains for Sydney every weekday morning and in the evening they return. There is nothing special about them as trains other than faster than average schedules and fewer intermediate stops. Both have now become typical eight-car double decked air conditioned inter-urban EMUs, although the latter remained an older single decker set until 1988.

For a while there was another commuter express from the Blue Mountains area which was called *The Heron*. It was named presumably in honour of John Heron, with the added thought of a big scavenging bird that picked up the bits of fish and chips left behind by the other two trains. *The Heron* did not terminate in Sydney itself, being switched at Central station to the suburban lines of the City Railway and then over the famous Harbour Bridge to terminate at Hornsby in the northern suburbs. This must have made it one of the few examples (if not unique) in the world of a named train traversing the centre of a capital city to end its journey somewhere on the outskirts.

In some countries trains bearing names have at times become almost an endangered species. D.W. Winkworth noted in a 1978 review in *Railway Magazine* that named trains in Britain had declined from 79 in 1958 to only 22 that year. By 1981 the total was down to 18, but more recently they have proliferated. British Rail in the 1990s developed a mania for naming almost any train that differed from its regular interval services, including some unromantic and otherwise ordinary trains without refreshment facilities other than a trolley. The names of these undistinguished trains could be found only in the printed timetable or perhaps from pieces of paper stuck in the carriage windows - names like *The Ayrshire Trader* (Newcastle –Girvan) or *Y Cwmro* (translated - The Welshman) which boasted some first class seats but had no sign of any catering. As the English might themselves say, "A jolly poor show, what?" The Welsh might have a more colourful way of expressing their view. Like Spanish and Arabic, it is a good language to swear in.

The Atchison Topeka and Santa Fe Railroad in the USA had the right idea when they refused to let Amtrak use the title 'Chief' for a service they considered lacked the glory of the former *Super Chief*s. The best they could manage in the 1970s for their Chicago–L.A. service was *South-West Limited* but by 1985 when I travelled it was the *South-West Chief*. This was indeed a very fine train, marred only by little things such as the plastic or treated cardboard crockery which, when you applied a knife to cut the meat (good steak), allowed gravy to discolour the resultant grooves in the plate. Hardly a first class service worthy of pre-war days.

There has always been something special, at least to me, in a train with a name. One of my earliest train memories, vivid to this day, was my first and only trip on the *Silver Jubilee* which, as its name implied, ran from 1935 – the year of Jubilee for the then King and Queen of England – until the exigencies of war ended its career. It was beautiful.

We sat in the dining car and I had green ice cream – which to a kid of about nine was heaven. The train went so fast that instead of the usual de-de-de-dum of the wheels on the rail joints there was just a steady di-dum, di-dum, di-dum, di-dum, very fast, with a ting, ting, ting, ting of the dining car cutlery in time with the wheels. I think this was something to do with the articulation and different spacing of bogies but that would have been too technical for me at the time.

With the train pulling out of London and accelerating northwards I recall that the less important trains, expresses in their own right, halted respectfully at signals as our streamlined silver streak swished smoothly past. Even the engine was called 'Silver' something or other: the engines had names too and this practice has continued from the earliest days. I remember one called the *Hush-hush* but I never discovered exactly what it was. I suppose it was very hush-hush, but subsequent research suggests it was the LNER experimental 4-6-4 high pressure boiler locomotive number 10,000. I saw it once while we were crossing the Forth Bridge, where everyone tosses pennies out just like they do at the Trevi Fountain in Roma.

I am often asked what are, or have been, my favourite rail journeys. Does one judge on speed, on the route followed, on the amenities or on some combination of these? Like picking dishes in a Chinese restaurant, so many trains are so good! Personal preference will prejudice any selection and different trains are memorable for different reasons and to different people.

Some passengers seek comfort and luxury, some scenery, some speed and some the 'way-out' or unusual. Edna St Vincent Millay said there wasn't a train she wouldn't take and I am with her in that, but there could be some she, or I, might certainly not want to take again.

As another form of trivial pursuit I listed the trains I have particularly liked and would travel on again given the chance, excluding those where the memories were primarily due to incidents or to the people I met.

I came up with a list of 32 trains. Then, as in a league football series of matches, I set them in random order, paired off one against another, then matched the winners until I came up with the favourite. Eliminating this, I repeated the process to find the second favourite and so on – a lengthier process than simple knockout soccer competition (as in the English FA Cup) in which the unsuccessful finalist might not in fact be the second best team.

How did I weigh the respective merits? A subjective assessment based on the things that were memorable – comfort and scenes from the train and refreshments on board – were weighted heavily; speed seemed to count for less. I could have adopted a more scientific approach, assigning a weight to each criterion and then giving a score on each criterion to each train – as a university colleague and I have done in comparing features of suburban train networks and services, but this is not a treatise on multicriteria evaluation techniques. Overall impressions are what count to the rail traveller, and those are what I remember. Thinking of each of them I asked myself 'Which of these two would I most like to travel on again?'

The results? Perhaps I should have used a more objective method because I did not agree with the final ranking of even the top 10, let alone the whole lot. I tried pairing them differently, and came up with different answers, still unsatisfactory. It depended on what factor I took as most distinctive when comparing different trains. Uniqueness was one (yes, I know a thing is either unique or it isn't but it is a neater word than the proper term 'unusualness'): factors such as scenery from the train vied with comfort and amenities on board – sometimes I leaned to one, sometimes to the other. There was at least no doubt that however I juggled with the ranking, the *Queenslander* came out on top, and the top 10 invariably included the *Ghan*, Switzerland's *Glacier Express*, British Columbia's *Cariboo*, the former *Lufthansa Airport Express* and the indeed unique 'Forsayth Mixed' of Queensland's outback.

I was asked once to write an article on the top 10 train journeys of the world. Not limited by my own experience but going by reputation and probably some hearsay as well, I included trains like the trans-

Siberian *Rossia* and the *Orient Express* as well as the five named above (except the Forsayth train which I then felt might appeal only to rail buffs but how wrong I was!). My list also included the privately run *North Yorks Pullman* and a complementary pair comprising the BR night sleeper *The Royal Highlander* and the Inverness–Kyle of Lochalsh train they used to call *The Hebridean*, a train which passes through some of the most heart-rendingly beautiful scenery in the world.

Some trains are legendary. People talk of the luxurious *Blue Train*, but one can never be sure whether they mean the formerly luxurious *Train Bleu* sleeping car service between Paris and Nice, now quite an ordinary overnight express, or whether they mean the exclusive South African travelling hotel between Pretoria and Capetown.

Once famous in Europe were the all first class Trans Europ Expresses (TEE trains) which included France's *Mistral*, Italy's *Settebello* and the magnificent *Rheingold* (Amsterdam to Genève and München). These three, alas, are now all gone. Even the title 'Trans Europ Express' has all but vanished, replaced by the less aspiring term 'Euro-city'. Are they no longer expresses?

This raises the question of what an express really is. On the line between Bundaberg and Rockhampton in Queensland there were, up until July 1989, only two passenger trains a day in each direction. These were the *Sunlander*, which normally stopped at up to 12 stations depending on demand, and the *Capricornian*. The latter was scheduled to stop at 31 of the 42 stations on this part of the route, but would stop at all the others if required. In other words it was a stopping train.

But even with its extra stops, the *Capricornian*'s schedule between Rockhampton and Brisbane was faster than that of the *Sunlander*! So it should have been regarded as the express, and so called. In fact it was a named stopping train; not a common species but by no means unique. The former *Hebridean* from Inverness to Kyle of Lochalsh in northwest Scotland, known locally as the 'Skye Train', was a British example.

The word express comes from 'explicit' or 'expressly stated' and dates from the fifteenth century. It was first applied to trains in 1845 and signified a 'special' train which operated for an 'express' purpose and was not necessarily fast.

Terms like 'high speed train', 'very fast train', 'bullet train' and initials such as TGV, AVE, and ICE have replaced the mundane but time-honoured word 'express'. But are these reputedly faster than average trains really the 'best' and how does one judge what is best anyway?

Vicarious enjoyment can be had from diligent perusal of the Thomas Cook timetables, travel guide books and a good atlas. This is also much cheaper than actually travelling when some of the top trains are intended only for the rich.

For sheer luxury, nothing would quite match the opulence of the resurrected *Orient Express*, which for $A 2426 (in 1992) would take you from Paris to Venezia, berths and table d'hôte meals included. Should Sea Bass in vermouth sauce with caviar, followed by beef fillet and asparagus tips, baked potatoes and French cheeses not satisfy you, there are extras à la carte. Broiled baby lobster at $64.75 perhaps, or would Eggs Benedict with leaf spinach (is there another kind?) at $17.50 better suit your pocket?

Wines? Half bottles of 'el cheapo' come at $24. You may prefer champagne to celebrate. A Dom Perignon would knock you back $210.50. But on such a trip of a lifetime why not that Grand Cru of all wines, Chateau d'Yquem? A mere $337.25 the bottle. Cheap at half the price, as they say.

"Gratuities," the menu adds, "are at your discretion" – provided you have any money left. As an Australian of course, one does not indulge in this legalised form of bribery. Instead, emulating Crocodile Mick Dundee, you shake the waiter's hand and say 'G'Day' – as at home.

If you want to say you have travelled the *Orient Express* – as I have – truthfully and without such extravagance, then it is worth knowing that an ordinary European train of that name still runs daily from Paris to Budapest. There are first and economy sleepers as well as really cheap couchette berths. A restaurant car is attached at Salzburg in which a good meal would cost less than a cheap wine on the luxury version!

The *Blue Train* and the *Orient Express* are not the only luxury cruise trains. Spain's *Transcantabrico* wanders along little known routes of northern Spain's coast and interior, the home of Rioja wines. The food and wine on all Spanish trains is excellent and reasonably priced but this one is different. Over an eight day tour it is parked at night and meals other than breakfast are taken at local restaurants. *Al Andalus* does something similar in southern Spain.

Britain has similar tours by *The Royal Scotsman* but priced well out of reach of the average tourist. The North Yorkshire Moors Railway's *North Yorks Pullman*, lately re-named the *Pickering Pullman*, which runs between Grosmont and Pickering through the lovely moorland and valley scenery made familiar through the BBC television series *Heartbeat* offers a taste of *Orient Express* type luxury. This leisurely summer evening trip in 1992 included a five course dinner in the $65 fare. Motive power may be a gleaming ex-LMS 'Black Five' steamer or perhaps a retired 'Deltic' diesel. The rolling stock comprises former Pullman cars from such trains as the *Queen of Scots*. To me the highlight of the dinner was real Wensleydale cheese (what else!), arguably the finest cheese anywhere – mild yet sharp, crumbly without disintegrating, and which does not crawl, live, of its own accord across the plate onto your biscuit like some cheeses do, nor does it cling like plasticine or reek of urine like some of those cheeses that are actually matured in the stuff – or taste like it. But I digress.

(Forgive a little plug for something I have learned to like after eschewing cheese of all kinds for most of my first twenty years. The point is you can get really good food on a train if you choose your trains carefully. It was on trains I first learned to appreciate fruit cake [Pelaw Co-operative Society slab cake on the Middlesbrough–Newcastle buffets] and I have enjoyed little packets of Bel Paese cheese with Californian wine on Amtrak, and Brie with Grand Champagne Cognac on the TEE *L'Arbalete* in France.)

LEGENDARY JOURNEYS

For the ultimate in mountain scenery viewed from a moving train, many would vote for Switzerland. The *Glacier Express* will take you through the heart of the Alps past the Rhone Glacier to Zermatt at the foot of the Matterhorn.

Leaving Chur at 10.55 the journey takes under six hours and an excellent lunch can be pre-booked. I found especially fascinating the way the steward would pour wine into your glass from high in the air without spilling a drop. There are souvenir glasses, too, tilted to match the incline of the track, but remember to turn it around when the train starts downhill!

Even higher mountain railways exist. At La Cima on the Central Railway of Peru you ascend over 4800 metres above sea level. India's Darjeeling railway with its tight spirals is unique but another more accessible and spectacular – which I have sampled – is the Jungfrau Railway in Switzerland.

From Interlaken it is a 70 km round trip amidst breathtaking scenery, past the Eiger Glacier to the Jungfrau summit. The train divides en route, there being two separate ways up to Kleine Scheidegg where the final ascent begins. Whichever way you go a change of trains is also necessary at Grindelwald or Lauterbrunnen.

Sightseeing stops at Eismeer and Eigerwand, in the mountain face itself, let you look out from windows cut in the rock sides of the tunnel. I viewed the final ascent with a certain amount of trepidation, being unsure whether the extreme cold of the high alps, coupled with the rarefied atmosphere, would affect my breathing or my heart or whatever. Queensland's enervating heat is not the best preparation for venturing into the land of eternal snows, but there was no problem. Although Jungfraujoch station is 3457 metres above sea level it is enclosed. Visitors are warned not to venture far away from the railway when the train stops as they will be short of breath if they stay out on the snow of the high alp too long. I took a short stroll outside, then waited for the return train in the well-heated restaurant at the summit.

Environmental groups have insisted that some high speed lines, particularly in Germany, be built in tunnel or between high walls. Great though German ICE trains are, cruising at 260 km/h is not particularly impressive with little to see beyond the lineside. The French TGV is like a jet plane hurtling down the runway without taking off. The song *Leaving on a Jet Plane* could well apply to it. Awareness of the extremely high speed of travel is awakened only when cars and trucks on the adjoining highway seem to be going backwards.

My choice among high speed trains for top ranking would be the earlier *Lufthansa Airport Express* which the publicity referred to as "ground level flight" by the Rhine. This combined moderately fast speed, replacing air travel between Düsseldorf and Frankfurt, with quality service (including wine tasting), comfort, and the romantic vistas of river, castles, vineyards and small towns along the banks of the Rhine. I enjoyed two trips on this train by courtesy of Lufthansa and later sneaked in an extra couple of kilometres by hitching a ride from Köln Deutz (close to Lufthansa HQ offices) to Köln Hauptbahnhof on

Climbing the Jungfrau by train, one of the world's highest railways – both in altitude reached and ticket price. (Geoffrey Churchman)

the pretext of asking one of the girls for picture postcards of the train (not to mention her address and telephone number).

In Sweden I had a memorable cab ride in the Stockholm–Göteborg X-2000 tilt train. Sweden's railways are much more tortuous than one might expect from the country's topography and Statens Järnvägar (SJ), after thorough research, made a deliberate decision to invest in tilt technology rather than build new high speed lines. The result: a saving of 20 percent in journey times between major centres like Stockholm and Göteborg and a ready-made recycled infrastructure.

The way these trains lean into the sharp curves is astonishing. I do not recall seeing check rails as one would expect on curves of tight radius, but there was certainly some screeching and scraping noise as we hurtled through one reverse curve after another with the speedo clocking a steady 190 km/h. Accompanying me in the cab with the driver was now retired Per-Arne Dahlin, of SJ Passenger Group.

One of the worst problems the Swedes faced was the number of level crossings on the route. And here came the unexpected. As the train sped along the driver answered a call on his radio: an unscheduled stop had to be made. The train in front had struck a pedestrian on a crossing at Flöby – a tiny station barely on the map and no longer a passenger stop. We were to pick up passengers and crew to take them on to Göteborg. The driver of the set involved in the collision would not be allowed further driving that day but a relief driver must have been summoned because later on that evening while awaiting another train at Göteborg I saw the damaged one come into the platform. Its sleek nose was disfigured by a great dent, such had been the force of the impact. I hate to imagine what it did to the pedestrian, but there had been police and ambulance activity evident when we passed through Flöby.

On the Göteborg platform, waiting, was a railway road truck and a group of workmen. From the truck they took a brand new nose cone and within minutes had replaced the damaged one leaving the train fit once more for service. I could just imagine how long such a job would have taken in Britain or Australia. There would have been forms to fill in, inspectors to come round, head office authorisations to obtain – and they probably wouldn't have had the spare parts anyway. No, the train would have been out of service for months.

A quick nose job for the X-2000 at Göteborg. (Colin Taylor)

Unlike the German ICE trains and Italy's ETR services, none of the X-2000 trains as yet have a distinguishing name, although their performances differ markedly. For this reason they, like most of the French TGV and Japanese *Shinkansen*, are less memorable individually. People can say, "I went on one of those regular 500 km/h [they tend to exaggerate] expresses – what do you call them, X-something, bullet trains?" but to me it has always seemed better to be able to recall a journey on the *Riviera Express*, the *Ligure, Settebello, Golden Arrow, Royal Scot, Denver Zephyr, Southern Aurora* or *Rheingold* any day.

The TEE *Rheingold* was a truly marvellous train. The club car was in essence a first class and roomier version of the old buffet cars found on BR before the HST days. Its dome car had disappeared by the time

LEGENDARY JOURNEYS

I travelled on it but it still gave a great feeling of satisfaction to be on it. I am happier on an express train of this kind than I am on 'terra firma'. When on an extended rail tour but not on a moving train I feel like a fish out of water.

One kind of train that fails to excite me is the European privately run 'holiday train' species, mainly because they cater for organised tours – and I could never abide being organised. "Why don't you just fit in?" my folks used to say to me. I never did. As the bard Robert Service put so well in verse, "There's a race of men that don't fit in" and I am clearly one of them.

On one journey in Austria I came across two of these holiday trains in the same day, both named the *Alpensee Express*. One, loaded with passengers, was standing in Schwarzach St Veit station bound for Klagenfurt but had to await the departure of my train, the regular *Gasteinertal* express which takes the longest route from Linz to Wien via Salzburg, Klagenfurt and Leoben, a 687 km journey against the direct 190 km main line and which obviously needed priority on that account alone. The other *Alpensee* was standing empty at Spittal-Millstättersee, its passengers massing into waiting buses with a folk music group entertaining them.

The *Thomas Cook European Timetable* lists a dozen or more of the regular named holiday trains. Of more interest to rail enthusiasts are the charter trains put on by preservation societies, works social clubs, and others including (once they saw there was profit in it) railway systems themselves. Thomas Cook himself first conceived the railway excursion idea back in 1841 when he organised a special shilling return outing on the Midland Railway from Leicester to Loughborough, the start not only of rail excursions but of travel agencies.

Special excursion trains tend to cover unusual routes, or have unusual or historic motive power or carriages and are particularly popular in Britain. Sometimes they are given one-off names like the *Centenary Express* (celebrating 100 years of rail catering in Britain), *Glamorgan Growler*, *Yorkshire Ranger*, *Deep Duffryn Diddler* and

A Eurailpass takes you to one of the most northerly rail destinations in the world – Narvik in Norway. Here the waters of the Ofotfjord are viewed from a descending train. (Geoffrey Churchman)

Welsh Collieries Rambler, the last two clearly intended to attract coalmining enthusiasts as well as branch railway aficionados. Others adopt names once proudly borne by regular scheduled trains but follow different routes. An example of these was a *Heart of Midlothian* advertised in 1982 by the LNER Society which went to Edinburgh not from Kings Cross as its namesake did but from Euston via Northampton, Carlisle and Carstairs, an itinerary which LNER purists would deem sacrilege!

Unusual itineraries are one thing: there are also unusual, weird, fantastic way-out trains and lines. Rack railways and funiculars are common in mountainous country but I have only once come across an underground funicular. At Haifa in Israel the *Carmelit* climbs from a downtown terminal to near the top of Mount Carmel – underground all the way. Saltburn, on the English north-east coast, has a funicular powered by water and gravity. Similar incline railways were features of other coastal resorts: how many remain I have no idea but one was at Lynton in Devon in 1980.

Monorails are thought to be a new idea and were once seen as the railways of the future, but they have never been developed for long distance or fast rail travel. One of the earliest – and certainly the most successful – is the Langen suspension railway at Wuppertal, affectionately termed the 'Danglebahn' by many who appreciate it. This working monorail is of the suspended type in which the cars hang from a two-wheels-in-tandem bogie running on a single inverted 'T' rail, as distinct from the 'straddle' monorail, the car balanced over a single beam with side guide wheels, of which that at Sydney Harbour is a recent Australian example.

The 'Danglebahn' or, to use its proper name, the *Schwebebahn*, has operated for almost a hundred years without ever an accident. It has 18 stations and runs mostly above the river Wupper but also over city streets for a total of 13.7 km from Barmen to Elberfeld in the Ruhr. Although limited in scheduled running to 50 km/h maximum, tests have demonstrated that curves of 366 metre radius could be safely negotiated at 150 km/h. At maximum line speed around 275 metre radius curves the car tilts at up to 10 degrees, so perhaps it could legitimately be called the world's first tilt train as well.

By no means unusual but still legendary and worthy of a place in any railway roll of honour is the 'Ratty', as the steam-hauled tourist train on the narrow gauge Ravenglass and Eskdale railway is affectionately known. Over a century old, this line originally served iron mines. The trains later carried stone, but passengers were always catered for. Most unusual among these would have been the fictional but plausible two dogs that hid in the 'Ratty' during their escape from the inhuman animal research establishment in Richard Adams' moving book *The Plague Dogs*. In 1992 I was privileged to join the driver of the 'Ratty' and shovelled coal into the firebox as it steamed and chuffed its way deep into the English Lake District. Ravenglass is its still operative interchange with the BR system, being on the Cumberland coast line, where one need never be surprised to meet historic locomotives like streamlined A4 Pacific No.4498 *Sir Nigel Gresley* running 'light' or heading an excursion train from Steamtown at Carnforth.

The 'Ratty' does not have an official name but quite a few short distance trains on preserved and narrow gauge railways do. Melbourne's *Puffing Billy* in the Dandenong Ranges is one: there are many in Europe and America. I have often wondered what gave a name like the 'Skunk' to the California Western Railroad's tourist train which takes anything over two hours to cover the 65 km of track between Fort Bragg and Willits.

It is interesting to note the origin of train names and to the English language speaker foreign ones are not always obvious. *Flèche d'Or* was readily recognised as the train the English knew as the *Golden Arrow*. I guessed when I travelled on *Freccia del Sud* (that fateful journey when I had my case stolen) that the name meant 'Arrow of the South' or perhaps just 'Southern Arrow' and it was not difficult to realise that many of the German and international train names derived from national figures like Tirolese hero Andreas Hofer, printing inventor Gutenberg, Walter Gropius the architect, and Alfred Nobel, founder of the world-famous prizes. Scientists, writers, artists and musicians have also featured prominently among European train names, the *Jules Verne, Otto Lilienthal, Gustave Eiffel, Rembrandt, Hans Holbein, Mozart, Chopin, Beethoven* and *Franz Schubert* among them.

Literature was commemorated in some of the former British train names – like *Fair Maid* from Walter Scott's *Fair Maid of Perth*, *The Talisman* and my old favourite *Heart of Midlothian* from the same writer, yet Scotland's favourite bard and national poet, Robbie Burns, is strangely unrepresented in train names. Less surprisingly perhaps, Scotland's (and the world's) reputed worst poet, the 'Great' McGonagall, is not represented either, despite his several poems concerning trains which, like the bridge over the River Tay, "will be remembered for a very long time".

Glasgow's founder, St Mungo, was remembered in one of a quartet of Glasgow–Aberdeen expresses which used to take the old Caledonian main line through Coupar Angus and Forfar.

When this closed in 1967 the trains were re-routed and as diesel power took over it was not many more years before a two-hourly interval service replaced the named expresses. As Cecil J. Allen commented in *Titled Trains of Great Britain*, "names in such a uniform service are superfluous".

Geographical names are widespread, some quite prosaic such as the *Roma Express*, the *Brighton Belle*, the *California Zephyr* and the *Yorkshire Pullman*. Others are less obvious unless you know the places or districts – Austria's *Pongau*, *Pustertal* and *Ötscherland* represent geographical regions: the *Yenesei* of Russia is named after a mountain range. Language limitations preclude any explanation here of Polish, Finnish or Chinese train names unless they are anglicised in Cook's timetables in which you can look them up but it might not help in trying to book on them at the local ticket office.

Australian named trains are not widely known overseas. The trans-Australian railway is widely known but the train of that name less so, especially as it no longer exists. Most Australians would have heard of the *Ghan* but fewer know the *Indian Pacific* which was born only in 1970 and even in books I have seen the *Overland* wrongly called the "Overlander".

'Aurora' is a train name found in several countries. There was one in Yugoslavia – it may have been the 7.08 to Rijeka I was supposed to be on during that first Eurail tour in 1977 – and there is another in Alaska, the principal train running from Anchorage to Fairbanks.

Australia's *Southern Aurora*, named after the southern hemisphere's night-time counterpart of the Northern Lights was introduced in 1962 to mark the opening of the new standard gauge line south from Albury and became one of three daily trains using the standard gauge between Sydney and Melbourne. South of Albury the line is double track but with a difference. One line is standard gauge, the other is in Victoria's 1600 mm 'Irish' gauge. So the line comprises two single tracks running parallel. During Australia's bicentennial celebrations simultaneous steam trains were run in the same direction on this route, though not as a race like those ones in America between steam and electric back in 1905 on the New York Central when they demonstrated the superior speed of electric to steam locomotives hauling trains of identical weight.

The bicentennial runs in Australia included trains of NSW stock hauled by the LNER *Flying Scotsman* locomotive, visiting Australia by courtesy of its current owner Sir Thomas McAlpine.

Introduced first as a non-stop Sydney–Melbourne all first-class service, although always with operational stops for locomotive purposes, the *'Aurora Australis'* is now among the honour roll of departed glories in railway legend. In its latter days it lost its name and much of its glory. On one of my last trips on it (and since it was one of the first named trains I had travelled on in Australia I was faithful to the end) it broke down before leaving the station. At least the power car failed, not the locomotive. This car provides the air-conditioning, not to mention lighting and electricity for cooking and refrigeration.

Being scheduled to leave Sydney at 20.00 just ahead of the semi-fast *Spirit of Progress* at 20.10, the *Aurora* clearly had some problem as passengers realised when the other train left first. Knowledgeable regulars sought the dining car to pass the time. Into the next platform then came the empty *Brisbane Limited*, a less important train due to leave at 20.50 but which, for some reason – perhaps deferring to our train's priority – did not.

At 20.45 our power car had been fixed and was operating. Would we go before the *Brisbane*? The race became tense. By 20.52 the *Brisbane Limited* was still there but looking ready for the 'off'; service was under way in its dining car and the stewards looking across were sneering good naturedly at us.

Not until 21.00, exactly an hour late, did we slowly pull away to a spontaneous burst of applause and a few derisive gestures to the stewards on the *Limited*, left forlorn and lonely at platform two.

LEGENDARY JOURNEYS

Once having started from Sydney, *'Aurora Australis'* sped on its way with great purpose, lesser trains standing back everywhere to give us passage. We roared through Strathfield in XPT time, then took the direct line through Sefton Park junction. Sometimes journey time is lengthened when main line trains are routed through Granville. This was the scene of one of Australia's worst rail disasters in 1977, a full account of which is given by Kenn Pearce in the book *Australian Railway Disasters*.

After the brief conditional stop at Campbelltown, the train I was on went haring off after the long departed *Spirit* into the Southern Highlands of New South Wales. We passed the *Spirit* somewhere around Cootamundra, but *Aurora* passengers were well asleep by that time of night.

I travelled overnight on the *Spirit* several times. It was once the only way you could go between Canberra and Melbourne without using a feeder bus to Yass Junction. Some highly praised the *Spirit*: I am not sure why. The dining car was of the long bar-counter type with stools and thus not very sociable. There were no individual sleeping cabins. But the seats were comfortable enough to recline in and a passenger lucky enough to have a double could curl up and enjoy a modicum of sleep. They say it was more sociable than the all-first class *Southern Aurora*, but I think this is just an example of that curious inverted snobbery that regards the company in Economy or Second Class as more exciting than your average travellers in First. Some of the popular railway guide books tell you this but I wonder how much of such travel the authors have really experienced. If your idea of relaxation is being kept awake half the night by squalling children, by groups in party spirit, and possibly a strumming guitar or, worse, a transistor or cassette player, well... I agree, it can be sociable for a while, but give me somewhere to get my head down for a decent sleep when I need it!

I had an unexpectedly pleasant encounter once when travelling overnight on the *Spirit of Progress*. I was booked in a sitting car to join at Yass, but through a delayed connection was forced to join at Harden, an hour later at two in the morning. The carriage interior was in darkness as I groped my way along looking for my seat number. A figure huddled in a double seat stirred and spoke:

"You looking for seat 37?" it asked. The voice was husky and female.

"Yes," I answered. (What else could I be doing, wandering along peering at the numbers in almost total darkness?)

But how could she guess it was the one next to her I was looking for? I didn't ask, but realised later it was because the Conductor had come through the carriage at Yass, anxiously seeking his passenger, like the Good Shepherd not content with the "ninety and nine that safely lay". These on-train conductors really are first class in the way they check all their charges, assist with baggage, and wake you up when you are near your destination.

She moved over to make room and I settled myself down. Although it was midsummer, around the end of January, it can be cold on an air-conditioned overnight train when you are a sitting passenger. I made to spread my warm Italian leather jacket over my legs to keep cosy, but my seat-mate had other and better ideas.

"You can share my sleeping bag," she whispered, her voice in the darkness sounding full of warm promise. When the lights are out and people are trying to sleep it is incumbent on those awake to speak softly. Although we had not been formally introduced I felt it might give offence to spurn such a kind invitation. Not for lack of experience of the fair sex, surely, had Congreve remarked two centuries before that even Hell had not "a fury like a woman scorned". It clearly behoved a gentleman to rise to the occasion so without demur I turned in my seat and snuggled in close. This was better than a lonely sleeping berth on the *Southern Aurora* and I felt no more cold until they spoilt it all by putting the lights on somewhere near Albury around five in the morning. There she had to leave the train, but the rising sun shed no warmth for me. Now if only the rival *Southern Aurora* had been late that morning I could have transferred to it at Albury!

LEGENDARY JOURNEYS

Some people get themselves in the *Guinness Book of Records* for things like visiting all the stations on BR in one day (well, not quite: 18 days is the record). There was one intrepid traveller who visited 10 different countries by train in 24 hours. In my first book I gave a list of seven Australian named trains I had travelled on in one day, which I called my 'name train marathon'. Seven may not sound many to people used to European rail travel but it was not bad for Australia with its sparse rail network, infrequent services and disconcerting lack of connectivity. For the curious or unbelieving the date was 25 February, the year 1984, and the trains the *Gold Coast Motorail Express*, the *Mid-North Coast XPT*, Down *Riverina XPT*, Up *Riverina XPT*, *Newcastle Express*, *North Coast Daylight Express* and *Brisbane Limited*. You can check the timetable if you like to see how it was done.

But I easily achieved a better record in Europe when, on one day in the course of only five minutes I travelled on three named trains, the *Dachstein*, the *Transalpin* and the *Blauer Enzian*. "How was this?" I hear you ask. Simply that on that particular section of line the three trains (or parts of them) were all marshalled together and I travelled on all three by simply walking along the corridor! And then, quite without trying, I found myself on another three trains simultaneously the very next day when I took train D516, the *Steiermark Express* (Graz–Bischofshofen) from Selzthal to Stainach Irdning only to find that it was also the *Tauern Express* (Graz–Oostende) and the *Kärnten Express* (Graz–Hamburg)! This marshalling of bits and pieces of different trains together reaches its peak in Europe but is not an unusual principle in the railway world. Australia has, however, one curiosity which could well be unique – two named trains coupled together for the whole journey. In other words a train with two names, one for the front portion and one for the rear. These are the *Queenslander*, all first class with dining car and piano lounge bar, and the *Spirit of the Tropics*, economy sitting and sleeping with 'Club Loco' buffet disco. The whole train runs from Brisbane to Cairns and back from Sunday through to Wednesday but on the Thursday only the 'Spirit' portion makes a shortened run to

Proserpine, returning to reach Brisbane on the Saturday. Australia has also revived the age-old practice of naming separate carriages on premium trains. Well known to pullman car frequenters in the old days, this is now seen in both the *Queenslander* and Australian National's *Ghan*. In fact the much older *Overland* adopted the same principle.

Undoubtedly the most famous Australian named train was the old *Ghan* of narrow gauge days on the Central Australia Railway. It was one of the now disappearing breed of mixed trains, with passenger and goods vehicles combined, and certainly one of the few such trains to bear an official name. They used to say "if you want to see the land, ride the *Ghan*" and in fact a song was written about it. You had plenty of time to do it in. Without allowing for delays, of which there were many, caused by such trivialities as floods washing away mile after mile of track or intense heat bending the rails, the old *Ghan* was allowed a generous 31 hours or so to cover its 870 km of shaky narrow-gauge track, laid slap on the desert floor without any proper foundation. At 28 km/h overall, it may well have merited the title of the slowest named train in the world, at least among officially named trains.

The *Ghan* ran only from Marree to Alice Springs on narrow gauge track. Another train of the same name started from Port Pirie on the standard gauge line and reached Marree at 22.20 when passengers had to change trains. The name is an abbreviation of Afghan and owes its origin to the Afghan drivers (actually they probably came from what is now Pakistan) of camel trains who first pioneered the north-south route across the Australian continent. Just north of Adelaide you can still see camels, apparently parked waiting for drivers and loads. The name has been retained in the new *Ghan*, an up-to-date luxury air-conditioned train which comfortably swallows up the 1335 km new route via Tarcoola in 20 hours.

The old one, of course, was a journey of a lifetime and always something of an adventure with the possibility of being stranded in the red middle of nowhere for days on end.

The train usually comprised a motley assortment of coaching stock of different vintages, including some luxurious old sleeping cars like the wagon-lits of 19th century Europe, with brass fittings and inlaid polished wood, the decadent luxury of yesteryear. Such coaches were still to be seen in Portugal in 1977 when on my first European visit I travelled (for only $A 10) in an old blue sleeping car on the overnight mail between Porto and Lisboa. It was heated by a coal fire in a cubicle at the end of the car, giving an atmosphere in the station nostalgically reminiscent of steam traction days.

Many are the tales told of travel on the old *Ghan* and much has been written. One of the best, oft repeated, is that of the female passenger who became increasingly agitated as time went by.

"When will we reach Alice Springs?" she enquired.

"Should be there any week now," replied the Conductor. "Why, what's wrong?"

"Can't you see I'm pregnant!" she exclaimed.

"Well, really, lady, you shouldn't have made the journey in that condition," remonstrated the Conductor.

"But I wasn't in this condition when I got on this train!" she retorted hotly.

This fits in with what was written in praise of train travel in a popular women's magazine: "Trains have a special meaning to Australians ... how many and varied are the proud variations on the tale; how I was conceived/born/seduced on a train!" and as Ludovic Kennedy put it:

"You are transported in comfort, even style, to the wild places of the earth ... you can move around ... read, sleep, snore, make love."

And you can! A young woman once told me there was nothing like making love in a tent. A male friend said he preferred it while sliding down one of those enclosed water flumes you get at warm climate fun parks like they have in northern Queensland. I suppose there are others who favour it while in free fall, or in outer space. Shipboard romances are always popular while some must make do with the back seat of a car.

But Ian Fleming had it right when he wrote of James Bond's

experience with Goldfinger's secretary on the *Silver Meteor* from Miami.

"To the rhythm of the giant diesels pounding out the miles, they had made long, slow love in the narrow berth" he says (after they had enjoyed a flagon of iced champagne), in the way known only to those who have felt the rhythm of the wheels beneath. And the earth moved for them, too.

An American on the *Ghan*, believe it or not, said "We have nothing like this in the States"! The earth must have moved for him. Or perhaps, as Pliny might have described it if trains had been invented in the first century, it was a case of '*in treno veritas*'.

Chapter 9

Slow Train to Biloela

And the Lord God made everything that creepeth and crawleth upon the face of the earth.
– Genesis 1.25 loosely quoted.

A few years ago, a man of the cloth told the station-master at Earlesfield junction in Central Queensland that Queensland Railways (QR) were mentioned in the Bible.

"What!" exclaimed the station-master, who clearly disbelieved the worthy minister, "Whereabouts?"

"In Genesis," the minister assured him, quoting the above words.

Queensland easily takes the honours for the slowest trains in Australia and has boasted some of the slowest in the world, at least as far as regular scheduled passenger trains worked by adhesion go. In 1980 the Queensland average speed (not counting suburban trains) was just over 32 km/h when the Australian average was closer to 50. By 1988 the figures were 41 and 61 respectively and they have since further improved – but as much owing to the withdrawal of slow mixed and other country trains as to the speeding up of main line services.

In early steam days there was a Queensland train known locally as 'The Wild Beaudesert Train' which allegedly took nearly seven hours to cover the 76 km from Brisbane's Melbourne Street terminus to Beaudesert, gateway to the border ranges. There are still some weird and wonderful journeys to savour, "journeys for masochists" as one newspaper described them.

In 1981 the crown belonged to what was dubbed by one journalist as "The Thangool Rocket". This was the four-times-weekly 7.30 ex-

Thangool mixed, or rather "goods with passenger van attached", whose 178 km crawl to Rockhampton via Mount Morgan was punctuated by lengthy stops at various places en route, especially at Biloela. There it waited an agonising six and a half hours. With a total of at least nine and a half of its nearly 16 hour journey spent at scheduled stops, it is not surprising that its average speed throughout the whole sorry performance was thereby reduced to a mind-tearing 11.2 km/h.

By the time the news of this phenomenon hit a startled world (newspapers and radio all over eastern Australia featured it when they obtained a preview of an excerpt from a rather unusual thesis), the schedules had been altered and there was a dramatic acceleration: an hour was slashed from the schedule and the journey was accomplished in just under 15 hours.

Queensland Rail built a new station at Biloela – just before withdrawing the train altogether and severing the line in the middle. Yet they could have introduced a fast railcar service on the direct coal line linking Biloela district with Gladstone on the coast – and they could even now do so if the government cared about rail services to rural centres. Governments who think only in terms of balance sheets should read Hillman and Whalley's revealing book *The Social Consequences of Rail Closures*.

A journey on the 'Thangool Rocket' was unforgettable. Primarily a goods train, it trailed an iron-verandahed passenger coach in which one could stand and watch the receding track in the setting sun as the train wended its leisurely way towards Mount Morgan, with silly cars and trucks hurtling past on the adjacent highway. One could look out at the wild flowers festooning the half-buried track and look forward to the next lengthy refreshment stop which, though unadvertised as such, was always within sight of a cool country pub.

Railway systems naturally like to boast about their achievements, their 'crack' trains, their modern signalling systems, and the like. They are not keen to have attention drawn to curiosities even when some of them might well earn a place in the *Guinness Book of Records*, say as the slowest train in the world. Managements tend to ignore or be unaware of the potential of the unusual but I believe that any railway system which for whatever reason, thoughtfully attaches passenger coaches to pick-up goods trains, should not only be commended for it but be proud of it!

In law, an advertised train which has passenger accommodation and runs to a timetable is a passenger train, no matter that it may carry only one passenger to every 20 or 30 goods wagons. This was established as long ago as 1885 by the House of Lords in the case of Burnett v. Great North of Scotland Railway Co. (10 Appeal Cas. 147.)

But there remains the question: Why did this Queensland train, No. 5C, take so long and what did it do for six and a half hours at Biloela? This could only be resolved by going for the ride, and the answers were not what I expected.

First of all, I found that although Biloela – or Billo as the locals call it – was a pleasant enough place, the train did not in fact hang around for six and a half hours doing nothing. Only part of it did. What happened was that the engine and, more importantly, the van – that is the guard's van cum passenger carriage, an ancient red Queensland wooden job with its little open verandah at each end and a toilet in the middle – left the rest of the train standing in Biloela station and jaunted off down the line to Earlesfield, 22 km and 50 minutes away.

It became a different train – goods No.1 – although it only consisted of engine and coach, and was not advertised. At Earlesfield it picked up the odd truck or two that had been standing there, probably discarded by another train on the twice-weekly occasions when one came over the ranges from Gladstone earlier in the day.

Having done this, it set off back for Biloela as train 2, where it shunted around for another hour or more while the original crew went to the pub for a counter lunch. Then it left for Rockhampton as train 5C once again.

From that time on it was go-go all the way. Rockhampton, 167 km, would be reached in a mere eight and a quarter hours, assuming there were no other delays.

What it did on the days it didn't have to pick up trucks at Earlesfield, I don't know. Frankly, I felt it might be impolite to ask. Expressing some surprise at the ingenuity of the arrangement I asked whether I could have found out by enquiry at Brisbane (but what on earth would I have asked them?).

"They wouldn't know anything about it," said the locals pityingly. Someone probably did once, I thought, and things had remained unaltered since.

Anyhow, as the one and only passenger that day, I recorded Train 5C's departure from Biloela as dead on time.

Within eight minutes we stopped at Caldaws, an unscheduled stop according to the timetable. The station name was indecipherable. No-one was in charge, but there was a truck in a siding full of pigs which stank to high heaven and made indescribable noises. Surely we were not going to attach this lot to the train? The owner was nowhere in sight. How long they had been left unattended I knew not but obviously we were there to rescue them from their present unenviable predicament, squealing with frustration in the hot afternoon sun, and to take them to their ultimate Nirvana, the bacon factory.

I am rather partial to a nice bit of pork, and would not wish to put anyone off travelling by any kind of train, but you can imagine that a truck load of frustrated porkers close to my nose for the next eight hours to Rockhampton was not something I greatly fancied. Fortunately the guard must have been of similar persuasion – he being in the other end of the same carriage – and I found that there must be an arrangement or understanding on the railways between guard and driver that livestock trucks go next to the engine. Apart from the occasional downwind scent (the reason for the fresh air smell of the country, as the eight year old put it in the famous essay), the pigs worried me little throughout the journey. I reckoned it worried them more than me, especially if the spirits of their ancestors had told them anything about bacon factories.

SLOW TRAIN TO BILOELA

We left Caldaws 14 minutes later and our next stop was to be Goovigen (pronounced 'Goo-VID-Jen') where there would be time for refreshment. But the junction at Dakenba delayed us for some time. The points there were set for the Callide mine branch and had to be adjusted for trains on the Biloela run which was secondary in importance.

In car number 528, with its wrought iron verandah from which, like Alexander Selkirk, one could be monarch of all surveyed, I felt a bit like an American president on an election tour, except that there was no cheering or bomb-throwing crowd, and it was a darned sight hotter than it would have been on the plains of the American west. The carriage had a carafe of water and a tumbler, but the guard could not recommend it wholeheartedly. "It may be of uncertain age," he said.

We stopped again at Callide, the train obviously acting as a pick-up or 'shunt' goods, whatever its nomenclature according to the timetable. At least it had a working toilet (with water, soap and paper towels), although with an open verandah and nothing in sight the lack of one would have presented difficulty only in certain circumstances. The train journey was leisurely; I found I could write notes with ease when it stopped, which it did frequently.

At a few stations we were timed to spend an hour or more, whether there was anything to pick up or not. Fortunately, and it could well be an example of thoughtful scheduling, these were without exception places where there was a most inviting Queensland pub just opposite, but hardly anything else in the way of civilisation.

We spent about six minutes at Callide, crossed a coal train at Koonkool, and I waved to children in a house adjoining the line at Jambin. There were quite a few houses there and the keeping of Guinea fowl seemed to be a local speciality. Those who have never tasted roast Guinea fowl: come to Queensland!

We reached Goovigen at 15.47 and the weather was hot. Just opposite the station was a cool, country pub, with friendly host and beautiful young smiling dark haired barmaid serving. A road sign at the level crossing heralded Banana, the Shire seat of government, some distance to the west. The guard said the train would wait at least 20 minutes, whatever there was to do. This was the way to go! Where else in the world could you enjoy such travel? A personal chariot, with horses attached (not to mention pigs); you standing on the verandah in the breeze, watching the track unfurl behind you, and stopping just about whenever you felt the need for refreshment and a taste of the local scene.

At 16.38 we reached Rannes, the junction with the Theodore line. I had not known what to expect. Something a bit short of Clapham or Crewe, but presumably a station at least, some station staff; perhaps even a refreshment room, toilets, telephone and taxi rank?

There was nothing. De la Mare's poem came to mind: "Is there anybody there, said the traveller, knocking on the moonlit door." There wasn't. QR were even then cutting down on staff at stations, and on trains as well. It was difficult to see how a junction between two extensive branch lines could reasonably operate on a non-attended basis even with only two trains a day calling there. It left the train crew

The author enjoying fresh air on the slow train to Biloela.

to do everything, and of course that added to the time involved. I was told that Mount Morgan, further up the line and once a thriving mining town, was to be similarly downgraded. This has since happened. In fact it has gone altogether. Operating on a shoestring budget is a policy of despair and a sure prelude to disaster.

With only the guard and the driver's mate to do the work, engine No. 1637 then set about collecting four empty cattle trucks from a siding. We moved forward again a few minutes later but stopped after joining the 'main' line from Theodore. At five o'clock we were still at Rannes, apparently ready to go but standing in silent contemplation in the hot blue-white glare of the afternoon sun.

I realised this was the crew meal break (strictly BYO) and we were late leaving Rannes. But after five in the evening, goods trains are allowed to go ahead of schedule and so we did from there onwards. Times were arranged to the mutual satisfaction of the guard and myself. Indeed, by the time we reached Mount Morgan, the biggest intermediate stop, we were nearly half an hour early. The crew wanted to get there quickly because that is where both driver and guard went off duty and others took over. Once there, the guard led the way across the tracks to the local so fast I could hardly keep up with him. But there was time for only a quick drink and not the meal I had hoped for. The new crew had no intention of hanging around Mount Morgan longer than was necessary for loading the train.

But although we left Mount Morgan ahead of time, an unamused Signal Control at Rockhampton would not deign to recognise the early arriving Thangool Rocket and kept us waiting outside Kabra junction for an hour or more and then again at Gracemere before allowing us to crawl home to Rockhampton at 22.42, exactly 14 minutes late.

The second slowest train in Queensland in 1981 was the 5.45 Tuesday "goods with passenger" Wandoan to Miles, at an overall 13.4 km/h for its journey of just under 70 km. What ghastly secret did this train conceal beneath its seemingly innocuous schedule, which showed three timetabled intermediate stops and five other calls "as required" before its Miles arrival at 10.55?.

Study of the Working Timetables revealed that if the train stopped at the next station, known as Whitleys' Siding, it would leave there at 8.15. This was advertised only as a conditional stop and the arrival time was not given. Two and a half hours to cover the barely one and a quarter kilometres between stations that were probably in sight of each other seemed excessive. You could safely miss the train, have a cup of tea, then stroll to the next station to find it waiting for you, with an hour or more to spare before you need board it.

But close study of the working timetable footnotes revealed something even more startling: number 465 from Wandoan did not waste its time idling. It was scheduled to leave Whitley's siding after about an hour there, go another kilometre and a half down the track to the next station, Wubagul, where it remained a further half hour—just to get the feel of the place? Then back to Whitley's siding, its first love. The train that went backwards!

If you missed it at the starting point you had time to walk to the next station, and if you missed it again there, dilly-dallying on the way, then "no worries, mate: she'll be right," as Australians say, the train would condescendingly return for you.

Did it turn round or merely reverse, and why? I never found out, because to travel on it would have meant an inordinate amount of time getting to Wandoan for five in the morning in the first place. Such a departure was not possible without a prior night stop, which meant finding a connection from Miles, the junction on the main west line. There was one at 12.18 on the Monday but no connection from Brisbane any later than the preceding Friday night.

I deduced that I could discover the irresistible charms of Whitley's siding by taking one of several other trains at that time running on the Wandoan branch.

But the "best laid schemes of mice and men", as the Bard observed, "gang aft agley". Trains which are liable to "cancellation without notice" (as all the "goods with passenger van attached" specimens in

SLOW TRAIN TO BILOELA

Queensland were) must perforce be checked. Here was the first snag. It was Christmas week. The train I had selected was cancelled.

But another train had been rescheduled, and by leaving Toowoomba just after midnight on the Monday I could change at Chinchilla for train 464, due to reach Wandoan at 8.57. This allowed plenty of time to study the surroundings, perhaps have a couple of beers, a good lunch, and maybe a siesta in the afternoon before rejoining the train in the evening for the return journey. One way or another I would see what made Whitley's siding tick.

My connection from Toowoomba, number 6676 express freight, was supposed to include a passenger carriage, although not so advertised in the public timetable. If what is not advertised is not provided one can hardly complain. Instead of a passenger carriage there was one of a more recent style of crew vehicle which are half guard's van and half crew rest compartment. There are full length seats and you can lie down, but they are horribly bare, some have no facilities, and the windows are tiny. For a comfortable ride, even overnight, I preferred the old fashioned wooden carriages with black leather seats, toilet, big windows you can look out of and open, and a handy carafe of drinking water. QR used even to put old sleeping cars on some of the inland overnight goods/passenger trains, though did not advertise them as such or offer the usual amenities.

At Chinchilla the sun was showing its golden influence in the eastern sky, and this took some of the bite out of the wind. I was glad to leave the cold bare van, which had no heating except in the guard's part. Why did I not go in with the guard? Three reasons: I wanted to lie down and sleep awhile, I don't believe in distracting railway staff from their jobs, and I didn't know he had a heater!

I induced a little internal warmth by a swig from a small flask of medicinal preparation my doctor had recommended as appropriate to such travel ventures: an extract of malt made in the Scottish Highlands.

Where now was the Wandoan train? I did not have far to look. There it was, in the final stages of assembly in Chinchilla yard. I found the passenger coach, an old one that had seen better days. A good clean up would have done it good, and so would a spell in the repair shops. The inside was, to put it mildly, filthy. Old newspapers littered the floor; there was thick dust on the seat, and the windows and doors were partly broken. Incongruously, a neatly folded pair of grey trousers, fresh from the cleaners with the tab attached, lay on one seat, but there was no sign of the owner. What was he wearing now?

I was interrupted in my speculation by the totally unexpected demand to produce my ticket. Every railway servant has the right to ask to see a passenger's ticket and I commend the station-master for his diligence, but it came as a surprise. Somehow, Chinchilla station at five o'clock in the morning on the Wandoan goods is not where you would expect to find ticket collection actively pursued.

The hotel at Wandoan served a good counter lunch, and had wine on tap as well as beer. Resolving on an afternoon siesta I checked hotel unit prices, but settled instead for a lie down in the empty railway carriage still standing in the station. It was rather hot, and dust and flies were something of a nuisance, but it saved paying for accommodation and it ensured that whatever happened I couldn't possibly miss the train back.

The train was late leaving Wandoan but that was of no concern, as it merely reduced the waiting time for my westbound sleeper onwards from Chinchilla.

Oh, I nearly forgot. Whitley's siding was nothing more than a cattle yard and a few extra tracks. With no sales that day I was spared the 'fresh air' of the country that I otherwise might have enjoyed. As for missing the train at Wandoan, while they still run livestock trains there as and when required (so they say), people as travellers are catered for no longer, with or without their trousers.

Chapter 10
Through Irish Eyes

"And watch the sun go down on Galway Bay" – from Irish song

Actually, it goes down over a council housing estate – at least when you are approaching Galway Bay by train at that time of day in late summer.

I had a great night in Galway. Bridie was manager of a very reasonably priced guest house-cum-pub (almost every business in Ireland is part-pub, even the butchers and the post office in small country towns) and I stayed in a kind of dormitory with several other visitors. Perhaps Bridie believed there was safety in numbers. There was a folk group performing that night in the bar and we had a wonderful time singing the old songs, not only of Ireland but of Liverpool - regarded by some as the biggest Irish city next to Dublin. To the strains of *Dirty Old Town* and *Johnny Todd* – the BBC *Z Cars* theme tune – I eventually got to sleep.

You don't wake up too early in Ireland. At least the natives don't. The Irish are late risers and late to bed. Early breakfast in guest houses is almost impossible. Normal breakfast times are from 8.30 to 10.00 and none of the trains I took in Ireland started before eight.

The Irish, like the Scots of the Western Highlands and Islands, have a cavalier attitude to time. They do not even measure distance the way they do in England. A Scottish mile, for example, though officially obsolete, is longer than an English mile (and you would know if you walked one) while an Irish mile at 2240 yards (2.048 km) is longer still.

I once attended a Council meeting at Stornoway in the Outer Hebrides. "What time does it start," I asked the town clerk, "because I would like to be there beforehand".

"At seven," he said, "come along about a quarter to eight".

The Irish railways do have timetables and the distances are in statute (English) miles. Also the trains, by and large, run to them although in my 1985 tour covering 16 countries I found that punctuality was worse in Ireland than anywhere else; in 3674 km of travel by 41 Irish trains, the total lateness amounted to 628 minutes, representing a mean addition of 19 percent to the scheduled duration of the journeys.

The first time I went to Galway was in 1953, using a 'Freedom of Ireland' pass – or something like that. Not all trains were late: some could be early or at least on time from the starting point, so it was no good arriving after the scheduled time in the hope the train would not have gone. In any country it is best to be at the station early. On this occasion I had arrived at Dublin Westland Row in what I thought was time for the Galway train at 8.40. "She's just after going," they said. Taking "after" in the colloquial sense of 'wanting to or being about to do something' I hurried forward to the platform. It was empty. The Irish use some expressions literally. "After going" meant precisely that: the train was indeed "after" going – it had gone!

There was a popular song some years ago called *Does your mother come from Ireland?* Well, mine didn't but my father was born in County Galway. I was aiming to see the town of his birth near where, he had told me, he was nearly drowned in the Shannon when a young boy. He must have been something of a wanderer like me, because the Shannon was at least 32 km from where he had lived. The town was Newbridge; not the better known Droichead Nua in County Kildare, but a little place halfway between Roscommon and Galway. Having missed the Galway train, I found there was a Westport train at 9.10, calling at Roscommon. There I met an Irish barrister, motoring down to Galway, I assume on holiday. I make that assumption because he was fairly well 'under the weather' before we started and we called at two or three bars on the journey down. Indeed at one stage he drove almost into the ditch and I was quite relieved when we actually reached Galway in safety.

Irish place names are fantastic when you see them in Erse or Irish

Gaelic, and in parts of the west the authorities don't bother to give the English translation. I did not see the famous aggressive cats of Cil Choinnig but I recognised the Rose of Trali at the end of another day's trip past the lakes and fells of Cil Airne. Somewhat surprising and hard to explain was a place named Rathluirc between Tipperary and Mallow, translated as Charleville. For a moment I thought I must be back in Queensland!

It is only "a long way to Tipperary" (Thiobrad Arann) going by train if you go via Wicklow, Wexford and Waterford, as I did. Otherwise, you take the 14.55 *Cork Express* from Dublin and change at Limerick Junction: you'll be in Tipperary in just over two hours.

One regret of travelling by rail in Ireland was that the remote branch lines serving the rugged Atlantic coast were all gone, right from Burtonport and Killybegs in the wilds of Donegal right down through Clifden in Connemara to Kilkee, Dingle, Valentia Harbour and Baltimore in the south. Irish railways, like those in Britain, had their heyday around 1923. Less than a tenth of that would now remain. The lines long gone include the almost unique Ballybunion railway, a 15 km single line – and single rail – link with the Limerick and Kerry Railway at Listowel. An invention of a Frenchman, Charles Lartigue, this was in effect a monorail of the straddle type. As the train approached maximum running speed of around 20 miles an hour (32 km/h) a pitching motion developed, which was found to simulate seasickness, and the line finally closed in 1924 after 36 years of mostly less than marginal profitability.

The same pitching motion is evident on some of the British Rail (BR) four-wheel passenger carriages which have replaced Metro-Cammel and other bogie diesel multiple units on local lines. Truck-type wheelbases were reserved for goods trains after the Americans introduced railways to the bogie, and for a long time now most of the better goods vehicles have had bogies too. It is not only sad to see railways reverting to the more primitive wheel arrangement; it shows a lack of consideration for passengers. Economic criteria are all they consider, forgetting that a short-term cost reduction per passenger will soon disappear when discomfort causes a fall in patronage.

Among the minor Irish railways the lines of the County Donegal Joint Committee lingered longer than most. These were narrow gauge (three feet or 914 mm), and although I hitch-hiked round that area in the 1950s it is to my regret that I did not sample travel on this system before it closed finally at the end of that decade, to the sound of many detonators followed by the press obituaries for County Donegal's last piece of railway. I had thought this to be the end of railways in this wildly scenic part of the British Isles but no, in 1978 an inquisitive wanderer of remote places, Hugh Dougherty, reported in the *Railway Magazine* his discovery of a little-known surviving narrow gauge line (two feet or 610 mm) a mile out of the town of Glenties. Built in 1946 to transport peat from an extensive peat bog in the area, the train includes a home-made passenger coach in the form of a tin shed on wheels. This line could be high on my list of railways to visit the next time I go across the sea to Ireland: the only problem, as with so many preserved railways, would be that they are so unconnected with the main line system. It takes a very dedicated rail enthusiast to suffer hours of bus travel to reach a remote and tiny railway. My criterion would be that the length of rail journey at the end of it should at least balance the duration of the ordeal in reaching it. One cannot help feeling that official tourist bodies are failing to coordinate public transport effectively – or at least failing to make representations to the major transport undertakings at the appropriate time – before convenient links are severed.

My first experience of Irish railways (and of the Emerald Isle itself) had been not long after the end of World War II when rationing of some commodities was still in force in Britain. I had several trips there in the 1950s and one I remember well was when we ventured over the border from the north into County Monaghan. There in the town of that name you could buy sweets without coupons, and no doubt a lot more besides, but my pocket money would not have covered anything significant. It was there that I first indulged in smuggling.

Most of my travels being then "with knapsack on my back" (actually a huge frame rucksack) and either on foot or by public transport, I had secreted a tube of 'Rowntrees Clear Gums' (as Rowntree Fruit Gums were then called) in the top flap and when the customs people came along as we re-crossed the border into Armagh, to my horror the officer felt this hard tube when examining my luggage.

"What's this?" he barked. "Sweets," I confessed.

"Oh, I just thought it might have been a fountain pen," he said, in tones suggesting that possession of such an item would be on a par with stealing the Ruritanian Crown Jewels. I wonder if he just had a warped sense of humour. Anyway, I doubt if taking lollies across the border was really a criminal offence.

Going to Ireland from the north of England in those days meant one of several possible journeys. You either went to Stranraer for the Larne boat and then by train to Belfast or you went via Heysham Harbour, from whence you could sail to Belfast (Donegall Quay) or to Dublin (North Wall). There were also boats from Liverpool, Holyhead and some other remote place in Wales. In busy seasons a 'sailing ticket' was needed as well as rail and steamer tickets. These were a passenger numbers control feature, rather similar to the boarding passes you need in addition to your ticket to board an express on the railways of Spain, or to board the Vale of Rheidol railway to Devils Bridge in Wales, and there was a limit on the number issued.

If you were going to Belfast the Larne-Belfast train would be waiting at Larne Harbour in Northern Ireland. Since it was the shortest sea crossing by far, one naturally looked to this route, and on my first visit to Ireland as a teenager it was the way we went. The 'midnight special' (actually 24.30) from Newcastle, ran non-stop to Carlisle and continued via Castle Douglas and the now abandoned Portpatrick and Wigtownshire Joint railway, unfortunately arriving at Stranraer Harbour early in the morning and so missing the scenery of the route. We later found out this was not the cheapest way to go since the steamer fare was insignificant compared to rail.

Heysham Harbour therefore was to become my favoured route from north-east England - especially when the girl I loved went to live there! On that first trip a group of us were to stay at a teenage camp at Lough Fea in the beautiful Sperrin Mountains of County Tyrone. The nearest railway station was at Cookstown, reached by a branch from the Belfast - Omagh line at Dungannon. Cookstown was a dead end but another branch went out northwards to join the main Belfast–Derry line just south of Coleraine. Having heard about the legendary 'Girls of Coleraine' may be one reason my friend and I took the train there after the camp ended, or it may have been to see the famous Giant's Causeway at nearby Portrush. In the event we did. At Portrush you changed to the Bushmills electric tramway to Giant's Causeway and there faced a short walk along the cliffs. I remember being infuriated on arrival to find that the Causeway itself was on so-called 'private' land and payment had to be made to enter upon it. So we contented ourselves with viewing from a distance. Had we been a little older we might well have paused at Bushmills on the way back to console ourselves with a sample of its special product.

I am not sure by what route I first went to Dublin; it was probably from Liverpool and I well remember arriving in the Republic around seven in the morning to find the pubs open and dozens of foaming pints of Guinness waiting on the bar for the thirsty travellers. Draught Guinness, locally known as "Liffey water" from and of similar consistency to the river of that name which flows through the city, is very frothy. Bar staff can draw it only slowly from the wood, pausing frequently to wipe the creamy excess froth from the top with a little plastic spatula. That is why they need to have glasses half-poured ready when they are expecting a crowd.

Many of the boats crossing the Irish sea for Dublin came into the nearby port of Dun Loaghaire (pronounced 'Dunleery') and this is now the main ocean terminal, served by the local DART suburban railway but without its former branch right onto the quay. The railway-owned hotel adjoining the station serves a first class meal, but not at budget prices. Dublin itself has a fairly extensive network of rail lines, relic of the days of rival companies. Amiens Street and North Wall served the Great Northern and Midland Great Western routes, Westland Row the Dublin, Wicklow and Wexford line, and Kingsbridge the Great Southern & Western main line to Cork. A loop line crossed the Liffey west of Kingsbridge and linked the last-named into North Wall and Amiens Street, while the City of Dublin Junction railway linked Amiens Street junction to Westland Row. It was therefore possible to run trains through the capital between any two routes, with the exception of a branch from the Wicklow & Waterford system which terminated at the dead-end station of Harcourt Street. Another dead-end station was Broadstone, on a branch from the Midland and Great Western at Liffey Junction.

All this has changed. In effect, Amiens Street has become Connolly, linked to Pearse (formerly Westland Row) by the old Dublin Junction line, and Kingsbridge has been replaced by Heuston. Broadstone and Harcourt Street have gone, but North Wall and the loop west of Kingsbridge remain for goods traffic.

I should mention another Dublin terminal which is rather special and was even more so in early days. At James's Gate, Dublin, well known to the drinking fraternity from labels on the bottle, is the famous Guinness Brewery, linked to the system at Islandbridge Junction just west of Heuston. From 1874 to 1975 there was also an internal rail network at the brewery, and they had four passenger vehicles used in a "Visitors Train". Most of the internal system was narrow gauge (559 mm) and it included a spiral tunnel linking two levels of the factory floor which must have been unique. As they say, 'there's nothing like a Guinness' yet, quite surprisingly, this railway is not even mentioned in the *Guinness Book of Rail Facts and Feats*.

In Ireland the trains have two classes, standard (second class or economy) and "super standard" (first equivalent) plus, more recently, a "Gold Seal" service which in essence is an Irish version of BR

Pullman class. Super standard seating followed the '2 + 1' layout with head cushions for added comfort, although there was a different kind of first class on some of the trains. The Cork line always had the most up-to-date rolling stock. On other trains they had what we might call a 'Clayton's' first class. It was often not used as such. Decisions appeared to be up to the ticket collector of the day.

Joining the inter-city express at Limerick Junction I found the "super standard" sitting car next to the buffet was occupied by 'ordinary' passengers. I am not sure now how I came to that conclusion: for one thing it was full, and some of them just did not look the type likely to have first class tickets. It was obviously in use, with official blessing, by standard class ticket holders – perhaps there were notices on the windows to that effect, like BR often had, but if so I did not record the fact. Two coaches further along the train was the 'proper' super standard coach, though there did not appear to be any at-seat service as would normally have been expected. Always curious, I sought the reason.

The train had obviously been wrongly assembled at Cork, the steward told me, or even at Dublin the day before. He was seething mad about it and was swearing at the inspector: one could hardly blame him because it made it very difficult for the buffet staff to provide the expected service three coaches down the train.

On another occasion I found a dining car which was not advertised, but neither was it open. This was an Athlone–Westport train on a Sunday, and people were commenting unfavourably about it while busy unscrewing their thermos flasks and unwrapping their 'pieces' – obviously not expecting a dining car and therefore hardly justified in complaining about its absence.

To be fair to the Irish (who were very generous in allowing me to explore their railway network free and supplying me with literature, not to mention an excellent welcoming lunch), the weather had a lot to do with any minor inconveniences I experienced. Ireland is so wonderfully green because it rains a lot. And on this trip the weather really showed why the middle of Ireland is one big bog. Ireland is like a saucer, with mountains all round the rim and wet in the middle – and most of my travelling was in the middle.

The weather during that month in 1985 was really awful, with violent thunder and rain storms washing out signalling so it is hardly surprising there was some chaos on the system. I had hoped to cover all the lines still open for traffic, including a link northwards from Limerick to Claremorris in County Mayo through Athenry in County Galway. This route was traversed only by freight trains apart from the 'Knock Special' passenger services which operated during the annual religious festival to Cnoc Mhuire, where the Virgin Mary was reputed to have appeared back in 1879. It was the pilgrimage season but the special trains were only on Sundays, so I had to look at the scheduled paths for cement and fertiliser trains on which I could have travelled with the driver or guard (if any). There were timeslots at 5.30 and 7.30. However, enquiry at the station after a night in Limerick produced a negative result. If there was a train, it had gone, or maybe there wasn't one that day. So it was back to Dublin for a tour of a different part of the country before ending up at Westport in County Mayo after all. I made a round trip of 709 km in place of the 194 km direct line, but I was able to include an hour's break en route at Athy in County Kildare, the town where my grandfather had worked long ago as a farrier, tending the horses on a local estate. County Kildare is still famed for equestrian pursuits.

In terms of time the roundabout route, with breaks between trains, took 13½ hours: had I successfully found a bulk goods train it might have taken (the operative word being 'might') about half that.

Still, on that tour I covered every passenger line then remaining open for regular services, except those in northern Ireland. Dundalk was the furthest north I ventured on the main Belfast line. This was at a time when the IRA and the 'Protestant Boys' were at it hammer and tongs up in the north, knee-capping and all, and railways can easily become a target for bomb practice in such an environment. It is wise to keep

TRAINCATCHER

out of other people's politics, especially when they get violent. Thus I did not visit Ulster again - I had been there before, and though I joined in singing Irish songs in Galway I refrained from offering a solo rendering of *The Sash my Father Wore* in Dublin's O'Connell Street.

A night at the little seaside resort of Balbriggan preceded my return south to Dublin and then Rosslare from where I had considered taking the boat over to France – this crossing being covered by the Eurailpass. The train ride down the coast past the Wicklow Hills is one of Ireland's most scenic routes, but it was not without incident. At Rosslare Harbour, a woman discovered she had left her spectacles on the train. Another couple had left their baby carriage in the compartment. I wondered how they could possibly have missed it since they stepped out of the train carrying the baby. But the guard leapt to the rescue as soon as he became aware of these problems. On the quay a young man lay sprawled, his knapsack lying beside him in a pool of vomit, sleeping off the effect of over-indulgence and certainly likely to wake up to find the boat was 'just after going'.

Our train was making ready for the return trip. Chatting to the kindly guard, I opted for a return to Dun Loaghaire to catch the boat to Holyhead instead. One of the highlights of this Irish jaunt was when after leaving Rosslare I joined driver Bill Watson in the cab. Coming into another station the platform was on my side, and Bill allowed me to lean out to exchange the 'token' as we drew in. The station-master caught my hoop beautifully but I dropped the one he held out for me – never any good even at catching a ball, that was me.

Among my other happy memories were the little coincidences, like arriving in Mallow on my return from Killarney, not to meet the legendary wild rakes of song (always fighting, always swearing) but nicely in time for an international festival. However, this meant no chance of accommodation for the night and since the railways of Ireland ceased to smile on sleeping cars a long time ago I resolved to make for Cork instead, or better still some small place on its outskirts which would be cheaper.

The buffet car was just closing when I joined the *Cork Express*, but the conductor and the cook – the only train staff left apart from driver and guard – succumbed to my blarney and provided me with a drink. It was not that I was dying of thirst but I always liked to test the catering facilities. When a train is advertised to carry a buffet between one place and another it should do so, and it should be open. Good naturedly pointing out that we were only 15 minutes out of Cork they had no objection to an additional late customer and suggested a place in nearby Cobh where I could find a cheap night's lodging.

At Cork the Cobh train was along at the platform end, but obligingly came right back to the buffers just a few minutes before departure – by which time most of the passengers had already walked the length of the platform to it. At least it showed some consideration for last minute arrivals.

Cobh (pronounced Cove) was where the ships to America used to sail from. The railway itself almost went to sea. Vast expanses of water appeared, covered by ghostly mists. Dark castles loomed up ahead as the train bounced along the uneven track like a bucking bronco. It went up and down like the body of the Loch Ness Monster and I feared we would be off the rails in no time. The ballast of the track was scattered with seaweed and other jetsam: I wondered what would happen at high tide.

Then in the mist a ship appeared off our starboard bow, then an old fort, I think called Black Rock Castle, then more ships. "Spanish ships of war at sea?" – the poem about Sir Richard Grenville's Revenge, about the first I ever learned and liked, came back to mind. I did not count to see whether there were "fifty three". After more wild bouncing a forest of cranes appeared and then we were at Cobh, end of the line, the last place some emigrants saw of old Ireland in the days when at £5 steerage class they shipped out in their hundreds to take their chances in the New World.

Anna at the Well House combined youth and beauty with old world charm and I had a good fish and chip supper before retiring for the night.

Some days later I found myself arriving at Mullingar on the now little used line from Athlone (once the principal route to Galway and Westport) right in the middle of its two day show. At the pleasant little hotel to which I was directed, I was relieved to find that scampi and chips with a glass of wine cost only £2.95. The weather was again deteriorating and although I had intended to make for Sligo, I decided that rather than risk arrival there after closing time with nowhere to stay I should opt for a night in Mullingar and work out a new itinerary for the rest of my trip.

It had been a bad day for connections. Starting my return from the round trip to Westport our train reached Athlone at 10.54. There I had to wait for the Up train from Galway which came in a little late at 11.09. The weather was foul. We stopped for three minutes about 13 km down the line, and somewhere else a bit later for another 14 minutes. Another stop, of four minutes, was followed by yet another of three minutes which brought the time to noon. We were then just outside Clara. The cause of delay was signals out of action because of rain and the electrical storm. At Clara, a former junction, the Down Galway train was waiting in the loop line near the platform. Here I left the Athone–Dublin train, which caught a green light, dropped the 'pilotman' and roared off south, catching a further green at the end of the loop. The Down Galway train left at 12.33, packed full of Sunday trippers on their pilgrimage to Knock, plus yours truly.

Years ago, connectivity at Clara was cause for comment. In what is probably a masterpiece of understatement, Doyle and Hirsh comment in *Railways in Ireland 1834-1984* that "connections with the GS&WR trains at Clara were not always well arranged". Well, my connection from the former GS&WR was at Athlone, to which I returned, the Clara–Streamstown link having been severed long before. In spite of the weather and late running of trains (over 40 minutes late at Clara and 20 late leaving there) I arrived back at Athlone by 12.30 and the connection I wanted was waiting. I had time for a quick out and back trip to Ballina before completing my travels for the day.

Later that evening as we were approaching Mullingar the conductor came round to make an announcement. With a beaming smile in his eyes, he proudly proclaimed that the train was 40 minutes late. "A breakdown at Clonsilla" was the cause, probably an aftermath of the storm which some said had been the worst in living memory. But was 40 minutes late supposed to be an achievement? – a new record for lateness – or was the train just unexpectedly early? Perhaps it was usually much later? We could only guess. Most passengers took it philosophically, but I still wonder. The Irish have their own inimitable way of putting things, and perhaps to understand you have to see events through Irish eyes.

Chapter 11

Britrail Revisited

"Second class travel only" – heading in BR Regional timetable, Durham, Cleveland, North Yorkshire 1985

The thing I noticed most on British Railways when I returned after 18 years absence was probably this. First class coaches there were, to be sure, but they were almost as rare as hens' teeth.

In the '50s and '60s you could nearly always find at least a few first class compartments on any but the most mundane of workmen's suburban trains. I don't mean the workmen were mundane, just the trains the railways gave them. But in 1985, apart from the Greater London commuter area and InterCity, first class seemed almost a thing of the past.

Even some overnight and long-distance trains seemed to lack first class. I found none on an Inverness to Edinburgh train in 1985. By 1992, all the Liverpool–Newcastle trains were second class only. Yet sometimes whole coaches of first class accommodation would be marked 'second class', with or without (as often as not without) the supplementary 'bargain fare' which British Rail (BR) seemed to consider popular.

This bargain first class consisting of a £2 supplement for any journey seemed to me a bit odd. While in the early days on Britain's railways there were three distinct classes – first, second and third – now it seemed there was first class for exclusive use of first class ticket holders, then the £2 bargain first class, then other first class marked "for the use of second class passengers" (that was the way BR described them, not 'passengers with second class tickets') and then there was the ordinary second class or "one class only" trains, which always meant the same thing. But at the other end of the scale there was '1st class Executive' – something better than first class, a premium first class or 'Pullman' service. Five different classes in effect: this seemed unduly complicated.

In the United States sleeping car accommodation is sometimes referred to as 'first class'. It seems also that some travellers regarded a first class ticket as automatic seat entitlement. An American visitor who occupied a lady's reserved first class seat on an afternoon train from Holyhead which was referred to as the 'Up' *Irish Mail*, declared "I paid first class" as though this entitled him to any or anyone else's seat.

On the 17.30 Newcastle to Kings Cross InterCity the 'Bargain First' occupied almost all the non-smoking first class coaches. The only first class non-smoking available to full first class ticket holders was half a coach of which the remainder was smoking. Naturally it reeked of smoke. I thought, why not have a composite 1st/economy smokers car? – or why not reserve the dining car seats when meals were not being offered and have them available for full first class fare paying non-smokers?

It was all very confusing. Yet first class on the InterCity services was very good. There was ample luggage space between the backs of the seats. The only minor defects were that the seats in the Mark IV coaches were not quite comfortable enough for complete relaxation nor were they quite correctly adjusted in height or spacing for you to sit up in a proper position to use the tables, which were fixed. The seats were not reversible but only Australians seem to want to face the direction of travel all the time.

I thought the Mark IV coach ride was also rather rough compared to the earlier Mark III. Perhaps the springing was not adequate for the train's speed, but the ride was still quite smooth. I decided I could not quite agree with a couple of travellers I encountered on an Italian train in 1992. One was Swiss, the other a Dane and they were speaking in English – presumably the only language they had in common. When I mentioned having just travelled on BR they rubbished it – it was the 'pits' as far as they were concerned. While I would have had to concede that the ETR 450 train we were on had something of an edge on BR in a number of ways, they overlooked the fact that many Swiss carriages, and the Corail type found in France and elsewhere in Western Europe, were very far from comfortable. Shortly after that encounter I travelled on a Danish inter-city train. Although beautifully appointed, it was one of the roughest rides I can ever recall.

On BR the *Gatwick Express* airport shuttle was excellent. Fast, frequent, with first class and well-stocked mobile buffet, it was far above the standard of the miserable LT stopping train to Heathrow or the London airport bus which was its alternative. Of course the *Gatwick Express* is run by InterCity rather than Network South-East and since even the latter's ordinary trains tend to be a cut above some of BR's other regional services it is not surprising that InterCity put on their best to impress the newcomer arriving at Gatwick.

The Pullman services were generally very good, as were the premier executive trains bearing the InterCity label.

On the East Coast Main Line these were either diesel 125 or electric 225 sets. I had sought a cab pass but BR, though helpful in every other possible way, were not disposed to allow travel in the cab. They did, however, arrange for me to board a stationary unit at Kings Cross. The lady to whom I was to report revealed she was from Hartlepool. Friendly relations were soon established. I said, "You would know where they hanged the monkey". From then we got on like a match factory on fire. She took me to meet the engine drivers. About half an hour's conducted initiation into the mysteries of the IC 225 and IC 125 power cars came to an abrupt end when suddenly the set we were in revved up in readiness for departure to the sheds. Not being in the driver's end at the time we were unaware of the imminent departure and I very nearly had an unauthorised trip after all.

Naturally it was to these types of train I gravitated. Not only were the trains first class; some of the passengers were first class too.

One girl I met on the train was definitely first class and beautiful. Perhaps it was her Spanish heritage. She was from Ecuador. I had never met a girl from Ecuador before and asked her if all the girls there were as beautiful as her. They were, she said. Olive skin – no, that's what people say but olives are green or black. Her skin was definitely neither. It was more a creamy yellow with a touch of duskiness, like the flesh of ripe avocado in colour and texture.

With another female companion and a small child she occupied the table across the aisle in the *Scottish Pullman* out of Kings Cross. It was the Easter holiday period and the catering service was barely operative. The girls were well prepared so must have travelled on BR before. Scarcely had we passed Grantham before they had polished off most of a bottle of red Rioja between them – a favourite wine with me too. Then to show their good taste they opened another bottle – this time a rich Australian red from Morris of Rutherglen. It was this, naturally, which started our conversation.

They were bound for Glasgow. I was due to leave the train at its first stop, Northallerton, a most unusual stop for the particular train. I had earlier remarked on the beauty of this girl to the man in the seat opposite me – an Australian who had worked as consultant on Queensland Rail electrification. It's a small world. "You'd never get to first base," he said.

I've never had anyone explain to me the exact location of this evidently sought after destination, but social intercourse was surely a step in the right direction. The Ecuadorian beauty shared with me an appreciation of good red wine at least and owing to the lack of active waiter service it was not long before I unpacked a small cask of Australian claret from my travel bag for an exchange of tastings. By now I was rather regretting my commitment to disembark at fast-approaching Northallerton. "I'd like to go all the way with you," I remarked. I think this comment may have been mis-interpreted. "I expect you would," she answered with a knowing twinkle. How could she possibly have guessed my secret desire to go to Glasgow?

There must be something about train travel that makes people lose their inhibitions. It is easy to strike up an acquaintance. Even the English can lose their traditional reserve. The story is told of a catholic priest travelling first class on a London-bound train who was joined in the compartment by a Jewish rabbi.

After a brief exchange of nods, an hour or so of silence ensued. Then the priest felt some conversation might be acceptable. After all, they were both men 'of the cloth' despite their difference of race and religion. "Tell me, rabbi," he said after an opening exchange of pleasantries, "I cannot help being curious, and forgive me for asking. But just between the two of us, have you ever eaten pork?"

There was a long silence. The rabbi looked out of the window, then down at the book he had been reading. "Yes," he confessed, and went back to his book.

But he kept quietly chuckling to himself. After a while he looked up again, tapped the priest on the knee and said, "Tell me, father, have you ever had sexual intercourse?"

The priest blushed and averted his eyes. When he raised them to face the rabbi again, he shook his head and with barely a whisper said, "No".

The rabbi beamed. "Better than pork!" he declared.

That was one thing about the old compartment idea on railways. If you got to talking then it could become quite sociable, but no-one rushed to make it so. First one in and you tried to get a compartment to yourself. We nowadays stress the sociability of railway travel but it certainly wasn't always like that. The first railway passenger coaches were virtually private carriages linked together and each seating no more than six or eight people. Corridors began the move to sociability, but probably more so that ticket collectors could pursue their unwelcome trade than out of any consideration for what the passengers might want.

In fact in Britain it was hardly the done thing to attempt a conversation with a fellow compartment-mate unless you had been introduced. People already in the compartment tended to scowl at newcomers, especially if the train was full. In the third class, which was what we now call 'budget' or 'economy' and is second class in mainland Europe, but which still retained its old name in Britain long after second class proper had disappeared, a full train meant you had to raise the armrests between seats so that four to a side rather than three would fit in where there was a corridor. With non-corridor carriages there was a tendency to pack in as many as six a side.

"Is this seat taken?" could be met by all sorts of evasive replies. There were also well-known techniques to discourage would-be passengers. If you were in the window seat facing the engine, then it was recognised as your right to decide whether the window should be open. A blast of icy air, so long as you could endure it, could soon discourage other passengers. Of course having bawling children with you, or exhibiting disgusting eating habits with sticky things out of rustling paper bags were methods sometimes practised, but the best was the one so beautifully described in Jerome K. Jerome's *Three Men in a Boat* — the saga of the cheeses. Over-ripe Stilton in a closed compartment is not conducive to friendly social intercourse.

A modern example on the same lines was reported in a 1992 *Australian Action for Public Transport Newsletter*. Describing it as a "hitherto unrecorded method of clearing a railway carriage" it told of a man seen in a peak-hour train at Town Hall (Sydney) who was "deeply inhaling eucalyptus oil, aggravating the dose by rubbing liberal amounts on his face and neck."

"Needless to say," said the reporter needlessly, "we didn't hang around!" Not much social intercourse there.

Segovia in his autobiography expressed his belief that outside of Spain "travellers can spend days together and address each other only in the most dire necessity".

"Spaniards," he wrote, "are fond of telling the story about an Italian, travelling in the United States, who attempts to start a conversation with his neighbour.

"'It's a nice day,' he says tentatively.

"Annoyed by this display of foreign boldness, the American answers aggressively, 'Who said it wasn't?' and turns his back on the Italian.

"Such aloofness is not possible in Spain" said Segovia. "The closed compartments of the trains in those days became convivial centres of conversation. On reaching their destination, passengers who had spent many long hours together bid each other farewell like lifelong friends or, if they had been irritated by some heated argument, parting is the time to make solemn promises to crack the skull of the other at the first available opportunity."

How friendly can you get?

In wartime Britain everybody was crowded in together, a mass of often unwashed humanity. Soldiers, airmen, clerks, manual workers, young women, old men, children, with their baggage in battered cases, kitbags, brown paper parcels, wedged into seats, standing in compartments, thrust together double deep in the corridor, sitting in the lavatory or even lying on the overhead luggage racks, it was dirty, smelly and uncomfortable for any length of time – but that was war and you smiled and put up with it – or as Winston Churchill might have said when castigating English language pedants, it was something 'up with which you put'.

I did not mind this. It was a train and it was going somewhere even if it often took a long time doing it. I think it was on such a train I experienced my first awareness of sexuality. The London train of about 20 coaches was packed solid and my father and I were both in the corridor. I would have been somewhere around the age of 14 at the time. My back was to the compartment wall and wedged in front of me facing the window was a young woman in WAAF uniform, her well-upholstered bottom constantly being pressed hard against my body as the train swayed to and fro. I became aware of things happening to me I did not fully understand and found it rather pleasant; the scent, the closeness... Of course I had by then cuddled and kissed girls from time to time, no more than little pecks mainly on the cheek, but this was different. This was woman, this was a new closeness in a different way, intimate, exciting. The WAAF probably had no idea of the effect she was having on the little lad behind her – or had she? I wonder. Older than I, about 20, she would be wise in the ways of the world and all females know full well how to tantalise a male. Nowadays it would be branded as sexual harassment but no male in his right mind would object to it. Pure pleasure, good clean fun, and like sugar, a 'natural part of life'. I am not condoning sex with violence but in most normal situations one can always say "no", "stop it" or, as a girl I once knew used to say, "gerroff". To my mind there is something sick about a society which regards normal male-female interaction as anti-social or worse, and people who take offence at any approach or even at a compliment by a member of the opposite sex should be seeing their psychiatrist rather than their lawyer.

I did not seek counselling or legal advice. I only remember a sense of loss when the corridor crush thinned out as some of the passengers left the overcrowded train at Grantham.

British Railways, or as they were in those days, the LNER, LMS, GWR and SR, did a fantastic job in wartime. There were many more lines than now, yet they kept them all going in the face of rolling stock shortages, air raids, coal shortages, and shortages of manpower. I think the railways were a 'reserved occupation' – or at least some of the jobs were, but I remember seeing women porters, something unheard of in pre-war days. A wonderful BBC radio documentary programme, *Junction X*, later published in booklet form, dramatically depicted the problems and the way they were overcome.

When I recall what was then achieved it makes me wonder why with far fewer routes to maintain and all nominally under one management, far newer motive power units and rolling stock, and far better maintained track, services should still suffer from breakdowns, delays, and missed connections.

But the thing that saddened me most on revisiting the BR network was the dereliction, the abandoned routes, the vacant industrial sites, the vanished railway yards, sidings, station buildings and passenger facilities at all but the largest centres. I felt like George Orwell's character in *Coming Up for Air*. Some of the industrial areas were like the imaginary but ever-so-real place called 'Grotton' by a columnist in the Journal of the Royal Town Planning Institute – in a word, grotty. It was sad and it was depressing, in spite of the sleek HST units, the greatly accelerated services and the overall cleanliness and smooth advertising.

Saltburn station was the end of the Darlington–Middlesbrough branch. It used to have several platforms, all covered, stone buildings, and an extension of the line under the adjoining roadway ended in the cellars of the railway-owned Zetland Hotel, where presumably in former days the dining cars were provisioned.

By 1985 all that remained was a single short platform, formerly the 'bay', with no shelter, enclosure or anything to keep passengers from the elements. Gone were the waiting rooms, chocolate vending machines, weighing machines with their little white tickets saying, "You are 10 stone, 5 pounds and have an engaging personality" – in fact most of these disappeared during or just after the war, but the worst thing was that there was nothing to attract passengers. It might as well have been a bus stop. And the trains! No longer was there the London-bound restaurant car train of corridor stock on which, when I lived in nearby Redcar I would sometimes get my breakfast before Eaglescliffe, where I changed back to the local for my work destination of Darlington. Even the diesels were different, with crowded bus-like seats and wide empty spaces for prams. This was actually a good point but it gave the atmosphere of a goods van, and the goods truck wheelbase helped in producing a far from comfortable ride.

Eaglescliffe was also depressingly altered and bare of amenities. This was a junction where the Leeds–Newcastle and Darlington–Saltburn lines interconnected and was part of the original Stockton & Darlington route, though in 1985 only one or two trains a day used the link south over Yarm viaduct to the East Coast Main Line at Northallerton. Since my last visit this has improved with an interesting Manchester Airport–Middlesbrough hourly interval service, but it is only second class. It is especially interesting because it at last recognises Manchester as the national capital as far as northern English people are concerned. In my youth we looked up to Manchester: we looked down on London, the home of southerners with their fancy talk. Professional people took not the *Times* but the *Manchester Guardian* newspaper.

At Eaglescliffe a sort of plastic glasshouse with a few hard seats in the middle of one long island platform was all the passengers were offered in the way of shelter. The refreshment room, in which I would often stop for a drink on the way home from work, had vanished along with all the other station buildings. There must have been a ticket office somewhere but having a Britrail Pass I did not need to look for it.

Thornaby, the next station along the line, was even more depressing. This used to have solid architect-designed station buildings and plenty of shelter, and one of its features was the variety of carving on the string course below the roof line. There was even a notice drawing attention to it and in 1982 an article featured it in Britain's famous *Railway Magazine*. With the same disregard for history as led them to remove the signs and even the track of the Stockton and Darlington Railway where it crossed the main line north of Darlington, the powers that be demolished Thornaby station buildings in 1982.

Even Stockton station is today barely recognisable and in 1994 there was a proposal to convert it into flats. What would happen then to the railway is not clear. Quite apart from its historic associations Stockton was for many years the most important junction on Tees-side, with lines radiating to West Hartlepool, Sunderland, Durham, Newcastle, Ferryhill, Bishop Auckland, Darlington, Leeds, York, Middlesbrough and the North York moors and coast. A massive goods yard occupied an area north-west of the station, which itself boasted a splendid arched iron roof. Unlike nearby Darlington, no passenger trains passed through Stockton without stopping. By 1985 the goods yard had gone and so had the arched roof.

The demolition and closure mania on Britain's railways had of course started well before 'Thatcherism' became a synonym for the economic rationalism that is neither economic nor rational. Beeching really started it, under orders from the then anti-public transport Tory government, but it certainly rose to a new pitch in the '70s and '80s, and we may yet see the almost total disintegration of a former proud network under the banner of 'accountability'. This is a process which starts off as 'rationalisation' (savage pruning), then becomes 'corporatisation' (breakup of management and abdication of responsibility). Following this comes franchising, which means giving away public assets, leading finally to the inevitable privatisation. No, not finally, because that in itself often leads to extinction.

Against this, there may be a growth of local community involvement, not just by private individuals and groups of conservation-minded citizens, but by local authorities conscious of their wider social responsibility and more responsive to local feelings and needs than a central ideology-driven government.

Even the many times threatened Settle and Carlisle line which I travelled on in 1985 has survived the efforts of government and rail management to close it.

Community concern and public determination has saved many lines in Britain and has led even to the reopening by BR regional management of lines previously closed and to the construction of new stations. Belatedly, government has come into the act, at least to the extent of approving new financial arrangements and co-operating with local authorities so that trains can still run on tracks owned by the State, but the scene is far from serene and astute observers warn of perils ahead as fragmentation and devolution of responsibility continues.

Even the privately run boat services of western Scotland have suffered. Caledonian McBrayne's Mallaig–Kyle of Lochalsh boat service linking these West Highland railheads had deteriorated by 1985. There were only two tiny lounges on the boat. Both allowed smoking. The buffet did not open until about 12.30, a full half hour after departure, and it closed at 13.20, forty minutes before arrival at Kyle. There was no announcement about either.

BRITRAIL REVISITED

If you wished to "make your way to Stornoway" nowadays you would no more find the wonderful old *Loch Seaforth* plying the Minch from Kyle of Lochalsh with Captain Smith pitting his skills against a force 10 gale; a car ferry from Ullapool is the modern substitute – and despite plans many, many years ago, Ullapool has never had a rail connection.

No-one ever built a railway on the Island of Lewis either although they prepared the roadbed for it, which crossed the island from Stornoway to Carloway, with a branch to Callanish, home of the standing stone circle which is more sinister to some than the better known one at Stonehenge. I travelled this rail route once by car, right to its end where it crosses under the coast road and tried to imagine how long it would have lasted if Beeching or Thatcher had ever heard of it.

The Isle of Lewis is renowned locally for tasty Lewis mutton from highland blackface sheep, and for succulent Broad Bay prawns and it is the home, ironically, of the cloth popularly known as Harris Tweed, almost all of which, though woven in the island crofts, is finished in the mills of Stornoway.

'Lovely Stornoway' became infamous for a time as the scene of an alleged early indiscretion of Prince Charles. Not in connection with women, but rather in a hotel there he was reported to have drunk a cherry brandy when strictly under the then drinking age. The licensee (you don't use the term 'landlord' in the Highlands) assured me it was all a storm in a teacup, or rather a lemonade glass. The tipple was 'Cherry Bee', a popular soft drink of that time. "Mind you," he added, "he had a few whiskies afterwards". To refuse a dram in the Outer Isles is not the done thing.

In the latest timetable there is no mention of a boat between Mallaig and Kyle, let alone one from there to Stornoway. But you can still get to Kyle by taking the *Royal Highlander* or some other train up to Inverness. In your sleeper on the *Royal Highlander* you will find pure Caithness Spring mineral water (non-fizzy), a pack containing clothes brush, shoe shine, soap, and foot-mat, besides individual temperature control and the obvious things like a bed. This is now a much more civilised train than when I travelled south in 1967 on the first leg of my journey to Australia.

By whatever train you reach Inverness you then take the diesel sprinter service across the width of Scotland to Kyle. After clanking across a swing bridge over the top end of the Caledonian Canal – assuming the fearsome An Niseagh is not exploring this possible outlet from her Loch Ness home and rears up to frighten the driver and stop the train – you come to the first stop at Dingwall – an old name of Norse origin. Here the track branches away from the northern Thurso route and starts its climb to Achterneed, for many years station for nearby Strathpeffer, spa resort of Victorian days. The Strath once boasted its own railway station and still enjoys popularity as a centre for a regular Highland Gathering.

Beyond Achterneed, itself now closed, the railway enters a deep cutting under the lower slopes of Little Wyvis (and out of sight but just north of where I used to live) to emerge on the other side above Rogie Falls, a popular local spot where salmon could be watched leaping upstream. After Loch Garve some of the scenery has been modified by hydro-electric works, but by and large the effect has been minimal. Unlike some of the conspicuous hydro-electric works such as the Loch Sloy scheme near the top end of Loch Lomond (which you pass on the Glasgow–Mallaig run), those in Ross-shire have been more carefully integrated. At Lochluichart, west of Garve, realignment of the railway gave enhanced views, while at the nearby power station on the Conon river the Hydro Board built special salmon ladders to enable fish to reach their spawning grounds in the upper reaches. So genuinely concerned about preserving scenery were the electricity people at that time that when a new hydro-electric power station was to be built on the eastern shore of Loch Maree under the majestic Slioch mountain, they agreed to put the line underground from the power station up to where it would be behind the ridge and out of sight of the tourist road on the opposite shore. Underground power lines are commonplace in residential areas – but this was a 250,000 Volt national grid line!

Apart from a somewhat bleak stretch across open moorland between Achanalt and Glencarron (though even that is livened by a number of small lochs) the scenery of the Kyle line is in my view unsurpassed for its beauty and variety. It is friendly scenery, its magnificence tempered to a human scale. A magnificent view is had of peaks and a gorge to the north just to the west of Achnashellach, but the landscape does not intimidate, as some of the wilder and grander mountain and gorge scenes found in the European Alps do.

After Glencarron (the small platform there long since closed) you reach Lochcarron and the track wends along its shores to Stromeferry. Then follow the picture postcard views of the village of Plockton, seen across the water, before you enter the final winding cuttings to come out at Kyle of Lochalsh with the Isle of Skye just a stone's throw across the water.

In the 1960s there was a proposal to close this line. I attended a public inquiry by what was called the Transport Users Consultative Committee. The proposal fell through, mainly I think because the road alternative was unsuitable but it could have been partly through the strength of the public opposition. I remember the chairman saying to the BR representative when the case was nearing its end that he did not think he had heard a weaker case in any of the previous hearings he had attended.

Rail closures were not the only subject of public inquiries I attended in that area. When I was County Planning Officer for Ross and Cromarty there was a crofter who wished to build a house on his croft. The site happened to be on a 'raised beach' area of flattish ground above and forming the background to the village. The existing houses were strung along the landward side of the main street just above the water line. A house on the land above would have stood out like a sore thumb, and the Council refused permission. Other land could be made available for the crofter's house. It was nearly all owned by the National Trust, who were equally concerned to preserve the landscape.

The Inquiry lasted three days. The crofter pleaded that if he could not build where he and his young wife wanted they would have to emigrate to Australia. As planning officer I was seen as the villain of the piece but the Council stood by me and the crofter's pleas did not sway the government reporter.

Subsequently he built his house in a lovely spot down in the village right on the edge of the loch and only a stone's throw from his croft. He was delighted with it and had no need to emigrate, but shortly after that I did, and I seem to remember a farewell bottle of whisky being enjoyed together on my last visit to Plockton.

The Kyle line is not the only one for memorable scenery. The West Highland line to Mallaig and the Oban branch are also noteworthy and still accessible. There are great views over the Gareloch from the bridge just after Garelochhead not long after leaving Glasgow, and then of Loch Goil and Loch Long before the train climbs away up the side of the 'brae' and crosses over to Loch Lomond side.

There, as you would expect, are many fine views of the 'bonnie bonnie banks', with the wooded lower slopes, and the mountains – Ben Lomond, Beinn a Choin and Beinn Chabhair – beyond. Further on lies the magnificent pristine unspoiled country of Rannoch Moor and after Fort William the scenery all the way to Mallaig is unsurpassed, Loch Eil, Shiel Water and Prince Charles' Monument, then by Loch Ailort and Loch Morar to the sea – the iron 'Road to the Isles'. Much the same applies to the route to Oban, past lovely Loch Awe and through the Pass of Brander; water, rivers, mountains and mists – unforgettable from a moving train especially when it has a buffet car. The loco on the Oban train was a reminder of more highland songs: it was named *Jimmy Shand* after Scotland's best known folk band leader.

There were still some scenic routes in other unspoiled, or little changed, parts of Britain. The rail network of Wales, like that of the Scottish Highlands, had remained virtually unchanged from 1971 to 1991, nearly all the actual closures having been carried out in the first few years after the Beeching Report. Forty percent (467 out of 1153 km) of major Welsh rail routes outside the South Wales coalfield area disappeared during that time.

Here and there in Wales were little privately run narrow gauge lines, but mostly only accessible by road which from my point of view ruled them out of consideration. In the limited time available I wanted to see what was left, for better or for worse, of the main system. That there had been no closures for 20 years was not for lack of trying on the part of BR. The Mid-Wales line, for example, between Craven Arms and Swansea, which includes the marvellous stone single track bridge at Knucklas just before the Llangynllo tunnel, looking like a Brunel design with turrets at each end, had been proposed for closure twice, in 1972 and again in 1977. Its survival today is proof that local determination can sometimes vanquish the destroyers.

There was, surprisingly, one British Railways route still operated with steam in the west of Wales, between Aberystwyth and Devil's Bridge. It was also BR's only narrow gauge service. Since it traversed the scenic Rheidol Valley it was natural I should wish to include it in my visit. This proved easier said than done.

To reach the main line terminal at Aberystwyth in the first place required a journey right across mid-Wales from Shrewsbury. There was no way in from the south, the former Great Western line from Carmarthen having gone in the '60s and the Caernarvon link from Afon Wen to Menai Bridge (with its branch to Llanberis and the Snowdon Mountain Railway) also having gone; the only way out to the north was up the coast past Harlech Castle to the privately owned Ffestiniog Railway and thence down to Llandudno on a surviving BR North Wales branch.

Thus I went in from Shrewsbury, finding to my surprise the diesel set was one of the older Metro-Cammel ones and included a comfortable first class section but no longer marked as such. There was also catering on this train, but privately run by a volunteer organisation. This rather showed BR in a poor light. Further north, as I found on my return from Aberystwyth, the Ffestiniog narrow gauge private railway not only operated its own buffet cars but also had draught beer in them, something never thought of by British Rail or its miserable 'Passenger Fare' catering subsidiary in their wildest dreams.

The "Great Little Trains of Wales", as a popular documentary TV series called them, seemed to outclass the not-so-great 'Big Trains of Wales'.

On reaching Aberystwyth I was in for a disappointment, not having obtained a "control ticket". The train was full anyway, they told me. But there had been no warning; no mention of this when I had asked the times of trains, nor did the BR timetable say anything about it. This was rather surprising because the BR timetables of the time were quite informative. Since 1985 or before they had included information and instructions in more than one language – French and German as well as English – a welcome change from earlier times when if people spoke no English they were beneath notice.

But at Aberystwyth there was not even a notice up on the station, not even in Welsh, let alone German or French, about control tickets being needed for every train. They were only available half an hour before departure, yet there was nothing to warn the passenger until it was too late. Could I have reserved in advance? I asked. No, that was not possible. The timetable said the railway might put extra trains on in peak periods, but there were none.

At least the Chief Clerk gave me back the 60p I had paid for luggage which I no longer needed to leave at the station and I went over the road to the pub to await the next train back while musing on the waywardness of BR. It seemed a funny way to run a railway.

On my most recent return in 1992 I arrived in Britain by air from Australia and at first seemed unconscious of the cold, going straight off to Peterborough by train to say hello to the Thomas Cook people. Next day there was a weather change. It was colder, wet and windy. Also, the delayed action of jet lag hit me.

I was staying on a barge on a canal near Southall, Middlesex with my nephew, and took the train again to Peterborough, arriving about midday. Crossing to the bus station I realised I could not face the cold wind any more, so turned tail straight back to the station for the next InterCity to London. There, having time to kill, I opted for a trip to Brighton – the south coast of Britain being potentially warmer. At Brighton I was reluctant to venture beyond the station, and seeing a fast train with buffet car about to depart for London Bridge I returned from whence I had come, taking the Underground back to Kings Cross to await my nephew in the warmth of the station bar.

I found one good thing about Britrail passes in comparison with the Eurailpass. The latter expires at midnight on its last day of validity. But with a Britrail Pass you could finish the journey on any train on which you started that day. This was especially useful if you had a flexipass which could be used on odd days. For example, on one day, after travelling around, you might take an overnight train leaving at, say, ten at night, and arriving somewhere at eight in the morning. Provided you did no more rail travel on the day of arrival it would not count as a day of ticket use. By doing the same thing a few times you could increase considerably the value of your pass.

This was of little use to me, since I rarely stopped in any place long without going somewhere else by train. I also did less overnight travel than in Europe. One reason for this was that in Britain the choice was between sitting up or taking an expensive sleeper. The popular European couchette never took on in Britain. Nor did the seats in compartments fold down and slide forward to meet those opposite so that you could lie down even if the train was crowded. You needed the full width of a compartment in Britain. Another reason was the pragmatic, or economic, one of having more friends and relations in Britain with whom I could stay a night, and the third reason was that there remained fewer overnight trains, with or without sleeping accommodation.

For example, no trains ran south from Edinburgh overnight on the East Coast Main Line, there were no sleeping car trains serving Newcastle, Sunderland, Durham, or York, and since 1992 the sleepers from Stranraer, Barrow-in-Furness, Holyhead and Fishguard have all disappeared.

But one encouraging sign on revisiting BR was the number of cross-country trains linking places that, so far as I know, would never have been linked by direct services before – at least not on a regular timetabled basis. Examples were Glasgow to Newcastle via Carlisle, Newcastle to Girvan, Middlesbrough to Carlisle, Blackpool to Cambridge, Liverpool to Middlesbrough, Brighton to Milford Haven, Manchester and Liverpool to Brighton and Dover and, in an amazing latterday discovery of the versatility of the greater London network, trains from Cardiff to Waterloo and Edinburgh to Paddington! The opening of the Channel Tunnel has now brought trains to Waterloo even from the BR East Coast Main Line.

Except on the premium InterCity services, catering services in Britain since the 1980s have been a disappointment. At one stage BR refused even to indicate in their timetables whether a train carried a buffet or restaurant car. This has since been remedied – how could anyone expect people to use facilities they did not know were there? However, cross-country trains and almost all trains at weekends and holiday times can be barren of sustenance.

The need of passengers for substantial fare when travelling merits a chapter by itself.

Sortie at Waterloo – the new *Eurostar* train for 'Chunnel' travellers. (BTA)

Chapter 12

Food for Thought

"For I was hungry and you gave me no food. I was thirsty and you gave me no drink"
— Matthew 25:42 RSV

"Dinner in the diner, nothing could be finer" went the words of *Chattanooga Choo Choo*. But is it "Food, glorious food!" as another song put it, or Railway Meat Pie? This is now promoted in Australia as a gourmet choice and well worth trying at least as a snack.

In their well-known *Eurail Guide*, K.S. Turpin and M.L. Saltzman warn that "food in train dining cars is expensive, and the choice is

Welcome to the Stuart Restaurant on *The Ghan*. (Australian National)

limited". Paul Theroux, in *The Kingdom by the Sea*, describes an excellent though "overpriced" four course lunch with waiter service in a British Railways restaurant car "with tables set for eighteen", in which he was the only customer.

Criticism of railway food is not new. That great railway engineer Isambard Kingdom Brunel personally complained to the caterer at Swindon about the coffee tasting of "bad roasted corn". In 1869 novelist Anthony Trollope condemned the railway sandwich as a "real disgrace". Two of the poorest three course meals I have ever had were, one, on the *Flying Scotsman* in England at the end of World War II; and the other in 1974 on Queensland's *Sunlander* which consisted of reconstituted potatoes, tinned peas and semi-rancid half-cooked bacon with the rind still on. Only the eggs were palatable. But I have enjoyed excellent meals on trains, from the gourmet dishes of Spain's *Catalan Talgo* to the fresh 'home roasted' lamb and full flavoured but tender steak of Western Beef you could once get on Queensland inland trains. The cheese and greens platter offered at the conclusion of the evening meal on the short-lived *Alice* in New South Wales could not be faulted, nor can the succulent array of prawns, oysters and crab comprising the 'Pacific Coast Seafood Platter' frequently offered on the *Queenslander* between Brisbane and Cairns.

Yet what was once the expectation of every traveller is becoming the exception – hence the resurrection of the famous railway pie. Snack foods are in: full dining car service is regrettably on the way out – or is it?

A cartoon in wartime Britain depicted a traveller walking through the corridor of a train. He reaches the last coach, steps through the concertina connection (which has been carelessly left open at the end) and out onto the track. The caption, his remark on falling to the ground, is, "Dammit, no dining car again!"

This could be true of quite a few rail journeys anywhere in the world and the traveller may well be disappointed if the timetable is not carefully consulted first. It is no good simply expecting that a train, because it takes a long time on a journey, will have provision for meals on board, or that because one of the carriages is marked 'buffet' or 'snack bar' there will be anyone in attendance and any food for sale.

A surprising number of long distance trains have no dining car or even a buffet. A survey in 1990 of all the trains listed in the International section of the *Thomas Cook European Timetable* showed that in any one week, out of 329 inter-city trips lasting over 16 hours, 35 or just over 10 percent had no advertised refreshment facility. That is not to say that some provision for refreshment might not have been made, either by the sporadic appearance of a trolley or by food vendors materialising on the platform when the trains stopped for any length of time at a station.

Passengers occupying first class sleeping berths can usually obtain at least a continental breakfast on overnight trains of long journey duration, but some long distance day trains have little to offer, especially some that cross frontiers. Railway systems seem to put on their best mainly for trains within their own borders. I was surprised to find in 1985 that a named train, the *Gondoliere*, starting its 11-hour journey to Wien from Venezia in Italy at 7.00, carried only a 'minibar' instead of the usual full restaurant car typical of Austrian railways.

Refreshment services on trains began in the USA, when George M. Pullman conceived the particular style of luxury service known to this day by his name. The first regular dining car was introduced in Britain in 1879 and since then restaurant and buffet cars have increasingly replaced the refreshment stops which provided such uncivilised eating conditions, delayed the trains, and militated against their advertised advantage of speedy travel.

In New Zealand even as recently as 1988, unlicensed refreshment room stops were the only relief from famine or thirst offered on train journeys between Christchurch and Picton (six hours) and between Wellington and Gisborne (10 hours). At one time NZ Rail used to have refreshment stops at pubs but abandoned the practice because the trains were kept waiting for passengers.

"Didn't you hear the whistle?" the guard would ask when trying to round up his charges.
"Never heard a thing," they would lie.
"Are you coming on this train or not?".
In 1985 the train staff rang a bell a few times before the train's departure but since the tearooms were all 'dry' it was hardly necessary. They were not places where anyone would want to stay. I am glad to note that on-board catering has been the regime on all long distance trains in New Zealand since 1988.

Travelling refreshment rooms and bars are a response to public demand. Market research has confirmed this response to have been well-founded. A "significant proportion of medium and long distance InterCity passengers expect some form of on-train full meal or buffet service" said Brian Perren in the magazine *Modern Railways* in 1978. Dr A Giesl-Gieslingen in the November 1981 *Railway Gazette International* confirmed this by Austrian experience: "ÖBB recognised that full dining car service is not a paying proposition, but considers it an essential adjunct to inter-city rail travel".

Numerous complaints, he said, had been received from disappointed patrons when self-service 'Quick-Pik' cars had replaced full dining cars on some services to and from Germany.

Railway catering generally is far from perfect. On some trains it has long been reminiscent of the sort of food you would expect at a transport cafe: not bad, but nothing to write home about.

British Rail (BR) boasted recently of their "Great English Breakfast", a meal offered in restaurant cars (and at station refreshment rooms) at various prices; the quality varying in proportion. Best was the full works (bacon, sausage, egg, mushrooms, fried potatoes, etc.) on trains like the *Manchester Pullman* at typical hotel prices, with the mandatory addition of a tip. According to BR figures, over half a million such breakfasts a year are sold on board InterCity trains. The BR 'continental breakfast' is just over half the price, but you have to be careful when ordering. The time-honoured principle that the customer is always right

FOOD FOR THOUGHT

may not apply on the railways of Britain.

On one occasion on the *Manchester Pullman* I found the conductor to be an insolent pig. I believe a Pullman menu should always include à la carte as well as table d'hôte meals but since the choice was either continental or full British Breakfast, I opted for the latter. For 'starters' I chose fruit juice. Following this the conductor brought the main course.

"What about the cereal?" I asked.

"You didn't ask for it," he replied.

I pointed out it was on the menu and I had not been asked whether or what kind of cereal I wanted.

"You should ask for what you want at the beginning," he said. Needless to add, this attendant got the tip he deserved – zilch.

Nevertheless I have found railway train staff generally, even in restaurant cars, and in Britain too, to be pleasant and courteous, but two or three really bad examples can give the breed a bad name.

Whether on BR or elsewhere things are not quite as bad as painted by author Ian Fleming in *For Your Eyes Only* where hero James Bond takes the train:

"The best train from Rome to Venice is the Laguna Express [i.e. *Freccia della Laguna*] that leaves every day at midday ... the Laguna is a smart, streamlined affair that looks and sounds more luxurious than it is. The seats are made for small Italians and the restaurant car staff suffer from the disease that afflicts their brethren in the great trains all over the world – a genuine loathing for the modern traveller and particularly for the foreigner."

Most of Britain's HST services have a buffet where full restaurant fare is not offered, but the queues of passengers can stretch through adjoining coaches, and service may finish an hour or more before the final destination. While it is true that there is usually some form of catering on all BR InterCity services this may at times be only from a mobile trolley.

British Rail publicity asserts that more on-board refreshment is provided in Britain than in the rest of Europe. Ernest Turner, in his book tracing *The Shocking History of Advertising*, shows that exaggeration has always been part of the advertiser's art. BR's Intercity magazine of May 1992 specifically stated that their On-Board Services operated 250 restaurant and 1000 buffets daily: "more than the rest of Western Europe's railways put together", a boast that unfortunately was not supported by the facts. It would be true that Britain had more restaurant and buffet services than any other single country but as for Western Europe, there were at that time at least 1305 daily trains with restaurant or buffet service without counting any in Spain, Belgium, Holland, or Italy. If the former Deutsche Reichsbahn services of the then newly united eastern part of Germany were counted, there were 788 restaurant and buffet trains daily in or through Germany alone. And with a big difference, that by and large the European services were maintained at weekends and throughout the journeys.

At weekends in Britain the traveller was well advised to carry emergency supplies. Apart from the irritation of finding that advertised catering services were simply not available or were less than advertised (especially at weekends) a major disincentive was the failure to have them open during extensive periods of travel. I give some examples:

On 5 August 1985 the 17.00 Euston to Manchester train's buffet opened about 17.15 but no announcement was made of it. The "last final call" for buffet orders was announced at 18.41, about an hour before the final destination. The dining car was also open but only for full four-course meals with very limited choice of fare. This was a far cry from the standards set by former restaurant cars of the London Midland region (formerly LMS); the 'Traveller's Fare' regime did much to damage BR's reputation for meals on wheels.

On 6 August 1985 the IC 125 buffet was already closed and locked when the train came into Macclesfield, on time, at 15.38. The catering staff were seen calmly reclining in comfortable seats, finished work for the day. Granted that the buffet had been attached to the train four hours earlier at Exeter, there was still almost half an hour to go before its

FOOD FOR THOUGHT

Manchester destination. Had it just been about to close at Macclesfield that could have been seen as reasonable but by the look of things the shutters must have been put up not long after Birmingham.

At 20.19 on 25 October 1985 the buffet of the 18.30 out of Euston was announced as "now closed and will not reopen" when the train was still 50 miles (80 km) away from its Manchester destination. The dining car was full and would be having no more sittings, although its opening time had never been announced. I assumed that the regular passengers, if any, knew about it and went straight to it at Euston.

On 27 October 1985 on the 11.00 Kings Cross to Edinburgh HST, it was announced at 11.16 that the buffet would open in about 20 minutes time, that is, 35 minutes after departure. By that time there were the usual long queues for the inadequate catering provision at weekends, this being a Sunday.

Travelling south one day on the *Flying Scotsman* I noticed the queues extending out from the buffet car through two entire coaches and they remained like that all the way from Newcastle to south of Darlington. The train was packed.

On 4 August 1985 the buffet of a Birmingham to Glasgow train was already closed when the train reached Carlisle – or perhaps it had never been open because it was a Sunday. There was no buffet on the 17.45 Carlisle to Glasgow (ex Euston) on the same day, although one was advertised, nor was there a buffet on the 17.30 Carlisle–Euston (ex-Glasgow at 16.05).

One interesting minor point was that 'Traveller's Fare' management did not see fit to give their on-train catering staff a cash 'float'. To me, this told its own story.

Even worse than Travellers Fare was an innovation I first noted in Scotland. In place of a BR refreshment room, was a joint called 'Casey Jones'. Granted Casey Jones was a railwayman but he had nothing to do with Scotland, nor with railway catering unless he was the one who invented the 'firebox grilled breakfast' experienced by Ronald Ransom in his youth and described in the *Railway Magazine* of March 1980. The article also quotes the following recipe produced by the then Catering Manager of the former Great Central Railway for a Tourist Board 'Taste of England' promotion:

Footplate Fry-Up (serves two)

Ingredients: 4 eggs, 4 rashers of English bacon, 4 sausages, 2 tomatoes (halved), 2 thick slices of white bread, 6-8 oz. of lard (dependent on size of shovel)

Equipment: 1 fireman's shovel   1 steam locomotive

Method: Prepare shovel by scrubbing down thoroughly, using slacking pipe from injector. Ensure blower is almost closed. Melt lard on shovel. Place ingredients in melted fat. Fry in a slow to medium firebox (800 deg. F) for 1½ to 2 min. or until whites of eggs have begun to brown, holding shovel well down towards back of firebox. If eggs are preferred without coal dust flavour, they may be cooked separately. After ensuring shells are sound, wrap in cloth, tie to injector overflow pipe and turn on steam valve. Cook for 3-4 min. as required.

Alas, it is hard to find a working steam engine these days, so this great culinary treat must remain an experience known only to the favoured few. At the 'Casey Jones' catering outlet the food was appalling and the coffee worse. One was bombarded all the time with a really awful pop song racket.

By 1992 under the newly formed 'On-Board Services' division of BR a new name replaced Travellers Fare, at least in the mini-buffets carried on some trains. 'Snack on the Track', they called it – and probably it was no more popular with British travellers than the Quick-Pik restaurant cars of Germany were with European travellers. I think

FOOD FOR THOUGHT

it is important, if railways want a good image, not only that they offer a good service – and a continuous service – but that they adopt an attractive name. 'Snack on the Track', like the 'Food bar' cars of Queensland Rail (QR) and the 'Cafeteria' cars they had in Britain years ago are not slogans nearly as likely to bring in eager patrons as are names like 'dining car', 'the Coral Cay (or whatever) Restaurant', 'bistro' or even 'griddle car'.

In Western Europe the standard of train food varies according to country and train. I have usually found there to be a choice between simple à la carte snacks and a full meal. Popular 'business' trains in Switzerland, France, Austria, Germany and elsewhere still feature full meal service at tables – as they do in Britain on weekdays.

But if the Swiss railways, for example, can still provide proper restaurant car services on Sundays why cannot BR do the same? Are Britons not supposed to eat at weekends?

To be fair to BR, one of their difficulties is the penalty payment they evidently have to make to catering staff at weekends – hence little or no service. But this is a problem of the hospitality industry the world over. Others manage to get round it: catering on trains does not vanish at weekends in Europe or even in Australia, although tourist hotels certainly face problems. Surely there are minds capable of working out a sensible system where they pay an appropriate rate for the job irrespective of the time of day or day of week.

In Switzerland I found the restaurant cars particularly good, and the DSG company in West Germany also did well with its catering. It was more consistent and, with the exception of the breakfasts, beat the British and also the Italian catering easily.

In the dining cars of Deutsche Bundesbahn (DB) I found beautiful steaks with mushroom on the menu, although at first the name 'Toast Mozart' did not catch the eye. The service on their inter-regional trains was also excellent. The catering vehicle was called a bistro bar; it was like a café-cum-pub, with tables on different levels and seats informally arranged. The menu was chalked up on a board, and the place decorated with pot plants.

Gulaschsuppe and *Nürnburger Bratwurst* were among the hot dishes available. You placed your order at the bar and an attendant brought it to your seat when ready. The red wine was good, too. There was a public telephone kept at the bar. In these trains the first class carriages were superb. A non-smoking compartment I found on IR 2074 had only four seats, with ample luggage space, curtains, and a table convertible to an extra seat for a child. There were occasional seats in the corridor as well and the floor was carpeted throughout. A train like this, running from Fulda through Hamburg to Flensburg was the DB equivalent of something like a BR Liverpool–Newcastle regional express, a six hour rather than the latter's four hour journey but far superior.

Especially attractive is the idea of going along for something as and when you like, whether just a bottle of wine, a snack, or a full meal.

Some of the dining cars in France are now let out to a special catering organisation, Servirail, which offers gourmet meals in the best French tradition at a price you cannot afford. But on the TGV there is no dining car. The best they offer is a pre-ordered tray meal, airline style, and not very much better than what you would be served on an aircraft (albeit in first or business class) but there is also a buffet bar with tasty (and more temptingly priced) snacks.

In Denmark the catering on inter-city trains is nothing special, although in first class you have complimentary coffee and newspapers as well as mineral water. The catering on the boats is much better, and reasonably priced, so since most of the trains go by sea part of the way, the traveller is well catered for when leaving the train carriage to enjoy the amenities of the ferry. The ferries also accept all credit cards which the trains do not unless they are issued by a Danish bank.

All major credit cards are acceptable on SJ in Sweden. The X-2000 seats are spacious (as are seats on the older Swedish expresses), equipped with armrests, music socket and complimentary headphones as in aircraft, and overhead light switch. Tea, coffee and mineral water are complimentary. The tables have folding flaps for ease of ingress and egress and the meal, attractive and nourishing though not outstanding, is included in the fare. In the newer sleeping cars, which have individual showers and were meant to have radios but someone with access to a key stole them all, the passenger finds a tucker-box full of goodies: a large French roll filled with ham, cheese and salad, a carton of orange juice and a can of mineral water. A can of beer or a small bottle of wine would have been a welcome addition! There was also a breakfast thrown in on arrival at Stockholm station.

Particularly commendable is the variety of hot and cold snacks available on some of the mini-diners on the ÖBB Austrian system. On the Stainach Irdning–Attnang Puchheim line, for example, one attendant would serve a four car trainset. These restaurant cars had 17 seats, yet the steward coped with a menu of six different hot snacks, five cold snacks, four different kinds of soup (including their superb *Leberknödel*) and an assortment of supplementary items, plus wine, beer, spirits and other beverages.

"No trouble," said the steward. This friendly service coupled with good food made BR's Travellers Fare look sick by comparison.

On the Pustertal approaching Lienz the restaurant car crew were busy having their own meal, an unidentified but appetising-smelling stew with lashings of Knödel in it. Yet they still broke off to serve any passenger seeking refreshment, even if just wanting a beer. I was most impressed. The Austrian crew changed over for the return working at Lienz while the train carried on into Italy sans refreshment.

Austrian restaurant cars are an example of what restaurant cars used to be and ought still to be. Usually open throughout the journey, they offer service with a smile. Patrons can come and go at almost any time and choose from an à la carte menu anything from a full meal to just a drink. Half bottles of local wine are there on the table to tempt you. They will accept all the usual credit cards, Diners Club, Amex, Mastercard, and a host of local European ones, and even foreign money at current rates of exchange. The atmosphere is relaxed. There is no rush to make you pay or to consume and get out, yet everyone is served efficiently.

There is only one snag, and not peculiar to Austria. It says something on the menu about 'service' being included or not. This probably means sometimes you may be expected to tip. Only once was I ever asked for it but after I showed my ignorance of the language and kept pointing at the price list and the money I was proffering to cover it the attendant gave up with a shrug of despair.

Yet, in my judgment, the best of all catering in Western Europe, as far as normal scheduled trains are concerned, were the main meals on the Spanish *Talgo* trains and on the *Linha do Norte* in Portugal. Rich soup, delicious sautéed medallions of tender steak in sauce, a half bottle of wine, sweet, fresh fruit, coffee and brandy, with impeccable service.

The price? For this in 1985 on the *Tejo* (20.15 ex Lisboa) I paid the equivalent of only $A 12 including tip. But be careful in Portugal: you can pay a great deal more in a restaurant, especially if you ask for prawns and especially if you go down to the Allgarve district on the south coast.

In Australia it would be difficult to imagine interstate or long distance trains between major cities like Brisbane, Sydney and Melbourne without a restaurant car – unless of course you were one of the bureaucrats in New South Wales who thought they knew better and managed to replace all the dining cars with takeaway buffets by 1994.

In terms of price, and more importantly value for money, Australian on-train catering compares reasonably well with food at restaurants and cafés. The variety is not great but exceeds what the airlines can offer, i.e. Hobson's choice. Top of the range in dining car menus are those on the *Queenslander*. Lunch offers choice of soup or two appetisers (e.g. terrine and salad or curried prawns one day; fruit compote or ravioli another), four main courses and three desserts, followed by coffee or tea. The dinner menu has soup, choice from three entrees, four main courses, four desserts or cheese and fruit, again with coffee or tea plus after dinner mints. Only an epicure or a complete berk could fault such delightful offerings as the *Queenslander*'s Emerald Terrine, of pork and chicken with biscuits and continental salad, or the Pacific Coast Seafood Platter of king prawns, oysters and sand crabs (or, if you are lucky, Moreton Bay Bugs). Reef Fish Yeppoon, Lamb Torquay (rolled loin stuffed with raisins, herbs and Queensland bush nuts), and Sunshine Salad of cold meats, smoked ham and chicken are other delicacies, to say nothing of the tantalising Cherry Pancakes Cooroy or the Redlands Romanoff – fresh strawberries liqueured and served with cream. Even the breakfast menu includes a bowl of tropical and other fruit – cantaloupe, pineapple, banana, kiwi fruit, strawberries. It approaches *Orient Express* standards – and at a far lower price. With all this and more, it would perhaps be churlish to question the difference between Capricorn Grill (lunch menu 1) and Fitzroy Fillet (lunch menu 2), the descriptions of which were identical. Some advertising licence has to be allowed! As well, menus change from time to time and some of these dishes may now have different names or be replaced by others which will usually be equally interesting.

So enticing and generous are the meals on the *Queenslander* that one lady who could not finish it all asked for a 'doggie bag'. This practice is well developed in restaurants in Australia and the United States, when people want to keep some tasty leftovers for subsequent re-heating for a meal at home – whether they have a dog or not – but it was the first and only time I have ever heard anyone ask for one on a train.

The meals on the *Ghan* of Australian National also merit high marks. There is never any shortage. If passengers want another helping, or even a different and additional course, then, as on an ocean cruise they have only to ask.

Until recently, when some of the railways contracted out their catering to airline companies, breakfasts on Australian trains were usually superb, whether on the *Ghan*, the *Indian Pacific*, or even the friendly old *Westlander* out west of the Darling Downs. You can still nearly always get eggs of some kind with bacon, sausage or even lamb chops or steak; these are part of the traditional Aussie breakfast which can hold its own against the best on BR any day or for that matter, Amtrak or the Wagon-Lits Company of Europe.

However, trying to eat bacon and eggs from a plastic plate in a high-sided cardboard tray perched on your lap or on a folding, swinging and sometimes tilting mini-table, as on the XPT, is difficult. Possibly the greatest of many mistakes made by the State Rail Authority of New South Wales when they introduced the XPT was in the catering area. Other blunders like having no sleepers or couchettes on overnight trains have been rectified to some degree.

Amtrak's best dinner menu would probably be that on the *Southwest Chief* (Chicago–Kansas City–Los Angeles). At least their publicity would have you believe so. It is admittedly inferior to what it was before the Reagan Administration cut railway funding, but it is still good, especially at dinner. Typical à la carte fare includes oven baked half chicken, the day's seafood catch (where they catch it out there in the Rockies is a mystery), a select cut of beef, grilled New York strip steak, vegetarian lasagna, or the chef's speciality, which when I travelled on it was Spanish chicken, and excellent. They also offer hamburger as a main dish. These are not made on the train but come in packs and some are better than others. That on the *Southwest Chief* was so good it made me realise why, in contrast to what people have served up to them as hamburger in most other countries (including some well-known chain restaurants) the Americans are so fond of this particular dish.

Amtrak dining cars usually have set hours of service but no specified sittings, but the whole effort remains just that little bit spoiled by the lack of proper crockery. Sometimes, too, and a fault by no means confined to Amtrak, pre-cooked or partly cooked dishes reheated in the microwave would not be heated thoroughly – or overheated to the point of mouth-scalding discomfort. This was not a problem with hot drinks. One practical innovation I found on Amtrak was the little slit in the lid of takeaway coffee cups which greatly reduced the risk of spilling hot liquid from the top of an opened cup when the train lurched.

One of the great attractions of eating meals on trains is the ability to

FOOD FOR THOUGHT

look out of the window at the passing scenery between mouthfuls; it can make a modest repast seem like a banquet. It is an advantage the railways should make every effort to exploit. When 'Tavern Cars' were introduced on main lines in England – with no windows to look out of, these were one of the great non-success stories of BR passenger developments.

Amfleet cars in the USA have rather small and often dirty windows. I suspect they are made of perspex rather than glass, in which case this would be the cause. It was noticeable particularly in the observation cars where the windows appeared double glazed.

Food on American trains is reasonably cheap, but I encountered one old-timer on a train up in Oregon State who was far from happy. He wanted a cheeseburger, but these were available, according to the steward, with salad or some other accompaniment only as a 'meal' in the diner after 12 o'clock noon.

"This is baloney," he said. "Just so you can charge $4.50 for them!"

"Not so," said the steward. "This is not a lounge car nor is it on *The Chief*. It operates as a diner".

"Baloney," repeated the old timer. "I was travelling on this train before you were born".

But the poor fellow still did not get his cheeseburger, and he had disappeared by the time my lunch came. I opted for the 'full works' but later sought just soup and crackers for an evening meal. This was not to be; I faced the same problem: a full meal or nothing. The main course, I later learned, was halibut and I had cause to regret a decision to postpone dinner until my intended destination of Vancouver (Oregon, not Canada). There, to my disappointment, the place I was booked in, Inn on the Wharf – which had sounded like a nice budget-priced dockland pub – turned out to be an up-market joint with rip-off prices to match.

This fault of Amtrak catering – having to go for the 'full works' in a dining car is found equally in Britain and in Australia, but is rare in Europe where you order what you want and pay for what you get.

Another curiosity of Amtrak was that the dinner menu did not include soup, whereas the lunch menu did. But the supper basket in the sleeping car merited top marks. Included with the 'accommodation supplement' (berth fee) this contained:

1 quarter bottle of French white wine
1 packet Danish pumperknickel black bread
1 packet Nabisco Waverley wafers (salt coated biscuits)
1 tin Grissini breadsticks
1 packet honey roasted potatoes (a bit like potato crisps)
1 container of "Smoky" pasteurised cheese spread
1 mini Bonbel semisoft cheese [Bel paese, I think]
1 mint wafer sweet
plastic wine glass, plastic knife and paper napkin

It has long been one of the criticisms of travel in the USA that when the train crossed certain frontiers, your drink was snatched from under your nose lest you unwittingly broke the law. You cannot drink in forbidden territory even though the train may not stop there at all. But on Amtrak trains it is not really all that bad. They do give you timely warning of approaching danger in the form of a 'dry' area and of the fact that you are not allowed to drink there – at least not in the buffet or diner. Presumably you can consume what you like in your own sleeping compartment. I found no warning notice enclosed with my supper basket and who would be there to check what passengers did in the privacy of their own 'accommodation'?

The 'dry' counties are little more than an inconvenience to residents as well as tourists since there is nothing to stop people bringing in drinks from elsewhere. In fact, they boost businesses in adjoining areas. Some of these could well be owned by the wowsers who invented the dry areas – since the overriding consideration in the USA always seems to be money and the making of it.

Although British trains are not subject to local variations in the licensing laws, BR themselves have imposed restrictions on certain trains and at certain times. I found warnings at Aberdeen one Saturday. "No alcohol to be taken on train," it was announced. This was the day of a big football match and this could cause trouble. Football matches in England, too, are not immune from hooliganism. I found the refreshment room and bar on York station closed one Saturday for the same reason, yet it was inconsistent with reality in that there were no crowds and no signs of trouble. One could still buy drinks at an off-licence just down the road and they were also available on the northbound train. Britain still has to come of age in its drinking laws. Some attitudes are still reminiscent of Australia in the 'six o' clock swill' days or America under prohibition. Oddly enough Scotland, which in my younger days was more restrictive than England, has now moved further to liberalisation.

By and large in most countries the catering staff interpret whatever regulations there are reasonably flexibly, on the grounds that what the head office desk-wallahs don't know they won't grieve about.

Although York station bar proved 'dry' that day, an obliging steward in the buffet of the *Cleveland Executive* found a drink for a thirsty passenger while the train was standing in the station, and this even though the steward was getting off there with only four minutes to go. It is good to report such examples of patron care, rare though they may be.

In Britain the licensing laws which apply to premises do not and have never covered moving trains (or buses or boats for that matter), and the Railways can make their own arrangements. It was always one of the delights of BR (and its predecessors) that whenever the utterly ridiculous licensing laws of that country prohibited drink, you could hop on a train with a buffet car and be served. Drink starved Welshmen on a Sunday, when that rain-sodden land was 'dry', have even been known to take a day season ticket on the narrow gauge Ffestiniog railway, where they could drink all day.

A curiosity in New Zealand which, like Australia, imported some of the worst as well as the best British habits, was that the hostess could only serve drinks to seats in 'smoking' carriages. I found this on the *Southerner* in 1985 as I did some 10 years previously on the former *Endeavour*. I could not understand why. But at least there was a licensed buffet where all could get drinks. Was the idea to keep smokers out of the eating area? If so, a good idea, but NZ Railways had a tendency to use smoking and non-smoking carriages interchangeably. Non-smoking coaches would have conspicuous ash trays and a lingering smell of tobacco smoke.

Although wine was nominally available the New Zealand trains were not well stocked. Miniature sherry, a local brand, was all the *Endeavour* could offer in 1974. Eleven years later, on the *Southerner*, when the wine ran out on the southbound trip the hostess said there should be 10 bottles loaded on the train at Invercargill for the return trip. "I'll pack one in my luggage just in case", I replied, unable as always to resist a pun.

On another trip I sought a drink at 18.04, 41 minutes before the train's destination. "Oh, sorry, we're finished now - all the stocks are done". They were quite apologetic but why hadn't they announced it? I could wait 40 minutes without a drink but it is the principle of the thing that matters. A clear "Last orders please: we will be closing in 10 minutes" would avoid all, or most of, any disappointment or irritation.

On the *Southerner* drinks could be taken to any seat or consumed at the buffet but on the *Northerner* drinks were allowed in the buffet only: the law prohibited taking them to one's seat. On the North Island's *Silver Fern*, however, drinks were served at all seats. Were these distinctions due to liquor laws or a departmental bureaucratic stipulation by small-minded and out-of-touch-with-reality middle management officials? Probably, as it was so often in Australia.

Even those sufferers from tender stomachs who, like Timothy, were 'drinkers of water' would not find it readily available on New Zealand trains (nor on those in Europe). There were no drinking cups and no water taps except in the toilet where at least the water was potable.

FOOD FOR THOUGHT

The *Silver Fern* was a premium train on which even off-duty staff had to pay a supplementary fare. But it was nothing particularly special. Unlike the *Northerner*, the night train between Auckland and Wellington which had a dining car though not offering full meal service, this daylight railcar set had no on-board catering other than the bar service. Curiously, this was not advertised, perhaps because they only carried six little bottles of white wine.

Meals had to be ordered in advance and were provided at a refreshment stop. This lunch stopover offered a chance to meet and talk to fellow passengers. Although in New Zealand there are sheep, sheep everywhere there were surprisingly no succulent lamb chops on the menu. The hot chicken and chips looked good but the ham and pineapple salad was poor; not real off-the-bone ham but a wodge of pressed or canned stuff. The pineapple was not fresh or even tinned chunks or rings but only a mush of crush. The salad was largely coleslaw. There was no bar at the refreshment stop, yet mealtimes are when a lot of people like to drink.

Hugh Bennett, writing in the *Railway Magazine* in 1980, extolled the delights of "taking wine with the train": "A jug of wine, a rushing train, and thou" (he plagiarised Omar Khayyam). This highlights one of the insufficiently publicised but unquestionable advantages rail has over other forms of land transport, particularly the motor car. As a motorist you are embattled by the constant exhortation not to drink and drive and the threat of heavy penalties if you do.

With so much concern, rightly, over drunk driving on the roads, the ability to drink on a train journey is one of the pleasures of railways.

In Australia there has long been a curious, and somewhat uneasy marriage of wowser and boozer attitudes. Queensland Rail, having plunged rather late into the 20th century with the daring *Queenslander* lounge bar introduced in 1986, and which is open, like the pubs, all day from 10 o'clock, later retreated into the dark ages for its inland services, with the timetable showing a reversion to the "liquor only with meals" syndrome. One is reminded of the old *Punch* cartoon of the very fat fellow whose friend commented on how he had been putting on weight. "Yes", he said, "Doctor said I was only to drink with meals - got to eat such a deuce of a lot of meals, don't you know!"

Before the mid 1970s it was rarely possible to obtain wine on Australian trains. Beer was the staple drink, and buffet cars usually stocked beer, soft drinks, and miniatures of spirits and possibly sherry. Wines have usually been available in the proper dining cars, but stock was often very limited indeed.

Queensland is the only Australian State to offer wine by glass or carafe, in the lounge and diner of the *Queenslander* and on the service-at-every-seat (in the old BR pullman style) *Spirit of Capricorn*. The wine drinker still tends to be discriminated against in other states. Red wine has generally been unobtainable on the InterCity services of Victoria and since about 1988 V/line have banned wine altogether; offering instead a fruit-based concoction known as 'cooler' whose principal function appears to be an attempt to turn children into alcoholics.

For most of the last 20 years the only beer on the InterCity services of Victoria has been the light variety. World-wide, hardly any systems offer the beer drinker draught ale. Those who seek well can find it on some of the private railways in Britain.

It is still a cause for wonder to me that in Europe you can find a railway refreshment room packed with people drinking jugs of beer or other alcohol at six in the morning – I have seen this in France, in Germany, in Switzerland and in Croatia (then Yugoslavia) – and you can drink all night on trains in Portugal if so inclined.

The rail systems of many European countries carry the local wines as part of a national image and as an attraction to tourists. On the *Romulus* express from Venezia to Wien I found half-bottles of wine temptingly placed as part of the dinner place-setting in the dining car - a most effective advertisement. Some Spanish and Hungarian trains also followed this practice. How sad that in Australia, Victoria's V/line did not adopt the idea on its former *Vinelander* service to Mildura in the rich wine growing district of Sunraysia!

Drinking on trains is best at a table, where one can watch the scenery. I used to derive wicked amusement from sitting drinking a glass in British buffet cars while passing through stations on which hungry and thirsty passengers would be waiting for lesser trains, especially if it was outside legal boozing hours. Drinking at a bar is not quite so attractive, especially if you cannot also see outside. The French TGV bar is excellent but the window sill is about half a metre too high, preventing the average passenger from enjoying the view while having a drink.

Also, I think it is nice to be able to order a drink from a steward or hostess, whether over a buffet bar counter or at a dining car table or from one's own seat. I disliked the system on Switzerland's *Panoramic Express* where bottles of wine or beer were obtainable only from a slot machine – and then only if you had the right small change.

On the former *Lufthansa Airport Express* drinks were free. "Anything on this train is yours for the taking," the hostess said. "Anything?" I questioned, with an unholy gleam in my eye. Poor lass, how could I have thought of taking advantage of such unintentionally careless use of English? But the staff were very friendly and helpful. The *Airport Express* seats had no hostess call button; they were not needed because the train staff simply pampered you all the way.

At least one Australian service, the long-running former *Albury Express*, had no liquor whatever in the buffet, a travelling "pub with no beer" which, if not unique outside Moslem countries, was certainly unusual in the railway catering world. The railway tradition has long been that whatever else you could or could not get in a buffet, you could get a drink. Jerome K. Jerome's story of the man with the cheeses tells of the traveller and the undertaker repairing to the buffet where they stamped and waved their umbrellas until they were served with double brandies.

That would not have been possible on some Queensland trains for many years in the past. They would not serve you a double of any spirits but, in the inimitable contortionist reasoning of the bureaucratic minds responsible, there was no problem about two single measures, even at the same time!

In some strange way this must have kept the wowsers happy and it gave the staff more washing up to do, lest they frittered away their time in idle chatter. But the rule was not written anywhere, either in the timetable or in the buffet car itself, and a lot depended on the personality of the staff concerned whether it was followed to the letter.

Another curious ruling of that period was when drinking was restricted to brief liquor sessions but was also allowed with meals. You were permitted two drinks with a meal but you had to order both at once when ordering: you could not come back for a second drink if you only decided to have one in the first place. Possibly this is not the way the rule was meant to be interpreted but it placed staff in an invidious position. They risked facing derision or abuse on the one hand or reprimand from superiors on the other.

Discrepancies between what is advertised or implied by the advertisements and what is actually obtainable, and when, are not good for the railways' image, and should be corrected. That is a well-known principle of advertising, that the product must be available as advertised, quite apart from whether it is good or as good as proclaimed.

As distinct from on the airlines, refreshments aboard most trains have to be paid for directly by the passengers requiring them. The price of meals and sleeping berths may be included in the first class fare on premium long distance expresses like Australia's *Queenslander*, Spoornet's *Blue Train* and the ETR 450 and X-2000 services of Italy and Sweden. When a meal is included the traveller must of course take it or leave it. It is commendable that even with an inclusive fare structure some railways still offer a choice.

But inclusive meals can sometimes be taken for granted. Arriving in Melbourne one morning from Sydney on the old *Southern Aurora*, Mira the hostess told the conductor of a couple who had breakfasted well but neglected to pay. Waylaying them later on the platform, she was told "we thought it was included". But they paid up.

FOOD FOR THOUGHT

Even if occasionally there may be "one that got away" there was really no call for an irritating Queensland practice, peculiar to QR, which has persisted for at least 10 years recently on the *Sunlander* – that of asking for payment in the middle of the meal when the main course arrives, although this practice is being reviewed.

"Dinner is served – but let's see the colour of your money." It is not conducive to friendly relations between passengers and staff. The unwelcome taste which it leaves may be remembered more than the succulent mouth-watering dish placed before you. Why not a bill afterwards? Even to ask for payment in advance, on ordering, would be more acceptable. There is not very much room to manoeuvre with four seats to the width of the car, and fishing for wallets and change while your tempting freshly-cooked breakfast or dinner is steaming hot in front of your nose is most uncivilised and annoying. The dining car only seats 24 passengers. Up to mid-1995 the menu and price were fixed. Dining car patrons are virtually a captive clientele, so there was no real justification for such a practice.

"I think we've always done it that way," an official said to me. "Don't the others?"

One final curiosity deserves to be mentioned. Before the standardisation of the Port Pirie to Adelaide track, there was an arrangement whereby passengers arriving in Adelaide from the west were provided with a meal at the Adelaide refreshment room. It was quaintly described in some of the timetables as a 'compulsory meal', bringing a mental picture of a diner being physically restrained and force-fed.

What terrible fate awaited the passenger who could not, or would not, eat his compulsory meal one does not dare to think. 'Ve haf vays of making you enjoy yourself!'

All it really meant, of course, was that the meal was included in the fare whether you felt like having it or not.

I am not aware of any railway which requires passengers to partake of a 'compulsory drink', but perhaps it is an idea some systems should take up.

Chapter 13

The Long Straight

"Too many chiefs and not enough Indians" – Anon

From Sydney on the western rim of what Australians call the "old Pacific Sea", runs Australia's best known train and one of its finest. The *Indian Pacific* or simply the 'Indian' or 'IP' to railwaymen and regulars, travels between the Pacific and the Indian Oceans, hence the name.

It is mostly composed of first-class cars, is air-conditioned, and includes dining, club and lounge cars. There are single and twin sleepers, showers and even a private suite. It was once called the second

Driver's cab view of the 'Long Straight'. (Colin Taylor)

most luxurious train in the world. This was when South Africa's *Blue Train* was considered to hold first place honours, but a Brisbane friend who had travelled on both hotly disputed this, asserting that even the *Indian*'s 'older brother', the now defunct *Trans-Australian* was a cut above South Africa's best. Perhaps it was, but towards the end of the 1980s the *Indian* gradually deteriorated, through lack of government funding. A 1992 injection of Federal funds and a switch to "line management" by Australian National (AN) promises to make this train once more rank among the truly great.

The *Indian* was called a "dinosaur" in the well-known BBC television series *Great Railway Journeys of the World* on the grounds that it was one of a disappearing breed of long distance transcontinental trains of the American type. Once as common on the plains of the American west as the Indians and the buffaloes, they have now been largely eclipsed by the motor car and the aeroplane. The dinosaur appellation is not really apt or, if it is, dinosaurs would have to have been popular, friendly and 'Pacific' beasts.

The *Indian Pacific* is potentially the flagship of the Railways of Australia and it attracts a steady tourist traffic from all over the world. This is not to say that the train is always full. Even in the height of the tourist season it is often possible to obtain a berth at short notice. There is still something wrong with the Australian booking system. Computerised in the last decade or so, it still appears to err on the side of caution rather than optimism as the airlines do. Over-booking, or double booking, which the airlines have developed to a fine art, is rare on the railways. More often than not a train reported as fully booked seems to run half empty.

A few years ago, in one of the regular disputes between management and the industrial unions (of the three different rail systems which then operated the train) a compromise resulted in the former economy class sleepers on the *Indian* being withdrawn. It is not clear who the compromise satisfied, if anyone. Certainly the travelling public were among the losers. But instead of becoming all first class, which appears to have been what the rail chiefs then wanted, the train ran with mixed first class sleeping cars and economy sitters, but only the first class sleepers went all the way. It was impossible sometimes to distinguish between first class and economy on NSW sitting cars which were attached for part of the way only, and even the timetable was not much help. In fact you never quite knew what to expect in the way of non-sleeper accommodation on the *Indian Pacific* in those days.

Now under single 'line management' with AN the winner, plus a Federal funding injection (niggardly and belated though that is in comparison with Federal road funding) the *Indian* has new-style 'holiday' class accommodation for those unwilling or unable to afford first class – but even this would be justly labelled 'first' on many rail systems in the world.

When the *Indian Pacific* was inaugurated in February 1970, it brought Australia together "in a way that the Constitution could never do", according to former National Party leader Ian Sinclair (who took his honeymoon on that very train).

Granted that a man on his honeymoon with a young and beautiful wife might tend to take a rosy view of events, his comment was in fact far from exaggeration. Express container freight trains now thunder across the continent daily. In one week there are seven express freight trains and three Super Freighters across the Nullarbor in each direction, while the prestigious *Westliner* and *Eastliner* services have up to nine scheduled runs each way. Altogether a busy single line thousand mile railway! It is over 1600 km across the Nullarbor from Port Augusta to Kalgoorlie whereas the famous 'long straight' – the longest in the world – is only a third of it at 296.2 miles (476.7 km) from just east of Watson to a few kilometres before Nurina. Since both of these are only passing loops you would notice only if the train happened to stop on meeting another (which it may not be scheduled to do) or if you just happened to be looking out of the window in the right direction and saw the nameboard, you may not know when you enter or leave the long straight unless you ask the Conductor. To the casual glance the scenery is unchanging hour after hour. There is no more impressive way to appreciate Australia's vastness than by taking this trip. As Anthony Dennis expressed so well in *Ribbons of Steel*, his commemorative tribute to the *Indian Pacific*'s coming-of-age in 1991, the journey on this train is "a rite of passage, a vehicle which embraces like no other the enormity of an enormous country, which should be travelled at least once in a lifetime".

The long straight alone equals Euston to Carlisle in distance, the almost uninhabited desert stretch between Port Augusta and Kalgoorlie compares with Calais to Wien, while the entire crossing from the Pacific Ocean to the Indian Ocean at 4348 km is just about equivalent in distance to a rail journey from Moskva to Madrid.

The year 1970 marked the first time it became possible to go right across the continent by one train. In earlier days, passengers had to take one train to Albury, another from there to Melbourne, yet another to Adelaide, another from there to Port Pirie, another from there to Kalgoorlie and then a final one to Perth. Some of the train changes were in the middle of the night. It was impossible to operate through trains because of differences in the track gauges.

The last link to be completed was between Broken Hill and Port Pirie. Before that the *Trans Australian* had been regularly linking Port Pirie with the west and the 'Trans' kept running between Adelaide and Perth for many years after the *Indian* was introduced on the direct Sydney–Port Pirie–Perth line. Together these offered a daily service between Port Pirie and Perth and between Adelaide and Perth five days a week with a train change on the other two days. The Sydney–Perth direct service ran twice weekly and on four other days passengers could connect via Melbourne and Adelaide.

In the last few years the service frequency has been reduced, and around 1990 almost looked like disappearing altogether. Starting with a twice-weekly service, the *Indian Pacific* was increased to thrice weekly in 1973 and from 1975 to 1982 ran as many as four return trips weekly. Between then and 1984 its frequency again declined, first to

Crossing of *Indian Pacific* trains in the middle of the desert. (Jean Campbell)

thrice-weekly then back to only twice. Meanwhile the *Trans-Australian* ran between Adelaide and Perth on the other days; five times weekly to 1972, four times weekly in 1973, and thrice weekly from 1975 to 1982, after which things were complicated with the appearance of the new *Alice* direct Sydney–Alice Springs service. Together, the passenger trains crossing the Nullarbor were down to five a week by 1984 and four a week by 1991. Another year later the *Trans-Australian* had vanished, at least by name, but in fact it still ran twice weekly as an Adelaide-Perth *Indian Pacific*, while the original Sydney-based *Indian* was reduced to a once weekly service. By 1994 the curtain had fallen on the last remnants of the once-proud *Trans-Australian*, usurped by the more up-market *Indian Pacific*. This, however, reverted to a twice-weekly run in place of the once almost daily service across Australia.

But this summarised history hides other developments. The *Indian* has regained much of its former glory and incorporates the best aspects of the train it replaced. Adelaide, which was once served only by connecting train, has been included in the route. This resulted from the construction of a Port Pirie by-pass line at Coonamia and the standardisation of the gauge of the Adelaide link. Yet it added over 400 km to the total journey and involved a two and a half hour re-tracing of route. This must seem incredible to European visitors used to highly developed networks. Not surprisingly it gives rise to the occasional complaint. It is certainly odd that having built a short connecting link to avoid the few kilometres of travel and reversal of direction at the dead end in Port Pirie, the trains should now be diverted hundreds of kilometres to another dead-end reversal.

Apart from the inconvenience of the distance of the new Adelaide terminal from the City, the new arrangements serve Adelaide well but historic and interesting Port Pirie (which at one time boasted the longest station platform in the world and where the main street was virtually a continuation of the railway) is neglected. The reason has little to do with passengers. AN centralised their offices and administration in Adelaide. Some staff formerly located at Port Pirie and as far away as Port Augusta had to commute or relocate there. The hour and a half the train formerly stood in Port Pirie is now spent standing in Adelaide. Although Adelaide passengers no longer have to change trains, they had to make the connection by bus when the broad gauge was being converted in 1983. This was as popular as a concrete parachute, and especially irritating to those who knew that freight trains still used the line as far as Dry Creek in Adelaide's northern suburbs.

This was not the first change of route. Fred Talbot in *Railway Wonders of the World* (published 1910) describes how severe gradients over the Blue Mountains of New South Wales, originally accomplished by means of a zigzag, were replaced by a series of tunnels. The zigzag still remains as a tourist line operated with steam-hauled trains. West of Lithgow the passenger will see other signs of realignments where tight curves have been eliminated.

Beyond Broken Hill the standard gauge line replaced the narrow gauge Silverton 'tramway', the formation of which can still be seen after Cockburn where it mostly runs parallel with the new line. Further west still, beyond Kalgoorlie, the standard gauge line swings 50 km north of the original West Australian narrow gauge route (which followed the Great Eastern Highway), by-passing the old gold mining centre of Coolgardie and going through towns like Koolyanobbing which prior to the West Australian mining boom of the 1960s were not even marked on the map.

From Northam westwards, most of the last 120 km is dual gauge, combining the West Australian 1067 mm with the standard 1435 mm.

On the trans-continental trip you will meet tourists from New Zealand, the United Kingdom, the USA and Canada; from South Africa, Japan, and Europe – especially Germany and Switzerland. A surprising number of Australians, young and old, will also be among your fellow-passengers. Not all will be travelling the route for the first time. Some will be making their annual 'cruise', just going for the ride. No-one is likely to be in a hurry so it does not matter if the train is late on the way, though one likes to know that it will arrive punctually at the other end, when time resumes its normal ruthless dominance of our affairs and connections have to be made, relatives and hotels contacted, onward bookings confirmed and planes caught.

Broken Hill marks the first time zone change on the westward journey. The town uses South Australian time which is both geographically sensible and recognises the possibly greater affinity it has with Adelaide than with Sydney. The *Indian Pacific* in 1995 was the only rail passenger link Broken Hill had with anywhere else at all. Before 1990, this city enjoyed other thrice-weekly passenger rail connections with both Adelaide and Sydney. The former was by a 'Bluebird' railcar set named the *Silver City Limited* and the latter by Australia's first air conditioned train, the *Silver City Comet* diesel railcar set, modelled perhaps on the *Zephyr* sets of North America, or at least suggestive of them and dating from the same period, the 1930s, although they were not in the same speed league.

The 'Bluebird' lingered a further couple of years as an occasional 'pokie train' (gambling) excursion, but the latter disappeared altogether in 1990 to be replaced by a bus to the XPT rail terminus 743 km away at Dubbo.

From some 20 trains a week in the 1970s to as few as four a week now (total of both directions), this warm mining centre of the outback has been badly let down by all sides – the State of New South Wales in which it lies, the State of South Australia whose time zone it has adopted, and the Federal Government whose refusal to fund rolling stock replacement condemned Broken Hill (as well as Port Pirie, Whyalla and Mount Gambier) to virtual railway isolation.

I visited Broken Hill often when you could go there on one train, stay a night or even a few hours, and continue or return by another. Once, to check out how railway passing loops were operated, I took the *Indian Pacific* to one of them at The Gorge, the last station before 'The Hill', where I descended to await the eastbound *Silver City Comet*.

Passing places are important on Australia's largely single track network, but they can soon disrupt the timetables when trains are late. Do not believe the transport economists and engineers who will tell you (and try to prove it mathematically) that a single track properly operated has as much capacity as a double track. Anyone who has ever travelled on single lane highways, the kind common in the Highlands of Scotland and surprisingly not unusual in Hong Kong's New Territories, would know this for the nonsense it is.

Passing loops vary in length and if two trains are both longer than the loop, passing is rather difficult. Very precise signalling is needed at all times and the *Indian* itself once came to grief through a miscalculation or malfunction involving a crossing freight near Crystal Brook.

The legendary Casey Jones, famed in American folk song, was in fact a certain Irish-born John Jones, driver of an express train which came to grief on a passing loop at Vaughan, Mississippi on the single track Memphis-New Orleans main line in 1906.

When the *Silver City Comet* operated one could take a daylight run back into mid-west New South Wales, calling at little places like Roto (a junction from where now abandoned tracks led south to Melbourne), Condobolin and Ivanhoe. These towns cannot now be accessed by passenger train services, buses having ousted trains on almost all the inland routes in New South Wales. When trains stopped at such places, residents other than passengers would often turn out to greet them, as is still the case in the few rural centres of Australia still enjoying a train service.

At Ivanhoe a group of young women, girls in fact, were gathered on the platform to wave. Smiling, beautiful and oh so natural that they brought reciprocal smiles from the passengers. I remarked to a fellow traveller on their exceptional attractiveness. "Yes, they're creamies," he replied. A new word to me at the time, I took it to mean something similar to the term 'octoroon' used in the USA to signify someone of racially mixed parentage, 'white' with a touch of 'black'. Not that this gives an accurate impression: white with black in any proportion produces grey and though they may well have been grey-haired when much older, their complexions were far from it. 'Creamy' was an excellent appellation, suggestive of choice quality and fullness of flavour. I did not take it in any way as a term of abuse nor did my informant use it in such a way.

I was astonished some years later to read in a Queensland newspaper of writer Paul Theroux being accused of inventing the word 'creamie'. A North Queensland resident who allegedly travelled with that author for several days, accused him of making up the terms 'gin jockeys', 'gin burglars', 'creamies' and 'halfies', and said that he himself had never used words like 'boong'. He may have been right about his conversation with Theroux, but these terms were certainly not made up by that author and are in quite common use in Australia, particularly in the outback.

'Gin' has long been a shortened form of 'aborigine' and is applied particularly to aboriginal females by 'whites'. It is not difficult to work out the origin of the expression 'gin jockey', used derogatorily to describe a 'white' man partial to what in other former colonial outposts would be called 'black velvet'. The Queensland *Hansard* records use of this term in the parliament, and the Macquarie dictionary, 'bible' of authentic 'Strine', recognises all the words quoted.

'Creamie' is a term applied to a light coloured horse but colloquially to a person of mixed race. It signifies a quarter-caste Aboriginal and is no more derogatory than any other word signifying a person of mixed race or colour.

The aboriginal word, 'Lubra' is sometimes used derogatorily by uneducated whites, when in fact it simply means 'woman' – a term which, despite the views of some extremists among us, is not yet regarded as a term of abuse in the English language.

On the train across Australia the time changes so often you can become bewildered. It's not a bad idea to leave your watches alone and rely on the conductor to tell you when the meals are. No wonder that in the former USSR, Moskva time was kept wherever the Trans-Siberian *Rossia* was; it did not change its clocks every few hours. Neither for that matter does the *Indian Pacific*! There is a clock in the lounge car and the only thing that can confidently be said about it is that whatever time it shows is almost certain to be wrong. But as long as you get your breakfast, lunch and dinner at a reasonable time, a drink when you need it, and can go to bed when it's dark or when you feel the urge for it, then it doesn't really matter what the time is. You don't have to listen to the news or check the mail at the office. You can relax as on a holiday even if you are not!

John and Anita from New York were on holiday. They hailed from Upper Montclair, a rather highbrow suburb in the view of most of its residents, but this friendly couple were far from the flamboyant and arrogant type of American tourist that one sometimes expects. They were very down to earth.

"The basin fell on Anita in the 'John' this morning," announced John at breakfast. He had told us that when the *Kinsey Report* came out, with its revelations of *Peyton Place* type promiscuity the saying was "it couldn't happen in Upper Montclair!" Montclair prided itself on its propriety.

We agreed that basins falling on you in the 'John' couldn't happen there either.

Another character was a woman with a weather-beaten face – typical 'salt of the earth' country Australian with a voice as harsh and strident as the call of a white cockatoo. All the crowd listened – it was impossible to do otherwise. Describing a previous train journey in a sitting car, she told any who wanted to listen about a young lad who wouldn't give up the next seat for her. Why he should have done so was not explained. He cannot have been all that young either, for next: "He squeezed my toe. He got his legs round me and I thought he was on to me." For some obscure reason she must have thought him both immature and sensitive. "I couldn't say anything to him!" she said, but "I told my daughter about it." We could imagine the reaction.

Then she told us about the meat sandwiches the morning after her "rough night".

"I was real sick," she said. She had spent an hour in the toilet on the approach to Sydney, and then, unable to contact her folks on the telephone (it was never clear why) she had "walked the streets" for five hours.

"The sandwiches upset me," she explained. "It must have been the meat one".

The passengers were by now in fits.

"My son had warned me not to buy sandwiches on the train," she added.

Her friend was trying diplomatically to edge her through to the dining car. She was already late for the call.

"I had a valium tablet," she said. "It made me go yackity yak".

Her friend was discreetly moving on, but had to come back, because she was still 'yackity yacking' about the sandwiches.

At last they got her off to lunch. "Have a meat sandwich," someone called as a parting shot.

THE LONG STRAIGHT

One of my most pleasurable experiences ever was playing the piano in the lounge car of the *Indian*, though sometimes going round the curves near St. George in New South Wales it was difficult to keep on the stool. Singsongs would easily develop if a pianist with some knowledge of popular songs was among the passengers. Personally I just play things I know and that usually seems to be appreciated, so much so that one can be plied with drinks by grateful passengers, or even given a free one now and then by the staff – doubtless on the basis that a bit of entertainment keeps the customers going.

The lounge cars are usually best patronised just before and during meal sittings, when people are assembling near the dining car awaiting the call. At other times people will spend time playing cards, conversing, having drinks, reading, or merely looking out of the window. Not many find it boring. I did meet a woman who liked travelling by train but insisted "Australia is boring". So is an ocean cruise if you do nothing to make it otherwise.

I met the late British comedian Jimmy Edwards in the lounge of the *Indian Pacific*. He found it boring, he said, but spent most of the waking part of the journey just sitting there with a glass of whisky. I enjoy that myself, but you need something to go with it – and I don't mean water. Music, company, looking out at the scenery, hearing about what other people have done – if nothing else just chatting to the stewards who have all 'been there, done that' many a time.

"Oh I liked that *St Louis Blues* you played last night," the bar steward told me one morning at eleven when I sought the hair of the dog. "You got better each time and the last rendering was great!" That had been when the bar had closed and everyone but the steward and I had gone to their beds. "Play it again, Sam," he had said, and I must have put everything I had into it – there was blood on the ivory when I finished.

If you stay up late and have a few grogs with friends to while away the evening after dinner, you should see a wonderful sunset when out on the Nullarbor. Those who say the finest sunsets are in industrial towns where the smoke of the furnaces fills the air with particles which catch the setting rays and turn the sky red have never seen a sunset over the desert. Sand and dust can do just as much for the artistic eye when it comes to painting the night sky.

If you have difficulty getting to sleep on the train, you may care to look out for Tarcoola. This is one of the major outposts of Australia in the desert, a rail junction which boasts several permanent houses and a pub. Tarcoola is named after a racehorse. An annual Tarcoola Cup is held there, a horse race of which it is said few can remember the winner from one year to the next. Unfortunately, whatever regular passenger train you travel on you are likely to see Tarcoola only in the middle of the night.

At Cook the clocks must again be adjusted for the different times of Central and Western Australia, and the tourist is wooed by trinkets, souvenirs, and the chance to photograph the town's original jail cells. Like dunnies, his and hers, they stand alongside the railway station. A notice, crudely painted, invites people to "come to Cook when you're crook": the hospital needs patients. It may be necessary to explain to non-Australians that 'crook' in this context is nothing to do with crime – in spite of the juxtaposition and local importance of the cells. A 'crook' Australian is one who is sick, possibly a corruption from the German *krank*.

A friend told of a transcontinental journey in the old days when the train stopped somewhere in the outback where there was a pub about a kilometre from the station. I have never yet identified this location – it might have been Tarcoola or possibly Cook, where the local club is a modest distance from the station. Anyway, according to him the beer on the train had run out, or was warm. This was in the days before air conditioning and efficient refrigeration. The passengers were told there was plenty of time to go over for 'a cold one'. To their dismay, on reaching the inviting desert oasis, they were refused admission because they were not wearing ties or jackets.

One still comes across such antiquated Pommie-based dress rules in unexpected places. At one hotel in Alice Springs (there are not many apart from the motel type) staff would not serve anyone in a tee-shirt either in the lounge or any of the other reasonably respectable bars. Out at the back I was told to go, to a bare tiled room with spilt beer and wine covering the few tables provided. The clientele, all Aborigines, seemed used to being directed to such an environment. It was in fact nothing more than racial discrimination disguised as dress rules and it still occurs in parts of Australia. But there are far more examples of easy inter-racial mixing. In an outback Queensland hotel I found a happy mixture of local workers, women, children, Aborigines, dressed much as they liked, that is, in normal Queensland bush fashion.

Fortunately another, and better, hotel in Alice Springs had no such hang-ups, even being content to allow workmen in singlets in the lounge bar. What moves these crazy people who import London winter dress standards to the tropical heat of north and central Australia?

There can be nothing else quite like the Nullarbor in the world. The line is straight, but you would hardly notice any modest curves in the preceding few hundred kilometres. The straightness is not something you are acutely aware of except when there is a stop, as at Cook, where you can get off the train and look back, or forward along the line. It looks about the same either way. If standing waiting for a train at night it is amazing to see how the headlights appear miles away long before it arrives. Not that it is going particularly slowly; it is just the sheer distance, the straightness of the track, and the absence of anything else to attract attention.

The Nullarbor begins very suddenly at Ooldea (pronounced 'Oolday') after curving through a maze of sand hills which start at Wynbring Rocks about an hour's journey west of Tarcoola. This is actually the tail end of the Great Victorian Desert, a vast sandy waste lying mostly north of the Nullarbor Plain. The long straight begins almost immediately after Ooldea. Known to few passengers is the fact that Maralinga, scene of the infamous atomic bomb experiments by the British, is barely 40 km north of this point.

When I joined the driver along the long straight the son of a former driver was lifted up into the cab by his dad.

Obviously a very young potential railwayman, he was enthralled. "Where's the steering wheel?" he asked.

Silly but by no means unusual. Adults are capable of the same mistake. A woman in a car stalled on a level crossing in Melbourne was planning to sue the driver of the train that crashed into her. "He should have swerved," she asserted. Travelling north on Queensland's intercity *Spirit of Capricorn* where you can sometimes watch the driver, a passenger observed he had his hands behind his head.

"Shouldn't you keep your hands on the wheel?" the passenger asked. Some mothers do have 'em!

In the Nullarbor the sun rises on a bare brown horizon all around. Ahead you forge into a silent world, and as evening falls the setting sun turns the brown earth to golden red, as far as the eye can see; the entire horizon like an ocean of rust. But it would be wrong to think there is nothing there. Spotting things in the desert becomes one of the pastimes. The Nullarbor, as its name implies, is devoid of trees but there are some fairly substantial bushes here and there and all sorts of scrubby growths that presumably afford sustenance for the lizards, rabbits, roos, emus, wallabies and dingoes you may see if you are lucky enough to be staring into space at just the right time and in the right direction. There are birds too; big black eagles perch on the telegraph poles, ruffling their feathers and flexing their talons as the train passes. Sometimes they fly off languidly; at other times they seem unconcerned. If you see a roo it will be hopping away in great bounds, but will obligingly stop and look back at you when it thinks it has reached a safe distance. Have your camera handy with a telephoto lens.

While the *Indian Pacific* is allowed ample time to cover the 1690 km from Port Augusta to Kalgoorlie (25¼ hours), another less well publicised train takes a lot longer.

This is the 'Tea and Sugar', the unofficial name given by locals and railway people to the 'slow mixed', as the official tables described it for many years. Although it carries passengers, it is not advertised as a passenger train and passengers are not really encouraged. Nor is it a mixed or a goods train in the normal sense, although it conveys plenty of goods wagons. It is something probably unique on rail, a travelling shopping and community centre, hence its well-deserved appellation. (Tea and sugar sounds more discreet than, say, beer and chips: the fact is, a whole refrigerated van is stacked with cartons of the amber fluid.)

For many years up until November 1983, when it was re-timed, its journey took a total of five and a half days; three quarters of this time being spent standing motionless at tiny settlements where it fulfilled its primary function of bringing essential supplies and comfort to these remote communities, or perhaps it simply languished overnight to gather sufficient strength to continue its harrowing journey over the plain with no trees. ('Nullarbor' may sound like an aboriginal name but is Latin for 'no trees'.)

It is now called a 'shunt goods'. Apart from ballast trains, this category covers the slowest of the slow in railway parlance. The British called them 'pick-up goods'. Its consist is virtually unchanged but no longer includes the famous butcher's van. As concrete sleepers replaced timber, the number of railway settlements declined and fettlers' families now have to order their joints and steaks in advance and pick them up from a fast goods, or go out into the desert and shoot rabbits.

With the consequent reduction in the number of trading stops there came a marked acceleration in timing, some former overnight stops being eliminated altogether.

To travel on this remarkable train is easier said than done. In the first place, the 'Tea and Sugar' does not appear as such – or at all – in the public timetables. You have to know about it, or have access to the 'Working Timetables'. These are not easy to come by. They cannot be bought on the station bookstall, and they can be altered at any time by a 'special traffic notice' which you will not know exists unless you are a railway employee or have a special arrangement as some publishers do.

The difference between working and public timetables is a subtle one. The working timetables contain a little more information about what is happening, or is supposed to happen. If the working timetable says a train leaves at 12.20 and the public one says it leaves at 12.15, then it will leave at 12.20 (or later), but never before. The traveller relying on the public timetable will not miss the train so long as he is in time for it. He will only think it's late if it leaves after the time stated. It isn't really. The unpublished working timetable shows it to be dead on time. I hope the distinction is clear!

Goods trains also follow timetables, but there is more flexibility. They are a rough guide to whether a train may operate on a particular day, but unlike most passenger trains, goods trains are often allowed to leave a station early.

To meet up with the legendary 'Tea and Sugar' I had carefully arranged an itinerary to travel on the *Indian Pacific* from Sydney to Rawlinna on Saturday 14 January (Sydney depart 15.50, arrive Rawlinna 14.30 two days later); then to wait around an hour and a half and catch the 'Tea and Sugar' to Parkeston, Kalgoorlie; an overnight journey with unknown complications but worth the adventure.

It proved surprisingly difficult to find out from tourist agencies or anywhere else what, if anything, there was at Rawlinna. Nor could I ascertain what provision, if any, there was on the 'Tea and Sugar' for travellers to eat and drink. Knowing it was a travelling shop made it reasonable to surmise that I could buy a steak or a few chops – but what about cooking? One thing I knew the train did not have was a dining car, but were there any facilities for warming food? Was there take-away fast food in the travelling shop? On the other hand, could I obtain cold beer? Was the shop open only when the train stopped and if so, for how long?

Since there are limits to what one can safely leave to chance when travelling through Australia's outback, even by train, I tried to find out what I could in advance. Even this was a formidable task, involving letters and phone calls to Adelaide and Port Augusta. In the middle of it all, and after I had made advance bookings, came a revised timetable.

I checked. A key service in my itinerary, one of the 'Indians', had to my astonishment disappeared, even though I had a confirmed booking on it! Of the 'Tea and Sugar' there was not a trace! But train number 543 looked suspiciously like it. Several trunk calls later I had this confirmed, but its schedule was drastically altered and the 'connections' I had carefully planned were 'fubar'.

The new schedules meant adding two whole days to my itinerary. A Sydney departure on the Thursday would give an arrival at Rawlinna at midday Saturday. The 'Tea and Sugar' would not reach there until 18.50 the same day, a longish wait, with what, I wondered, in the way of amenities or even shade.

But I booked to Rawlinna anyway, making sure of lunch on the train before arrival. I had met a few people on the train and was not the only passenger to alight. Tommy, a genial Maori, was with the railway and had been away on the Eyre peninsula where he had been offered a new posting.

Tommy introduced me to his friends at the railway club which was the social centre of the tiny settlement.

After a siesta in the railway rest house I awoke to find it was dark outside. What time was it? The 'Tea and Sugar'! Had it gone? Where was it? Peering at my watch I found it to be going on for eight at night. I hurried towards the railway.

No sign of the train! Passing an open door I saw two men having a cup of tea. They invited me to join them. "I have to catch a train," I said, feeling rather stupid. What else would a complete stranger be doing there?

"No hurry," they said. "Have a cuppa first". They knew perfectly well who I was and what I was waiting for, and suggested I make my way to the crew cars at the front, where there would probably be a spare sleeping berth. But there was time to visit the club again while the various wagons lying about in Rawlinna sidings had been assembled into something recognisable as a train, and there I met the guard of the 'Tea and Sugar' and the girls who staffed the community services car.

I did not find any empty berth: the vehicles were spread out over what seemed like miles of track and I judged it dangerous to go wandering about the sidings in the dark with shunting in progress. I therefore settled for the ordinary passenger coach, which was then nearby and unlocked. Once sure I was on the right train – the community services car was almost next door and the travelling shop a little further along, I curled up and fell asleep.

The guard had assured me the train would not leave without me and I felt perfectly confident in his assurance.

Leaving without your passenger is unthinkable to railway people in these remote parts of the continent. One time at Dimbulah in north Queensland, having been assured by the guard that the train would wait for me, I had asked what would they do if I simply didn't turn up. This posed no problem whatsoever. "We'd just get the police to find you," they said.

The thought of being dragged out of a bar by the Queensland police was not altogether appealing: it could be open to misinterpretation by a critical public who tend to regard the mere sight of a policeman as an invasion of civil liberties!

A sudden lurch of movement in Rawlinna sidings signalled our departure, which I recorded as at 1.43. After that, sleep was fitful; the next stop I noted was in the cruel early hours around four o'clock. Zanthus, perhaps – another 'major' railway settlement of half a dozen houses or so. But no, we waited only a few minutes.

We reached Zanthus with the dawn at 5.16, shoppers coming to meet us in search of weekly bargains like early birds seeking morning morsels.

This is too early for breakfast, thought I, and settled for a further snooze after I had bought a tin of lambs' tongues in the shop to eat when I woke up.

Around midday we passed through Golden Ridge which meant it would not be long before we came to a final halt in Parkeston yard. From there some fellow passengers I had not previously seen offered me a lift in a railway van for the final 6 km into the famous Golden City.

On the *Indian Pacific* Kalgoorlie is reached in the evening. There is time for a short walk around town or, if preferred, a convenient coach tour of Kalgoorlie and its surroundings can be made while the train waits. Kalgoorlie boasts many hotels, some old and with great character: it also has some good restaurants and other attractions.

The station itself is worth looking at carefully: the platform is 526.5 metres long and there are over 20 hydrant points for filling the water tanks in the carriages of long passenger trains. I am not sure how AN managed after the floods of 1974 when they ran combined *Trans-Australian* and *Indian Pacific* train consists, 42 coaches long. This was well matched early in 1984 when the first train through to Alice Springs after unprecedented flooding comprised 34 coaches and 29 car carrier wagons, well over a kilometre in length.

Gold was discovered in Kalgoorlie by an Irishman, Paddy Hannon, and his name was perpetuated for years in the beer brewed there. You used to find it on the train too, but nowadays the beverage all comes from the Swan brewery at Canning Vale in Perth.

There is one quite famous, or infamous place in Kalgoorlie where you can stay, and the coach driver will be sure to point it out. Only a street or two away from the station, it is unprepossessing externally, resembling a row of tin dunnies but comfortably furnished inside. Always open, it lies at the corner of Hay Street and Lane Street, but it is not listed among the city's hotels in the directory and is very expensive. Upwards of $200 a night is rather high for a smallish Western Australian town, but although the amenities are few, it is said the personal service is exceptional and guests enjoy complete satisfaction within a short time of entering. Who am I to contradict them?

Chapter 14

Great Circle Routes

Great circle/ - 2. the line of shortest distance between two points on the surface of the earth.
— *Macquarie Dictionary*

The trans-Nullarbor or any other long straight railway notwithstanding, it is rare to encounter a truly straight route in a surface transportation network. Even the Nullarbor is not level, and therefore not straight if viewed in elevation rather than plan. The old saying "as the crow flies" was meant to indicate the shortest straight-line route, but the earth is not flat (even if we ironed out the hills and filled the valleys) and whatever map projection is used, the representation of a curved surface on a flat sheet distorts distance, area, direction or a combination of these.

The Romans had a reputation for their straight roads and there are lengths of railway, as well as streets in cities which, for all practical purposes are straight and the shortest distance you could hope to achieve between two points on that straight line. But usually one has to change direction and turn corners, whether to avoid obstructions or simply because the direction in which the sought-after destination lies does not match the lie of the streets. As we know from Pythagoras, if the street layout is a square grid, the road distance of a diagonal journey will be 1.4 times the direct distance.

Studies have shown that actual road and rail distances between any two points can vary tremendously from the straight line distance. In a well-developed network a typical ratio would be in the range of 1.1 to 1.4, but in mountainous or other difficult country much higher ratios are found. With a sparse network where links are missing it can be a very

GREAT CIRCLE ROUTES

long journey indeed between places that geographically may not be very far apart.

In Australia for example, between Armidale and Coffs Harbour in northern New South Wales, the road distance of 190 km is less than 1.2 times the straight line distance of 163 km, yet by rail you have over five times as far to go, and the 802 km trip will take not less than 15 hours (thanks partly to one of those delightful non-connections so dear to the hearts of railway timetable planners).

Of course, you simply do not make this trip by rail unless you are a masochist, a rail 'buff', or both.

To the road planner sometimes a roundabout way is best. The well known hazards of a crossroads, while capable of some alleviation by traffic lights, are best avoided by the roundabout, a little circle route devised by a Frenchman M. Hennard in the days of horse drawn carriages. It is still the best way to negotiate a crossroads as long as the right rules of the road are followed. I tried to illustrate this once by a physical model. Built in 'N' gauge model railway track it was operated with model trains since I could not obtain model cars and buses that ran on railway wheels. It had three 'lanes' of entry from each of four directions and the trains could 'weave' across on each side of the squared circle depending on the desired exit. It became quite a feature at the annual 'Expo-Uni' show but I suppose not too many understood its teaching function – so much so that my assistant saw fit to put up a notice that said: "Anyone referring to this model as a 'toy choo choo' will be severely frowned upon"! (See diagram in Apendix II.)

I do not know of a real railway roundabout, though the principle would be capable of application. There are certainly railway crossroads which, unlike those on our highways, are universally controlled by signalling of one kind or another. Few are complete 12-way junctions (four routes of entry, each with three possible exits): Darlington North Road crossing was one; there was another at Mossend near Glasgow, a distorted one just south of Wigan and a more spread out version near East Boldon on Tyneside, all since emasculated. I found one still existing in 1985 at Fort Worth, Texas, where the westbound *Texas Eagle* from Dallas turned left along the southern exit before reversing straight across into the passenger station on the right.

Roundabouts are of necessity one way only. The balloon loops found at the end of many coal and other industrial lines are on this principle but with only one entry and exit and negotiated at creep speed, such trains would hardly interest the average traveller – especially in a coal truck likely to tip up or lose its bottom at any moment.

A railway roundabout on a larger scale would be something like London Transport's Inner Circle or the ring encircling Berlin on which, I suppose, with the right kind of ticket and nothing better to do, you could go round and round all day. But otherwise the idea of a 'round trip' has a lot to commend it, as against say, a normal 'out and back' return. Suburban systems apart, there are now only two opportunities in Australia for an out and back trip to be made using different routes each way: these being from Sydney to Moss Vale (at weekends only) and from Sydney to Adelaide (twice a week).

When rail cuts are made, often it is not only an alternative route which is axed; it is sometimes the shortest and best route. In 1965 British Rail closed what was known as the 'Paddy Line' from Dumfries to Stranraer, which had served not just local traffic but boat trains from many parts of England to the Irish ferry. There was even a through sleeper from London (popularly known as 'The Paddy') and a direct service across northern England from Tyneside. The case for its reopening was eloquently put in an article by Hugh Dougherty in the *Scots Magazine* in December 1992. He pointed out that England-bound trains from Stranraer Harbour (still running and until very recently with a comfortable sleeping car) were "forced to go north via the Girvan line, before making their way across country, to regain the rail route south to Dumfries, an additional 70 miles (113 km) and two hours compared to the direct line".

"No wonder," he added, "so many deserted the trains for private cars and buses". This story must have echoes in almost every country.

GREAT CIRCLE ROUTES

Between Melbourne and Mount Gambier there used to be a passenger rail service. You took the *Overland* on the main Adelaide line to Wolseley, where you changed in the middle of the night. The total distance is 653 km and the thrice weekly service took 11½ hours. But there is another rail route to Mount Gambier from Melbourne. It is via the Portland line, turning off at Heywood and coming into Mount Gambier from the east. This route is far from direct, but substantially shorter than the main line via Wolseley. There are also three different ways of reaching the Portland line. This branches south from the main line at Ararat, which is reached via Ballan and Ballarat, via North Geelong and Ballarat, or via North Geelong and Cressy. The line through Cressy joins the Ararat to Portland line at Maroona. The North Geelong–Ararat route was selected because of its easy gradients for conversion to standard (or combined) gauge as part of the final link up of Australian mainland capital cities at a uniform gauge.

A round trip was possible using goods services on these connecting links and I therefore set off one night a few years ago on a circular tour of western Victoria and the South Australian border country by this means.

The *Overland*, one of the oldest of Australia's regular trains (it celebrated its centenary in 1987 although its name has twice been changed, from *Inter-Colonial Express* in 1901 and from *Melbourne Express* in 1936) was long noted for its comfortable ride and the way they brought you breakfast in bed. Now re-gauged and following a different route it used to afford wonderful panoramic views back toward the lights of the city as it climbed away nightly from Melbourne on the east as it still does from Adelaide on the west.

To avoid having to leave my warm bunk at three in the morning to change at Wolseley junction for the Mount Gambier 'connection' (due 10 hours later!) I stayed on board until we reached Bridgewater up in the Mount Lofty Ranges from where the train wends its way down the hillside to Adelaide.

At Bridgewater I did not have long to wait for the *Mount Gambier*

Bluebird, a quite civilised one-class railcar, with a small buffet bar at the end. It meant the ubiquitous meat pie for lunch again, and I was glad of the continental breakfast I had already enjoyed. The journey takes you down from the mountains, then over Australia's greatest river, the Murray, at Murray Bridge, some 60 km from its mouth on Encounter Bay.

In early days a posting to Wolseley was regarded as penance for a railwayman who had blotted his copybook. A serious case of goods hijacking occurred on this line. Goods in trains waiting in a yard were off-loaded onto road trucks and never seen again. The vans were re-sealed and only an unusual display of affluence on the part of an employee led to the racket being unveiled.

From Mount Gambier I planned to take Vicrail goods No. 9122 through to Melbourne via Heywood, Maroona, and North Geelong. The loco had not arrived – it was due on a goods from Portland which was running late. There was time for a wander round town. Mount Gambier is famous for its volcanic lakes and its creamy and easily worked limestone, a building material of exceptional quality and beauty.

It was dark when the goods finally left Mount Gambier and a black night, so there was little to see for the first part of the journey. I stayed awake with the guard and we naturally discussed how the railways were planning to manage in future without guards – once the most important person on board and having overall charge of the train. One of the tasks of the guard is to look along the train at night from his periscope. A show of sparks can indicate a derailed truck which might otherwise go unnoticed. When shunting or passing or crossing other trains the guard may be responsible for setting and re-setting points and giving signals. If someone from the cab has to do all this, delays will be significant. There seemed to me to be more case for doing without the fireman or observer but more case still for doing away with some of the administrators and advisers who dream up these so-called economies!

At Heywood the loco changed ends, and the guard had to move to another van. I stayed put, making the most of the extra room before the next crew changeover at Maroona. Before we left Heywood the guard brought me a box of matches to light the wood stove which was the only form of heating in the older vans. He showed me where the fuel was stored so I could keep it going. Soon I had a roaring blaze and to my horror the metal chimney began to glow red hot. A fountain of sparks in the night sky marked our passage through the rich wheatlands of Victoria's southwest.

The fire tended to stink the van out with fumes so I opened the window for fresh air. This militated against my attempts to keep warm. The exercise of alternately stoking the fire and opening and shutting the window kept the blood circulating until the sky began to lighten with the approach of dawn. By the time we reached Maroona the fire was nearly out. "Shall I keep it going?" was my first question to the new guard.

He was not keen. "The local wheat cockies are not too happy about the sparks," he said.

Bush and grass fires are a regular hazard in many parts of Australia and it is easy to understand the concern of farmers, but how did they cope in the days of steam?

The track from Maroona to Cressy was rough and seemed more so in the rocking, shuddering guard's van (I mean the van was shuddering not the guard – he was used to it). Track always seems rougher when you are in the locomotive, too.

"We rarely lose a guard's van," he said, as I cowered at the back of the seat, trying to cling to the wall as we lurched and clattered down a steep bank at what seemed a breakneck speed.

By the time we reached Cressy, I began to worry instead about my intended connection at Geelong with a Melbourne passenger train. Although there is a frequent service around morning rush hour (we were due at North Geelong at 7.26), it is only once every hour later on, and I was booked on the Albury InterCity north again from Melbourne around midday.

Then there was the problem of how to travel from North Geelong 'C' box to the platform – a distance of about a kilometre through a busy railway yard. It was not clear whether the train would go into Geelong yard or take the curve straight onto the Melbourne line and the guard was beginning to worry about his relief.

As we approached Wingeel a taxi was seen waiting. The train was to go straight on to Melbourne and the relief crew had been sent out to meet us.

It did not take long to work out that my best chance of catching the Melbourne passenger train was to go with the crew by road to Geelong. We made it with half a minute to spare. I rushed through the barrier just as it was being closed and sank breathlessly into a seat.

Mount Gambier to Melbourne by overnight goods, taxi and InterCity: 482 km in 14 hours and 40 minutes. Had I waited in South Australia to make the return trip by the *Overland* I would not have been in Melbourne until a day later. Sometimes a goods train and a roundabout route can get you to your destination quicker.

The longest rail journey of all in Australia, by regular passenger service, is from Mount Isa to Bunbury, W.A. at 7442 km, nearly three times the direct distance of around 2700 km. In terms of deviousness, Mount Isa to Alice Springs is worse still, the rail trip of some 6150 km being nine times the straight line distance, yet it is a fascinating journey of considerable variety and if the 'return' leg is done by air (barely an hour's flight) it makes an excellent round trip for anyone interested in train travel or wishing to tour Australia in an unusual way.

An even longer and doubtless harrowing journey by rail could have been made in the 1970s when trains ran to Meekatharra in north-western Australia. From Mount Isa that was 7795 km by the shortest possible rail route ('crow-fly' distance about 2200 km), with no less than 10 changes of train at little known places like Stuart, Wallangarra, Werris Creek, Binnaway and Mullewa but it was not the quickest route. To go by the shortest route would have taken seventeen days, four and a quarter hours but the quickest route, via Townsville, Sydney and Goomalling, was 228 km longer and could have been accomplished with only six train changes in less than nine and a half days. Alas, this journey for masochists is no longer possible, the line to Meekatharra having been abandoned 30 km beyond Mullewa, trains having been withdrawn from all cross country links in New South Wales and the link from Toowoomba south to New South Wales having been cut by road works just south of the border.

The last-mentioned is now one of the saddest 'missing links' in the Australian passenger network, for historical reasons alone. The 18 km link between Tenterfield NSW and Wallangarra, Queensland was the original interstate route before the Kyogle and Border Loop standard gauge line was constructed, and all passengers changed at Wallangarra from the standard gauge of NSW to Queensland's narrow gauge trains. In the old days the *Brisbane Express* ran this way on what was known as the north main line, and the station there testifies to its past glories. There remain plans for alternative routes, some never and some once partly constructed, for what was called the 'Via Recta' route, shortening the Warwick–Ipswich sector of the Queensland part of the route by

Wallangara station seen on 19 March 1995: the (former) New South Wales tracks on the left, the Queensland tracks on the right. (Geoffrey Churchman)

crossing the Great Dividing Range south of Toowoomba. This would have been a highly scenic journey, as is the remaining line south from Toowoomba and from Toowoomba down the ranges to Brisbane, regrettably not exploited as a tourist attraction.

When it was still possible to travel part of this route by using goods trains I ventured south to see what scenery most tourists now miss.

Leaving Brisbane with the commuting hordes I took a railcar to Helidon (no longer possible) and there waited in the station bar (well patronised but now gone) for the Dirranbandi 'Passenger' (which no longer carries a passenger car). This took me over the ranges to Toowoomba where I paused for a meal break, and to obtain provisions for breakfast next day.

The Wallangarra goods left Toowoomba at one in the morning (it still runs but now leaves two hours later from a somewhat inaccessible yard north of Toowoomba) and the weather was cold indeed. Toowoomba is high on the ranges and snow is far from unknown. I slept fitfully and woke in the early dawn at Cotton Vale. We were dead on time but the guard felt a chat with the station-master was important and we left late. The train consisted only of diesel locomotive, three bogie goods vans, two tank wagons and an empty truck, plus the guard's van I was in. There was less 'roadside' work to do than usual and we reached Stanthorpe ahead of time. Stanthorpe station is way above the town where you can see all the granite outcrops of the surrounding hills.

The guard brewed me a billy of tea and I opened the 'doggiebag' I had brought from the Toowoomba restaurant the night before. A local character visiting the station handed us some peaches, fresh fruit of the district, the 'granite belt' being noted for its stone fruits, apples, and wine. Here we discarded all our remaining wagons and for the rest of the way to the border, it was engine and van only. I was the sole passenger but was told there had been two the day before, both busy taking photographs.

At the lonely Wallangarra station the train could go no further owing to the change of gauge. Although the line remained intact there was no sign of any train from the New South Wales side. Expecting this, I had arranged for my wife, making the journey south by road, to pick me up in the car for the short hop to Tenterfield, then served by the occasional passenger train from Sydney. The *Tenterfield Mail*, as it was then called, was ready to depart later in the day, but the station was a long walk from the town and that could partly account for its demise.

A caravan park behind a building that could only have been the Railway Hotel in the old days, advertised "no train noise". Its location, a stone's throw from the track, was mute testimony to departed glory and a portent of the future.

Some rail buffs collect engine numbers but others are notorious for boring fellow passengers with remarks about the train running – the kind that will pull out a stop watch a short way into a journey, sniff disparagingly and remark that the train is two minutes late. The only kind of rail buffs with whom I have much affinity is the kind that go on special excursions on unusual routes or on lines closed to normal passenger trains. It can be a pleasant surprise to the incurable wanderer when some mishap, engineering work, Act of God, or whatever causes a train to diverge from its normal route and take a different one, even though this may add to the journey time. That is, provided I have no strict appointment to keep and do not mind being late, and provided I am not dumped at some obscure place far from civilisation in the middle of the night.

British Rail and, I suspect, many other systems, have a habit of carrying out engineering work at weekends and trains are advertised as subject to delay through diversion. It has frequently been possible, for example, to take an East Coast Main Line HST 125 via Hertford North instead of the main line through Hatfield, or via Yarm, Stockton and Ferryhill instead of Darlington, or via Leamside and Gateshead East instead of through Durham. I remember once a Leeds–Manchester diesel set shunning its usual route through Dewsbury and following a tortuous course round the edges of the Pennine foothills on a now abandoned LNWR route through Gomersall. Then there was a time when the usual Newcastle–Middlesbrough train I was on was diverted at Sunderland onto the Durham branch south of the river Wear where, according to legend and song, the young Lord Lambton went fishing and caught the famous Lambton Worm, distant cousin of the Loch Ness Monster. The buffet car crew panicked and closed the bar, not knowing where and when their spell of duty would suddenly end. They need not have worried. The route we followed through Penshaw and Leamside led to the Ferryhill–Stockton line which was not markedly longer than the normal coast route through West Hartlepool.

In Queensland when floods swell the lower reaches of some rivers, trains may have to be diverted inland. If Rockhampton area is flooded trains like the *Queenslander* can have hours added to their schedule through diversion to the coal lines of the central Queensland basin. The train has even been sent as far as outback Winton on occasion, adding over 750 km to its normal run.

Returning once from northern Queensland on the *Sunlander* we were held for a while at Yukan yard just south of Mackay where the heavy coal trains to and from Hay Point cross the main north line. This was somewhere around midnight and sleep overwhelmed me before we started moving again, but I woke later to find we were in unfamiliar territory, not on the coast line but somewhere inland. Steel columns spaced alongside the track signalled the presence of catenaries overhead. Clearly we had been diverted to the electrified coal lines of the central Queensland basin. Indeed, by the time it was fully light we were passing Burngove, junction with the midland route from Rockhampton.

Obviously the floods had not subsided and Rockhampton would be by-passed. It was certain that our train would have to take the Gracemere diversion from just west of 'Rocky', a line that is intensively used by heavy coal trains but not by passenger traffic. I had been on it once before when an Institute of Railway Engineers' special had taken this direct route to Gladstone after a tour of mine sites in the Blackwater area, so I looked forward with interest to the diversion. At Gracemere, where a brief stop was mandatory in the circumstances, I opted to join

GREAT CIRCLE ROUTES

A train at sea — floods near Rockhampton in Queensland, seen from the cab of a QR electric locomotive. (Colin Taylor)

the driver in the cab and what an amazing sight lay ahead as we descended to the lower ground of the coast route! All around was water. The roads were closed: ahead the track was barely visible. It was like being at sea. As we continued on the driver suddenly said, "Better hold your nose here". Good God, were we going under?

Not quite. He had spotted a dead cow floating in an inundated paddock beside the track and knew what the smell would be like, having been that way before.

Unexpected pleasure was mine once when returning from Adelaide by the *Indian Pacific*. An announcement was made that the train would be diverted through Forbes and Cootamundra, thence via the main Melbourne–Sydney line, because of bridge repairs somewhere in the middle west of New South Wales. After reversing at Parkes, junction for the Forbes line, we trundled along at a leisurely pace past the grain silos of this now mainly wheat line to Cootamundra West where a crowd of railway photographers obviously in the know were waiting to catch us rounding the curve into Cootamundra.

Here the train again reversed and there was time for some passengers to make emergency phone calls. I was amazed to learn that a local station official refused to allow the dining car steward to use the official phone for a similar purpose. A poor example of solidarity. This was when some of the staff belonged to Australian National and some to the NSW State Rail Authority (SRA), producing a rivalry and sometimes antagonism between a few of them which did not go down well with the passengers.

The big question, then, since the train was obviously going to be at least five hours late in Sydney (where it was normally due around four in the afternoon) was whether the SRA would look after our need for sustenance and put on an extra meal they had not budgeted for in the fares. The SRA had long been notorious for being alone among *Indian Pacific* operators in not providing sleeping car passengers with morning tea. Would they even have enough supplies? I am glad to say they did and the only sour note to me was in losing my camera or having it stolen—with the snaps of Forbes and Cootamundra taken along the way.

This is par for the course with me, being probably the world's unluckiest photographer. On my first tour of Europe I had my camera stolen somewhere between Firenze and Napoli, probably at Roma Termini station. On my next European tour I had the camera set for the wrong film speed and most of the pictures were a whiteout. And then this! A few years later I was again visiting Sydney and found that because of electrical work on the track north of Strathfield all main north line trains were being diverted via the City Railway and Harbour Bridge. Since the sight of trains like the *Brisbane XPT* and the *Tablelands Xplorer* (that's the way they spell it) using this route was rare I hurried to a local train and disembarked at Milson's Point at the northern end of the bridge to catch a photo (as did two or three others who saw this opportunity). But with all the diversions and the consequent messing up of suburban timetables through most of the Sydney area the train I was waiting for was horribly late, and I spent much of the day there. Imagine my chagrin when on attempting to photograph the famous Tree of Knowledge at Barcaldine in Queensland a month later to finish the film I found to my horror there was in fact no film in the camera.

Even without a diversion through Forbes and Cootamundra the *Indian Pacific* journey between Sydney and Perth is one of the longest continuous journeys by one train in the world.

The place of honour belongs to 'Train 41' from Pyongyang, Korea to Moskva, departing at 10.10 on one day of the week (which may vary) and arriving at 18.50 seven days later.

The total duration of this marathon journey is 206 hours 14 mins (8 days, 14 hours, 14 mins) and the trip is 8666 km, nearly twice the distance from Sydney to Perth. The train carries soft and hard class berths and restaurant car facilities for most of the journey. At Khabarovsk it becomes part of the Trans Siberian *Rossia*.

If one allows a change of train then much longer train journeys than that are possible, without going by a roundabout route or re-tracing any section which of course could extend any trip virtually to infinity.

As another 'trivial pursuit' and possibly in the hope of one day being able to make such a journey I thought it worthwhile finding out what would be the longest train journey possible worldwide by taking the shortest route between the most distant places.

As already noted, a journey of 7442 km is possible in Australia. In North America, Vancouver B.C. to Miami by the shortest route is 7858 km. There are no long continuous rail links in South America or Africa comparable with these.

It is to Asia and Europe we have to look for the record. The longest possible journey that can be made by rail on passenger trains without deviating from the most direct route – or, to put it differently, the shortest route between the most distantly separated places which are connected by rail services – is from Ho Chi Minh City in Viet Nam to Vila Real de St António Guadiana in Portugal, a distance of 16,677 km. The 'great circle' route between the same places is about 11,333 km.

The shortest rail route runs through Hanoi, Lizhou, Aktogay, Barnaul, Karasuk, Tatarsk, Omsk, Yekaterinburg, Kazan, Moskva, Brest, Lukow, Pilawa, Skierniewice, Lowicz, Poznan, Frankfurt an der Oder, Grunow, Luckau, Falkenburg, Leipzig, Erfurt, Bebra, Frankfurt am Main, Mainz, Bad Keuznach, Idar-Oberstein, Saarbrücken, Metz, Nancy, Toul, Dijon, Moulins, Clermont Ferrand, Brive, Périgueux, Bordeaux, Hendaye, Burgos, Salamanca, Guarda, Entroncamento, Setil, Casa Branca, and Tunes.

To undertake this marathon journey as quickly as possible by present (1995) services you would need to spend nearly three weeks in almost continuous train travel, leaving at 19.40 on a Friday and reaching your destination at 7.44 on a Thursday. But, and this again illustrates the frequent difference between the shortest and the quickest routes between two points, you could go from Ho Chi Minh City in almost a week less if you took a longer route! Leaving at exactly the same time and going instead via Beijing, Ulan Bator, Moskva, Köln, Paris and Madrid, you could be at your journey's end just after midnight on the fifteenth day from the start and would cover 19,241 km in the process.

Complete timetables for these journeys are given in the Appendix for the guidance of any rail enthusiast or masochist keen enough and with time enough and money enough to do it. I would enjoy it myself (so must be a masochist) – but "wish I were a rich man" too!

If any reader knows of a longer trip, let me know and I will send a signed copy of the next edition.

Chapter 15

The Far Outback

"The train, passing through twice a week, was more of a diversion than a means of conveyance; the townspeople came down to meet it like an old friend."

— Jon Cleary: *The Sundowners*

Remoteness is a relative quality. When they used to explain the remoteness of the Shetland Islands, the Scots would assert that the nearest railway station to Lerwick, Shetland's capital, was Bergen in Norway. The distance, as the crow flies, is about 380 km but it was not true anyway. Thurso on the Scottish mainland is only about 220 km away. By comparison, some places in Australia are remote indeed. Birdsville is on the edge of the Simpson Desert, over 500 km from the nearest town of more than 6000 population. This is what Australians call real outback, a term sometimes defined as 'beyond the Black Stump'; the only problem being that just about every State except Tasmania claims to have the original Black Stump, just as several of them also now claim the 'Pub with No Beer' of Gordon Parsons' bush ballad fame. There is certainly one in New South Wales, at a place called Taylor's Arm, 26 km from Macksville on the NSW North Coast main line, but there is another in Queensland at Ingham on the main line north of Townsville. So you can take your pick, but give me a pub with beer any time!

Birdsville is not on the railway, nor is it ever likely to be, but Tarcoola – that place the traveller sees crossing the Nullarbor in the middle of the night – is, and Tarcoola is about as remote a place as you can get on the railway. It is a junction at which all trains stop, but the nearest town of any size is Port Augusta, 412 km east by rail. Alice Springs is twice as far to the north, while Kalgoorlie, the next place west of any size, is 1277 km away.

I have never seen the Tarcoola Cup run, nor have I visited the local pub, but I have spent some time at this tiny outback rail junction on two occasions. There is of course nothing much to do at Tarcoola station in the middle of the night. The station building consisted of a shed. I think there was a seat in it, but pacing the platform gazing at the sky was a better way to pass the time. I have never seen a night sky so clear.

I had left Adelaide at 12.40 on the *Trans Australian* and reached Tarcoola on time at 1.42 next morning. There I planned to await the 'Tea and Sugar' which was due to arrive at 3.25, a pleasant wait on a balmy night – I thought. The station-master was there when we arrived, but went off in his utility after the 'Trans' departed. He returned an hour or more later with the news that the 'Sugar' was running late and would not be due till about five o'clock. He had come back to see to the *Alice* which was running early and was soon to arrive on its return journey to Adelaide.

Now a few moments' thought was enough to cause a re-think of plans. Being in this remotest railway junction was an experience but why hang around for another two hours when here was a train about to go and meet the one I intended to catch? Being on a single track the trains could only cross at a passing loop, and there I could hop from one to the other. I checked with the station-master. No problem! The guard would look after me: I could rest in the lounge car of the *Alice* and they would radio the 'Tea and Sugar' so that I changed over smoothly.

We left Tarcoola at 3.42 and arrived at Kingoonya 78 minutes early at 4.38 where I changed trains, leaving two minutes later. By then the 'Sugar' was running close to three hours late. It had left Spencer Junction, its eastern starting point 3 km west of Port Augusta, 80 minutes late but made up time over the first 100 km and was seven minutes early at McLeay. It then lost hours at Pimba, junction for the disused branch to Woomera, the rocket range settlement which once had its own thrice-weekly railcar service from Port Pirie.

My second visit to Tarcoola was a quick out-and-back trip from Port Pirie on the *Indian Pacific*, returning on the *Ghan*. Both were late and I had nearly three hours to admire the outback sky once more, yet amazingly, it started to rain. This is fairly rare in those parts. The would-be rail traveller in the outback therefore has to be ready for anything. Almost anything can happen, and probably will.

The story is told of a couple staying in the outback who went to the station for their return train, on which a booking had been made.

"Sorry," said the station-master, "these tickets are no good".

"Why not?" they asked, the train being there waiting.

"Sorry mate, but this is yesterday's train," said the official.

"What about today's train?" they asked.

"Better come back tomorrow," was the reply.

Apocryphal though the story undoubtedly is, it does have a message. In general, once a train is late it tends to get progressively later, and other trains on the line become late as well. On suburban systems this can be remedied after a while by simply missing out a few of the scheduled services. The nine-twenty running 25 minutes late can simply be held back an extra five to become the nine-fifty.

With longer distances the delays can mount up. In England there was a train that arrived two months late after it had been held in 42-foot (12.8 metre) snowdrifts in the Pennines between Barnard Castle and Kirkby Stephen, but the passengers would have been taken off first. Not so fortunate were the passengers on the rescue train of the Florida East Coast Railway in 1935 when a hurricane swept it away together with miles of track linking the coral quays. This train of events established a world record for lateness when another train on that line stranded at Key West was barged back to Miami months later.

There have been trains running days and even weeks late even in my own experience. I essayed to travel on Australia's *Ghan* not long after the new route from Tarcoola had been opened in 1983. This was supposed to be a flood-free line, unlike the old route which crossed creek beds and was continually being washed out. Unfortunately it had rained heavily the week before I was booked, and the new *Ghan* had been cancelled. When it finally did run, over a week later, it consisted of over 40 carriages, two or three trains all in one.

While trains like the 'Tea and Sugar' and the *Ghan* certainly traverse the outback they do not let the traveller experience the flavour of real outback towns, the places where the people come out to greet the train, either to collect goods from it, meet friends or family, or just sit and watch it while it is there. Many outback rural centres have been deprived of rail services in the last two decades. Some still remain in Queensland, but all are threatened by the pseudo-rationalist forces which seem to be raging out of control.

When Queensland's *Westlander* ran twice weekly in each direction between Brisbane and Cunnamulla in the far south-west of the State (which it did until 1994), 'Flying Flea' was the name given by railwaymen to a single sitting coach which, with van, loco, and power unit, was marshalled at Charleville (now the terminus of the whole train) to serve the branch to Quilpie.

Quilpie was the end of the line, the furthest west you could go in Southern Queensland, and one of the two nearest stations in Queensland to the South Australian border. Yaraka, further north on a branch from the Midland route, shares this honour and is slightly nearer by road to remote Birdsville, start of the sandy trail to South Australia known as the Birdsville track, and home of the annual Birdsville Races, but Yaraka was even less accessible than Quilpie.

When I first travelled to Quilpie the land was greener than it had been in years. There had been 'good' rain shortly before, and the locals were pleased about it – an unusual thing for farming people who, to the city dwellers, appear always to be grumbling either about drought or floods – some of which are the result of ignorant land use practice by farmers and graziers over several generations.

Near Mitchell I had an excellent bacon and egg breakfast. Bacon and eggs is one thing the Queensland Food Bar cars do well. Beyond

THE FAR OUTBACK

Mitchell the place names have a poetic quality: Womallila, Ulandilla, Amboola, Mungallala, Dulbydilla, Morven, Angellala, Lurnea, Sommariva, Arabella... and then a sudden crash back to reality – Glenroy Scour Siding. Perhaps not reality, or not any more. There was no sign of any scour or siding, though doubtless they must have existed in the past. As for a glen – nothing remotely like one could be seen. The place seemed rather to be a habitation of white ants – termite mounds thrust their way through the hard soil all around.

In the timetable those days there was a lunchtime break at Charleville while the train divided into the Cunnamulla and Quilpie sections. Once past Charleville you feel you are really in the bush. The train would roll uncertainly along the slender rails, which railwaymen refer to as "two wires in the grass". The sun beats down through the windows and a blue-white haze obscures the horizon. Most passengers go to sleep, but some become talkative instead. There were nearly five hours to go when the trains ran: the flashes of interest, perhaps a passing truck held up at a crossing, a goods train going the other way, and the brief stop at Cheepie, aboriginal for 'Whistling Duck'. There the old Royal Mail

The *Westlander* seen approaching Westgate – the junction of Quilpie and Cunnamulla lines – from Cunnamulla in Queensland. (Colin Taylor)

Hotel, a stone's throw from the station, promised some relief in the event of any unforeseen delay. The train buffet was detached at Charleville and went with the main part of the train to Cunnamulla.

On the Cunnamulla line the track is said to be ballasted with local soil or creek sand, tamped not by conventional machines but by the 'patter of Merino pegs' – sheep's feet. Sheep are something of a nuisance on the track. There are few fences: sheep are often beside the line and in their sheepish way when they hear a train coming, decide the other side is safer and run across in front of the train with the rest of the flock following. Loco crews are not allowed to put injured sheep out of their misery: they say such action would be classified as 'Slaughter in other than Primary Industries Department Approved Premises' and consequently illegal. But it is also said that in times of severe drought when sheep farmers are reluctant to spend money on bullets to shoot starving stock, they drag disabled sheep onto the railway for the train to finish them off. Not everything you hear in the bar of an outback town pub is necessarily true: it is a favourite Australian pastime to spin a good yarn and occasionally pull the leg of gullible city people. At holiday periods the 'Flying Flea' was well patronised but there were times when the *Westlander* itself carried less than a dozen passengers – at least according to statistics produced in support of its truncation.

In the old days the Railways could always be sure of at least one passenger a week on this train, a barmaid travelling from Brisbane or returning. One of the former publicans apparently believed in a sort of *Droit de Seigneur* and was constantly advertising in the Brisbane newspaper for barmaids at his Quilpie hotel. Their fare was paid.

Once there, they were expected to sleep with the landlord. If they didn't, he sacked them. If they did, his wife sacked them. I was told there were always three on the go at any one time; one travelling to Quilpie, one there, and one on the way back.

Interestingly, the hotel I stayed at had an attractive barmaid, and I had a very affectionate companion in bed with me that night, one that crooned softly to me while gently kissing my ear. It was not the barmaid, alas, but a very large mosquito. Mosquito shooting is probably the major local sport: they are the size of horses and twice as vicious.

There is an abundance of miniature wildlife at Quilpie. Ordering a counter tea of pork chops and salad, I found a number of little green crickets anxious to share it with me. Quilpie was one place you could do with a mosquito net, to say nothing of fly-screening. I spent a better night on the train, but the pub at Quilpie was a friendly place, with the happiest mixture of different races, ages, and sexes I had seen in Australia for a long time.

A crowd of workers from an oil drilling site further west came in. They were travelling by coach to Brisbane (to me an abhorrent thought) but they took the opportunity of anaesthetizing themselves before leaving, loaded with suitable 'medicinal' supplies for the long journey.

At Quilpie the whole train would be turned round on the reversing triangle, backing into the cattle yards. I joined the driver for the first part of the trip back, leaving the train at Westgate Junction to wait for the *Westlander* proper.

Standing at Westgate waiting for a train conveyed very powerfully the remoteness and loneliness of the 'bush'. As a junction Westgate was not quite the thriving hub of a railway system the name might imply. Here the single track Quilpie line diverged from the Cunnamulla line. The points at Westgate were set for the Quilpie line, which carried more traffic than the branch to Cunnamulla. There was a short passing loop and a little used curve linking the two branches. It was known as a 'totally unattended Train Order crossing station' and there was a page of instructions on how it had to be operated. All passenger trains beyond Charleville had to be worked by three-man crews. There was no platform and the station architecture consisted of a tiny hut.

Rarely would one see two trains together at Westgate, although I did the last time I travelled beyond Charleville. Our train, the Cunnamulla section, was running late and the 'Flying Flea' from Quilpie – which by then had been expanded by the addition of a sleeping car – was already at the junction. Since our part was scheduled to go first the

'Flea' had to wait while the points were changed and we went ahead. This brought us nicely into Charleville with time for a last drink in the hotel opposite the station before the trains could be connected up for the return to Brisbane. In those days, not long before passenger services were taken off the Quilpie and Cunnamulla branches, the trains were so well patronised that I was forced to occupy a sitting car from Cunnamulla to Charleville because the only vacant berth was on the Quilpie section. The berths were in 'twinette' compartments and sharing with a stranger was normal, but since the schedule has been truncated, it is not unusual to find an empty compartment.

On the earlier occasion the trains ran to a different schedule and left the western termini at breakfast time. By the time the main portion arrived at Westgate at midday I was ready for a cold beer and was probably their first customer since breakfast, getting in ahead of the crowd who thronged the bar at Charleville.

The beer was cold but the buffet was not. The air-conditioning had failed and as we left Charleville it became hotter and hotter. The car had seats for only fifteen and was packed. An incredible rush taxed the ability of the one girl who worked heroically in the ever increasing heat to cope with the demands of hungry and thirsty travellers. I have nothing but admiration for the way one girl coped with the demand, occasionally wiping the perspiration from her brow, and very early in the process divesting herself of the hostess uniform and serving only in a towelling dress. The Conductor came to 'muck in' with the dishes, but still noticed a couple of youths smoking when they shouldn't and dealt with them with firm politeness.

At Morven a railwayman joined who was on a 'busman's' holiday, going by sitting car all the way to Cairns. I did not envy him his three day journey but he had made a good start before the buffet closed that day. With buses a few years later replacing the Quilpie train he might now remember that trip with nostalgia.

I had two farewell trips to Cunnamulla before the service was withdrawn, the last one by accident. By accident because I intended going only as far as Roma and returning by the thrice-weekly Toowoomba railcar. This was to enable me to reach Brisbane in time for a new train to Longreach in the evening. I checked the details and made all necessary bookings in advance. Surprising then it was to find on arrival at Roma in the dawn's early light no sign whatever of the railcar. I hurried over to the station-master.

"What time does the Toowoomba railcar go?" I asked.

"It doesn't," he replied. "Not since Christmas." Incredibly, it had been taken off without even the Queensland Rail Travel Centre being informed. Later in the week at Toowoomba I found a small typed notice on the station announcing the withdrawal but there had been no other announcement about it as far as I was aware.

Now I had a problem. Roma, Qld, is not exactly a metropolis like its Italian namesake. Waiting a couple of hours for a railcar was fine but without this service the next train would be the *Westlander* coming back from Cunnamulla at five o'clock the following morning. There was no way I was prepared to wait that long. The *Westlander* was being signalled away. I made a quick decision, hurried back on board and back to my comfortable berth. If I had to wait a whole day for the train I might as well be on it!

A shower and a breakfast later we arrived in Charleville. Here the train always waited at least half an hour while it shunted around and split into its two main parts, discarding a few vans in the process. There was time to explore the town, make a couple of phone calls and investigate possible alternatives. My first stop was the station-master's office. "Would there be a freight train going back to Toowoomba?" I enquired. "You can't travel on a freight train," he replied. "I can," I said, since I had special permission to do so. He remained adamant. "No-one can," he declared, but when I invited him to take a look at the letter I held from the Chief Executive of the railway, he immediately became most helpful. "Yes, there is one," he said, "but it will only be going as far as Roma". This was no good. At a local tourist office I enquired about air service back to Brisbane. Yes, they had a spare seat on the midday 'plane, and I seriously considered this for a few minutes. But the price put me off. Over $200 would be something of a waste. For that I could have a slap up meal (insofar as that would be possible on the train) and I could always get the Longreach train another day.

Thus settled, I returned to the *Westlander* for my second 'last trip to Cunnamulla' in a fortnight. Somehow it had lost part of its attraction, but I had a book to read and settled down to make the most of the unintended journey. Writer Paul Theroux seemed to spend much of his rail journeys through South America reading books: he tells the reader about them in *The Old Patagonian Express*. I struggled through a book on the history of town planning in Sydney once on a long train journey but found it much less interesting than the conversation of fellow passengers. But this time I was lucky in having a book I had been given as a present, a moving story with the slightly off-putting title of *Love in the time of Cholera*. I think there is nothing more boring than hearing about books other people have read (except possibly looking at other people's family photo albums) so that is all I am going to say on this subject.

Talking of family, I usually telephone my wife at some time when I am away on a train trip. Provided I am not interstate this is fine, but if there is a time zone difference I am sure to get it wrong, and face trouble and strife when my calls have roused her out of bed.

With its terminus at Charleville, and a long wait before its return, the *Westlander* is not now such an attractive two day trip as it was. There used to be a saying in our family. Whenever we had a slight tiff about nothing in particular and I lost an argument I would jokingly threaten to temporarily leave home by declaring: "I'll get the *Westlander!*" My wife could not threaten to go back to mother, the conventional threat of a disenchanted female, since her mother then lived with us, and whenever I threatened to "get the *Westlander*" my mother-in-law would say "I'll pack your bags". But she never did.

Queensland's *Midlander* and *Inlander* services were similar in consist to the *Westlander* and travelled a similar distance. The former ran inland twice-weekly from Rockhampton to Longreach and Winton and the second from Townsville to Cloncurry and Mount Isa.

The *Midlander* has since been replaced by the new through service from Brisbane to Longreach which I failed to catch after my unintended Cunnamulla trip. This new train is named *Spirit of the Outback* although Longreach is regarded merely as the 'border' of Central Queensland's far outback. Winton is 177 km further northwest, close to the Diamantina River which flows right across Central Australia to empty into Lake Eyre (when it flows at all, that is, since according to song "the rain never falls on the dusty Diamantina"). Winton is much more of the real outback, and is the birthplace of both Qantas, Australia's own airline (originally Queensland and Northern Territory Air Services – which explains why there is no 'u' after the 'q'), and Australia's own national song *Waltzing Matilda*, first performed publicly at the North Gregory hotel in that town.

There is a good museum in Winton which arguably contains more of interest than the recently constructed Stockman's Hall of Fame in Longreach. Winton is also noted for its scalding hot water from artesian sources and the dinosaur tracks at Lark's Quarry some 130 km south on the Jundah road, for which a four-wheel drive is needed. Winton is served now only by weekly freight trains to and from Longreach and Hughenden on the Mount Isa line, although in times of coastal flooding main line trains have been diverted by this link.

I liked Winton. You met friendly people there and friendly people on the train. Winton station had a metal arched roof and it was wonderful to visit such an outback place on an air-conditioned train with single berth roomette sleepers equal to the best anywhere in the world. Arriving there one hot afternoon, I helped a large fellow who seemed to be having some difficulty climbing down from the carriage. He turned out to be a visitor from Alaska. I thought, what a change in climate! He was postmaster at a little place called Tenakee Springs and was just visiting Winton for the day (as I was also on that occasion after a three day town planning conference in Longreach). The train allowed about two hours in Winton, while the goods were unloaded and Sadie (yes, she was the cleaning lady) prepared the passenger carriages for the return trip. This was not enough time to visit the dinosaur quarry but plenty for anything else, including a taste of fresh-caught yellowbelly from the river in the Winton hotel next door to the station. 'Bright eyes' Kneen, the conductor, who knew everyone who mattered at Winton, was there to welcome me back to my sleeper and he as well as Sadie and buffet attendant Suzie are among my happy recollections of journeys that can no longer be taken.

Trains on the midland line negotiate some very difficult country in the coast ranges as well as inland west of Bogantungan in the Drummond Range, where five chain (100 metre) radius curves and steep gradients abound.

Here the trains have to travel very slowly and need to stop from time to time to allow brake pressure to build up. On one occasion I was travelling back from Yaraka and joined a cattle train at Alpha, sharing the two compartments in the passenger van with Ted Stewart, a stockman. Ted was responsible for the well-being of the cattle on the train – nearly a million dollars worth, he said. After we came down through the Drummond Range he insisted on going along to check the condition of the beasts. He carried an electric cattle prod, presumably to check that any lying down were still alive after the rough journey. In conversation, as I shared with him some biscuits and cheese spread from his 'swag', he casually mentioned a previous trip when there had been a 'pile up' on these ranges and a lot of cattle had been lost. The passenger van being the first vehicle behind the engine, I was not a little perturbed at the possibility of all those big cattle trucks piling into us if we came off the rails.

Surprisingly, some of the express livestock trains nearly match the *Midlander* in scheduled timing, and were even faster on some sections.

Talking of speed, not many people realise that Queensland has a TGV. Not quite the same as the *Train à Grande Vitesse* of the SNCF but it is one of a group of crew cars constructed to replace Queensland's

THE FAR OUTBACK

old wooden passenger brake vans. There are also TLV, TDV and TGVS vans. I am not familiar with the exact differences: they are all intended for spare crew and some are better than others to travel in. Passengers other than drovers are carried only in an emergency or by special permission and even drovers are not allowed in the TGV. Queensland has its own ICE as well – the railway people's acronym for the *Spirit of Capricorn* inter-city express. With ICE and TGV here already, France and Germany watch out! Queensland will be having the tilt train next.

When I went down the branch to Yaraka, there was a TGV at the rear with spare crew, while I was directed to a less salubrious TLV van at the front. Nevertheless the passenger compartment was equipped with fluorescent lighting and ceiling fans. There was a toilet with wash basin, mirror and toilet paper, but no soap or plug for the basin outlet. The water pressure was vicious

I had wanted to see why Queensland's then Transport Minister, David Hamill, had particularly mentioned this out-of-the-way place as one to which continued service (passenger as well as freight) was guaranteed, since there was no return service actually advertised. I went there early in 1991 to find out.

To reach Yaraka required disembarking from my sleeper on the comfortable and well patronised *Midlander* at Jericho horribly early on a cold morning. The Yaraka train did not arrive until 6.10 and I was glad that even in the Queensland outback I still carried my faithful Italian leather jacket.

The countryside seemed very empty and I began to wonder why they ever built a railway here anyway. But the train was very long, and all the stuff had to be going somewhere. Later on I realised some of the major cattle stations were in this area.

We stopped at Blackall at 10.02 and left again 23 minutes late at 11.17, allowing ample time for a pie and a 'pot' in the pub. There is supposed to be a rare railway ambulance here still but I did not see it and it would probably be no longer used anyway.

The longest 'section' in Queensland (Blackall–Emmett) of 104.58

km is no longer significant to drivers since the Train Order system means that drivers can change anywhere. Ours changed at Benlidi at 13.03. The Yaraka train carries a crew car from Alpha which has spare crew who take over after eight or nine hours, then the first lot take over again. Each crew consists of three, a driver and a driver's assistant in the cab, plus a third man who assists in the shunting. It seemed a lot of crew for such a train and I wondered why no railwaymen were stationed at Blackall or Yaraka itself. This was probably because with only a once or twice weekly train there would be too little to keep them occupied, so it was easy to see in this case why QR might wish to close the line. However, this has not happened to the time of writing, though other seemingly much more important and frequently used lines have suffered from the branch line closure mania sweeping Australia.

The only other station appearing on the map as anything but a rail halt was Emmett. It was totally derelict. They still leave and pick up mail bags on this route. I wondered if the tradition of 'the mails must go through' would apply to the 'Yaraka Mixed' in the event of a rail strike. There were not many trains left where Queensland Rail still had the mail contract.

On the return journey, after a pleasant interlude meeting the locals in Yaraka including, importantly, learning how to pronounce it correctly (accent on first syllable) the train reached Alpha at 5.20 the next morning. Here I was advised to leave because the van was to be taken off and the train would not go further until nine o'clock, despite what the timetable appeared to say. Hence I ended up on the stock train which came in at six thirty.

Ted told me that often he had arguments with drivers when he had to check the condition of his beasts, the drivers being concerned not to have the train delayed. The drover, too, does not want delay because the cattle are watered only at the start of the journey. But it is still an essential part of the job to check them regularly. This was done immediately on the train's arrival at Alpha and again after the ranges at Bogantungan. The latter stop enabled me to check something I had puzzled over a long time. Bogantungan used to have a refreshment room advertised in the timetable. One friend recalled having to order meals in advance to have them supplied when the train reached there. Another friend reported in 1983 that the room had been "closed for years". In fact, it is still open, but of no use as far as passenger trains are concerned: they stop there for only a couple of minutes. I assume its function is more as a corner store for the surrounding district.

After Bogantungan our train showed how fast an express stock train could go, and we arrived comfortably in Emerald in good time for a counter lunch before I continued east by McCafferty's bus at 15.12, so as to be sure of catching the *Capricornian* from Rockhampton back to Brisbane. Ted was unable to join me, having not only to check his charges again but go with them all the way.

In contrast to the tortuous routes through the ranges, the Midland line boasts some long straights, one being of 127 km between Ilfracombe and Barcaldine. Australia not only has the longest straight railway line in the world, it has quite a few other contenders for a place in the top twenty, including one of 110 km through Barcaldine and one of 77 km on the Yaraka line north of Blackall. Though little in comparison with the Nullarbor such distances compare well with the longest straights in the USA, only 12 of which are over 80 km with the longest at only 126.9 km, while Britain's longest is less than a quarter of that.

The *Inlander* is a train whose character stems partly from the route it follows and partly from the passengers who travel on it.

In railway terms it is a loco-hauled air-conditioned passenger train, with first and second class seating and sleeping accommodation and a small buffet/dining car.

Like other Queensland inland trains a few years ago, the buffet had restricted "liquor sessions" when I first made a journey on this train and, knowing Mount Isa to be a down to earth hard-working industrial town, I was curious to see how religiously the rules were followed.

Just before session time, my fellow traveller Mike Kent decided to go up on the locomotive. Mike drives passenger trains on the Mulgrave

Mill cane line south of Cairns and had a professional interest. I told him I would have a 'cold one' awaiting his return.

But the end of the session came with no Mike in sight – hardly anybody in sight, in fact, because the official session was rather early and most people only came along when it was about finished.

The staff agreed to keep a can of beer for Mike, in fact it was decided to regard the session as starting an hour later – and why not? Time is a human invention – we acknowledge that it varies with longitude – and Mount Isa is far west of Townsville, the main population centre on the coast. If the real time was eleven o'clock in Townsville, it must be barely ten in Mount Isa. The spirit of the regulations, if not the letter, was therefore kept.

The buffet was full of drovers, ringers and assorted travellers of every description. There were two young girls, barely 15, whose burning desire was to return to Gladstone to be with the boyfriends they had met on holiday; a Mauritian girl on her way to Darwin – wearing a tee-shirt top with the slogan, "If I owned Australia and heaven, I'd rent heaven and live in Australia"; a somewhat sloshed Cockney woman and a crowd of happy kids.

We also had a stowaway – or so I was told. A character who joined the train at Stuart, south of Townsville, and kept changing seats to avoid the ticket collector.

Stuart is known for its jail, and it was believed he had just been released (or escaped?). They never caught up with him.

One of Queensland's favourite railway stories is told about Cloncurry, or 'The Curry' as they know it there. A drover had joined the train there with his dog – a blue cattle dog bitch. You are not supposed to take dogs in the carriages – there is a place for them in the guard's van – and in any case you had to have a dog's rail ticket. He hadn't, and a passenger complained when the train left Charters Towers. Along came the guard.

"I know there's a dog in here," he said.

"No dog," said the drover. "No bloody fear, there's not!"

"There is a dog," said another passenger. "Look there!" An old overcoat was bunched on the seat next to the drover. The guard pulled back the coat. There lay a blue cattle dog bitch.

"What's this then?" he asked.

"That's the wife," said the drover, "straight-up, mate, and she's a damned sight cleaner and more sober than I am!"

"You'll have to pay," said the railway officer, unimpressed. And pay he did, for the whole journey back from Mount Isa too!

'The Isa' itself has to be seen. It is an industrial massif. Soaring chimneys, huge buildings piled seemingly one on top of the other – as impressive as most industrial megaplants are – like the Ruhr or Teesside – but the more so because it appears so starkly in the outback after miles of comparative nothingness.

Mount Isa also lays claim to being the largest city in the world. This is another of those 'trivial pursuit' type questions, and it is true. Mount Isa's population is barely 25,000 but its local authority area is 40,977 square kilometres, roughly twice the size of Wales.

Some of the countryside between Cloncurry and Mount Isa is very rugged and wild camels may sometimes be seen. There is a tale about one that used to go into the pub at Duchess, the junction for the Dajarra branch, and drink with the locals. This is probably another of those tall Australian stories but it is astonishing how much truth there sometimes is in them. Near Mallacoota in Victoria there is a pub where a kangaroo is said to be one of the regular customers. It comes up to the bar, reaches in its pouch for the coin, and quaffs a beer. I never met this discerning roo, but have a press clipping photo of it doing just that at the pub at Gypsy Point.

There is another story about a roo that escaped from a zoo in Britain and, being thirsty, hopped into a nearby pub and asked for a half of beer. The landlord, presuming that the beast would have little notion of the price of things, overcharged. Then, seeking to make conversation started off with "We don't see many kangaroos in here," to which the roo replied, "I'm not bloody surprised if you charge £5 for a glass of beer".

Chapter 16

The Sunshine Route

"I'll walk beside you" – song disrespectfully credited to inspiration by Queensland Rail's *Sunlander*

The flagship of the Queensland Rail (QR) passenger fleet of 'traveltrains' is now the *Queenslander*, arguably most luxurious of all regular trains in Australia and a better bargain than most of the privately run premium trains elsewhere.

This is a comfortable, well appointed train, first introduced in 1986 as an up-market version of the ageing *Sunlander* which itself replaced the old *Sunshine Express* on Queensland's main line linking Brisbane to the tropic north of the State.

The *Queenslander* runs once weekly between Brisbane and Cairns, The first class fare includes superb meals, berths, unlimited coffee, entertainment and magnificent Queensland scenery. It takes 31 hours to Cairns and while there you can add a half day trip on the Kuranda Tourist Train, but not if you want to return on the Queenslander next day. You will have to wait for the older and less well-appointed *Sunlander*.

Even so, to travel this route all the way between Brisbane and Cairns can properly be considered what it is claimed to be – one of the World's greatest train rides.

The scenery alone makes it memorable; fascinating mountain shapes – the almost phallic Glasshouse Mountains rising from among the pineapple farms south of Nambour, the canefields of Bundaberg and beyond, the glimpses of the coast. Mighty rivers, fearsome in flood, flat plains where brolgas dance; the myriad islands off the coast; and

THE SUNSHINE ROUTE

A view of the Cairns-bound *Sunlander* on 17 July 1994 near Bowen. (Jean Campbell)

the dense rainforests and cloud-covered mountains of the north. The towns are varied, too. There is Brisbane with its straggling suburbs; the old gold mining town of Gympie (which unfortunately is now by-passed and is out of sight of the railway); Gladstone with its power station chimneys, aluminium refinery and coal terminals set against a background of gleaming waters dotted with small boats; Rockhampton where the train goes along the middle of the street; Mackay – flat but fascinating, where the sunsets flare over the fields of cane and the largest bulk sugar terminal in the world is situated; bustling Townsville, the most 'townish' of Queensland provincial centres with its grand historic station building and modern pedestrian mall round the corner; and finally Cairns, the heart and essence of North Queensland, hospitable, warm, extrovert, and the sort of place you will want to go to again and again.

I did. I tend to make instant judgements about places. First impressions count a lot. Sometimes one has a favourable opinion preconceived – or an unfavourable one. I had heard nothing favourable about

Gladstone, but liked it. As a town planner, I fully expected to find Surfers Paradise abominable, but the worst thing about it turned out to be the highway between there and Brisbane. Alice Springs I looked forward to, but was disillusioned as far as the town itself was concerned.

The fact that I liked Cairns at once had absolutely nothing to do with the good friend and former student who welcomed me with a couple of girls on his arm and took me for lunch and a bottle of ice-cold Seigersdorf Riesling beside a most inviting swimming pool. Little things like that would of course never sway my professional judgment. (He lies.)

Having said all this, prepare yourself for a long slow train journey if you go to Cairns. If you feel that the day and a half allocated by QR for the *Sunlander* or *Queenslander* is rushing it a bit, at all of 50 km/h, they will let you take five days over it instead. This is by travelling on the *Sunshine Daylight Rail Experience*, a tour train which stops for the night whenever it gets tired — usually half way through the afternoon.

The *Sunshine Daylight Rail Tour* (as it was originally named) started life as a railcar service but in the last few years has been a two or three coach air conditioned train. The seating is marked 'economy' and there is no on-board catering except 'morning tea' (although in some advertising material it was shown as having a club car — which it did, for that one occasion!).

No sleeping accommodation is provided; the passengers are booked in hotels for the four overnight stops and the special fare is inclusive of accommodation and meals. The morning 'tea' of fruit salad is served after the first stop, which is for photographs of the Glasshouse Mountains.

The trip may include a detour to Hervey Bay, opposite Fraser Island, which is made by bus in spite of the existence of a rail line almost to its shore at Pialba. At Ingham, north of Townsville, passengers may enjoy a launch trip through the Hinchinbrook Channel to re-join the train at Cardwell on Rockingham Bay.

I once travelled part of the way with this train, pursuing it by

THE SUNSHINE ROUTE

Sunlander two days after it left, overtaking it en route later, then returning south to Home Hill where I spent an evening with friends before joining a goods train back to Townsville. There I caught up with the Sunshine Tour which was stabled for the night.

It was quite a gathering of trains that day. There were two other 'specials' in addition to the Sunshine Tour. Both had been chartered by educational establishments and consisted of old non-air conditioned sleepers with a griddle car operated on the do-it-yourself principle. The Queensland University Agricultural Department ran an annual field trip in this way. Their special 'train' had to be attached to various goods trains to travel from one place to another, but it made a cheap and convenient travelling hotel.

While waiting at Townsville, the overnight freight from Cairns came in. This had a passenger carriage attached. Two girls stepped out.

"How was the trip?" I asked.

"Great," they said. "Better than the *Sunlander* – you're not cramped in a little seat".

This was an understandable reaction. In the old carriages that used to be attached to goods trains – there were a lot in Queensland – you could lie full length across the compartment and thus enjoy some genuine rest, whereas in the 'proper' passenger coaches with a centre aisle you had only your own narrow seat, or at best two together on which you could squirm into a foetal position if so inclined.

The day before there had been questionnaires handed out to *Sunlander* passengers, seeking comments on the comfort and other features of the service, in particular whether passengers would welcome a lower standard of accommodation without air conditioning (presumably at a lower fare).

Well, two at least apparently did – but whether they would feel the same if their carriage had been packed is perhaps another matter! What happened to the questionnaire and its results I never found out. Perhaps QR didn't like the answers. Sometimes this sort of thing is little more than a public relations exercise, not intended to improve anything or affect decisions already made but just to give the impression that someone up there cares about what the public think. The government has recently been amalgamating local authorities throughout Queensland. Everywhere it goes for an expensive public relations exercise. Nowhere is any notice taken of the fact that 90 percent of the public are against the proposals!

The message is: beware of management bearing questionnaires!

I joined the *Daylight Tour* as far as Ingham, two hours journey north from Townsville, and was able to brief Margaret, the tour hostess, on one or two things about the line that weren't in her script.

Just north of Townsville, and less noticeably just to the south, the railway runs alongside the main highway, which is unfenced, for several kilometres. Here the trains are restricted to a 12 km/h crawl, yet road traffic can go five times that speed. It seems ridiculous that a long distance passenger train (or an express freight for that matter) should have to spend over 10 minutes to cover the less than 5 km between Townsville and Garbutt. To console the tourists I mentioned the fact that the five a.m. train took an hour and a quarter on that same stretch. In fact it is so timed because it is one of those 'shunt' or 'pick-up' goods trains. I hope it made them feel better about our slow progress, but probably they didn't care. Slow travel is no great problem if there is plenty to see: no-one would want to hurtle through the Swiss Alps at a hundred miles an hour and perhaps the rail tour passengers found the Townsville northern industrial suburbs equally fascinating. It was a change from the canefields, after all.

On my first trip on the *Sunlander*, from Brisbane to Gympie, people told me about *I'll Walk Beside You*, and said the song had originated there. Here the narrow gauge track used to wind endlessly and climb steadily, but a realignment has now removed the most difficult parts. It was reputed to be the longest continuous gradient in Australia and probably still is. At night the train seemed to be going so slowly you wondered if it had stopped. It used to be said that seeds thrown out from the engine germinated and flourished as the train passed, allowing the guard to harvest the crop. This was as much a testimony to the rapid plant growth promoted by Queensland's sun and moisture as it was a serious comment on the speed of the train.

Queensland's coastal rivers are not long by world standards, or compared with the Murray and its tributaries and the great seasonal flows from the other side of the ranges which sometimes find their way south to Lake Eyre, but they make up for it in sheer volume of water. By rail you view them from bridges near the mouth; the Mary, which rises in the Conondale Range behind the Glasshouse Mountains and flows north close to the railway from Gympie to Maryborough, the Isis, which is crossed north of Howard and flows into Hervey Bay, and the Burnett at Bundaberg. The first two are quite small, but notorious for flood capability. There is the Fitzroy at Rockhampton (the railway swings across it just north of the town), the mighty Burdekin at Home Hill (which you cannot possibly miss) and the Herbert at Ingham.

Some railway bridges are astonishingly narrow when viewed from the engine, and there is an optical illusion when you are not used to it. When crossing a narrow bridge by road, drivers usually slow down, because the reduced side clearance makes it unsafe to go at speed: a slight swerve could spell disaster. Swerving, of course, is unheard of on a railway track, except in the Polish joke about the Russian soldiers on the line: (the train tore off across a field):

"Why?" asked a passenger.

"Didn't you see the soldiers?" replied the conductor.

"But why not go straight on then? said the mystified passenger, to which the conductor replied: "One of them got away!"

The result is that the engine rushes towards an opening that looks far too narrow to go through. On one of my journeys, coming down from the ranges near Charters Towers on the Mount Isa line, I was photographing the Burdekin bridge ahead and instinctively shied away from the side of the cab as we entered the girders. The tale is told of a train driver on the Brooloo line that panicked as the train approached a tunnel. "It won't fit!" he shrieked.

TRAINCATCHER

Around Giru and Cromarty, between Bowen and Townsville, are flat marshes, swarming with wild birds; Brolgas or 'native companions' in their hundreds, Burdekin ducks, great cranes in dozens, egrets, and ibisis. It is wonderful sedgeland country.

The countryside north of Townsville towards Cairns also deserves to be seen in daylight, with the impressive peaks of Hinchinbrook Island, the channel, and the Cardwell Ranges behind the little town of that name. You then go north through Tully (station for dreamlike Dunk Island) and up through Innisfail in a valley of canefields flanked by ranges on both sides, past the Bellenden Ker range which includes Queensland's highest peak, Mount Bartle Frere, and through Babinda, Gordonvale and Edmonton.

It is worth breaking the journey at Babinda, where a long walk or a short taxi ride will bring the visitor to the Boulders Reserve, set in tropical rainforest and rich in legend. Oolana, a beautiful young woman of the local tribe, was said to have been given in marriage to a respected elder. All went well until the visit of another tribe brought a handsome young man along. Love stricken at first sight, the young ones fled, but were overtaken by the searchers under Churichilam, (Mount Bartle Frere) where they were camped by a gentle pool. Dyga, the man, was forced away and Oolana was seized, but she broke away and flung herself into the waters. At once there was a giant upheaval which thrust up the huge boulders that remain to mark the spot. Oolana was never seen again but the legend says her spirit lives in the boulders. Among them, the stream plunges into a limestone cavern and foolhardy swimmers diving into it have disappeared for ever. Keep to the deep pool further upstream where it is safe!

Until recently the club car was the only part of the *Sunlander* where smokers and non-smokers were separated, one end being for each. The dining car prohibited smoking altogether and now this applies to the whole train. On one of my journeys a youth of about 16 entered the club car, sat down at a table under the 'no-smoking' sign and promptly lit up. I drew attention to his error and he moved to the other end.

THE SUNSHINE ROUTE

An elderly gentleman opposite criticised the no-smoking rule. "Why should people not smoke if they want to?" he asked. It was supposed to be a 'club' car. I pointed out there was plenty of room for both, although the smoking part in those days usually became the most crowded. He then commented that drinking was worse than smoking anyway, looking down his nose at the can of beer I was just about to enjoy. He didn't smoke himself, and he didn't drink either; just sat there in silence (when I declined to let the conversation develop further) and scowled at the club car in general and my beer in particular. I wondered why he came there at all and was relieved when he went away.

Later he came back, this time with a woman in tow. She looked vaguely South African – how I could guess that I don't know: their accent was not Australian, but there was something about their demeanour that rang a bell. He bought two cups of tea, a big deal; then smilingly chatted to a young girl who was going to Mackay. Getting bold and fraternising with the natives, were we!

'Sport Australia', her T-shirt top said.

Then I heard him talking to some others who joined his table. The clipped accents were a sure giveaway.

"Ai haf lift here some time but haf lift in other countries – Botswana, Rhodesia..." I heard. That was it: Southern Africa it was. But he seemed to be enjoying himself more as time went by. Perhaps his woman had slipped a gin in his tea.

There was an old dear from Melbourne at the other end of the car. She neither drank nor smoked but enjoyed the company. A younger crowd, travelling to Cairns, were from Perth, from South Australia, Victoria and the Gold Coast. They had met for the first time on the train and were going to have a whale of a time if they lasted as far as Cairns.

One of the menu items in the dining car is Silkwood Platter, which is really bacon and eggs with tomato and hash potato – a 'proper' breakfast. It takes its name from Silkwood, a small station on the railway between Tully and Innisfail where traditionally the dining car staff would put out their scraps to feed the 'chooks' on a property adjoining the track. This was a regular occurrence, just one of those delightful little traditions that build up around regular long distance trains going through isolated places.

I broke one of my journeys north at Proserpine. This is a small town set among canefields with a range of hills between it and the coast. Forty minutes' bus ride brings you to Shute Harbour, gateway to the Whitsunday Islands.

At one of these, Hayman Island, transport is by rail from the jetty to the resort complex, with an intermediate stop at the heliport (with flights from Proserpine). Built around 1954 by Ansett Airlines, the railway is 0.87 km long, with three engines, four covered coaches, and five other vehicles. Except for the working parts, the trains are made on the island. The open passenger trucks have a sunshade roof, and 25 percent of stores for the resort are conveyed by the flat cars. Brampton Island, further south towards Mackay, has a similar arrangement and was reputedly the first in this field.

Returning south on a relief *Sunlander* I met a family group who boarded the train at one of the "conditional" stops before Ingham. The father, a Polish migrant, was fond of beer and didn't like to lose drinking time by going for a set meal. This was when QR stipulated session times for drinking which tended to clash with meal times. The man was not going to be hurried. Their 20-year-old daughter did not drink and kept mostly to herself. She seemed half asleep, and came to breakfast next morning very late, bleary eyed.

"She stays up late at night," explained Mum. "Lives it up. Never in bed before two o'clock."

I wondered how she managed to "live it up" on the *Sunlander* at that time of night. They were going on holiday together, I think for the first time in years. The girl had a child and Mum usually had to look after it for her at home. Where was it now?

Nobody told me. "Ungrateful, she is," said Mum, but the daughter's own story, when she told me, was uncomplimentary of both parents. They were all nice people, but there seemed very little rapport between them. I wondered how they came to be going for a holiday together. Three in one economy sleeper for two days did not augur well for a restful break from the stresses of everyday life.

A younger group sat in the buffet. One of them, a slim girl with a vacant expression and childish features but extraordinary mammaries, took out a cigarette pack; then saw the 'no smoking' notice. They discussed it, then the young lad with her lit up. Later they moved to the other end where an older fellow in his twenties began showing keen interest in the girl. Her expression throughout remained vacant.

At Rockhampton I encountered them later in the evening as we sought a drink in the station bar. Their relationship was difficult to sort out. The young lad gave the impression the girl was his sister. She was 14, he said, but later, at Brisbane, he seemed not to know her and went his own way. There was an older woman who might have been the mother of one or both but looked like neither.

At Rockhampton refreshment room a notice says, "No glass bottles of drinks allowed on trains". The older fellow tried unsuccessfully to stock up on beer to take on the train, perhaps to break down the girl's resistance, if any, or to console himself if he got nowhere. By the time the train's departure was announced he was leaning over her with an arm round her shoulders; one knee almost between her thighs. Breathing rather quickly he was muttering words into her ear which were mercifully inaudible to others but did not require much exercise of the imagination to guess at. Mother, if such she was, simply looked on and continued her drink. The young lad smiled secretly, as though this was par for the course. Young Miss, Lolita-like, continued to look vacant and spoke not a word.

Almost all the way along the Sunshine Route, on the flat lands and winding up the sides of valleys, you find canefields. Their little narrow gauge railways run parallel to the main line; in some places cross it at a 'diamond', or here and there a bridge. Formerly some of these trains carried passengers but none now do so on a regular basis except at Mosman, north of Cairns, and Gordonvale to the south where the

Ballyhooley Express and the *Mulgrave Rambler* are popular tourist attractions.

I spoke to Paul, an entrepreneur who ran the comfortable, low-cost Avalon motel at Proserpine. Paul was interested in developing passenger services out of the cane season on the extensive cane railway network in that area. He would provide and run them, he said, but the local mill-owners and Council were not interested. Certainly there is scope for some entrancing tourist rail routes at places like Cairns, Babinda, Innisfail, Tully, Ingham and Proserpine. There are possibilities also at Giru, near Townsville; in the Mackay and Bundaberg regions, and at Nambour.

The Sunshine Route offers leisurely and relaxing train travel – a good way to begin a holiday, like an ocean cruise. Whether you like clubbing it, mixing with the younger set in the disco, or just reading a book, you can do it all on these trains while viewing scenery of great beauty and variety.

Arriving in Rockhampton on a southbound *Queenslander* there was quite a crowd waiting on the platform but it was not clear what they were waiting for, to take a place on the train or to meet friends. The place seemed somehow dead. Probably the station bar was closed. In contrast, our lounge car was swinging. Claudine, our entertainer, was in full spate, belting out songs in her powerful contralto to the karaoke backing. Even crew members were joining in and having a go. *Under the Boardwalk* was the number that got them all going. It was as though we were welcoming the people there. But nobody on the station seemed to show the slightest interest. One passenger, Lenore, was quietly enjoying every minute. She had joined the train earlier. Did she like the train, she was asked.

"Yes, I always enjoy a train trip, it's a great way to fly," was her answer. Lenore usually flew but preferred the train. So many do.

Among the innovations on the new *Queenslander* I thought the individual keys to sleeping cabins was a brilliant one. It is now being applied to other QR sleeping car trains. And what a pleasure to have a quality electronic musical instrument, a Roland, that actually sounds like a real piano! Participant entertainment is so much better than the canned variety.

Features like these, plus the superb food, put the *Queenslander*, in my estimation, just ahead of the *Ghan* but in the spirit of friendly rivalry I suppose Australian National may come up with something new yet! And indeed they have – since writing the above a new cuisine, yet to be sampled, looks like a winner.

On the return journey of the inaugural 'Whitsunday' *Queenslander*, a mid-week run to Proserpine and back, I had a slight accident which I mention because a similar thing just might happen to someone who could be litigious, like the woman who sued Australian National when she stumbled on the rocky ground at a photostop made by the *Alice*.

Several of us were engaged in an "Eye-Spy" game. This was from a booklet produced by Railways of Australia which we found in the lounge car, along with children's games and all sorts of other things to interest people if they became tired of the scenery or the readily available refreshments. In turning away from the door end window in the lounge I caught my forehead on one of the 'Roman column' type features of the lounge interior. Whether it was a lurch by the train or just my lifelong propensity for knocking my bald head on anything it can find, I am not sure. One of the men who had worked on the actual refurbishment of the car interior was also a passengers and we jokingly discussed the prospects of suing the railway for damages. Vexatious litigation is one of Australia's most peculiar and wasteful pastimes (since lawyers are the only beneficiaries). There used to be a photo stop in central Australia when the Alice Springs train passed the 'Iron Man' monument, a modernistic sculpture of twisted rails and sleepers near the South Australia/Northern Territory border, and the crew would let the passengers out to walk over and look at it. When one of them stumbled and sued the railway, that was the end of it.

Anyway, we resolved against any such meanness – this being a promotional trip in which all the passengers were guests of QR. But the spot affected rapidly came up in a noticeable swelling which attracted attention and concern, and although it was painful for several days afterwards I suffered no permanent effects. In fact the memory overall is a pleasant one. A delightful young lady passenger ministered to my comfort with ice from the bar, gently holding me and bathing my forehead. Ice numbs the nerve endings so you feel extreme cold rather than pain but it must have checked the inflammation.

"It's not coming up any more," she murmured, looking at me with concern, her fingers tenderly stroking my forehead. "Something is," I replied, *sotto voce*. "Cheeky," she said, with a playfully provocative nudge. Wink, wink. Say no more. Nothing like the old TLC to soothe an injured male.

Much worse misfortune befell those passengers who were on the first public run of this delightful train the following week. I was both saddened and angered by the actions of those responsible and although I always avoid taking sides in such matters I was not convinced by the union spokesman's attempts to justify the sudden strike which caused the paying passengers to be off-loaded on to buses halfway through their journey. It was distressing for them and bad publicity for QR. It also did nothing to advance the union's cause – however just or otherwise this may have been. It takes two to tango, they say, and both sides usually share some of the blame when worker/management disputes arise. Why cannot all concerned agree that whatever action they take, be it a strike, a lockout, or whatever, the public must not be allowed to suffer. Australia is notorious for things like airline strikes which always seem to happen at the beginning of school or other major holidays. I wondered what had now become of the old railway tradition that whatever else happened, the 'Mail' would go through – the 'Mail' traditionally being the principal express train on the line.

Like a lot of other good traditions, this seems to have been lost sight of. Perhaps it no longer applies because the mail now all goes by air.

Chapter 17

Suburban Shuffle

"Chaos is come again" – William Shakespeare: *Othello*

In contrast to the cruise-like atmosphere of Queensland's and similar 'traveltrains' are the suburban railway systems, or 'citytrains' as QR call them.

From time to time people come along who have proudly travelled on every railway route in one of our capital cities in one day. It can be done, but not many would really want to do it, and few would do it twice. The fact is that suburban railways are generally uninspiring – they are a necessary evil associated with the growth of big cities. You don't find many expresses, you rarely find a buffet car and you may even be lucky to find a seat.

Nevertheless, suburban trains are an excellent and speedy way of getting about a big city, provided you avoid the rush hour when all forms of transport are appalling.

What would London be without its Underground or Southern Electric – sorry! – Network Southeast. Where would Paris or Moskva be without their Metros, New York without its Subway, or Melbourne without its 'sparks' (and trams)? And where would Sydney be without its double-deck suburban trains? It was the first city in the world to have double-deck suburban electric multiple unit trains, just as London was first with an underground railway.

It only needs a rail strike to answer: chaos!

The suburban rail services in Australian cities are, by and large, nothing to be ashamed of – even if Melbourne a few years ago still had clerestory roofed carriages designed for gas lamps that would have been scrapped decades ago anywhere else; even if most of the systems have extensive single track sections and many are plagued by frequent level crossings, a mixture of suburban, long-distance and freight traffic sharing the same routes, and signalling systems that make up in variety what they lack in sophistication.

Sydney and Brisbane stand out as the scenes of the most substantial recent improvement, extension and modernisation, but all Australian capital cities have invested in new rolling stock and all except Melbourne in new or extended routes in the last few years.

The intensity of suburban traffic on Sydney's underground City Railway is reminiscent of London's Inner Circle, yet Melbourne's Spencer Street Station bears the title of the busiest station in Australia, with its constant stream of EMUs sliding in from the north and west, curving round the viaduct from Flinders Street, and popping up like weasels from the open tubes of the underground City Loop.

Before moving to Queensland in 1972 I was a regular commuter for a couple of years in Victoria, travelling up to 78 km daily though not always by train. The suburban journey from Lilydale to Melbourne's Flinders Street was tedious except when one caught the evening express which ran non-stop nearly all the way. There should be more expresses on suburban lines. This is difficult when there are only one or two tracks but with a little imagination (for which administrators are not often noted) it is still possible to intersperse express with stopping trains if there are extra platforms at some of the stations where fast trains can overtake slow ones. The Lilydale line in Melbourne had about six tracks for the first few stations out from the city and was then triple track most of the way, reducing to twin track and then single for the very last couple of sections. Three tracks are good, because the railways can adopt 'tidal flow' if the signalling and train control systems are geared to it. The same technique is sometimes used on highways to make better use of road space. On a four lane highway there can be three lanes inward and only one outward during the morning peak, with the situation reversed in the evening.

SUBURBAN SHUFFLE

The world over, the ubiquitous multiple unit train provides quick, stress-free transport from the suburbs to the centres of major cities. Left: a København electric S-ban set of the type introduced in 1966 (Geoffrey Churchman), and below, an elderly Adelaide 'red hen' diesel set near Lynton in the Adelaide Hills. The Adelaide suburban transport administration has so far not appreciated the benefits of electrification. (Jean Campbell)

TRAINCATCHER

In Melbourne the suburban electric trains are referred to as 'sparks'. Electric sparks mark their passage and there must be something about the rails, the type of current, or the Melbourne atmosphere that gives these trains that characteristic odour that seems typical of electricity and hot metal.

I find suburban train travel rather tedious on the whole, but that is more a reflection on our failure to plan cities sensibly than it is a criticism of this travel mode. If suburban rail journeys are tedious, what can we say of suburban bus journeys – or city driving? Perhaps of all suburban transport systems the tram is best; easy to mount or alight from, combining the smoothness of rail with the interest of being in the streets among buildings and people. Melbourne's rail, bus and tram systems are better coordinated than most and there are useful (if a little too complicated) runabout tickets which offer travel by any mode.

Vandalism can be rampant on suburban trains. Some routes have bad reputations which the condition of the seats confirms. Vandalism on Sydney's suburban system costs over a million dollars a year. A more visible police presence could be one answer. This is a problem of society, not of transportation. If young folk see their elders ignoring regulations they will adopt a similar attitude to society's restraints. The non-observance of 'no smoking' signs on trains was long a common offence before most systems banned smoking altogether but other infringements of regulations are frequently to be seen – the playing of radios (usually banned because it can annoy other passengers), and the placing of feet on seats are the most common. Even graffiti, such a distressing scourge of modern society in spite of occasional touches of artistic merit, may well owe something to the way we allow commercial advertising to disfigure our buildings.

I was travelling on the line past Brisbane Airport one afternoon when a group of teenagers joined the train. There were several girls and two boys. Some carried balloons full of water which they would squirt at each other, or over the seats, windows and floor. Having made a mess of one group of seats they moved on to another, giggling and indulging in horseplay. The larger girl, 14 or 15 years old at a guess, lit a cigarette. Naturally, it was a non-smoking area. One of the boys kept trying to grab her bottom, and she swore at him. Then he sat on her knee and put his arm round her. This seemed fine for a while but she tired of the intimacy and threw him off. He looked too immature to do her any good. With her smouldering eyes, sensual mouth and the taut yet lissome movements of a young lioness, she could have devoured a fellow twice his size for breakfast. He made a grab at her crotch and the expletive injunctions were repeated as she brushed him away. Then she let him sit close to her again: protesting yet enjoying and encouraging his attention.

Another girl, sweet-faced, slim and innocent looking with 'physical' emblazoned on part of her anatomy that still had a fair way to go before meriting such a description, looked on with mingled amusement and disdain – or was it envy? I wondered how they behaved at school – or how they would have acted if the train had been full. The carriage had felt the impact of their presence but at least they had not been violent or destructive. They kept glancing at me as if half expecting some sign of disapproval or a comment (I was taking notes) but I held my peace. There is a time to refrain from speaking.

Less forgivable was the behaviour of a gang of youths on a Sydney train who seemed to find amusement in shouting obscenities at passengers in passing trains and spiting at them across the gap. Only a partly closed window saved me from a face full of disgusting gob. Spitting on the floor, feet up on seats, a general disregard for the comfort or convenience of others and for public property, seem to be regarded by some elements as part of showing their maturity. When they are older they either settle down or just don't travel by train.

On a suburban railcar at Richmond in Sydney's western suburbs, two young ladies entered – I call them that merely to signify they were female, older than 'girls' but not quite adult. They plonked themselves down across the aisle from me, looked around (did they read the sign about not putting feet on the seats?) and promptly placed their feet on the opposite seats.

They had cigarettes but didn't light up, which was some relief. They saw my camera and decided to include me in the conversation.

"You a photographer or something?" they asked without preamble or introduction.

I said no, but was taking some photographs of the railway.

This started a new topic of conversation. One had a boyfriend – mad, he was, she said – he spent a fortune taking pictures of trains. This dismissed me as mad as well, I suppose. Her statement was liberally adorned with unnecessary adjectives of Anglo-Saxon derivation. I am not personally offended by the use of straightforward Anglo-Saxon four letter words or their derivatives, being brought up in the north of England where they call a spade a spade – or a bloody shovel – nor do I object in principle, as many seem to do, to the use of such terms by females.

Judiciously used, even as expletives (perhaps especially as expletives), they can be colourful and enrich the language, but I dislike their indiscriminate use when it adds nothing to the meaning. Taken literally, the girl's account accredited her boyfriend with remarkable ability, if rather unusual habits. No doubt she knew him well, but if people talk like that merely to shock others, they do themselves a disservice. I was not there to judge, but I found their speech and manner offensive. Perhaps I should have persevered, seeking some common ground, some topic of mutual interest that would transform this chance encounter of three human souls into a meeting of minds, but I 'chickened out'. Seconds before the train left, I suddenly noticed the pub across the road advertising counter lunches. There would be another train in an hour. I leaped to my feet and made for the door.

"You going?"

"Yes," I replied. "Wrong train!"

On the London Underground you meet all types. Most just sit enduring the crush and the rush stoically, some simply bury themselves in a book or a newspaper, but now and then you get the type that wants

SUBURBAN SHUFFLE

to harangue a captive audience.

There was a rough slag on the London Bridge to Kings Cross tube. That is all I can call her. Rough looking, sloppily dressed, and uncouth. With her loud voice she addressed anyone and everyone, but directly and individually, drawing the attention of other passengers to people she singled out as victims of her observations. One poor quiet fellow was trying to read a book: she picked on him, deprecating intellectual pursuits. I could see he was embarrassed. Then she told us all where she was going and what she would be doing. I do not recall all the sordid details because we were nearing my place of departure.

"Have a nice night," I said, seeking to forestall any remark of hers directed at me as I rose to my feet and she focussed her attention on a potential new victim. "Old enough to be my grandfather" she announced, as if presenting me to any passengers who were taking notice. "There may be snow on top, but there's fire down below" I very nearly retorted but held my tongue because such a remark could have immediately been relayed to the crowd in a cruder form. She might even have demanded a command performance as proof. I may be somewhat extrovert myself but I really found this woman revolting in every way.

A much more pleasant encounter with modern youth was on a train to Cronulla. This is a seaside resort south of Sydney where the railway goes almost to the beach and it is very popular with surfies and bathers. State Rail even ran excursions on holiday weekends from Penrith and Parramatta in the western suburbs, round a lot of back routes, to take people direct to the beach.

On this particular day there had been a signalling failure and the train was late. We stopped at St Peters just out of Sydney for nearly half an hour and no-one told us what was wrong. At Sutherland the guard called "all change", terminating the train (then 36 minutes late) so that it could return in its proper time slot. I had intended to go first to Waterfall (then the end of the electric route) but Cronulla was my major destination so I waited on the packed platform. It seemed that several trains had been reversed and had disgorged their contents. Surfboards, beach gear, bright colours and bare legs crowded the platform.

The train came in, already full, but some disembarked to leave a few seats vacant.

A young group obviously knew each other. The fellows would keep 'stealing' money from one of the girls, hiding it, passing it to each other, saying "No I haven't got it", then when she reached to wrest it back, popping it suddenly down her bra. "No, Damian, no!" she squealed (like "O, no John, no John, no!"), loving every minute and coming back for more.

At Cronulla they all poured out across the road, asserting the age-old common law right of passage on the King's highway, halting traffic as pedestrians should. Having crossed safely, they swarmed down to the beach like locusts to pattern the sand and surf with their bronzed bodies, bright gear, corn-coloured hair and glistening surfboards.

Not only on suburban trains have I found young people to be generally very open and easy to approach, sometimes rude, sometimes crude, but this is a lot better than being vicious and destructive. I would rather face verbal abuse than physical and it is wise to avoid empty suburban carriages late at night.

In Western Australia there is a little train that goes down the coast to Bunbury. Hardly suburban, but it is only a two hour trip and some features of it I found very reminiscent of the train to Cronulla. At Bunbury one can go down to the sandy beach, and also see the waves of the Indian Ocean crashing against rock formations that are rather like a miniature version of Ireland's 'Giant's Causeway'.

For most of the journey to Bunbury I was treated to a dissertation on 'modern youth' from an elderly lady who had brought her own children up to behave 'properly', she said. She couldn't understand how her daughter would let the grandchildren get away with such bad behaviour, using first name terms and refusing to do things when asked. "My daughter is good," she said, "Still wouldn't cheek her own mother."

Modern youth in the *Australind*, as this train is called, was meanwhile enjoying itself in the next carriage, adjoining the buffet. A group of school children in their teens with an older person I took to be a teacher, were obviously on an excursion or going on holiday. They were met by a coach at Bunbury.

One of the girls, conspicuously well developed, was playing footsies with a young lad under the table. Both had their shoes off and were getting each other quite excited, but out of the line of sight of teacher. Another young lass smiled and waved at me. Very forward, I thought, but not horrifying. Was this the 'modern youth' I had just been warned about? She had a tee-shirt with "beautiful Aussie" stamped on it, and was well on the way to becoming one, but she would have looked more beautiful without the bubble gum which splattered in her mouth whenever she opened it.

At Granada in Spain, I was subjected to a similar exhibition of American influence at its worst. Beautiful dark Spanish maidens in thin puffy blouses and kilt-type skirts (yes, tartan patterns), paraded the sun-drenched streets splatting pink bubble gum between their pouting lips. Ugh!

It might also be television influence (much of it from American programmes) that is a factor in changing the way young people act towards each other and towards adults. The one-time common chivalry, like giving an older person a seat on a crowded bus or train (or a man offering his seat to a lady), and the occasional friendly exchange or repartee that might accompany it, are tending to be replaced by rudeness and aggression. Harmless verbal play between male and female, of almost whatever age, used to be appreciated by both sides, but is now branded sexual harassment. It takes two to tango. But soon even "Shall we dance?" will be taken as aggressive sexual assault, and "that's a lovely dress" will be taken as a notice of intention to remove it!

I offered no such comment to the lady I was talking to on the *Australind*. She was too serious. Her remarks about young people were interspersed with a fairly detailed description of the chronic illness she suffered from. This somehow made the train a safer way to travel and seemed presented as an excuse for using it.

She told me the historic Rose Hotel in Bunbury was the place for lunch. There are a number of historic buildings in Bunbury but the rail enthusiast who used to find the rolling stock of the *Leschenault Lady* tucked away behind an engine shed at the far end of the station yard will now be disappointed. The government redeveloped the station as a shopping centre, moved the terminus out of town, and moved the historical items to another location altogether.

As well as its escape route to the beach at Cronulla, the Sydney suburban system used to have a branch to Royal National Park but this was closed for unknown reasons by an anti-rail government. However, the main north line goes past Kuringai-Chase, familiar National Park country of many Australian television scenes. You can also go by train up into the Blue Mountains. This is a particularly fascinating trip and the service is both frequent and fast. The best views are from the upper deck of double deck trains, and you can get off at 'Bottom Points' near Lithgow for a trip on the steam train plying the old Zigzag which was the main route through the mountains before it was replaced by a series of tunnels.

Sydney's suburban rail network is the most developed in Australia, one on which it is possible to make round trips rather than journeys merely out from the centre and back. This backwards-and-forwards suburban shuffle is characteristic of Australian metropolitan rail networks. They follow a radial pattern. Brisbane has only two cross-town links, one of which is used only on special festive occasions. Melbourne has its underground loop, but nowhere can you go round and round in a circle quite the way you can on the London Underground, or cross from one line to another without going most of the way back to the central area.

In Adelaide the authorities have tried to counter the modern increase in vandalism by introducing State Transit Police. These are a most discouraging looking lot and seem to have replaced guards. However, there are no tickets on sale at suburban stations and these fellows, despite conspicuous armament, do not act as train guards, cannot sell tickets or do anything for passengers at the stations themselves, which is often where the trouble starts.

In Sydney, Cityrail now have a magnetic ticket system which in theory means they can dispense with manned barriers. But there are so many problems of the magnetic strip failing that they seem to have ended up with more people manning the turnstiles than ever before. I wonder how well the costs and benefits of these new systems have really been worked out. There is nothing so reassuring as the physical presence of some railway staff at a suburban station at night, and no amount of electronic surveillance systems, automated barriers, 'help points' and emergency telephones make up for it. Authorities lock or take away the station toilets because of the dangers they pose but what when you have to 'spend a penny'?

And worse things could be in store for suburban rail users. In keeping with the philosophy of 'make the user pay' and a mania for private enterprise and de-regulation as the supposed panacea for efficient transport, bodies like the Industry Commission in Australia have recommended 'reforms' to public transport such as higher fares, more competition, fewer subsidies, fragmented management, devolution of government control, curtailed services and suchlike, presumably with the idea it will thereby become more efficient as an industry.

Such recommendations are based largely on untested theories and untried experiments. The commission shows little appreciation of the inter-relationship of transport and land use planning; indeed, they must regard 'planning' in any sense as anathema. Free competition and market forces will work together for the best, they imply. How several different operators could run trains on one and the same track is not explained: the notion that rival profit-motivated operators will co-operate with each other to co-ordinate services is surely evidence of utter ignorance of both human nature and transport history! Hopefully, their ideas will be ignored. If implemented, as an Australia-wide coalition of community interest groups and individuals with special knowledge and experience of transport, Transport 2000, warned, urban public transport in Australia and consequently our cities themselves could suffer irreparable harm. These views were echoed by several other concerned organisations and it is to be hoped that such a seriously flawed report will be unequivocally and totally rejected by Government. The alternative is chaos, a recipe for disaster.

Chapter 18

Through the Veil

"Nobody knew they were there" – from the song: *Oh dear what can the matter be?* (parody version)

They called it the Iron Curtain, but when I passed through it was more like a veil and no-one was quite sure where it began or ended. Certainly people living in some of the countries inside it had difficulty getting out, but to the international traveller it could be little more than a temporary nuisance. It may surprise many to learn that through all but the very coldest days of the 'Cold War', trains kept going, daily, from one side of the curtain to the other.

While trains like the *Ost-West Express* (Oostende–Moskva via Berlin and Warszawa) had been reintroduced long before the curtain started to fall there were still plenty of reminders of the political differences when I revisited Europe in 1985.

On a kind of reconnaissance trip I skirted the East German border by train from Bad Harzburg to Braunschweig. From the line one could clearly see the tall iron fence with its guard posts separating East from West Germany. Further south at Bayerische Eisenstein the railway ended in a no-man's land, with a notice 'This land is mined' separating us from the former Czechoslovakian station on the other side of the border. The mines must have been cleared since, because trains can now take you right through to Plzeň where the beer is just as famous as in Bavaria.

But I had resolved to go to Kraków in Poland. Why Kraków? I had been persuaded. My department Head, a professor who not long before had been one of the first people to 'escape' Poland after the internal political revolution which saw Lech Welenska become *persona grata* at last, insisted that to travel Europe without visiting his (and the Pope's) home town would be unthinkable. Also, the Tatry National Park was just south of Kraków, on the Czech border, and this, he maintained, was a scenic 'must'.

A Eurailpass, of course, did not include Poland or, for that matter, Czechoslovakia, East Germany, or anywhere else I could think of in between. But in planning the trip before leaving home I decided that Czechoslovakia was my best and shortest route into Poland, reached either via Germany or Austria, and I prudently obtained a visa for that country.

Earlier in the tour I had realised that to cart all my heavy luggage around from one place to another was not sensible. It was too much effort, in spite of the little wheels my monster suitcase was fitted with and the long strap by which I would pull it.

This suitcase saw some heavy wear. Pulled along on its lead over sometimes cobbled streets it performed admirably but would sometimes keel over, when taking a bend too fast, and I would stop and remonstrate with it while righting it. People watched with some amusement and I thought I would add flavour by christening it, so that I could call it like a dog on a lead. Somehow the name 'Pongo' suggested itself, perhaps because I was in a part of Austria called Pongau around this time. I had met a fellow called Daniel Strässle on the train from Switzerland and he and I with his father and mother had enjoyed a great party. It could have been Daniel who suggested a name for my suitcase: we met again later on the Swiss/Austrian border. They were a great crowd. I would walk along the platform trailing Pongo on the lead, calling, "Come on, good boy," but I felt it was not wise to subject Pongo to the unknown dangers beyond the Iron Veil. Poor thing might be quarantined.

That determined, I had to find a 'kennel' where I could leave him. Railway station luggage lockers are fine for short term deposits but I really needed a hotel for this purpose. I eventually established a base where I could leave things not wanted on a particular trip and be sure of a room to come back to. This was at Altenbeken, a small town railway junction near Paderborn in Westphalia. At the Bahnhof Hotel, right opposite the station, I found host Keith Gilbert, from Doncaster, England, who had married a German girl after the war and settled there to run the Station Hotel – sorry, the Bahnhof Hotel – and it was to Altenbeken I later returned to deposit Pongo in the care of my obliging host before venturing across the dreaded border.

I had also found a few good bases in Austria, but my limited German vocabulary made it difficult to make satisfactory arrangements for the stabling of Pongo anywhere in that country.

Of all European mainland countries my first prize would have to go to Austria, for prices, people, scenery and ease of communication. It is usually easy to find someone who can speak English (or readily understand a foreigner's attempts at German) and good accommodation and meals are obtainable at modest prices.

Although Austria is a participant in the Eurail consortium, the ÖBB was the first of only a few such rail systems to offer me free tickets for my proposed itinerary (the Irish were next). Apart from that, their railways are efficiently run. Their trains are clean, comfortable and well appointed and their timetables are the easiest of all to follow. You can hardly go wrong in Austria on the railways.

The connectivity of Austrian train services is almost incredible to one schooled in Britain and matured in Australia. Obviously Australians learned how not to connect train services, like they did so many other bad habits, from the Poms.

The very first table in the Austrian ÖBB Timetable is an example of what can be done by carefully scheduling a mix of fast and slow trains so as to afford connections at key stations. A typical pattern is shown in the following example:

At 6.00 a semi-fast train E740 leaves St Pölten for Salzburg stopping at several intermediate stations up to Linz (arrive 7.40, depart 8.00).

At 6.09 a stopping train follows from St Pölten calling at all stations

to Amstetten (arrive 7.11, depart 7.21) and Linz (arrive 8.32).
The express *Stachus* leaves Wien Westbahnhof at 6.00 for München, Germany, calling inter alia at Amstetten at 7.16, where it overtakes and connects both ways with the stopping train, and then at Linz at 7.52 where it does the same with semi-fast E740.

Thus all the stations between St Pölten and Linz are connected by stopping, semi-fast or express train combinations in guaranteed connections with minimum waiting time. On top of that, in the example just outlined, the 23 intermediate stations between Westbahnhof and St Pölten are also connected by an earlier stopping train reaching the latter station at 5.54.

At Ruette in Tirol where my free travel ended and I took up the Eurailpass for travel beyond Austria I had an encounter with the Austrian police. A friendly local, Peter, took me along to a *Pianokeller* – a pub with a piano, at which I had a great time playing a selection of everything I could remember – from *Waltzing Matilda* though *Lilli Marlene* and *The Happy Wanderer* to the *Horst Wessel* song (they were not over-enthusiastic about that one) and in return I had been plied with free drinks by mein host. Peter taught me the accepted salutation *Zum Wohl* (cheers!) but I had failed to notice my watch had gone kaput and it was rather late when we left. Arriving back at my hotel I found the door locked. I had a room key but had not counted on the entrance being closed, which was from an upper verandah. Knocking on the door brought no response. I wondered what to do – Peter had left for his own home. There were some wicker work easy-chairs on the verandah and I was thinking, okay, I'll just settle down for the night here, when in the street below a black car came to a halt and out stepped two policemen. I could see a possible night in the cells looming up! Showing my passport (and rail ticket) I explained that I was booked in the hotel but had been out to this wine cellar. There must have been some hidden intercom system I didn't know about as they very soon roused the proprietor and the door opened to admit the late night Aussie reveller. It was all very friendly – they were just making sure a visitor to their little town was safe.

Searching for a useful base in Austria I spent successive nights at St Anton am Arlberg in the Tirol, Waidhofen an der Ybbs, and Leoben (where I had briefly been before).

I eventually settled on Schwarzach St Veit in the Pongau as one of my main bases for this second European tour. Not that it was the most accessible place imaginable, especially for attempts at two-day or three-day trips into Spain or Poland, but the post office was right next to the station, and pension-style (*Gasthaus*) accommodation was just up the road. A wonderful rushing stream in the valley just near the *Gasthaus* with the sound of cow bells and the scent of mountain air made it a most restful haven. It was also a convenient contact point because, unlike those in some countries, the Austrian postal and telecommunications systems seemed to work.

Waiting for a connecting train at Stainach Irdning I met a couple of Australian girl tourists. "You don't sound Australian," they said. Maybe not to them: the native born Aussie can always pick a Pommie or other European accent yet to someone from the "old country" I would have been more identifiable as one. I had been in Australia only about four years when I had occasion to telephone my brother back in England. "Oh, Colin, you dewe sound laike an Orstraylian," he declared in typical toffee-in-the-mouth pommie tones – nothing like the flat northern English accents I remembered him having and thought I also still retained.

Anyway, I proved my credentials to the girls with my knowledge of Aussie places and expressions.

"What's a nice shiela from Melbourne doing in a place like this?" (pronouncing it correctly as 'Melbun' not 'Mell-bawne' as the Poms do). The place in fact might have been Aussieland. In fact one of the trains on this line was called the *Ausseerland* and went through a place called Bad Aussee. Just the place for my type. I left the cynical and wise Aussie shielas and chatted up the innocent hostess in the train buffet instead.

The six coach electric train *Hohensalzburg* – the one I joined –

consisted of two six-car units, each with its own mini-buffet, staffed by one. Customers, myself included, swarmed like bees round a honeypot as attractive hostess Andrea (no husband, no boyfriend, she said) coped easily with our culinary demands. Later, as the satisfied crowd melted away (once I find a buffet car I am not easily separated from it) we engaged in friendly conversation and she heated me a can of Austria's inimitable *Lieberknüdel* soup. Failing in an attempt to arrange a dinner date at the end of the trip (she had to check stock with the steward in the other buffet on arrival in Salzburg) I reluctantly kissed her goodbye – no, that is badly put: it was the goodbye that was reluctant not the kissing. She gave me details of her future movements and I hoped to renew her acquaintance on another train, or on the same train another day, but circumstances in the form of laundry and an accident intervened.

There being no immediate future in continuing to Salzburg I baled out in the early evening at Ebensee, a pleasant little spot near a lake with the station obviously located close to shops, hotels and the like – always an important consideration when travelling through unfamiliar territory. There is nothing worse than leaving a comfortable train at a chosen night stop and finding no sign of any hospitable buildings nearby – just desolate unlit roads, car sale yards, factories or dark and forbidding countryside.

But it was not like that. Nearby I soon found a *Gasthaus* with cheap accommodation and (another thing about Austria) a perfect willingness to accept traveller's cheques without exacting an exorbitant commission for them. In some countries even the banks practice this legalised robbery, and in one town in Germany even a travel agent would not accept a traveller's cheque in Deutschmarks! Austria has many smaller banks – I think of the savings bank type, called *Sparkasse* and here you can always get exchange currency. But ordinary shops often exchanged traveller's cheques too – as of course they should. It seems, though, that traveller's cheques are on the way out. Many would not accept American Express in particular, and the ubiquitous plastic card now seems to reign supreme. Even that can have its problems. Danish State

Railways would not accept a MasterCard in 1992 because it was not on a Danish bank. I had naively thought such cards to be world-wide.

But back to Ebensee. In what must have been the resident's lounge after dinner I met some friendly locals and we ended up having a great old singsong – of what songs I cannot remember but from my student days I knew a few traditional German songs and of course many more modern songs, through the efforts of people like Rolf Harris, the Beatles, and Abba are well known internationally. One of the characters, Rudolf, played an accordion and was the legendary life and soul of the party. Good-naturedly he identified himself with the red nose reindeer, one of the songs we all sang.

Revisiting Ebensee a couple of days later I was horrified to learn that Rudolf had had an accident and was in hospital in another town. He had been riding his bicycle home one night and had been blinded by the headlights of an approaching car, ending up in the ditch with a broken back and lacerated forehead. The hospital was in Bad Ischl, some 17 km away but what is that when you hold a Eurailpass? – just 20 minutes on the train. Forgetting my original idea of looking for lovely Andrea I thought, "Now, wouldn't it be a nice surprise for Rudolf to be visited by the Bad Aussie in Bad Ischl?" And so it was, for both of us. The poor fellow couldn't move and it was not possible for me to stay long because laughing made his back hurt, and he was the type who liked to laugh a lot, a happy approach to life. Austria seemed to generate a spirit of natural friendliness which was easy to reciprocate even if it meant going out of one's way a little.

Capital cities, when you are a total stranger, can be among the worst places to be lost in, or if not actually lost, just not knowing where to go. I was in Wien looking for a laundry. Could I find one – did anyone understand what I was looking for? Apparently not. But in a restaurant where at least the menu was clear enough for me to order and enjoy some delightful Hungarian *Cevacipi*, I met my Good Samaritan, Erich Kaiser, Vice-Director of a city insurance company who went totally out of his way not only to direct me to a laundry, but to take me there, explain my needs to the proprietor and tell me how to get there a day or two later when I would return to collect it. This quite changed my otherwise rather jaundiced view of Austria's capital city and I returned to my then favoured base of Kreilhof-an-der-Ybbs feeling, like Louis Armstrong, that it was a wonderful world after all.

The next day, in glorious sunshine I took the local train to Waidhofen (they called it the 'little train') where I changed for the main line connection to Wien where my laundry was ready for collection at the little *Wäscherei* not far from the Westbahnhof.

There was one train that travelled round the outskirts of the Wien central area from Westbahnhof to the lines going east and south from Südbahnhof, and this was the *Direct Orient Express*. Obviously a train to catch and, like so many European international services, it was made up of bits and pieces from everywhere to everywhere else. At Westbahnhof they took it apart and reassembled it in a different order. A very enticing Hungarian restaurant car was attached, with vases of flowers (and bottles of wine) on the tables and I began to regret that my rail pass did not extend to Hungary – nor did I have a Hungarian visa. My intended disembarkation was therefore at Bruck an der Leitr, just short of the border, which allowed no time for indulging the appetite.

Even so, I faced customs and ticket examination formalities not long after the train's departure and at Bruck station I was waylaid by a local con-man who just couldn't think why I should decline his generous offer to get me a Hungarian visa for only $US 16 and a taxi across to Hegyashalom in Hungary for another forty. Had he known that my average daily spending throughout my whole tour of 49 days up to that time was only $A 43 he might have understood. (That figure does not include some $A 6000 for air fares, rail passes, visas, departure tax and insurance which preceded the tour.) I had budgeted $50 a day for travelling expenses, board and subsistence, and was managing to keep within that (with a little help from my friends). To squander that amount just to go a few kilometres by taxi when I had a first class train ticket for the whole of Western Europe was not on my agenda. I could, and did, venture through the Iron Curtain another day and in a cheaper way so after a short spell in the railway station at Bruck I returned to Südbahnhof. There I caught a train to Murzzuschlag where I spent the night at a modest hotel with every amenity except soap and shower. A clean body and clean clothes naturally followed from having a clean mind. All the same, a note in my diary made a day or two later recorded my conclusion that "apart from other reasons, the trip to Wien just for laundry was ludicrous". It was! A 300 km round trip, and twice. I could have had it done in Waidhofen an der Ybbs.

But then I would have missed a trip on the Murtalbahn, one of the most delightful little train rides imaginable. The 65 km narrow gauge (760 mm) line of Styrian Railways, an ÖBB subsidiary, runs from Unzmarkt to Tamsweg and is operated mostly by diesel-electric trains. Had I been there a week earlier I could have taken a steam train with buffet car but no matter. The little tramcar-like train started away purposefully and when it reached Murau-Stolzalpe became packed with school children on a half day closing or long lunch break. It then wound its way up the pleasant little valley through tiny picture postcard villages. At the first of these, Kaindorf im Murtal, some humorist had chalked 'City' after the station name, but this was only a minor railway halt. The scenery was different from Austria's usual imposing mountains, somewhat reminiscent of mid-Wales or the Yorkshire Dales but more colourful.

Close to most of the stations were *Gasthaus*, post office, shops etc. and it was quite a problem deciding at which of these enticing places I would get off for a lunch break before the return trip. Preditz-Turracherhöhe Hu was particularly entrancing but what a mouthful! So was Kendibruck. Then followed one or two not quite so attractive places and with no *Gasthaus* evident in the station vicinity. Maybe I should go all the way and come back to one of the nicest places later? Checking the timetable I found that if I went on to Tamsweg at the end of the line the next train back was Saturdays only. I would have to wait till 13.40 and change again on the way back at Murau-Stolzalpe or one of the other little places noted on the way up. This would mean a very late return to my favoured nightstop of Schwarzach St Veit but if I was too late to find accommodation there I could still hop on an overnight train to somewhere else. After all, I had my clean laundry with me. Oh, the tribulations of a compulsive train traveller! But Europe is the train travellers's haven! One is rarely at risk of getting stranded in the middle of nowhere with no place to lay the weary head. Well, not in Austria anyway.

In the event, returning to Unzmarkt on the main line by a quarter past four, I was in ample time for the Villach to Wien *Wulfenia* express at 16.48 with full 32-seat dining car service which I was then ready to enjoy. The little place I had tried to get lunch at had closed at one o'clock. I came to the conclusion that Wednesday must have been half day closing – which might also explain all the school children going off home at barely midday.

Back again in Schwarzach St Veit I had found a little 'pub' where I got into conversation with Rolf, one of the locals. He was fascinated by the shape of the Australian 12-sided 50 cent piece so I gave him one to keep. He was quite overwhelmed with gratitude – I don't think he had worked out its insignificance in comparative value but to him it was a unique souvenir. Shortly after that he disappeared from the bar, then reappeared half an hour or so later. He had gone to his home to fetch a flask of Schnapps embossed with what I assume was his family crest. A delightful exchange of gifts, and a delightful drink too – at the right time. Schnapps, he told me, is for 'closing the stomach' – the last drink you have for the night. The French, he said, believe cheese has this same therapeutic value, but I think I agreed with Rolf. When in Rome, etc.... but back in Australia Schnapps did not seem quite the right drop. That half litre lasted me a long time back home. I still keep the bottle in the freezer though with Vodka substituted for Schnapps, and equally rarely enjoyed.

But Vodka was surely the Polish drink supreme. Before I left Brisbane my professor had introduced me to what the Scots would call the 'Reay Mackay' as far as Vodka was concerned (better known in American English as the 'Real McCoy'). This was Polish White Spirit at 140 proof. Would I be able to sample this at bargain prices in its place of origin, or would it be as ridiculously overpriced there as Scotch whisky was in the Highlands?

Before venturing into Poland I made a tour of part of Austria's southern border. Old maps had showed a railway which crossed into Yugoslavia east of Klagenfurt, from Lavamünd. I was interested to see these abandoned links between 'east' and 'west' in Europe, now that the barriers were beginning to come down, so I took a train from Klagenfurt first to Rosenbach, where I had first ventured into Europe from Yugoslavia some 10 years before. I had no visa for that country, but had not needed one on my earlier European trip – or if I did my travelling companions must have sorted it out with the officials when they sorted everything else out. But I had no such friends this time. "*Nicht,*" said the officials, which sounded distinctly negative. Thus I stayed the night at Rosenbach. Next day I took the railcar back to Klagenfurt and then a local train to St Paul. This, to my surprise, turned out to be a 'mixed' train, of the kind I knew in Queensland but had never expected to see in Europe. There were two or three passenger coaches coupled to several timber wagons.

We arrived at St Paul at 10.45 just in time for the railcar to Lavamünd.

There was almost nothing. The line of the abandoned and lifted railway was evident; some telegraph poles remained, but all was overgrown and it did not look like a rail route about to be re-vitalised. But at least there were no warnings about land mines!

I repaired to the local hostelry to await the railcar's return, less than an hour later, to civilisation.

Thus I journeyed to Wien on 26 September 1985 after these abortive attempts to penetrate the veil into Yugoslavia. Arriving at Wien Südbahnhof in the early evening I bought a single ticket for Kraków on the *Chopin* train departing at 18.40. Since the Eurailpass covered right to the Czech border, this ticket was only from Breclav and cost the equivalent of $A 32.70.

The train was advertised as having couchettes but I found it absolutely packed and only with difficulty managed to squeeze into one vacant seat in a first class compartment. It was to be then or never and I steeled myself for an uncomfortable overnight journey. The fare was remarkably cheap which was one consolation.

Not long after leaving Wien we reached the Czech border. There we stopped. No one was allowed out and a band of officials marched along the corridor. By the noises around it was clear that others were marching along the carriage roof outside. Thump, thump, thump went the boots. Then our door opened and we had a taste of military discipline. 'Stand by your beds' or words to that effect. The seat cushions were lifted, the floor searched underneath, the racks and our luggage examined. Apparently it was pornographic material they were particularly concerned about. They kept snapping their fingers officiously and demanding papers. A severe looking female in grey uniform glared at my passport, placed it against the wall, and stamped it heavily. She reminded me of one of the characters in the Australian TV series *Prisoner* and would have made a good prison warder. I wondered what it would take to make her smile. How would she react if told she was beautiful and asked for a date. I knew no words of the language so probably avoided the likelihood, nay, certainty of arrest. As it was, when they took my visa they kept it. I had assumed it to be valid for more than one entry. After all, I had to come back! But no, one visa, one entry. I could go back the way I came, or continue into Poland as my ticket showed, but I would have to find another way to the west from Poland or apply to their Consul for another visa when I got there. I could imagine how long that would take.

There would clearly have to be a review of options. Meantime, we all settled down in the warm compartment and I offered to share my seat with the attractive young married Polish woman on the seat opposite. It is easier to get some rest if you can get your feet up, so I moved slightly aside to let her feet onto my seat and I put mine on hers. It was nice and close and warm and rather naughtily intimate since we naturally took our shoes off and my arm rested across her stockinged ankles while my toes rested against her side just above the waist. As she was Warszawa-bound I was tempted to think of continuing on the train but having no Czech or Polish money and a ticket only to Kraków rather ruled out the idea as imprudent.

Crossing the next border into Poland was not quite as bad. The thaw had begun. The Polish officials were trying hard. 'Welcome to Poland' they concluded, after an unsmiling and rather severe examination of our documents and a close interrogation concerning our intentions.

To reach Kraków it was necessary to change at Katowiçe. There was no 'Cambio - Wechsel - Exchange' sign to be seen anywhere so my first priority once in Kraków would be money. Second priority would be how the hell to get out of there!

The Katowiçe–Kraków train was an early morning workmen's, without corridor and I think without much in the way of heating. There was no nice warm young thing in the opposite seat, just a group of workmen with whom I did not have anything to communicate. But I continued my progress to the east, and reached historic Kraków at breakfast time.

Since it was too early for the banks I tried a hotel for an exchange of travellers cheques and a breakfast. Not unless I was staying there, they explained. I wandered round town looking at the market stalls, selling revolting looking green and purple fungi, and at the half empty shops which had more the appearance of warehouses. There were queues everywhere. Overall there was a smell something like escaping gas in the atmosphere, the smell perhaps of decay, or of polluted drains. Only in the main square did I find a richness of architecture which spoke of Kraków's past glories. I sat on a bench and studied the timetables, puzzling over my next move. I had really wanted to go south to Zakopane, then make my way round back into Czechoslovakia to the other side of the Tatry mountains, but that was now out. Going back through East Germany was also out – I had no visa. I could fly back direct to Wien and avoid further border formalities but, first, that would be rather costly and, second, there was no plane for several days.

Meantime I went to a now opened bank and after much queueing and some minor hassles managed to change American Express dollars into Polish zlotys. In retrospect, what a mistake!

Ignorance is bliss, but only for a time. I successfully located a restaurant where I obtained a good meal with wine. I looked around the shops, thinking a bottle of Polish Vodka would be a nice thing to take back for my professor – or to sustain myself perhaps on the still uncertain journey back. But you could not buy Vodka or anything else there with zlotys – only with American dollars!

Then it dawned on me that Poland had a coastline, on the Baltic. Could there be boats to West Germany or Denmark, perhaps? And how to get to the coast? With money now in my wallet I returned to Kraków station and joined one of the many long queues at the booking office. I took a first class sleeper ticket to Swinoujscie on the coast, from where (thanks to Thomas Cook's timetables) I found there were steamers for Ystaad in Sweden, the nearest haven in Eurail territory.

The fare, including sleeper, was ridiculously low by other European and British or Australian standards. The train journey, over half way across Poland and taking all night, cost 1360 zlotys, the then equivalent of about $A 3. A bus trip cost only a few cents equivalent and a ferry I later took was free. It was difficult to spend more than about $10 Australian on a meal even including wine.

Kraków station had little to commend it. It had a large draughty refreshment room looking like a NAAFI canteen outside meal hours in World War II. I found my way to the 'gents' and barring the narrow entrance way were several elderly women handing out sheets of toilet paper. You got two, and there was a saucer full of zlotys which you were presumably expected to supplement by way of payment, or did this constitute the wages of these attendants? Since I was only intending to use the urinal I passed up the offer of paper, but was surprised when, along with others, we were staring at the tiled wall the way men do — so as not to be seen admiring what they have in their hand or looking at anybody else's — one of the women calmly walked through checking the cubicles, seeing they were flushed, and mopping the floor. They had a full working week, I felt sure, probably there from Monday to Saturday, and nobody — no, surely somebody — knew they were there!

When at last the train came in I had some difficulty finding my berth. In fact there was no car and berth number which exactly corresponded to my ticket. But I was directed to one that seemed roughly to correspond, although it had three berths. Three ladies (not those from the lavatory) then turned up, all with tickets for the same compartment. One was old and poorly: she was promptly helped into the lowest bunk. As I had not enough Polish to do other than explain my ticket and where I was going, any serious discussion on how to sort out the remaining sleeping arrangements was out of the question. I climbed up to the top bunk and left the others to their own devices.

The next morning I left the train at Szczecin Dabie junction for the connection to Swinoujscie. Here I took the free ferry over to the town and after a good meal at a cafe went to the sea shore of the Baltic and watched the swans. I had never seen swans on the sea before. They must be fond of herring, for which the Baltic is justly famous.

Returning to the port area, I booked on the Polferry service to Ystaad. It was nice to find an all night bar on board but I also obtained a berth to secure some sleep after two somewhat interrupted nights travelling within Poland. I had to pay the fare in US dollars, although I had some zlotys left. I asked the purser what I should do with them. He pointed to a collection box for some hospital or other good cause on the office wall. Its transparent sides showed it to be stuffed full of zlotys. I added mine. They had no exchange value and I wondered, why get them in the first place?

Breakfast on the boat was a good Swedish-style smörgåsbord, plenty of fish, hard boiled eggs, ham, but Ystaad in Sweden was disappointing. It was Sunday morning, hardly anything was open, and there was no train west for a long time. However, I was in Eurailpass territory once again and found a local train going to Simrishamn further up the coast. Better take a train trip than hang about in the station all morning! Most Swedes I met spoke excellent English: their telephones worked, the girls all looked like Agnetha Falskog of Abba and the bottle of cider I bought in a grocery proved to be non-alcoholic. You can't win 'em all.

Later that day I crossed on the ferry from Helsingborg (Sweden) to Helsingør (Denmark) and took the *Öresundspilen* international express from there to København.

I stayed the night in Lübeck, a historic city which was one of the Hanseatic ports. There was some marvellous architecture which I resolved to photograph on a future visit. The next morning I took the local to Hamburg and from there by fast train to Hannover. This particular stretch of line has featured some of the fastest runs by ordinary trains in the last 20 or so years, a particular 'racetrack' being the section between Celle and Uelzen.

There was no catering on the 9.14 Lübeck–Hamburg train but a Swedish 'captain' was well prepared. He claimed to be grandson of the King. He offered a bus ticket when an official asked for passport. Other passengers were getting a little disturbed by his behaviour. He was pretty full, drinking a mixture of Russian Vodka and French claret. Yuk! He ate from a huge slab of Brazilian chocolate, and offered to share it with me. I declined.

Visiting Europe again in 1992 I was taken by my German publisher friend Conrad from Kiel over the border to see the remains of the Iron Curtain separating east from west. There were still Russians about, rather lost and lonely, perhaps waiting to go home but not sure what would be there to meet them. A bit like Churchill's 'homes fit for heroes' after World War II which most heroes never saw. There were also signs of the change from communism to capitalism – the big multinationals moving in, prices rising, commercialisation in all its worst manifestations. Yet the new openness, seen in the abandoned border pillboxes and the smiles on the faces, was a welcome change from the Cold War. Some prices, also, remained at what to 'Western' eyes were at the ridiculously low communist country level. I remembered how I could go first class sleeper in 1985 right across Poland for little more than what a suburban trip would cost at home. So after we had motored through Lübeck and across the border to Bad Doberan it was no great surprise to find the train fare for the 40 minute trip on 'Molli' cost only two Deutschmarks.

Conrad had a camera with him and so had I. As is usual with me when I am anywhere specially interesting (I must be the world's worst photographer) I ran out of film before we had been two minutes on the train. Conrad's friend Marlis had taken the car to follow the train and pick us up again at the other end, and the first part of the journey was along the middle of the main town street. Here, traffic congestion caused a stop, and Conrad jumped out of the train, raced up to the car and grabbed another film from our bags which Marlis had taken care of. Thus re-supplied with film, and the traffic snarl clearing, we resumed our rail journey to the Ostsee resort of Kühlungsborn.

When Conrad had visited Brisbane I had taken him to a Scottish restaurant, one of Brisbane's many ethnic eateries and where you could get authentic home-made haggis and clootie dumpling. Returning to Kiel from the east he said we would go out for a meal. "We have a Scottish restaurant in Kiel too," he announced. He was pulling my leg, of course. Scottish in name only – a McDonalds, but to my relief he chose something rather more exciting – a Greek restaurant whose owner he knew.

From Kiel I took a train to Puttgarden and there waited for the night sleeper *Alfred Nobel* to Stockholm. Puttgarden, one of those out of the way spots known largely only because they are significant on the railway network, proved to be a disappointment. The restaurant was closed, and looked as if it had been so since World War II. There was really nothing to see and nothing to do – not even any trains due through until the one I was waiting for. So I rang my wife back home in Brisbane

— miscalculating, as usual, the time difference, and got the cold reception I deserved, nearly as cold as the weather outside. I was sustained only by a small medicinal flask I carried for such emergencies and, if I recall correctly, by a bag of crisps or something from a slot machine.

When the train came in things began to look up. The conductor was looking out for his passenger and I soon settled into a comfortable single berth compartment and placed my wake-up call and breakfast order. Then the train began its voyage to Denmark. After a lot of shunting to and fro it was split up into portions and we were on the train deck of the ferry. Here, passengers were invited to disembark (from the train) and visit the bars, restaurants and shops on board the vessel.

An excellent evening meal washed down with a bottle of Mateus Rose completed a satisfactory evening. I said "g'day" to a complete stranger in an obvious Akubra hat and bought a couple of hard boiled painted Easter Eggs with the idea of taking them home to my grandchildren. Yes, of course, I ate them myself later before they went bad.

One always seemed to be meeting fellow Australians in the most unusual places. When I revisited Altenbeken in Germany a few days earlier on this tour I was showing Keith the German edition of my guide

'Molli' at Kühlungsborn in the former East Germany. (Colin Taylor)

book and he said, "You should have been here a few minutes earlier — there are a couple of Australians working here who were just in."

I gave Keith a present of a slab of Harrogate Toffee as a reminder of the old country – one of those so very English specialities that you almost forget about when you are away for a number of years, and one I have not seen in Australia.

It was to Keith's place I came back after that first foray through the curtain in 1985. One thing I liked about the way people served you in German pubs was the trust they placed in your readiness to pay. On ordering a drink they would put a beer mat or coaster under your glass and mark it with pen or pencil. No money changed hands. Your next drink produced an added mark and after you had finished and were ready to go they totted it up and told you what was owed. What happened if a customer mixed his drinks I am not sure, nor can I guess how it would work with a mixed group 'shouting' each other. Trust of a different kind is seen in Australia, where on ordering you spill all your change – and often notes too – onto the bar and the barman or barmaid picks out the coins needed. You can even leave your change on the bar, go to the toilet, release any old ladies locked therein, and come back to find it still there. Try that in England!

Chapter 19

A Cook's Tour

"To travel hopefully is a better thing than to arrive"– Robert Louis Stevenson: *El Dorado*

Venturing through the Iron Curtain and the travels in Austria which preceded it were only a small part of the rail tour I took in 1985.

In all, my tour covered 131 days. I travelled on trains on all except eight of these, making a total of 651 rail trips with here and there connecting buses, taxis, trams, cars, boats and planes, not to mention walking even if only between stations or platforms. In the course of it all, I visited or passed through 17 countries.

This kind of itinerary can reasonably be described as a Cook's Tour, though Thomas Cook would probably turn in his grave if he knew the kind of trip people now attach to his name. For one thing, Thomas Cook was a teetotaller, and that historic first Cook's Tour in Britain was to enable people to attend a Temperance Rally. Cook was born in 1808, the same year that Richard Trevithick demonstrated a steam locomotive in London. He was born to a poor family and developed a concern for the lot of the downtrodden working classes, becoming not a socialist but a preacher and philantropist. He travelled many miles, mostly on foot, spreading the word against the 'demon drink' by which the well-off kept the masses in their place.

Cook saw the possibility of a cheap excursion by rail as offering a new form of relief from boredom. His 'market' was those who were not well off enough to own horse and carriage.

Ewen Anderson of Thomas Cook, Brisbane, gave me the following account of that first Cook's Tour:

A COOK'S TOUR

"On the morning of Monday 5th July, 1841, the 500 plus Temperance members gathered on the platform at Leicester station and when their train, which consisted of nine open carriages without seats, pulled in, they boarded, pushing and shoving to ensure that they were not left behind...

"Cook's train was pulled by an engine that resembled Robert Stephenson's *Rocket* whilst the carriages were completely open. There was to be plenty of fresh air mixed with hot sparks and showers of soot and smoke that billowed from the engine's funnel as they made their way through the green Leicestershire countryside to Loughborough. To make the outing as attractive as possible, Cook had arranged for many inclusions starting with a band which somehow squeezed into one of the carriages and accompanied the excursionists en route to Loughborough with bright breezy music."

The passengers had tea and buns, together with "speeches of high moral content" in a park after their arrival, and for a total cost of a shilling return (half price for children) they must have enjoyed it better than spending their time and money in the gin palaces, because it proved the first of many like it.

But that would not be my kind of tour. Steam trains are all very well, music is sometimes fine, open trucks are another matter, but without a buffet car the idea does not appeal to me.

When I arrived back in Altenbeken after my round trip from Wien through Kraków, Swinoujscie, Helsingborg and Lübeck, I caught up on the local news in my friendly Bahnhof Hotel. I heard there had been a fatal accident in the tunnel west of the town, when a railway worker had been killed by a train. However, my own urgent need after the drabness of Poland and the almost non-stop journey back to the west was – you guessed it, laundry again! Also, I was keen after the austerity of the Eastern Bloc and the high prices of Scandinavia to get moving again, use my Eurailpass to the full, visiting all those lovely places still beckoning me.

On my way back I had kept to the main Hannover–Ruhr line to

Bielefeld, then taken a local branch train to Paderborn. This was the nearest town of any size to Altenbeken and boasted a do-it-yourself launderette with a pleasant restaurant nearby. Paderborn was a place well-known from World War II days, something to do with the Luftwaffe if I remember correctly, or with British bombing. I was reminded of this as we approached Bielefeld, when a train going in the opposite direction consisted of military tanks and a troop carrying carriage – hurtling east for what purpose I could not imagine. Such trains had never been seen on British Rail (BR) since long before the end of World War II.

So once again I made a train trip just to get my washing done. A 30 km return trip was better than the last time I had done this. Although I had seen much of Germany earlier in the tour there were a few more places I wanted to see before venturing further south to Italy, a country I had enjoyed so much on my first European tour.

I had been to Berchtesgaden to see what remained of its wartime significance, I had been to München twice, not to visit a beer hall but to have a film developed and the second time was to collect it. It was fascinating to visit these places in Germany which in my youth we heard so much about but could not hope to visit while hostilities remained.

I had also already visited the Ruhr, travelled on the famous Langen suspension railway at Wuppertal, and on the *Lufthansa Airport Express* from Dusseldorf down the banks of the Rhine to Frankfurt. I had also enjoyed exploring by rail the Schwarzwald (Black Forest) country and tasting local venison at a small hotel in Donaueschingen in the upper reaches of the Donau (better known as the Danube).

But there were places in Germany I still wanted to see. South from Altenbeken there were branch lines meandering into the hills of Sauerland and Rothaargeb. Always hankering after places that were 'off the beaten track' I could not resist a foray south through Brilon Wald to Bad Wildungen. These were the sort of rail routes that BR would have closed by then if under their control, but I had a pleasant trip through scenic if unspectacular country and ended up cutting west from Giessen through Koblenz to end the day in the valley of the Mosel. While the little hotel I stayed in suffered from the usual European habit of not providing soap and charging for use of bath or shower, I did have the opportunity to find out that real Mosel wine was not the same as the sometimes over-sweet beverage producers tend to market under that name in Australia.

During the following four days I crisscrossed Germany, spending one night in Plochingen near Stuttgart and another in Plattling in the far south-east, with the last two back in Altenbeken. In between these I went to Hannover to check onward flights for the part of my tour after return to Britain and I came back through Hameln on the 'River Weser, deep and wide' but saw nothing of the Pied Piper. That was my 'day of rest' – only six trains. The day after it I rushed down to Austria again to see if any mail was waiting at the post office in Schwarzach St Veit. I was disappointed but the trip was not wasted because I went there via München and Salzburg on the *Tauern Express* and returned by a different route through Zell-am-See to Wörgl on the Austrian train *Pongau*.

Needless to say, on my last night before leaving Altenbeken I nipped over to Paderborn and enjoyed chicken liver and rice in the restaurant while a kindly local soul looked after my washing at the launderette. Thus I went south again, taking Pongo with me but leaving him for a week at the railway station in Horb. Why I broke my journey at Horb I am not sure. I had been there before but all my notes reveal is that I had an expensive meal in a restaurant which included snail cream soup (try anything once) but it was not as expensive as the meal a fellow at the next table bought for the very sexy young creature he was trying to impress. She ate as though food was going out of fashion and the bottle of sparkling Burgundy that she washed it down with would have cost a fortune. Well, he no doubt thought she was worth it.

Although the route through Horb and past the Rhine Falls into Switzerland, then through Zürich, Arth-Goldau, and the St Gotthard tunnel is the longest rail route between Germany and Italy, it is the most

TRAINCATCHER

One can be forgiven for thinking that the Swiss believe a mountain exists so that a railway can be built up the slopes of it to a restaurant on the top. On the Rigi there is not just one, but two rack railways — one up each side, meeting at the summit (Rigi Kulm). When it can be seen through the water vapour haze, there are views from here of Lake Lucerne. (Geoffrey Churchman)

central of the three routes and scenically perhaps the most varied and dramatic. It skirts the shores of the Zürichsee, Zugersee, Lauerzer See and Vierwaldstättersee (better known to English speakers as Lake Lucerne from the town of Luzern on its northern shores). Then it climbs through loops and spiral tunnels up to Göschenen, on the way passing the same church at Wassen three times. It goes on through the Gotthard tunnel to burst out into the deep valley of the Leventina, where the peaks tower above the valley and you can get a crick in the neck peering up at an angle of what seems to be about 80 degrees. The scenery between Airolo and Biasca defies description: it is almost overpowering compared to less dramatic but more serene beauty of British routes like the 'rail to the Isles' of the Scottish Highlands.

Switzerland generally is unsurpassed for dramatic and beautiful scenery. There is nothing quite like it anywhere that I have seen. I have already described the Jungfrau railway. A superb view back to the Jungfrau and Eiger can be obtained from the Grütschalp to Murren branch line, reached by a steep rack section from Lauterbrunnen. The rail routes running east-west across Switzerland are among the most dramatic. It is a pity that the *Glacier Express*, worth taking all the way from Chur to Zermatt under the towering Matterhorn, has lost a little of its attraction since the Furka Base Tunnel was opened south of the Rhône Glacier, but it does mean the trains can operate all year round instead of summer only. I found the more northerly of the east–west Alpine routes, between Luzern and Montreux, also entrancing. This comprises a metre gauge section through beautiful timbered country past the Lakes of Sarner, Lungern and Brienz to Interlaken, then the SBB standard gauge line past Lake Thun to Spiez. A Eurailpass will let you do this bit by steamer, but I found the Swiss Rail Pass to be better for exploring Switzerland by rail, steamer and postal bus, as it covers most of the many private railways too. At Spiez, a branch of the Berne Lötschberg Simplon (BLS) railway goes up to Zweisimmen to join the Montreux Oberland Bernois (MOB) metre gauge line to Lenk and to Montreux on Lac Léman (Lake Geneva). Here the main tourist train is the *Panoramic Express* which, apart from its rather sub-standard buffet facilities, is a beautiful train running through beautiful scenery. I thought the view just south of the first station down the line from Lenk looking back to the head of the Simmental and the views around Zweisimmen itself especially scenic.

There was a minor panic when an elderly man got off the Montreux–Zweisimmen train, meaning to board the Spiez connection at 14.20 but got on the 14.09 Lenk train, running late at 14.13, by mistake. His panic when it started was matched by his further panic to cross to a train going back when the Lenk train stopped at the first station down the line. One useful thing about railways in Switzerland is the way they display station names about half a kilometre in advance, so that provided you happen to see it (and are on the right train) you know where you are coming to in time to get ready if wanting to leave the train at that station.

TRAINCATCHER

Above: Martigny station in Switzerland seen on 15 October 1986, as the narrow gauge electric train enters the platform, on the other side of the SBB platform.
Below: The line leads to Vallorcine in France, where the SNCF has a metre gauge third rail electric line connecting to St Gervais. This view is taken at the alpine resort of Chamonix. (Geoffrey Churchman)

A COOK'S TOUR

On another trans-alpine route between Switzerland and France, the Martigny–Châtelard railway which at Vallorcine joins a narrow gauge SNCF branch from Chamonix, just under the slopes of Mont Blanc, there was a train buff with his camera in the vestibule just behind driver. He had that dedicated faraway look some such people have, and was meticulously recording numbers and types of every wagon, not to mention noting times. We were stuck for 12 minutes with some sort of engine trouble, or possibly it was to do with the rack not being engaged properly. Passengers were making remarks like 'lets all get out and push' (I could not be quite sure because of the foreign language) and these were greeted by ribald laughter. There was a great cheer when we finally moved onto the rack section. Possibly delay is normal there.

There are also three trans-alpine routes between Austria and Italy; the Brenner Pass south from Innsbruck on the west, a comparatively low level route from Villach through the Kanaltal to Udine on the east, and one in between which runs east-west from Lienz to Fortezza through the Pustertal, or in Italy Val Pusteria.

The last-named is interesting because, unlike most other frontier-spanning routes through the Alps, this line is not used by any truly international train service. Only one train, an ÖBB inter-city express, will convey passengers from Lienz in Austria to Fortezza in Italy or from there to its terminus at Innsbruck, in Austria again.

All other passenger trains between Lienz and Innsbruck by this line are 'corridor' trains. Corridor trains in Austria do not, as one might imagine, have passenger compartments connected by a corridor on one side. They may well have such an internal layout, but in Austria *Korridorzug* has a special meaning. It is a train that runs through part of another country en route between places in Austria, but does not serve places in that country. It is something that peculiarly results from Austria's geography and rail pattern. In Austria the direct rail route between Salzburg and Innsbruck necessarily passes through Germany; the only way to reach Ruette im Tirol is through Garmisch-Partenkirchen in Germany or to reach Oberloisdorf is through Hungary, while the line between Innsbruck and Lienz goes through part of northern Italy known as the Sud-Tirol.

Consequently, certain trains on such lines may be designated 'corridor' trains. They do not stop in the 'foreign' territory or if they do, passengers are not allowed to get on or off – the ultimate in the 'restricted stop' genre. That is not to say that people may not try. Not all Austrian people are law abiding. At St Polten station near Wien I saw a whole crowd of passengers hurrying over the tracks right under a large notice proclaiming it *verboten*.

There are no frontier formalities on corridor trains but the Wien – Innsbruck via Lienz express, doubly named – *Val Pusteria* in Italian and *Pustertal* in German – is an exception: it serves towns both sides of the frontier, and is boarded by Customs people at the last stop before crossing.

The Sud-Tirol is more Austrian than Italian. The people are a friendly lot and great football (soccer) fans. Station names, direction signs, etc. are all bilingual and even the places each side of the border have twin names. It is a scenic route but slow – three hours for the 143 km section between San Candido (otherwise Innichen) and Innsbruck. In these alpine valleys of Austria, like some in Switzerland, the squirrel-like struggle to combat the elements and prepare for the harshness of winter is evidenced by the constant cutting of grass and storage of hay. Near San Candido there used to be a branch line south from Dobbiaco through Cortina in the Dolomites to the Venetia region of Italy, but this has been closed since World War II between Dobbiaco and Calalzo with a bus substituted.

Station staff in the Süd-Tirol appeared to me to be sometimes in typical Austrian uniform, and sometimes obviously Ferrovie della Stato. At one place the Austrian station master, resplendent in magnificent uniform, stood there looking so proud as the train passed through his domain. Accompanying him was his offsider, a slim little Italian girl. I waved to him and he positively beamed with pleasure and waved back. I thought such response great – the kind of human interaction that makes life worthwhile in spite of frontiers, strikes, bombs, wars, wowserism, graffiti and all the other miserable things some people get up to. Such pride and pleasure in his job – but I wonder if he is still there. I had noted the place name in my diary as something like Pusteria 'valley'. The nearest I can find to that in the timetable would be Rio de Pusteria. The 1993 timetable lists it but gives no train times which to my suspicious mind could indicate that trains no longer stop there. The dismal hand of economic rationalism at work again? Add such attitudes to my hate list above!

Travelling across so many frontiers, and especially where two cultures, languages and currencies overlap, becomes confusing when you have to translate prices into a currency you know. There is a concurrent and consequent danger in Europe – that of becoming short of money without actually buying anything. It is the effortless way to become bankrupt without playing *Monopoly*. You will encounter plenty of tempting booths marked 'bureau de change, cambio, wechsel' and the like, but at many of them you face a rip-off. Your money will become less and less and after about a dozen moves you may have travelled all round Europe only to end up with nothing to show for it. Duty-free shops are another rip-off. Beware! They may be 'duty' free but they are far from profit-free, and many a time I have found it cheaper to buy something at normal local prices than from these specialised establishments owned by the vulture fraternity. Those at the airports are the worst. But at city stores offering duty-free goods to ticket-holding customers you can definitely get real bargains if you know what you are looking for and compare the prices carefully.

After some experience I found it best to carry a supply of small denomination notes in several key currencies, especially Swiss Francs and Deutschmarks, which seemed to hold their value and be accepted anywhere, and to resist the temptation to change money every time I encountered border formalities.

It had surprised me to find no border formalities at all between the Scandinavian countries. On the other hand, on my last trip I was unable to go into France at all. I had made arrangements with a French railway journalist to meet and possibly even travel in the cab of the TGV, but at almost the last minute found I needed a visa. This in spite of my having a British 'right of residence' endorsement on my passport which saw me through most other European frontiers as a 'common market' member. Incidentally, one advantage of the common market I noted on my tour was that the cheapest natural spring water in Germany, for example, was Highland Spring from Scotland!

Customs people rarely worried me. No longer a cigarette smoker I did not worry about carting cartons of duty-free cigarettes across every border. I certainly took some liquor but there is a practical limit to how much one can carry. A 1.125 litre bottle of Glenmorangie was obviously for personal consumption and passed through customs everywhere with no problems. I did not even have to declare the Polish vodka on returning home, because on one of my last trips through Austria in a couchette of the *Wiener Walzer*, I had met a Pole from Kraków Polytechnic and showed him the vodka I had bought in Poland. It didn't last long after I met him – its fate was inevitable.

One of the most attractive cross-frontier links in central Europe is the Centovalli railway between Italy and Switzerland. It connects Domodossola (Italy) on the Brig–Milano (Simplon tunnel) line with Locarno at the north end of Lake Maggiore in Switzerland, and thence by connecting service to Bellinzona on the main St Gotthard route.

Starting from the railway station in Domodossola at a normal platform, this narrow gauge railway quickly climbs well up into the mountains, and thence along the side of a deep and wide gorge to descend at the other end into a town street where it shares right of way with motor cars and finishes up at a tram stop. On the way the line crosses many side valleys. Attractive timber chalet-style houses with geraniums in profusion on their balconies, face across the main gorge to others which are often hidden among the trees and accessible only by flying fox ropeways.

The scenery is magnificent. I had taken this route in mid-winter on my first European trip and wanted to see it in its autumn colouring. The views cover almost a 180 degree vertical range from way down below to the tops of mountains way above. This time I joined the railway from the Swiss end. That part of Switzerland reaches down like a tongue into Italy, and the local train I took from Cadenazzo had 'FART' written prominently on its sides. Its destination board read 'Domodossola' but it went only to Locarno. The seats were uncomfortable, but no more so than those on the Centovalli. I wondered if FART represented something like 'Area Rapid Transit' but could not find a place beginning with 'F'. It would not have been in English anyway. I later found from the *RG Railway Directory* that the initial letters were Italian for Ticino District Transport (Società Ferrovie Autolinee Regionali Ticinesi) – so I was not too far out in my guess!

During my 1977 trip my favourite base had been Vernazza. This is an unspoilt little village of narrow cobbled streets and pantiled cottages clinging to the edge of an almost hidden narrow cleft in the cliffs around a tiny small boat harbour. It is backed by terraced vineyards and lies on a part of the Ligurian coast south of Sestri Levanti known as the Cinqueterre. I had booked in for a week there at the Pensione Sorisso, staying in fact for only four nights, and using it as a base while I visited Genova, Pisa and Milano, and then ranging as far as Paris, Avignon, Bern, and Locarno before returning at the end of my week. I recall particularly how I had left my heavy luggage, unlocked, all the time I was away, and all was safe and sound on my return, including my air ticket which was packed in a travel wallet. I do not think I would risk that anywhere in Italy nowadays.

On that trip I had spent more time in Italy than in any other country, principally seeking warmth but also entranced by its scenery, its food, and the ease of understanding and being understood. I think that to an English speaker Italian must be one of the simplest foreign languages to learn. German is full of guttural sounds and complicated adjectival word-combinations, Spanish is a bit like a harder version of Italian, Greek is Greek (the English expression of incomprehension being 'looks Greek to me') and as for French, well, they talk so fast they just don't want you to know.

So I was determined to include a visit to Italy in my 1985 Cook's Tour. In the event, I spent very little time there. The summer weather had lured me to spend so much time exploring Switzerland, Germany and Austria that Italy was very nearly by-passed. In fact I spent only one night in Italy out of just over 100 overnight stops, while only 10 out of my 651 journeys were entirely within its borders.

The nightstop was in Breccia, during a four day round trip at the end of the European part of my tour, and I found it very expensive. I started from Schwarzach and ended up at Wien airport. Scenically, this round trip was one of my most memorable. I had wanted particularly to see Italy's famous Lago di Como, so beloved by Winston Churchill, then to return to Austria via the Bernina Railway and include a side trip up the branch to Mariazell, one of the most scenic trips identified by John Price in *Cook's European Timetable*.

The scenery of the Rhätische Bahn up from Tirano through to Chur was excellent. This also was a John Price favourite. The Bernina Railway snakes its way across and up the valley to Poschiavo and then through the Bernina Pass. At Morteratsch, the last station 6 km before Pontresina, two hikers were seen running to catch the *Bernina Express*. Apparently they either did not have a timetable of when the train was due, or were late for it. In any case it was not booked to stop there. Poor souls, they were out in the middle of nowhere, but they would only have an hour to wait for the next train.

I was glad I was not hiking, since on this part of the trip I had to take Pongo with me all the way.

It was not until my 1992 trip that I managed to re-visit that part of the Italian coast I had been so enamoured with on my first European tour.

I then planned a flying visit to Italy, mainly to meet a friend, Renato, who had corresponded with me from Roma. He met me at the airport and found me a comfortable, moderately priced hotel near the famous

Spanish Steps. Next day I went with him to Roma Termini to book on the ETR 450 to Firenze, on which he was confident he could arrange a ride in the cab. This worked out fine, although his influence was not sufficient to avoid the queue for Eurailpass verification and seat reservation at a window which opened just a short time before the train's departure.

The seats on the ETR 450 proved far more comfortable than BR's Mark IV stock, but the one in front of me was somehow loose on its hinges and kept slewing round towards me. But the trip was not long and I soon went up to join the driver. Speeding along at 240 km/h plus we passed a row of carriages from the old *Settebello* which brought back memories of my first European trip. *Settebello* was one of the very best of the original Trans Europ Expresses and was the forerunner of other trains which adopted the semi-compartment group seating which is still found in some Scandinavian trains and was tried in Britain though without success. A most attractive feature of the *Settebello* was its nose-cone observation lounge, something I have not found elsewhere in any other train.

I had also arranged to meet a relation of one of my students who lived in Roma and worked for Interpol. He knew I was to be in Roma that day, so after reaching Firenze I changed to a cross-country local train for Pisa on the Genova–Roma coast line, so that I could slip up to Vernazza in search of *Gambaro alla Livornese* and local white wine for lunch.

On the train to Pisa a whole carriage was marked as reserved and was full of school children. There were some casual seats in the vestibule. One young lad offered me his: his girlfriend promptly gave him hers – and he took it! I wonder what the 'affirmative action' people would say about that display of distorted chivalry! Yet half the train was empty as I found out later.

The youths in the vestibule were all smoking. They were very law-abiding: their reserved seats in the carriage were all non-smokers.

On the train north from Pisa, there was an American woman and her friend in the next compartment, which was a non smoker. They came into my compartment (otherwise empty) for a smoke! Their conversation was all critical of Italy. They did not think Italians knew how to make pizzas (!) and thought American ones would sell better! I can imagine some big American fast-food chain investing on the strength of an opinion like that and quickly going bankrupt!

In an effort to show them something good about Italy I told them to look out at the glimpses of coastal villages we would soon be seeing as we went on through the galleria of the cliffs. I bid them *buon viaggiao* and 'have a nice day' as I prepared to disembark at the most colourful of these.

Vernazza remained exactly as I remembered it but my favourite restaurant was closed. I found another, and after a good lunch went back up the narrow, cobbled street to the station to catch the *Capodimente* express back to Roma. This did not stop at Vernazza. I took a connecting train to La Spezia. The *Capodimente* was something of a disappointment. It was comfortable enough, air conditioned compartment stock with curtains to pull over the windows, both on the outer and the corridor side, but there was no proper sit-down refreshment as I had come to expect on named trains of this category, just a small serving hatch along the corridor with nothing but water (at a price), beer and coffee. *Non c'è vino*! There should also have been a telephone but there was none or if there was it was not working.

Not until I reached Roma could I then telephone Enzo, who was expecting to see me. I learned later that he had taken the whole day off in the hope of showing me places I would like, so I was very sorry I had not made earlier arrangements with him. Too many half-baked plans with too many people at one time! As usual, I was trying to achieve too much in the time available.

But once I contacted him on the telephone he was delighted and arranged to come immediately to meet me at the station. He then took me to a nearby restaurant, although the streets we walked through were reminiscent of London's Soho and I was glad to be in the company of an Interpol man and not alone in the dark!

After a pleasant meal (Enzo knew the proprietor), he walked me back to the station as my plans were to take the overnight sleeper to Milano, after which God would provide. But there were no spare sleepers. The Italian reservation system did not extend to having any information about whether sleepers were all reserved or not. You had to wait until the train was in the platform and find out then. Not even Enzo could pull the strings to make one appear. Proceeding along the platform looking for a nice empty first class compartment we came across a car marked 'Sleeperette'. This was a reclining seat open saloon for first class passengers with no supplement added to the fare. It was very comfortable indeed. The 'pitch' or distance between seats would have been about 1.5 metres. I plonked my gear down in a vacant seat immediately and re-joined Enzo on the platform before the train's departure.

Enzo gave me a cassette to take back to his brother in law in Brisbane. Returning to my seat to put this in a safe place, I found another passenger had calmly moved my bags onto the rack and was occupying the seat. I endeavoured to remonstrate with him but my limited Italian vocabulary put me at a disadvantage. I went back to Enzo and told him the situation.

Like a flash, he was on the train, which was by then almost ready to depart. There was a great argument. The man who had been in my seat moved to the door, protesting. Enzo had asked him for his ticket and he hadn't got one. As the train started to move Enzo called to me from the door. "You won't see him again!" he said, and I did not, nor did I see Enzo again although I had so liked the bloke that I changed my plans and took the first train back to Roma when I woke up at Piacenza next morning after a very comfortable night. In Roma I called his number in vain. The phones, as so often in Italy, were out of order.

Italian telephones do not accept credit cards. I found out, too, that Ferrovie della Stato did not accept cards either. Nor can Italians, according to Enzo, take out travel insurance. Apparently people had been paying for their annual holidays through ficticious claims.

I also wanted to visit Spain and Portugal again, so much enjoyed from my 1977 winter trip, when I had actually found Portugal warm enough to go swimming in the Atlantic at Espinho just south of Porto. I still had pleasant memories of good food at reasonable prices, and as for the "ladies of Spain", famed in song, well! But I also had a sentimental reason: to visit and send a postcard from Lagos, the Portuguese resort after which my West African birthplace was named. And I did, but found it expensive. I also wanted to travel along the Spanish north coast on the narrow gauge FEVE railway and had written asking for a pass because this system was not covered by the Eurailpass. I would have liked to do the whole 773 km from San Sebastian to El Ferrol, but having had no reply before I left Australia I did not manage this particular journey. I decided I could afford a few short trips on some of the FEVE lines around Gijon and across the mountains from Mataporquera to Bilbao and thence along the coast to Santander. Only when I reached home again did I find the reply, enclosing a complimentary first class pass!

On this Cook's Tour I was struck by what seemed a similarity between Spanish and Welsh. At Cardiff I had noticed a sign reading *Croeso i Gaerdydd* (Welcome to Cardiff). The double 'd' at the end is pronounced 'ff', not at all unlike the 'dh' (pronounced as the 'th' in 'the') which is the way the 'd' is pronounced in Madrid or Valladolid.

I did not go swimming in the sea at Espinho again but I took the sleeper between Porto and Lisboa. Actually it was more of a couchette and cost the same as the sleeper had eight years previously. My best memories of Spain and Portugal this time were the huge serving of Paella at a little restaurant in Port Bou, the cheap but efficient haircut and beard trim I had at Evora, the little café at Vila Vicosa where I watched a bullfight on television – it is not nice for the bull but I found it most fascinating and colourful, and the way the horses danced backwards in front of the bull's horns was fantastic: I understood how it was so popular an entertainment – then there were the cobbled streets of Aveiro, where the pavements are decorated in incredibly intricate patterns and even the pedestrian zebra crossing is patterned in black and white tiles.

Memorable too were the intimate little arbours of the vineyard country of the Duoro. People climbed up on little ladders to pick their own grapes. The gardens were shaded and pleasant, and there were tiny arable patches here and there between buildings.

I had noticed on my earlier trip how people travelling into Portugal from Spain would take huge bunches of bananas plus cigarettes and biscuits. Cigarettes I could understand. Wherever you find smokers and a frontier someone will be taking cigarettes one way or the other, but bananas? Was it a case of "Yes, we have no bananas" in Portugal? I noticed in Spain and Portugal that people often carried flagons of wine with them, large ones done up in basketwork like the Italian Chianti bottles so popular among tourists (in Italy the best Chianti comes in perfectly ordinary wine bottles), and why they did this I could not fathom, since wine was available cheaply and in profusion all over the Iberian peninsula. Perhaps they just preferred to take their own with them.

In Portugal the Eurailpass covers the special carriage in the *Tejo* train, Lisboa–Porto, which I found more luxurious than anything else encountered in the whole of Europe. Its lounge car is somewhat similar to the lounge cars of Australia's *Ghan* and *Queenslander* but without a piano and without a bar. However, the restaurant car was just next door and the prices were dirt cheap.

Returning later to Britain with its much more expensive wine but equally memorable food – crisp bacon, new potatoes (Jersey chats), pork pies, black puddings, steak and kidney, field mushrooms, Tiptree marmalade, Cox's Orange Pippins, and rhubarb pie. You can forget the roast beef of old England: except in Scotland it's nothing like as tender as Australia's Western beef or the steak I was to experience in Texas. Britain still has much that is special and even BR was a welcome change from the generally slower trains of Spain and Portugal. Besides, on my last day or so in Britain before flying to Zürich to start the European tour there had been a rail strike, which meant I could not use the last of my

Britrail Pass. From Europe I had written to BR management suggesting that they do the decent thing and provide me with a pass or tickets to cover the few routes I still wanted to travel. Actually, I really wanted to re-visit some friends in Newcastle, Cleveland, Edinburgh and Manchester but BR were very obliging and sent me some free first class tickets to cover the lines I wanted to travel. This confirms my experience of many railways: when you get to the top management you usually find reasonable people, and down at the cutting edge, among the guards and drivers it is the same. It is just somewhere in middle management and among petty officials you are more likely to find awkwardness, incompetence or downright rudeness.

From London I flew to Chicago, scenically a fascinating trip coming in over Hudson's Bay and the Great Lakes, then by a connecting flight to St Louis where my daughter and family then lived. Being in the RAAF my son-in-law had been posted to an Australian unit at the McDonnell-Douglas plant at St Louis, where FA-18 fighter aircraft were being manufactured for Australia. We were always hearing about the United Sates having bases all over other people's countries: I liked to tell Americans that Australia had a 'base' in the USA. It sort of unnerved them a bit.

Dale picked me up at St Louis airport and we drove out to Lake St Louis, an artificial but pleasant outer suburb where Australian servicemen were stationed in spacious homes with 'all found' (including duty free grog from Australia). Here I relaxed for a while with the family before trotting off on the rest of my Cook's tour, Amtrak having kindly provided me with a pass for the western States.

The song *Shenandoah* has the line, "cross the wide Missouri". It is, especially near its confluence with the Mississippi just north of St Louis, wide man, real wide. The Missouri valley is very pleasant to the west of St Louis, where the main line to the west, the Missouri Pacific, runs along the south bank past historic Herman and most of the way to Kansas City, while the 'Katy' line, not normally used by Amtrak, takes the north bank. This line is frequently flooded and subject to a 20 miles

A COOK'S TOUR

an hour (32 km/h) limit but sometimes Amtrak services have to be rerouted. 'Katy' is the railman's pet name for the Missouri Kansas Texas railway which goes right down to Houston, crossing the Santa Fe line used by Amtrak at Temple in Texas.

I took a trip to Jefferson City and back, a quite small town but noteworthy as Missouri State capital; it was laid out by Daniel Boone, son of the frontiersman of that name and is named after the President who negotiated the Louisiana Purchase. Amtrak had an efficient booking office at the small 'country' type station there and I was able to make arrangements for my onward travel plans before returning to Kirkwood, the outer suburban station nearest to Lake St Louis.

On another day I was taken by car up the west side of the Mississippi to Hannibal, scene of Mark Twain's *Adventures of Tom Sawyer* and other sagas, and visited the museum there. From the lookout on the cliffs above town could be seen the marshalling yards of the Burlington Northern railroad which unfortunately does not carry passenger traffic any more. The nearest passenger station is West Quincy, 29 km to the north, but reached from St Louis only by going via Chicago (877 km and 15 hours, including a three hour wait in Chicago) or an even longer way through Kansas City and Galesburg taking more than a day and a night. Obviously Amtrak, however good a service they have in the North-East corridor, are not geared to cross-route travel in the Mid-West. Naturally, I went and returned by car. The train trips might have been interesting but the wasted waiting time would not have been.

My tour of the western USA involved a trip down into Temple in Texas to see a friend from schooldays who I had coincidentally met up with while visiting England earlier on my tour, and another trip on the *South West Chief* part way through the Rockies to Lamy beside the Santa Fe trail. I would have liked to see the Grand Canyon but the railway from Williams was not then operating. There was only a bus connection from Flagstaff. I note that this former Atchison, Topeka and Santa Fe branch has since been re-opened as the Grand Canyon Railway.

Instead of the bold scenery of the Rockies I remember this trip vividly for the Dallas–Fort Worth journey. At Dallas the train stops just opposite the building from which Lee Harvey Oswald allegedly shot President Jack Kennedy. They make a point of showing it to passengers, but what I remember most was the appalling urban landscape – the outer suburbs of Dallas are absolutely frightful with mile upon mile of used-car lots, garages, parking lots, warehouses and drive-in supermarkets, ugly industrial buildings, houses, and snack-diners, all mixed together with no evidence of town planning or civic pride. Here and there a multi-lane freeway cut through the mess, half full of cars going one knew not where. It was all the same all the way from Dallas to Fort Worth – 50 km of the most appalling desecration of the visual environment I have ever seen anywhere. Ogden Nash's *Song of the Open Road* parodying Joyce Kilmer's poem *Trees* might well have been inspired by such scenes. It goes:

"I think that I shall never see a billboard lovely as a tree, Indeed, unless the billboards fall I'll never see a tree at all."

There is reputed to have been an actual case in USA courts where an advertising firm sued a landowner to secure the removal of a group of trees which were obscuring a billboard. Even a 'scenic drive' consisting of nothing but billboards (one is supposed to exist) would have been a relief in Texas.

This was not at all like the Texas they sing about, where "the sage in bloom is like perfume", but it was quite pleasant at my friend Rolf's place out of town near Kempner, where his English-born wife actually taught horse riding to Texans and they both drove Cadillacs (what else?). The steaks were great but the 'diner' (restaurant) was more like a glorified drugstore.

Returning north on the *Texas Eagle* I opted for a large roomette which had its own toilet and shower. Designed for the disabled, this was an unusual kind of accommodation, taking the full width of the train at the end of one coach on the lower level. Most of the daytime accommodation on Amtrak is at the upper level: they advertise their trains as "See Level" but at night it is not important. Leaving Temple

A COOK'S TOUR

30 minutes late, this train reached St Louis dead on time next morning. It was a comfortable trip.

Less comfortable was my last overnight trip in the States, on the train in which I went west through Salt Lake City and Nevada after leaving St Louis and flying to Denver. There I arrived late in the evening owing to snowstorms in the Rockies delaying the 'plane and I was not in time, as I had hoped, to meet up with a girl I had met on the train in Spain (on the plain, near Medina del Campo). The friendly air hostess on United had presented me with a bottle of wine to take with me and a meal out on the town with the girl and her fiancée had been tentatively planned. But it was too late. All I could do was telephone from the airport to apologise, then take a taxi to the railway station. The taxi driver was a Nigerian from my birthplace of Lagos so we got on like a house on fire.

At Denver railroad station, a great empty mausoleum of a place, I faced a long wait for *The Pioneer*, the train in which I had booked to go west to Vancouver – not Canada, but a whistle stop in Washington State just north of Portland, Oregon on the banks of the Columbia River. *The Pioneer* was not due until next morning: it was still just evening and I did not favour an expensive city hotel. Denver is a big place. Instead, I found that by taking another train part way back east, I could cross over to *The Pioneer* earlier in the morning – and get in a sleeping berth. The train east bore a famous name, the *California Zephyr* and I found the coach class seat roomy, comfortable, and provided with a pillow. The conductor noted whither I was bound and made sure to wake me in the event I was asleep when we came to McCook, Nebraska, in the early hours.

The wait in beautiful downtown McCook was not exactly thrilling – there was only a soft drink machine in the way of amenities. As a place to await a train, Puttgarden, on the Scandinavian extremity of Germany would be its twin. At around four in the morning I joined the westbound *Pioneer* and this, my second last train trip in the States, provided the most spectacular scenery.

TRAINCATCHER

Climbing out of Denver, itself known as the 'mile high' city, the Denver, Rio Grande and Western rail line heads immediately up to the Continental Divide, the summit at 9211 feet (2807.5 metres) being the highest point on Amtrak, then passes through the 6.2 mile (10 km) Moffat Tunnel to come out along the upper reaches of the Colorado River – the South Boulder Canyon, a miniature Grand Canyon almost – and down to the resort city of Glenwood Springs. Much of the morning I enjoyed looking out at the magnificent scenery of snow-covered mountains, deep gorges and dense forests, chatting about travel and scenery to a lady named Barbara, who lived at Glenwood Springs, and to an Englishman, Malcolm, who worked for Allied Breweries of Burton-on-Trent which incidentally marketed Fourex, the lager from Castlemaine Brewery in Brisbane where my wife Barbara worked. What a small world!

After Grand Junction the massive sandstone walls of the Book Cliffs in Grand Valley give way to the open mesa country of Utah. Here were numerous sharp bends in the track and the lights kept going out. This was something to do with the electrical connections between coaches. On tight bends an automatic cutoff occurred, then the connection was just as quickly re-established on the straight. It seemed to me something that should easily have been rectified but this train had older coaches than those on the *Chief* or the *Zephyr*. To be more accurate, *The Pioneer*'s sleeping cars formed part of the *California Zephyr* as far as Salt Lake City, *The Pioneer* proper going from there to Seattle via Boise City and Portland, while the main train continued west through Reno to Oakland and other through cars turned southwards through Las Vegas to Los Angeles as the *Desert Wind*.

This has since changed. *The Pioneer* is now detached from the consist at Denver and no longer climbs through the ranges immediately west of the city. Instead it turns about to go due north into Wyoming, reverting more or less to the route followed up to the early 1980s by the whole train. An exception is that the train now by-passes Cheyenne, which is served by connecting bus from Borie, a junction somewhere on its western outskirts. Thus *The Pioneer* also by-passes Salt Lake City, following the Union Pacific route direct to Ogden, north of the lake.

I did not see anything of the famous Salt Lake itself, it being nighttime, but I woke several times in the early hours when the train seemed to be bouncing up and down like an Irish Jaunting Car. North of Ogden we would have been on Union Pacific tracks and must surely have been diverted onto a freight line, I thought, but there was no suitable route we could have used. At Pocatello the bouncing stopped: it had been something wrong with the suspension on the car I was in. We then continued through Idaho toward Boise City. That brought back the words of another popular song from my school days – "Away beyond the hills in Idaho, where yawning canyons greet the sun". Well, the sun was barely up, but Idaho is a curious State geographically. Shaped somewhat like a pregnant letter 'L' it is separated by the Bitterroot Range from Montana on the east and by the Snake River Canyon from Oregon on part of the west, with the usual surveyor's straight line boundaries everywhere else. Transportation-wise, Idaho is split in the middle. There is no railroad connection whatever between the north and south of the State, nor as far as I know has there ever been – the Salmon River Mountains intervene – and there is only one north–south highway, Route 95.

Beyond Boise City the rail route turns west to the State border where it follows the Snake River north for some 50 miles (80 km) before turning west into the Blue Mountains of Oregon at Huntington. After crossing the mountains the railway comes down to the Columbia River west of Hinkle and follows the south bank all the way to Portland. Another Amtrak route follows the Burlington Northern line along the north bank of the Columbia from further up at Pascoe. It seemed to me strange that two separate single track railways should parallel each other for such a distance, about 190 miles (300 km) but it must work. There is a link between the two routes at Wishram but crossing from one train to another was ruled out by the logistics of the timetable.

It would have been my intention to travel through into Canada from

Washington State if I could have done. For many years the *Pacific International* linked Seattle with Vancouver, BC. I had to do it by air, but this, like my London to Zürich, Wien to London, London to St Louis and St Louis to Denver flights, was covered by the British Airways 'Round the World' ticket I had purchased through Thomas Cook. As I had been unable to secure any travel concessions from Canada's ViaRail, financial constraints forced me to confine my Canadian travels, with some disappointment, to British Columbia Rail. But here there was no disappointment! The route of the little *Cariboo*, named after a gold rush of a century ago, goes up from North Vancouver into the mountains and lakes and along the rivers of British Columbia. The snow clad mountains, the rushing rivers with their leaping salmon and the sight of large, rather frightened deer running along beside the track through the woods was so reminiscent of the Scottish Highlands that I was thrilled at every turn. "Fair these broad meads, these hoary woods are grand," rang the Canadian boat song of Hebridean exiles. It could well have been written in British Columbia.

The full 744 km journey to Prince George takes 13½ hours and the first class fare includes a meal served at your seat. A day trip can be made from Vancouver to Lillooet on the Fraser River and back, and this is what I chose.

The train windows on BC rail were cleaner than those on Amtrak, excellent for scenic viewing. The first part of the journey, curving round Horseshoe Bay and up the side of Howe Sound, rather like a Scottish sea loch, is covered in summer by the *Royal Hudson* steam train from North Vancouver up to Squamish. My own northbound trip was by the 7.30 two-car diesel to Lillooet, where I waited for the southbound *Cariboo*, which operates thrice weekly. On the way north I sat with the driver for part of the journey and so learned much about the track and the scenery. Driver Eddie Patenaude, a French Canadian, now retired, had been to Brisbane, where his brother and nephew lived. As I found out only later, this was quite close to my own home at the time.

The lakes, salmon rivers, waterfalls, snow, mountains, fir, birch and alder trees combined to make beautiful and ever-changing views, reminiscent of Scotland at its best. The sheer joy of such a ride is that the scenery is of the heart-rending kind. I experienced that overwhelming feeling in which the soul just seems to melt with the beauty of the landscape, as at Loch Carron in the Scottish Highlands, in parts of Austria, at Vernazza on the Italian coast, or even in the suburbs of Brisbane when the Jacarandas are in full bloom covering the ground with their lovely violet blue blossoms.

Above the McGillivray Falls at Anderson Lake I saw the salmon spawning. There are three kinds here, the Red Sockeye, Cohoe and Chinook. Before leaving Canada I tasted some of the best at Vancouver airport: it was equal to any I have ever tasted, and that includes smoked salmon, tinned red salmon (which is all we ever saw when I was young and which I always liked) and salmon deep fried in batter with chips at a take-away fish and chip shop in Dingwall, Scotland. Best of all, I think, is salmon caught in a Scottish loch or even in the sea and baked in foil, but I am sure John West would not have rejected what I tasted in British Columbia!

The route of the British Columbia Railway is through the northern part of the Cascade Mountains but there are some incongruous station names. Garibaldi is one, the nearby 2678 metre high mountain being named after the 19th Century Italian hero. There is also a place called Ten Downing Street, also known as Gramson's. It was originally settled by Ab Gramson, a World War I veteran and the building remains have world war battle names painted on them. The driver told me of another place (probably the spectacular Cheakamus Canyon) where a sudden rock fall in a ravine on this route derailed a triple headed freight train. The engineer and fireman were unhurt although the leading loco fell a hundred feet (30 metres) down the ravine. The conductor in the caboose was injured, not by falling into the ravine but because the sudden stop made the door crash into him and it crushed his foot.

Returning from Lillooet on the *Cariboo* I took advantage of BC Rail's generosity and occupied a seat in the first class portion. First class includes a meal, served by a charming stewardess from a little galley behind a curtain. At night, travelling in this train is not unlike being in an aircraft; air conditioning, going along ever so smoothly, individual overhead lights, comfortable reclining seats, and hostess service. The bar is first class only. "I would like to be able to serve others but it's impossible," the hostess said. "What would one do if 40 people turned up for drinks with only little me serving?"

There is a ski train on some occasions, which does have a bar. However, one passenger was so anxious to get a drink he paid the extra $10 to change to first!

There is a basic tray refreshment service for non first class passengers.

I would liked to have seen more of Canada, particularly the other scenic routes through the Rockies. Now, regrettably, ViaRail have withdrawn the passenger trains from the route past Banff National Park and through the Kicking Horse Pass, although one train still follows the more northerly route through Jasper. Well, even a Cook's Tour cannot include everything.

My next stop was New Zealand, visited briefly once before but this time I had a rail pass by courtesy of New Zealand Rail and I meant to cover as much as possible on both islands, since passenger trains in New Zealand at that time looked like being in danger of disappearing altogether. Already the overnight first class Auckland–Wellington *Silver Star* sleeping car service had gone. So had trains on the Wellington–New Plymouth–Taumarunui circuit, and the *Kingston Flyer* had been truncated to a 13 km trip between two virtually uninhabited points on the map. The New Zealand railway timetable contained only six pages on trains out of 28: all the rest were to do with road services.

The New Zealand Travelpass covered these as well as the ferries and I did include one coach trip from Greymouth to see some of the alpine scenery of the South Island.

Although freight is carried by rail ferry between the North and South Islands, passenger trains do not cross the strait. The ferries run from a wharf 1.8 km from Wellington station and passengers are taken there by coach. Picton station, on the other side of Cook Strait, is within walking distance of the ferry terminal. But my tour of New Zealand was not as smooth as this might be thought to imply.

First, on arriving in Auckland I found the pub staff were on strike! The newspapers were on strike in Wellington, the ferry coming back from South Island was late, and mainline trains were to be replaced by buses because of electrification works at the weekend. But these caused only minor inconveniences: I had made sure of returning to Auckland before the weekend so did not have to endure a long bus journey and the only rail travel I missed out on was part of the suburban system there when I arrived to find the local trains on strike.

The scenery of New Zealand is unique; very good in most areas, especially in the mountains and on the coast. Most noticeable were wild flowers; gorse, broom, poppies, and lupins galore – and of course everywhere sheep, sheep, sheep, in their millions.

It is difficult to focus on what was specially memorable about New Zealand railways. So much was good, yet there was much that left a lot to be desired. I found the standard rail pass was not valid for the *Silver Fern* but they had given me extra tickets so this did not matter. Why it should have been an extra fare was not clear. It was advertised as a "luxury daylight railcar" but this was 'promoter's licence'. Although it offered at-seat service (from a very limited bill of fare) the seats themselves were far from comfortable: four to the carriage width is not first class standard, especially on less than standard rail gauge. The armrests were narrow and hard; it was somewhat reminiscent of economy airline, but the seats were well spaced in relation to the windows and all had a good view.

I found the seats on the *Northerner* night train between Auckland and Wellington much more comfortable, only three to the carriage width and somehow the carriages seemed wider as well. The berths on this train were as comfortable as any I have travelled in – but since my visit the economic rationalists have been at work and removed this amenity.

TRAINCATCHER

The Napier to Gisborne service has also been removed. This followed a very scenic route – the sort where most passengers look out at the countryside – a sure sign of scenic quality. A woman passenger's comment to me was, "It's different in the train. You can sit and look out. In a car, even as a passenger, you're always looking anxiously at the road ahead. In the train you're up higher. You can look down onto the scenery". I wonder what value the rationalists place on this?

North of Napier the track swings inland to skirt the Maungaharuru Range, then returns to run right round the coastline to Poverty Bay, plunging through a series of tunnels between which there would be sudden glimpses of the rocky coast from virtually inside the cliff, rather like the flashing glimpses of the sea on the Ligurian coast of Italy (though without the colourful houses perched on the edges).

I was dismayed to notice how many farmers had bulldozed the scrub out of gullies, precipitating visible erosion. It is always a wonder to me how people whose very livelihood depends so much on the land have so little awareness of conservation needs or elementary geomorphology. Near Longreach in Queensland I remember being proudly shown how a property owner cleared the gidgee scrub by dragging though it a heavy chain between two tractors. And they would be the first to complain when hit by wind erosion and drought. But as we continued on through New Zealand's North Island the train came to one place where an enlightened farmer had planted trees along the sides of a gully. There was hope yet.

The seat booking arrangements in New Zealand, at least on the Napier line, were a bit like the Italian sleeper reservations – unreliable. The guard was extremely helpful to those who wanted non-smoking seats – some had booked two months ahead and thought they were in them, but no. A block booking had been superimposed for a school camp group. At Hastings, when they got off, there was a mass transfer of non-smoking passengers from Car A to Car B.

Crowds of young people seemed to be a feature of New Zealand trains. Many carried radios or cassette players which they had on loud and blaring without any consideration for other passengers. I believe people carrying these sorts of things should be required to have earphones for them. I vowed next time to take earplugs or perhaps a cassette player of my own recordings of loud hot jazz, bagpipes, Wagner, steam train noise or an air raid. If they stuck on one programme it would have been not so bad but they would keep switching channels to get the noisiest or most up-to-date pop they could find. When we moved into the proper non-smoking part of the Napier train they were at least partly out of earshot.

I noted that the New Zealand Working Timetable stipulated that guards had to telephone ahead to catering stops to give a head count of passengers. This did not seem to do much good. Even if observed, the catering arrangements were rushed and inadequate.

There was a similar 'refreshment stop' on the bus trip down the coast from Greymouth. You can't write and hardly even read in a bus because of the vibration, so any stop is a welcome break. At Harihari, about half way to Franz Josef, "the bus stops a quarter of an hour here" said the genial driver – but we did not know what to expect there, what to spend time and money on – greenstone shops, refreshments, the pub (if any), fish and chips, toilet. The lack of knowledge meant time wasted, frustration and even anger. But there was a reasonable lunch break at Franz Josef before the bus returned and there I enjoyed an excellent meal amidst fine scenery. At Franz Josef you look right up at Mt Cook (New Zealand's highest mountain at 3764 metres) from the north.

The rail trip to Greymouth (however uninspiring the place name sounds) is a top quality scenic ride, marred only by little things like the high fences on each side of the bridges over the ravines. I assumed they were there for safety reasons and wondered if all New Zealand railway workers were really 10 feet tall? As I later found out, they were in fact windbreaks but they rather spoilt the view for a photographer.

Climbing west from the coastal Canterbury Plain just south of Christchurch, this rail route crosses the Southern Alps at Arthur's Pass, a National Park area. The Arthur's Pass tunnel is a long 8.5 km. Freight trains are hauled through by up to three locos, this section being electrified and with a gradient of 1 in 33. At Otira, the north end of the tunnel, the line skirts the Otehake Wilderness then turns north round Lake Brunner, while the highway follows the Taramakau River to the coast.

I stayed two nights in Greymouth. Bruce, one of the locals, had an extensive model railway but there was such a great crowd having such a great time at the little Royal Hotel I never got the chance to go and see it. Greymouth is not really geared for tourism, but has a friendly atmosphere, the sort of place you would come back to.

By comparison with the Greymouth route, the Pacific Coast line from Christchurch to Picton seemed somewhat dull. Although there are plenty of glimpses of the coast, much of it seemed to be black rocks and

New Zealand's long distance passenger trains have now been transformed into virtual tour buses on rails. Here the *TranzAlpine Express* is seen near Springfield. (NZ Rail)

there were few bays, headlands or islands to vary the scene. I somehow missed noticing the mountainous hinterland on the other side, perhaps through my eyes tending always to look to the coast or through being rather bored with the lack of amenities. The 'railcar' also seemed slow — but no slower than most other New Zealand trains, the fastest of which (as far as my travels went) I recorded as the *Southerner* from Invercargill to Christchurch at 60.8 km/h. The line speed limit was nowhere more than 90 km/h, though 100 km/h running is possible over some sections on this Pacific Coast route.

The Picton train was not in fact a railcar, but a three coach train, but it seemed the local fashion for every passenger train to be referred to as a railcar. There were rumours that the train was likely to be axed and replaced by a bus, which I was told would be quicker (in fact the existing buses took approximately the same time as the train — six hours) but the latest is that it now has a buffet, is proudly named the *Coastal Pacific Express*, and has had half an hour slashed from its journey time. Ten minutes of that would have been achieved simply by cutting out the euphemistically named "Time for refreshment" at Kaikoura station.

But the worst part about it was Picton itself. Here the timing of things, the catering, the announcements and everything else were unsatisfactory. The train arrived on time at 13.40 and the ferry was just coming in, late, from Wellington. It was supposed to leave again at 14.20 but this would clearly be impossible. Yet there was no announcement about when it would leave. There would have been time to get fish and chips at a local cafe, or even a counter lunch if passengers had only been told the estimated time of departure. There were no dining facilities at the terminal itself; only a little shop that offered a few sandwiches and cups of tea. Most of these had gone before many would-be passengers got near them, yet many people had not had a meal all day. People were heard expressing their disgust.

Trucks were still being unloaded from the ferry at 14.30, and waiting cars started boarding at 14.42. Once we were on board, of course there would be refreshments, but no, the bar and cafeteria were closed. The captain decided on a boat drill – why just then when late already? "Today of all days," commented one passenger. They had boat drill once a week. Boat drills are all very necessary but just after the 10.00 departure from Wellington on the outward voyage would have made more sense. No thought was given to the hungry and thirsty passengers! I wondered how often did management travel from Christchurch or Wellington to see for themselves what happened. Even one and a half hours after we had boarded there was still no refreshment. There could be no excuse for such a state of affairs. It left a sour taste, which New Zealand did not deserve.

Back in the North Island I spent a pleasant evening visiting an old friend from Lancashire in Te Awamutu, and made some new friends at Otaki, a little town 80 minutes by train out of Wellington which I chose as a temporary 'base'. My hosts, Queenie and Michael, at the Railway Hotel, knew Tees-side in England well, and even the little place north of Stockton where my wife came from. They also kept a good malt, Glenmorangie, which was a nice change from the rather flat (but tasty) New Zealand beer.

I have said little about touring Britain in this chapter, although my travels there were extensive. New Zealand reminded me of Britain: even some aspects of its railways did, although they hardly matched BR for speed. Although it is great to see new places and compare the scenery in different parts of the world, I still think some railway scenes in Britain are unmatched: the view of Durham Cathedral and Castle from the railway viaduct just south of the station I hold as one of the modern wonders of the world. Even the Royal Border Bridge by which trains on the East Coast Main Line approach Scotland is memorable. (People think they are entering Scotland but in fact it is only Berwick-upon-Tweed, part of England. The border is just north of that city!) Then, of course, where else is there a bridge to match the Forth, where even the rail tracks are nearly 50 metres above the water and the towers are 60 metres above the track. Whether seen from the shore, from the nearby new road bridge sometimes jestingly called the Fifth Bridge, from the top of the towers (if you were allowed to go there) or just from the train, this structure is certainly among the wonders of the modern world. But in almost every country where there are railways there are marvels. Railways seem to fit in. They are unobtrusive compared to highways: they enhance the landscape, emphasizing its contours and even when cutting across them, as with a bridge, bringing them together, as put so well by Graham Coster in his first novel *Train, Train* (based on British experiences of branch rail revival movements in the Thatcher era):

"There was a green road, winding across the landscape. A perfectly empty road: not a lead-grey road for glinting cars, but a green road, a grass road, a natural road – running level and still like a river...

"As it came nearer it was a green string across green fields, and then it disappeared behind a hill...then...merged into a gently, then steeply sloping hillside, and the line laid itself along a ledge around it as the ground dropped away beneath..."

"The line did not split the hills and the fields, like the road, but sewed them together."

It was of course an abandoned railway. There are so many. There are people who would want to turn them into highways but they are too narrow. A railway needs a lot less space to carry the traffic than a highway would. Old railways make wonderful long distance footpaths, but they make even better tram routes, and even better railways.

Although my last trip in New Zealand nearly had to be by bus, the last in Europe in my 1985 Cook's Tour actually was. Not because of a strike, but because I had spent the last night in a little lakeside town in Austria called Neusiedl am See. A very helpful fellow, Johann Allacher, gave me a lift in his car from the station and showed me a good *Gasthaus*.

Neusiedl was a good place to pick on for my last night because there was a railway bus direct to Wien airport next day, saving a double train change and station transfer in Wien, a significant consideration since by then I had all my full weight of luggage with me. Talking of which, on my arrival back home in Brisbane there was a letter waiting. Postmarked 'Suisse' it was from my Swiss friend Daniel Strässle. Among other things he enquired about Pongo's health. "How is Pongo?" he asked. Whether it was the manhandling of his overweight frame into the boot of the Neusiedl to Wien airport bus, or the baggage handlers at airports elsewhere, or just the over-long walks at high speed he had been subjected to, I am sorry to confess that Pongo had found it too much. As I took him out from the taxi at Auckland airport I found he had failed to withstand his harsh treatment somewhere along the line. One of his ribs had come sticking out through his skin, dangerous for anyone carrying him around. I managed to drag him home but his working life was over. Confined now to the garden shed (I did not have the heart to have the poor faithful thing put down), he is stuffed full of tax and expense sheets relating to my Cook's tour and other trips. One never knows when the dreaded Commissioner of Taxes will want to examine old records. Therefore I keep them – just in case.

Chapter 20
Against the Trend

"Everybody's out of step except our Johnny" – attributed to an elderly couple watching their son's graduation parade at a military academy.

The world railway scene today is confusing, full of contradictions. In some places vast sums are being invested in new lines, new trains, new stations: in other places services are being run down and railways abandoned.

But almost everywhere, what is being done is being 'justified', at least in the eyes of the doers, by some sort of rationale. George Orwell's "Newspeak" has been widely adopted. Sweeping changes to the world's railway systems, whether positive or negative are hailed as progress and development.

In Australia, Queensland is the latest victim of the 'rationalisation/ accountability/micro-economic reform' mania. Although there is a persuasive logic in what is happening it is the product of tunnel vision and in some cases total lack of vision. For example, while millions of dollars are being spent on main line upgrading, electrification, sophisticated signalling systems, and new rolling stock – technologically as up-to-date as can be obtained – existing assets are being abandoned with little or no consideration of their possible future potential. In the 1960s the then government abandoned and ripped up the railway between Brisbane, the State Capital, and the Gold Coast, its coastal resort counterpart then showing promise of development as a major centre (it is Queensland's second largest city). The Labor Party rightly criticised that decision as short-sighted and is, as government in 1995, building – at great expense – a new rail link. But it is itself repeating the same mistake with another, similar though smaller-scale city link further north. The coastal resort town of Hervey Bay is now developing just like the Gold Coast was 30 years ago and has already overtaken in population its regional capital of nearby Maryborough. Despite a significant increase in tourism as well as residential development, the Hervey Bay railway was first closed to passenger traffic, then to goods, and is now in the process of being dismantled. There are private buses serving Hervey Bay but no attempt has been made by the Transport Department – the licensing and controlling authority – to coordinate these bus services with mainline trains at Maryborough or anywhere else.

Again with undeniable logic of a kind, stations at some provincial towns have been relocated on the outskirts, effecting an operational saving but inconveniencing potential passengers. "Use it or lose it," the State Premier said, when warning of possible future cuts – a statement followed almost immediately by measures which effectively made it more difficult or even impossible to use the threatened routes!

In New South Wales a few years earlier the scenario was more complicated but with a similar intention, to produce what the rationalists referred to as a "leaner", more efficient operation. For "leaner" read 'meaner'. The process, which began in the late 1980s, took several years and involved much double talk and downright deception. Only part of this was attributable to changes in government: the railway administration appeared to have its own hidden agenda. Although at the political level there was a genuine concern about the mounting losses on the railway system there was little evidence of a genuine desire to investigate and remedy the root causes of this malaise. There was no overall plan or vision for the railways: branch railways were simply closed, passenger trains replaced with buses, goods trains replaced with road trucks, cattle trains abolished completely. Only mineral traffic was sought since what could not breathe could not voice complaint – but people did complain because they saw the stupidity of it, they suffered the inconvenience of it and they did not like it.

When the XPT, the Australian version of the British high speed diesel InterCity 125, was first introduced at the end of 1981 it seemed to mark

AGAINST THE TREND

a new beginning for Australian rail travel. I remember a feeling of considerable excitement as I saw it quietly easing round the bend from Telarah as I waited to board it the first time at Maitland. And then, when I joined the driver (by arrangement) in the cab and we went hurtling down the almost straight 18 km from Metford Box to Sandgate at up to 170 km/h I felt this was certainly the dawning of the age of, if not Aquarius then at least something significant in Australian rail travel. Other travellers thought so too. There seemed a great future for railways in Australia if the interest generated by the XPT and some other contemporary innovations could be held and strengthened.

The XPT caught the imagination of the public. Before it went into revenue service it was taken on a tour of New South Wales country towns and the only people unhappy about it were some transport economists. But country people did not stay happy for long. That first sight of the XPT on its promotional tour was the only sight some people ever had of it – and almost the last sight some of them had of any trains at all.

While in the early 1970s New South Wales had suffered a spate of branch line passenger train withdrawals (34 in all, totalling 3459 km of rail routes), these were mostly dead-end routes serving fairly small settlements, none of which had a population over 3000. Only seven of these routes, totalling 807 km, were connected to the network at both ends and had through route potential. But in the early 1980s, just after the XPT was introduced, the closure mania began to affect more significant cross-country links and more important country towns. Dismantling the network began in earnest. Not only were passenger trains withdrawn: lines were closed and taken up. The pursuers of this policy would refer to it as pruning: the analogy from horticulture being that this would be of benefit, promoting healthy growth. But this analogy is false. If a railway system, or any transportation system, is to be compared to a living organism, the animal kingdom affords more apt analogies. Amputate limbs and the patient may end up unable to move.

But even that analogy is not appropriate. The potential viability of any transportation network depends initially on its degree of development. A simple line from one place to another has limited chance of growth or development and no flexibility. If things go wrong – and as Murphy's Law so clearly declares, if they can, they will – there is no alternative route, no way round the derailment or whatever until it is fixed. Geographers have observed a correlation between the complexity of a nation's transportation network and its state of economic prosperity.

The severing of cross-country links between radiating main lines is therefore a retrograde process, quite irrespective of the health of the links themselves; of whether they carry much traffic, whether they 'pay' or whether they are even used at all. It is sufficient that they are there: they may be used only in an emergency – like the fire service or the ambulance.

In the 1880s a railway was built from Demondrille near Harden on the NSW main southern line northwards to meet the main western line at Blayney. The railway served the thriving country centres of Young and Cowra, the former an important fruit growing area, and formed a cross-country arc 177.5 km in length and 427.9 km rail distance from Sydney at its furthest point just north of Young.

In the decade before passenger services were withdrawn in November 1983, there were only two possible through 'connections' in each direction per week, both necessitating overnight stops in Cowra. Blayney to Harden took over 16 hours and Harden to Blayney over 42 hours, spending two nights and a day in Cowra en route.

It is clear that the line was regarded and operated as two separate branch lines that just happened to be linked at the extremity. This is confirmed by the fact that from Blayney to Cowra was regarded as a 'Down' line, while the continuation south to Harden was 'Up'. All trains entering the area, like Omar Khayyam, departed "by that same door" as in they went.

Yet if used by through trains, this route could have saved at least two hours on journeys between Canberra or Goulburn and cities west of

AGAINST THE TREND

Blayney like Orange, Dubbo or Broken Hill, and could have cut seven hours off journeys between central west NSW and the south of the State compared with travelling via Sydney. Even once a week, an XPT could have made a circular trip to achieve such improvements in connectivity.

And what did the State Rail Authority (SRA) do instead? They took away the trains, forgetting the occasions when the line had shown its value as a relief route for flagship trains like the *Intercapital Daylight* or *Indian Pacific* when things went wrong on the main Sydney–Melbourne line, or the earlier times when it was specifically advertised as an attractive alternative route from Sydney via the Blue Mountains to the south. As for the people of Young and Cowra, they got a bus. Well might they have echoed the words of A.D. Godley:

"What is this that roareth thus? Can it be a motor bus? Yes, the smell and hideous hum Indicat motorem bum."

I travelled on the last scheduled train, a sad but convivial occasion. Sad, because there was a feeling of hopelessness among the local people who turned out to say farewell to the faithful old railmotor the economists had axed: convivial because of their determination not to let the occasion pass unnoticed.

If the auditors of the SRA noted an unusual number of detonators being used at Blayney and Cowra at that time, I can confirm that there was dense fog on the line. A fog of incomprehension. Only recently had the new, sleek XPT been introduced. Sydney was now but four and a half hours from Blayney or Harden, something I suspect few people in Young or Cowra realised: yet instead of maintaining rail connections the Railways gave the people buses. Air-conditioned, sleek, smooth, and fast, but I heard what the locals thought about them when I travelled on that last regular railmotor service and I think it a pity the originators of the idea were not there to hear it. It is so easy to sit in a head office and make decisions affecting the lifestyle of people far away. My prescription for any senior rail executive would be – no car allowance: you travel by train (and live preferably in the bush). That way, the rest of us might get a better service – and there wouldn't be any bus substitutions either!

In the railmotors there was a toilet, room for luggage, chilled drinking water, and you didn't have to book in advance. Reservations were mandatory on the new service.

"You just cannot always book in advance: you don't know when you have to travel," complained one resident.

A couple with children were going for their last ride. "They just get it right," said the man, referring to the XPT on the main line from Blayney, "and then they stop it!"

I was later told that people now like the buses. "You are greeted by the driver: it is all so friendly". But it was an SRA apologist who said it. Some people believe what they want to believe.

The notion that buses are an 'adequate' substitute for rail is one perpetrated by cost-pruning managements and is not supported by published research or by those whose trains are taken away. In many thousands of kilometres of participant research in the field I have yet to meet a passenger who praised road-rail substitution. If management went out more and talked to the weary, bleary-eyed and cramp-ridden passengers transferring to rail from buses, often in the middle of the night (especially in Australia) or those forced onto buses when trains have been suddenly cancelled, they would not utter such platitudes.

A stewardess on New Zealand's *Silver Fern* railcar expressed a more common viewpoint. She hated the substitution of buses for trains, even when it was only for short stretches, and she confirmed that passengers absolutely hated it.

On the departure of that last train to Cowra, about two dozen people, including reporters, were there to photograph and record the event. About 30 detonators sounded the last post, and we were farewelled all down the line.

Julie and Madeleine were sisters – twins, they said, born two week's apart. They were among the last passengers and intended to enjoy the trip to the full. The railmotor was festooned with balloons – many of which blew off in the slipstream as we sped along the track – giving the

AGAINST THE TREND

Australian Railway Historical Society photographers a difficult task in trying to keep up with us by road!

We were nearing the tunnel. The girls were excited; they wanted the lights out to tell ghost stories. Then they started playing hide-and-seek. One hid half under my legs and half under the seat and the other couldn't find her and had to give up. They never sat in the same place for more than a few seconds – constantly getting up, going through into the next part of the coach, coming back, sitting down, talking all the time, and eating sweets.

I accepted a sweet from Madeleine. She was nine, she told me.

"Take me home with you," she demanded.

"I don't think your mummy would like it," I responded. (Now had she been 10 years older...)

Even with this last train, an overnight stop in Cowra was unavoidable. The next morning the last train left Cowra for Harden via Young. The railcar we had come on the evening before from Blayney was attached to it, either to cater for expected increased demand or because there was no scheduled return trip to Blayney and they could hardly just leave it at Cowra to rot – or could they? Anyway, it made the nearest thing to a through train the line had seen for years.

Small crowds from places on the route assembled to wave farewell. Cars raced along the highway – breaking all speed limits – in the historians' efforts to compile a photographic record of the last journey. A man with a movie camera on a tripod recorded it all from the driving cab.

A sign at the south end of Young station was like an epitaph: "No Thoroughfare".

At Demondrille we paused among the disused and overgrown sidings of this once-important junction to hand over the 'staff', and then crept out onto the double track main line. There we stopped, our gleaming brown and yellow paint standing out against the pale parched grass of our surroundings, as if we were out of our depth and didn't know quite what to do. With the doomed branch behind us and our remnant streamers and balloons dangling limply, the Blayney–Cowra railmotor and the Cowra–Harden railmotor stood forlorn on the alien main line, unsure whether to move any further towards their unknown ultimate fate.

I hoped we didn't stay too long. The *Riverina XPT* was due any moment on the same track and only a signal at 'danger' stood between us and its hundred-miles-an-hour approach (as the SRA then proudly advertised it).

At last we were off and careered down the track to Harden where the passengers alighted. Our railmotors backed away again and came into the bay platform, a stone's throw from the sleek and shiny road coach which had usurped them.

A year previously, Harden station had been notable for its display of totally out of date timetables. These had gone. Glossy red posters proclaimed the XPT and the new bus services that hadn't yet started – air-conditioned, tinted windows, reservations compulsory. Did they have a toilet? Was there chilled drinking water? What about carrying a bicycle? Could you walk about, change seats, play hide and seek, put lights out in the tunnel, tell ghost stories, wave to people out of the open windows and hang out streamers?

I had no intention of finding out. The withdrawal of branch line trains in favour of buses deleted a whole host of places from my list of tourist destinations, touring centres and potential nightstops.

When I started to write *Australia by Rail* I was going to recommend Cootamundra, 44 km west of Harden, as a base from which a visitor could make rail excursions. It was a junction of five rail routes. Now it is merely a stop on the main line. Gone is the picturesque run along Muttama Creek valley, over the River Murrumbidgee at Gundagai and up towards the Bogong Mountains at Tumut, with its short clickety-clack rails and the driver throwing out the daily newspaper to cottages along the line. I will probably never now visit Stockinbingal or Lake Cargelligo, and regretfully will have no occasion to renew acquaintance with Young or Cowra. Indeed, I cannot, as part of the line is no more.

AGAINST THE TREND

Railmotor CHP 38 'Creamy Kate' dating from June 1934 and named after the original colour, stands at Cowra in January 1983. In April it was condemned. (Jean Campbell)

It was instructive to note that there had been considerable track maintenance before the Harden–Blayney service ceased – a technique which assists in producing the figures the economists want, which show the line as loss-making. This technique is well-known to any who have witnessed similar rail closures elsewhere.

Such a technique was observed and reported long ago at the Transport Users Consultative Committee hearing into the closure of the trans-Pennine Barnard Castle–Kirkby Stephen line in the north of England. But to no avail. A millionaire quarry owner even offered to buy and run the line, but that would never do. It might have shown up the falsity of the case for closure. All efforts too, to suggest ways in which the line could be better used – by running through trains between NE England and Lancashire – were pooh-poohed. "There is not the affinity" said a railway spokesman. Yet the railways had been running a weekend service linking the major centres of South Shields and Barrow-in-Furness by this route. The only trouble, it was not advertised. Nor was another similar cross-country service on this route, as the working timetable showed. Nobody knew it was there!

Just as in the Harden–Blayney line's case, rational and imaginative uses of the line were ignored or not actively pursued while unproductive spending continued. This was the case with many country branches in New South Wales. As rail columnist Ken Date put it in the NSW *Railway Digest* in February 1990, the authorities did "not really want to provide a passenger train service on country routes". A *Thomas Cook Overseas Timetable* editorial a month or two later put it even more cogently: "There is obviously no longer any will to operate passenger services on the system".

As recently as 1994 similar techniques could be observed operating in Queensland. The government determined to close the branch from Toowoomba to Glenmorgan on the Darling Downs. Primarily a wheat line, it also carried goods trains "with passenger accommodation attached but subject to alteration or cancellation without notice". Partly due at least to the consequent uncertainty of such an erratic timetable no passengers had been seen during the previous 10 years.

Then someone came up with the idea of country "freight centres" – selected stations on the railway which would serve as a focal point for road trucks to the smaller places of which Glenmorgan was one, and the poorest. The *Brisbane Courier Mail* of 4 November 1994 reported the sole remaining railway employee there as saying his job consisted of unloading supply trucks once a week and storing necessities until farmers could collect them. There had not been a freight train for more than 18 months and "the last train that used the line was unloading replacement sleepers to upgrade the track". For what purpose, one wonders! Since then, a Task Force appointed to review the line's future has recommended its retention subject to achieving an improved cost recovery target. But without trains, how?

It is curious how management appears to treat railways or services they plan to close. At least two distinct techniques have been observed.

The 'unnecessary spending' technique, seen in examples already quoted, may not always be intentional. It could be sheer incompetence. But when it is deliberately planned it's evidence of brilliant but warped thinking on the part of some back room economists. How does one justify closure of a railway quickly? Easy! Spend a lot of money on it. Show that the costs so far exceed the benefits that it is a luxury the community cannot afford.

The difficulty with the heavy spending technique is that it may be indistinguishable from genuine investment in railway development. The context in which something is done is the clue. Clearly the West Australian and New South Wales governments were genuine in their investment in re-vitalising the Fremantle line (WA) and in developing the XPT (NSW) – the latter against the advice of the Bureau of Transport Economics.

Full marks to NSW at that stage! The XPT in itself was a success story – at least until SRA people got carried away and thought a train designed for fast daylight runs of not more than about six hours' duration would be a good replacement for overnight sleepers.

But what might well be termed the 'standard' technique is by the process of attrition. The track, facilities or service are reduced to the barest minimum. The whole thing is worn down to the point of being virtually unusable, when they can say "Look! There is no demand. We cannot afford to keep it going."

It is a subtle and gradual process and may even be practised unconsciously. Sudden changes arouse public indignation and reveal the truth – as happened in Queensland when it was proposed to eliminate 29 routes – a third of the total network, in 1993. When the plan was 'leaked' the public outcry forced the government (and a Labor government at that!) to back down, apologise – not for what they were planning but for not letting people know – and 'review' the proposals. This in the event meant reverting to the normal attrition technique. Nibble away gradually. Let things deteriorate to the point where there is little left to defend before wielding the final axe.

Of course this is what they had been doing anyway. Their mistake was in picking up the axe too quickly. Such a mistake has been known to lead, not only to public outcry but to loss of office. And in Queensland it very nearly did in 1995!

Westrail used the attrition technique with the Fremantle line – but it was re-opened later following a change of government. It was successfully applied in New South Wales in the sweeping closures of rural lines in the mid 1970s and again in 1983. Queensland used it with the original Gold Coast line and it has a long history of success in other countries.

Although British Rail became well known for their technique of scrapping unwanted railway carriages by putting them on football excursions and relying on drunken supporters to wreck them, there has been little sign of this practice extending to other countries. However, there is some evidence that the well known and widely practised Australian trick of burning down unprofitable country hotels in order to collect insurance may have attracted the attention of anti-railway manipulators.

Echuca on the River Murray was one of the earliest towns in northern Victoria to have a railway and the line from there to Melbourne via Bendigo was the first railway in Australia to seriously challenge the river steamers for trade. It was closed to passenger traffic in the 1970s but another rail link to Echuca from the north-east main line remained, served by passenger railmotors. Echuca itself is a historic town and has 'atmosphere'. When it was rumoured that the line was to close I decided to go on a rail trip there.

The railmotor had broken down – many of Vicrail's (as the State's rail system was then called) aged railmotor fleet being then almost beyond repair – and in its place was an ancient red clerestory-roofed carriage hauled by a Y class locomotive of the type more often used for yard shunting.

"Is this the train for Echuca?" asked a young lady on the platform at Toolamba, the junction with the Shepparton line.

"Yes, at least I hope so," I replied, since it could hardly have been anything else.

We had a compartment each, and so did about a dozen other passengers. The one-coach train set off briskly but gradually slowed down and lurched and staggered towards the first station, Tatura. It didn't make it. On a crossover leading to the platform it finally stopped, right on the points, and seemed to heave a sigh of resignation. The guard came along the corridor. "All change," he said.

We alighted on the track and were directed to walk to the platform, keeping clear of the engine.

It was easy to see why. It was on fire.

Underneath the frame a sort of revolving rod called the drawbar was glowing red hot; oil was dripping from it and flames were curling up. We finished the journey by taxi, so cramped together that conventions about the sanctity of 'personal space' had to be disregarded. She was a music student from Melbourne going on holiday. We agreed it was a funny way to run a railway.

For the confirmed train traveller the most ignominious thing of all is to face a bus substitution when there is a rail breakdown. But even this can sometimes bring a bonus. On my European tour I enjoyed a fascinating grandstand view of Monte Carlo from way above the town at night when the railway track – mostly in tunnels – had been blocked by a landslide. On another occasion I enjoyed the intimate street scenes of the little Spanish town of Antequara when our TER train broke down en route from Sevilla to Granada.

These, however, were very brief bus trips and much the exception. Up to about half an hour on a bus is tolerable but 15 minutes is really quite enough. Feeder bus services have their place but their journey duration needs to be sensibly proportional to the connecting train journey.

One of the worst examples is the Broken Hill to Dubbo service in New South Wales inaugurated by Countrylink when the SRA withdrew the ageing *Silver City Comet*. The Thomas Cook timetable editorial described the substitute service as probably the longest feeder bus service in the world – an eight and a half hour bus journey to connect with a six and a half hour train trip!

A decade or two ago in *Guide to Australia* Osmar White described Australian railways as "lamentable". At that time there was a fairly fast daylight train linking Sydney and Melbourne. Around the end of 1991 this train was withdrawn, leaving no daylight through service between Australia's two major cities. The two systems finally agreed on a timetable and crewing arrangements for a replacement XPT at the end of 1994. During the intervening three years passengers can only have been progressively put off travelling between these cities.

The rather pathetic history of this service is summarised below.

In January 1962 the first through passenger train between Sydney and Melbourne ran on the newly opened standard gauge line from Albury to Melbourne. In April the same year the *Southern Aurora* overnight sleeper was inaugurated and Victoria's *Spirit of Progress* was extended to and from Sydney.

From some time before 1970 to 1986 the timetables showed three trains each way every day except Sunday, when there were only the two night sleeper trains. The daytime *Intercapital Daylight Express* was then the fastest long distance train in Australia. A fourth service on three days of the week was also available by changing at Albury.

In 1984, replacement of the *South Mail* by the *South XPT* increased the fourth train frequency to five per week. This experiment (the XPT being overnight with no sleeping cars and an inactive buffet) was short-lived.

In 1986 the two overnight trains were combined into one, named *Melbourne* or *Sydney Express* according to destination. While maintaining the schedule of the former *Southern Aurora* the new service retained most or all of the stops made by its slower sister train. Although maintaining sleeping cars, sitting cars, lounge, dining car and buffet, this train, by general agreement, gradually deteriorated. The menu, the service, the amenities were all neglected. A telephone in the lounge car, introduced in time for World Expo 1988, soon fell into disuse and remained so for over a year until being taken away altogether. Another telephone was installed in the dying days of the service but I for one could rarely get it to work. There was also a relief express scheduled 'as required' but after 1988 it rarely ran.

At the end of 1991 the day train was withdrawn. The two managements responsible and the two unions (for Victoria and New South Wales) blamed each other for the failure to extend the successful *Riverina XPT* (Sydney–Albury) to Melbourne in a new time-slot. A Sydney bus connection from the morning Melbourne–Albury and to the evening Albury–Melbourne V/line InterCity services appeared in 1992; an eight hour bus link for a less than four hour train journey!

By 1994 the night train had been replaced by a new XPT, carrying one sleeping car in place of the previous four or more on the loco-hauled train, and without the dining and lounge cars. Any mention of a daylight service was absent from Countrylink timetables but Thomas Cook revealed the sordid truth – that V/line had axed its morning Albury service from Melbourne and its evening return working on five days of the week (Monday to Friday) and substituted a bus between Seymour and Albury. This meant that to travel by day between the two capital cities involved a 70 minute train journey followed or preceded by two ordeals by bus adding up to another 11 hours! At weekends the Victorian trains still went to Albury and the overall journey time was up to 50 minutes less because the fastest part of the line on the Victorian side was between Seymour and Albury.

Substituting buses for trains and bolstering it with arguments about how good it is, is like telling people shin beef is just as nice as fillet steak.

The rot in Victoria started around 1975. By mid-1980, Vicrail had closed 1500 km of passenger routes, and in their Annual Report for 1978-79, congratulated themselves on what they called 'rationalising' the rail system. The system was "On the right track," according to a feature in *Network*, a Railways of Australia publication which faithfully portrayed the management view. Yet in the 1980 July timetable, Vicrail advertisements urged people to "Travel relaxed with Vicrail ...

free from the traffic hassles and hazards of the highways".

In April 1981 Chairman Reiher, as reported in *Network*, said "The time has come to look very carefully at country passenger fleet sizes." An accompanying feature praised "Vicrail's new deal for country travellers". What was this new deal? – more buses!

There followed a further spate of rail closures. While withdrawing passenger trains from South Gippsland, Echuca, Cobram, Portland, and the Ballarat–Geelong link, Vicrail asserted that "the new country passenger services will see significant improvements in terms of reliability, presentation, journey times, cleanliness, comfort and on-train [sic] facilities".

In Britain, after the rash of closures initiated by the infamous Beeching Report (he was only doing his job – a railway assassin hired by the government), a study of the social effects of rail closures, including bus substitution, was carried out at the London Policy Studies Institute at about this time.

Researchers Mayer Hillman and Anne Whalley, in a detailed study of 10 rural lines in the United Kingdom, established the following facts:

1. That, contrary to what usage figures might suggest, usage of the railway had been widespread, extending to as much as half the population;
2. That many users travelled beyond the end of the line, i.e. used the branch as a feeder to the network as a whole, so that closure meant a loss of patronage to other lines;
3. That car ownership and usage of the railway were not inversely related to the extent that had been thought;
4. That substitute bus services attracted only half the former rail users; that the bus was considered a less acceptable form of travel, and that services had been further cut after rail closure; in fact, a major finding about buses was that "it would be an illusion to think that a bus service can fully replace or compensate for a rail service".

Most significantly of all, perhaps, and which should contain a message for the politicians, they found that many people were "considerably and adversely affected both in their travel and their lives in general". This ranged from mere irritation through sustained anger to genuine hardship, and was not confined to former rail users.

Interestingly enough, a 1990 random survey of travel preferences in New South Wales (the Grimwood Inquiry) found that while 90% of users of the then current service preferred rail for long distance travel, 48% of travellers by other modes (car, plane and coach) also preferred rail − but presumably were not using it because of some factor not identified by the survey. It was clear from public hearings and other evidence, however, that inconvenient schedules were among the reasons why some people did not use the trains. Significantly, coach travel as a preferred mode rated zero among rail travellers and only one percent among all others. By that time the SRA had already replaced the former sleeper services with the sitter-only XPT and an expanded coach network.

It was seven years after the successful introduction and initial popularity of the XPT in New South Wales that it began to be used for the long distance and overnight journeys for which it was never designed and for which it was totally unsuitable.

Among the submissions made to the Grimwood Inquiry was an analysis of the use then made in Britain of the High Speed Train (InterCity 125) on which the XPT was based.

The British HST was introduced as a fast inter-city day service. By mid 1978, they were operating between London and major cities in South Wales and Bristol, and to the north- east and Scotland on the East Coast Main Line. The longest run was London–Aberdeen, of seven hours duration. All were day trains except a summer Saturday train from London to Swansea, acting as a relief to the normal sleeper.

By 1989, a decade later, there were 1952 HST runs per week, averaging 346.2 km in distance, with a mean journey time of 3 hours 14.6 minutes. The median journey was half an hour less. In Australia, by a year after its introduction there were six weekly XPT services in each direction between Sydney and Albury, Sydney and Dubbo, and Sydney and Kempsey. The 36 runs per week gave a mean trip distance of 536.6 km and a median journey time of 6 hours 42 minutes.

By the end of 1989 XPT runs had increased to 60 per week, operating to 10 different schedules. The mean distance travelled was 533 km but the median journey time had lengthened to 7 hours 20 minutes, over twice the British average. Compared to its British counterpart, the XPT had less roomy seating and poorer catering, none having at-seat dining car service as did the principal InterCity 125 trains. The longest run of the Australian XPT at that time was by the *Holiday Coast XPT*, with a journey time of 9 hrs 50 mins. Extension of this service to Murwillumbah added a further three hours and 25 minutes to make a total of 13¼ hours, while the XPT service to Brisbane (989 km) taking 14 hours became the longest run by this type of train anywhere in the world.

In almost every country which has introduced high performance daytime expresses between major cities, overnight sleeper trains have been continued as an alternative.

At the time of the Grimwood Inquiry, an American resident in Sydney, Grant Gerrish, identified 11 steps a railway system might take if it wished to discourage passengers:

1. Do not go after new sectors of the market.
2. Do not retain the market you have.
3. Keep all co-operation with other States' railways to a minimum.
4. Discourage passengers finding out about other States' railways.
5. Ensure that timetables and maps are hard to understand.
6. Get rid of dining cars.
7. Scrap all sleeping cars and replace them with sitting cars.
8. Abandon motor vehicle carrying facilities.
9. Constantly drag out the cliché that Australia's population is too small.
10. Engage an American consulting company to tell you what to do.
11. Have your PR staff pursue not new business but pursue laying a smokescreen.

AGAINST THE TREND

Expanding on some of these points, Grant really hit the nail on the head with references to contemporary events and, if they ever read what he said, some SRA people must surely have writhed in discomfort:
"If there is, say, an airline strike and massive numbers of new customers are dumped in your lap, see to it that you have no extra facilities to carry them".

As columnist Ken Date remarked in his "Newsline" column in the *Railway Digest*, the policy seemed to be to "make the trains so unattractive or inconvenient that ... they can be safely withdrawn on the basis of lack of patronage"

The Consultant Report which the SRA used to justify its policies concentrated heavily on finance. While drawing attention, rightly, to wasteful practices and poor showing as against some other rail systems, the solutions offered did not address root causes. The philosophy was simplistic in the extreme. If it was true that an unacceptably high proportion of passengers enjoyed concession fares and there were some outmoded work practices which inflated expenses, the remedy was sought only in dismantling the service. As Grant Gerrish rightly observed, "No one can use a concession and no staff can possibly work in outmoded fashion on a train that isn't there"!

State Rail at this time suffered considerable loss of credibility, which it is still struggling to regain. Not only did their spokespeople try to maintain that their services were being upgraded to "world standard", in the face of overseas comparisons which showed the opposite, but statistics were put out which simply contradicted the facts. And this really got them into hot water. Even the Grimwood Inquiry found that some of the evidence given by the SRA did not correspond to reality.

It was asked in *Railway Digest* at the time: "Why has State Rail not promoted its sleeping berths, car carrying facilities and excellent dining cars? Has all the advertising budget been blown on ramming the XPT at the consumer?" No, a lot of it was wasted on fancy and glossy new timetables, obviously not designed by anyone with much experience of such publications, which were more than twice as difficult to read as any timetables I have ever known. It is difficult to avoid the conclusion they were a smokescreen designed to hide the facts.

As Walter Scott put it in *Marmion*:
"Oh what a tangled web we weave
When first we practice to deceive."

What a contrast between the SRA's policy at that time and the considered view of those most experienced operators of overnight services, the Wagons-Lits Company! According to General Manager Jean-Paul Camblain (quoted in *Railway Gazette* 151:4), they consider "four factors as essential for success in the overnight rail market: a well-planned timetable with convenient departure and arrival times; the quality of rolling stock and on-board service; comfort levels; and flexible, competitive pricing".

Columnist Leo Schofield, in the *Sydney Morning Herald* of 10 February 1990 commented on a debate on the Andrew Ollie radio show in which the then SRA chief kept "repeating that only 46 sleeping berths had been filled on the previous evening's service to Brisbane and Murwillumbah when he knows damned well [wrote Schofield] that the actual annualised occupancy figure is above 90 per cent." Schofield added that "More than 1,000 travellers a day telephone State Rail to book a train seat, can't get through, and hang up in frustration or disgust".

The facts were that on the night in question the train had been replaced by bus part of the way and this had put off many would-be passengers. It was quite atypical. Booking clerks at Sydney were so incensed over misleading figures presented at the time of the Inquiry that some were prepared to give Statutory Declarations on the matter.

The actual capacity of the trains was one of the contentious issues. From checks with the booking office, the train conductors, and actual counts on the trains, the normal capacity of the Brisbane and Gold Coast loco-hauled trains together was proved to be 834 or more seats including berths. The actual figure varied according to the number of sleeping cars; an extra one being added when demand was heavy.

AGAINST THE TREND

Trains were frequently packed to overflowing, taking close to two thousand passengers daily between Sydney and the north. With the abandonment of the two overnight trains, plus the *Holiday Coast XPT*, and their replacement by only two XPT trains daily, the available capacity on the route was slashed by almost a third, from 1266 to 864 places each way. This was represented by the railways as a capacity increase!

The loss of dining and sleeping cars and withdrawal of motorail facilities and refusal to accept certain kinds of luggage, e.g. surfboards, further discouraged substantial and important classes of former rail user. The SRA forgot (or they or the government did not at that time want to be reminded) that a pleasant journey at a convenient time, with sleeping compartments, dining cars, showers, the option of social mixing coupled with the security of a private compartment, are among those features of rail travel (quite apart from speed with safety) which appeal strongly to travellers and attract custom to railways against the competition of airlines and road coaches. Professional and business people and overseas tourists were among the groups who soon began to desert the substitute service.

This was not all. Even local passengers were discouraged. Effectively, at every station between Casino (805 km from Sydney) and Dungog (245 km, at the outer limit of the Newcastle-based local services of the Hunter Valley), the train service frequencies were cut by half or more or cut out altogether.

Where the Government and the SRA really lost credibility was in the aftermath of two major accidents on the Pacific Highway just before the introduction of the *Brisbane* and *Murwillumbah XPTs*. These bus crashes between them killed 55 people. The response of the SRA was no extra trains, no extra carriages, no bringing forward of the introduction of XPT as an additional day service. Hundreds of travellers were wanting to switch to rail but were denied the opportunity. The Countrylink view was that it would be in bad taste to use such a tragedy to extol the benefits of rail travel and entice customers from the road coach firms yet that is what travellers were seeking! Could the real reason have been that the railways themselves were about to force more people onto road transport?

As a *Railway Digest* columnist observed: "In response they peddled all sorts of misinformation about how much of an improvement the new services will be on the old and that they will more accurately reflect customer demand. But the facts are quite simple: the new XPT services to Brisbane and Murwillumbah will mean a decrease in overall capacity on the North Coast corridor. The removal of sleeping, dining and motorail cars will discourage patronage of the trains and can reasonably be expected to force more traffic onto the roads."

After the radio debate on ABC ended there were numerous calls, all condemning the views put forward by the SRA, so much so that I felt sorry for the bloke who had to be their spokesman. Meeting him some time later he confessed that he was really a rail enthusiast. It was clear that sometimes public servants are placed in an invidious position defending government policy. It is a pity in such cases that the matters cannot be thrashed out in a court environment with the rigor of witness cross-examination and the overriding constraint of possible perjury charges. In the town planning field, with which I am familiar, the realisation that planning witnesses might be forced to give their true professional opinion on oath acted as a very effective constraint on local authorities wishing to justify their own decisions by adducing professional evidence.

Politicians, of course, have to be careful what they say, since opponents will seize upon unfortunate quotes. The NSW Transport Minister (Baird), at a public meeting, stated categorically that "The north coast ... will never again have a daily sleeper service". Public pressure forced a re-think, and barely four years after the sleepers had been withdrawn, a brand new sleeping car coach was added to each of the north coast overnight XPTs. Public resentment does not quickly fade away, however. A year later, the government lost office.

In spite of the bright side, the present scene still has many of the

AGAINST THE TREND

ingredients of a tragedy. Are the improvements coming too late – are they already too late? Victoria's system was reduced almost to a skeleton before new coaches, new livery, and augmented and accelerated services appeared. But since then the Victorian government has again changed and the system is now more of a skeleton than ever dreamed of before, with passenger trains running over only a fraction of the network.

Almost every country in the world with a railway system operates passenger services between major cities and to many other destinations. Throughout the world there are 113 countries which have regular passenger rail services. Of those without, most are small or undeveloped (e.g. Haiti, Iceland, Lesotho, Rwanda) and have no railways anyway. The only countries with railway systems which have no passenger trains (barring changes in the last three years caused by political events) are El Salvador, Dominican Republic, Afghanistan, Uruguay, Liberia and some Pacific and other island nations which have narrow gauge sugar cane lines.

The combined length of these non-passenger systems is only 4021 kilometres, 75 percent of which are in Uruguay. Afghanistan, incidentally, is blessed with 0.8 km of railway.

With two exceptions every country which operates passenger trains serves its capital city. The exceptions are Mauritania (which has only one mineral line but carries passengers) and Venezuela. During the recent re-shaping of the passenger rail systems of Australia, it seemed likely at one stage, in 1989, that passenger trains might be withdrawn altogether from Canberra. Australia would then have joined Venezuela in the doubtful distinction of having a passenger rail network with no trains serving its national capital.

Passenger trains fill four main functions for which there is clearly recognised demand world-wide:
1. Fast inter-city daytime journeys averaging two to five hours
2. Overnight sleeper services between major population centres
3. Intensive suburban and outer urban commuting

4. Tourist travel over scenic routes or to specific resort destinations.

Almost every country in the world with a railway system offers these categories to a degree. The passenger trains of most countries cater for general and business travellers, commuters, families, the elderly, holiday-makers and tourists. They offer a great variety and range of on-train amenities such as dining, buffet, bar and cafeteria service, mobile refreshment trolleys; sleeping berths, couchettes and other 'lie-down' or reclining seats on overnight trains; car-carrying facilities (particularly on seasonal holiday trains) and they have a range of fares at different levels to attract different users at different seasons or times. They cover a variety of routes and they operate at a variety of times which are normally not only convenient but varied to suit the seasonal changes in demand.

The InterCity and InterRegio networks of Germany, the ÖBB network of Austria and the recent Swiss Bahn 2000 systems are examples of effective interlinking of services designed to yield the maximum benefit for the minimum cost. The stated aim of the German railways, for example, is "twice as fast as the car, half as fast as the plane", and this seems a practical formula for commercial success.

Ignoring international best practice – which the above represents, the Australian Railway Industry Council in 1990 produced a Discussion Paper entitled *Rail into the 21st Century* – an unfortunate misprint for the 19th Century in the opinion of many. The scenarios it postulated were fanciful and its evaluation methodology was unsound. In my own submission I expressed the view that a document which had taken at least 23 people over two and a half years to produce would have justified allowing others considerably longer than five weeks in which to comment on it. It was difficult to avoid the feeling that the invitation to public comment, however welcome and innovative, could be more a token gesture than a real desire to be influenced in decision making. Federal Budget and post-budget announcements at the time suggested that decisions had already been taken, particularly about the future of non-urban passenger train services. One had little confidence at that time in the Federal Government's interest in railways. In the 21 years from 1969 to 1990 Federal allocations to the States for rail development totalled less than the average allocation for one year to roads, and had in fact dropped to zero under the Hawke Labor Government.

I said I was conscious of a sense of futility; a feeling given substance by statements by the Federal Land Transport Minster at a seminar indicating that there would be no funding to support country rail services or subsidise pensioner concession travel, and by the announcement by NSW Minister Baird that daily sleeping car services on the northern main line from Sydney would never be restored – this in spite of the fact that the Review of this decision, agreed to in a case before the State Industrial Commission, had still at that time to make its report!

Even worse was an Federal-appointed Industry Commission Report on Rail Transport in 1991, which abounded in economic theory and selected every possible quotation or example it could find to downplay the importance and value of rail, particularly passenger trains.

In February the following year I was on my way to Sydney for the launch of *Steel Roads of Australia*. Naturally it would hardly have been right to go there other than by train. Having sampled the daylight XPT on previous occasions – a pleasant enough trip but with a most inconveniently early departure time from home and a rather inconveniently late arrival in Sydney, I decided to give the overnight XPT from the Gold Coast a chance to reveal its delights instead.

Strictly speaking, no railways serve Australia's Gold Coast. Queensland, in which it lies, tore up the track in the 1960s. New South Wales, with its border just south of the Gold Coast, has a single track branch from Casino which the SRA wanted to close a few years ago. Commonsense, or public opinion, prevailed, and the line was retained but the service reduced from two to one train a day. The terminus, Murwillumbah, is 56 km south of the Gold Coast heart at Surfers Paradise.

Although Queensland is constructing a new line to the Gold Coast, it is also single track, and ends at an as yet only partly developed civic and commercial centre at Kerrydale. The new station, some six or seven kilometres from the coastal strip as the crow flies, is to be named Robina after an adjoining suburb.

When the ubiquitous XPTs replaced the former *Gold Coast Motorail* and *Brisbane Limited* services, the SRA provided feeder bus connections for both trains. Only the southbound Brisbane–Murwillumbah bus connected with the train at a reasonable time of day and merited consideration, so in spite of the prospect of sitting up all night in the train, I settled on this option.

Knowing the train boasted a buffet with reasonably acceptable hot meals I postponed my dinner, which otherwise I would have needed to take around six in the evening before boarding time, since the bus left Brisbane Transit Centre at seven.

It was to be an express run, taking just under two hours. Almost the minute we were on board we were welcomed by Countrylink, the name chosen by the SRA when it substituted buses for most of its country trains. The welcome consisted almost entirely of dire warnings about what would happen to any passenger caught lighting a cigarette or taking a drop of alcohol. They would be put out – the offenders, that is, not just the cigarettes. Needless to say, there was nothing said about this when one made the booking. Ah well, I thought, there's plenty of time yet. When I join the train there'll be a good hot meal and some wine to go with it.

Meantime I acquired a pleasant seatmate. Lynne was a young lady from Hervey Bay I had met while waiting for the bus. Well, hardly 'met': she had been near me in the queue but had been hassled by some fellow she did not care to encourage. He was planning to sit next to her. Although we had barely exchanged a couple of words she came straight to my seat on the bus and asked if she could join me, as she wanted protection. Some of my friends would say that most young ladies would be seeking protection from rather than by me, but I was honoured by the trust of this innocent girl and acted as a gentleman should.

Regretfully, I found Lynne was booked in an economy carriage and I was in the first class at the other end of the train, but we were destined to meet again. (Music, violins!)

Once I had settled in my seat, I made my way to the buffet. "No wine except with a meal," they said. I asked for the menu. No meals!!

Whether they thought it too late to serve a meal or they had none left was not explained. The train had only just started its 13-hour journey and was advertised as having all night buffet service. Then what could they offer? Potato crisps, meat pies: at least the latter were hot. That was something. Would a meat pie count as a meal? No. Then what about three or four meat pies? Still no, that would not qualify for a mini-bottle of wine. They would be in trouble if they served it, they said. My own feeling was they ought to be in trouble for not serving it if management had any idea of what it was about but I could not prevail.

I took a couple of sloppy meat pies back to my seat and washed them down, illegally, with a paper cup or two of claret, which I had prudently smuggled aboard in my overnight bag so as to be prepared for the worst. How I missed the friendly girls that used to serve the Brisbane and Gold Coast trains when they changed train crews at Casino! When the SRA substituted the XPTs the Casino catering staff either had to move to Grafton, a hundred kilometres away from home, or lose their jobs. Some left, replaced by new staff with intensive 'multi-skilling' training but little customer experience. No, the girls from old Casino were, like "The Yellow Rose of Texas", the sweetest of them all! These saw their job as making customers happy, and they cried when the SRA took off the old *Brisbane Limited*. Take-away service can never be as friendly as personal attention and service at seat.

The journey south in the XPT was tiring. There is nothing much to see at night and a fitful night's sleep is all you can expect sitting up, as you fidget uncomfortably in the cramped seat. First class seats on the XPT were very little different from economy: the seat covers were a different colour.

Waking in the morning with the inevitable crick in the neck I was interested to see that a girl in the adjoining seat who had joined at Grafton had a little blow-up pillow to rest her head on. I resolved this would be a number one priority shopping item before my next overnight stint by XPT.

It was time to be visiting the toilet but it appeared to be in great demand. The 'engaged' sign was illuminated and had been so for rather a long time, longer than usual. Someone sleeping it off from the night before? Hardly likely, since drinks were so severely restricted. I guessed someone must be having a shave or something else time-consuming.

Then an announcement came over the train intercom. "This is the conductor. If any passenger on the train has a small Phillips screwdriver would they please contact the train staff immediately".

What was this? A wheel nut loose, perhaps? I hoped not. I had once been on the Melbourne *Intercapital Daylight* when a bogie came unstuck and the train came to a shuddering halt. Fortunately it was only crawling away from the platform at the time.

No. This time it was not loose wheels or bogies. The toilet light was still on. This fact and the announcement seemed related. "Three old ladies locked in the lavatory," perhaps?

Well, not quite. It turned out to be a small boy who had turned the sneck while in the lavatory and couldn't reach or work out how to unfasten it. The most amazing thing to me was that no-one on the train, that is, no official on the train, had a screwdriver among their equipment for the journey! In the old days New South Wales trains always had a travelling electrician to look after the air conditioning, lights, sound system, stoves and anything else electrical that could go wrong. Most Australian long distance trains still have them but if there was one on the XPT someone must have economised on the tool kit.

In fact, this was yet another example of the so-called micro-economic reforms designed to make the railways more cost-effective. In the campaign to cut staff costs some official had decreed that trains should not carry technicians. When a train developed an equipment fault it just had to continue with the fault un-remedied until a major station or the end of the journey was reached. If the fault was a major one, it would be held up waiting for someone to be summoned. This of course meant delay and inconvenience to passengers – resulting in turn in loss of patronage. I wondered what would have happened if no-one had had a screwdriver that day.

A screwdriver having been found, the XPT reached Sydney on time. On the concourse I met up again with Lynne. "How did the journey go?" I asked, and told her about the boy in the loo. "Terrible, but quite exciting in a way," she said, and told me the story about the bloke who had thrown people's luggage out at Coff's Harbour.

She said the offender had been drinking heavily from a whisky flask he carried. Over-indulgence from private supplies is to some extent only to be expected when management fail to provide reasonable facilities on board. It is like the old six o'clock swill of Australian pubs in semi-prohibition days. The pubs opened only for an hour or so and everyone got sloshed in next to no time. The airlines learned their lesson on this. When they went 'dry' people started to bring their own and policing became impossible. But when the airlines started serving drinks again, free or otherwise, the attendants would be coming round to people's seats and there was a greater measure of control.

I told Lynne she should have come along to me for more protection.

Curiously, it was only on the Brisbane and Gold Coast trains that Countrylink applied these strict liquor restrictions, as though they had something against Queenslanders, but they were inconsistently applied. On returning next day by the *Brisbane XPT* I found the buffet attendant to be one of the old hands I had met out Dubbo way on another XPT. No problem about wine, with or without a meal. I enjoyed both.

State Rail had a competition around that time to suggest new names for the XPT services to Brisbane and Murwillumbah. 'Stoic Express' for the day train and 'Masochist' for the overnight sitter were suggested but understandably not adopted. Instead, the new trains remained known simply as the *Brisbane* and the *Murwillumbah XPTs* – mundane and unimaginative appellations which was all they then deserved.

As mentioned earlier, sleepers are now restored. The mistakes of the past have not been explicitly acknowledged but there is a new enthusiasm and keen people. One sleeping car per train is better than none – and the new sleepers on the XPT are clean and comfortable, of a world standard and nearly as good as the new Swedish sleeping cars on the Göteborg–Stockholm run. The difference? The XPTs are two berths to a cabin, four to the shower and toilet compartment, and they don't give you a supper basket. But you do get a toilet pack and, if I remember correctly, the morning newspaper as well.

Who knows what the future may hold? Things that are taken away can sometimes, but not always, be replaced and improved upon. A problem railways face is in winning back custom lost by ill-advised decisions. The link to Darwin is still only on the drawing board – a drawing board long covered in dust. Little remains of the original North Australia Railway. How long will it be before anyone can do a round trip of Australia by train? Or catch a through carriage from, say, Brisbane to Canberra or Melbourne, or from Perth to Alice Springs? Or go from Brisbane to Surfers Paradise in half an hour?

Assuming sanity prevails and the situation gets no worse before it gets better, there are some glimmers of hope. A Swedish tilt train was trialed in 1995 between Sydney and Canberra while Queensland Rail has tilt train sets on order. June 1995 saw a historic Perth to Brisbane run of the *Indian Pacific* using the newly standardised Adelaide–Melbourne link.

Even now there is much for the visitor (and the resident Australian) to enjoy on Australia's railway system. The way to see Australia is by rail. Trains will still take people to outback places no other public transport mode can reach.

"The train can reassure you in awful places – a far cry from the anxious sweats of doom aeroplanes inspire, or the nauseating gas-sickness of the long distance bus, or the paralysis that afflicts the car passenger" wrote Paul Theroux in *The Great Railway Bazaar*.

AGAINST THE TREND

J. Tounard in an article "Travelling Hopefully" in the *Railway Magazine* echoed this: "There is all the time in the world... and the speed of travel, contrasted with the stillness in the train... gives a heightened sense of perception."

On a train, you can just relax; lie there and let it all happen. Trains can be pure travel pleasure — you don't have to have a seat belt — which you do in motor cars in most places and which are now becoming mandatory in some coaches.

Railways bring many benefits to rural centres. They are a link with history. They are a tangible link with the rest of the country and an existing asset in which the community has invested time and money. They provide employment directly and indirectly and they are used one way or another by most of the community. As Hillman and Whalley found, this is the case even where actual patronage in terms of seat occupancy is low, whether measured on any one train or averaged over a period of time.

The truncation of routes by cutting back railheads, reductions in train service frequency or capacity and downgrading of facilities divert passenger traffic to road transport, and ignore factors which are important.

"I love trains," said the lady in the seat behind me to her sitting companion. "None of the worry of driving". This was said, surprisingly, on New Zealand's *Silver Fern* railcar as it crawled at restricted speed on track recently lowered (for electrification) through a tunnel near Taihape in the North Island.

It makes me angry when people from a distance and in their comfortable offices, sustained by their publicly funded car allowances, make decisions which take away the lifeblood and the heritage of places in the country. It is particularly disturbing when governments allegedly of the Left (which is traditionally pro-public transport) seem to eagerly embrace the sterile pseudo-economic ideologies of the Right. Figures alleging great losses incurred by keeping trains going do not impress the people who feel deprived — who are a lot more numerous than governments sometimes imagine. Such people see the Government as being appointed to keep things going, to maintain established services, to preserve the ancient landmarks, and to have some vision for the future.

"Where there is no vision, the people perish."

On 20 October 1989, mothers with their children watch as DP 104 on WRM 45 departs Manildra station, just days before the final run of the *Silver City Comet* on 1 November 1989. This had given service to the rural communities between Orange and Broken Hill since 27 September 1937. (Jean Campbell)

Chapter 21

The Last Ride

"This train is bound for glory, this train" – Negro Spiritual

Described as "The World's Last Great Train Ride" when it emerged from virtual obscurity to travel the path, if not to glory, then at least to a brief period of fame, the weekly goods train from Cairns to Forsayth in north Queensland is now only a memory, thanks to the collective lack of vision of the Queensland cabinet and its dismal economic advisers.

Unlike the people who organised its demise, train 7A90, the 'Forsayth Mixed' will, in McGonagall's immortal words about the Tay Bridge Disaster, "be remembered for a very long time".

"The Last Great Train Ride" was the name given by John and Grace Smith of Forsayth's Goldfields Hotel to this last survivor of the railway which opened up the copper and gold fields of North Queensland at the turn of the last century.

It was then that Chillagoe Railway and Mines Ltd, a company formed in 1893, started to build a private railway system that became one of the largest in Australia, with a total of 494 track kilometres by 1915. The company's initial attempts to persuade the Queensland Government to construct the railway had proved unavailing, although the Government approved the project on a basis whereby they would have the right of acquisition within a set period.

The Chillagoe Company main line from Mareeba to Mungana, 166 km, was soundly constructed with 60 lb rails (30 kg/m). Rail historian John Kerr states that, although five chain (100 metres) radius curves were freely used, "it was a better standard of line than most of the QR".

The ore reserves at Chillagoe did not live up to expectations and in 1906 the Company, in a curious arrangement with government, undertook to build a railway to the Etheridge area where gold and copper deposits had been found. This 229 km Almaden to Forsayth branch was never built to the same standard, the rails being of 21 kg/m or less, with four chain (80 metre) curves, many 1 in 40 gradients and timber bridges.

The first ore train ran from the Einasleigh mines to the smelters at Chillagoe in 1910. In addition to Forsayth–Chillagoe ore trains, a regular mixed train operated three days a week between Forsayth and Almaden and 'connected' there with the 'main line' trains to and from Mareeba.

During and after World War I the mining boom gradually collapsed and by 1919 the government took over the whole undertaking, of which the railway by then was probably the most profitable part. Even so, the regular service was reduced to one mixed train a week and in 1927 after serious floods washed away bridges the service was suspended and the government wanted to close the line because of its losses. However, it was re-opened using only railmotors hauling one or two trailer wagons for goods. New low level bridges at the creek crossings featured 'momentum gradients' where the train would take a run downhill to the bridge and rely on the addition of momentum to help it up the other side.

In 1939 a 2-6-0 diesel mechanical loco was built at Ipswich works, numbered DL1 and named 'Etheridge'. Three others of this class followed. One, DL2, is preserved at Forsayth station and another, DL4, still works on the Normanton Railway. Later, after World War II a somewhat similar type of loco became the standard motive power used west of Mount Surprise. These were the DH class B-B (diesel-hydraulic) engines designed by Walkers of Maryborough. They were specially adapted for multiple working on the Forsayth line and it was not uncommon for trains to be triple or even quadruple headed. Since many of the dips in the track, dropping down almost into the creek bed, are preceded and followed by curves, someone at the end of the train could view the whole thing like a snake twisting over the ground, with the front end disappearing round a curve, the bit in the middle sagging down and up again, while the rear end was still climbing round the previous bend.

THE LAST RIDE

The Forsayth Mixed crosses the bridge at Einasleigh. (QR)

From about 1970 until 1988 the service beyond Mareeba was more or less regular with two mixed trains a week in each direction to and from Forsayth, one to and from Chillagoe and a weekday railcar across the Atherton Tableland to Ravenshoe. The Mungana extension of the Chillagoe line was worked only by cattle trains as and when such were required. Two other branches, from Dimbulah to Mount Mulligan and from Lappa Junction to Mount Garnet had been closed in 1958 and 1963 respectively.

The Chillagoe Mixed service, number 62 Up, was a daylight train, leaving Cairns at 6.45 on a Wednesday, Mareeba at 10.45, Almaden 16.35 and reaching Chillagoe at 17.30. The Forsayth trains were at 18.30 on Monday (number 98 Up) and 22.10 on Wednesday (number 100 Up), returning from Forsayth at 7.45 on Wednesday and 9.00 on Friday as 99 and 101 Down respectively. The Chillagoe service returned at 8.00 on Thursday as number 63 Down, reaching Cairns at 17.30 the same day.

My first trip on the Cairns Railway as it was then called was partly out of curiosity about the Chillagoe 'Mixed', timetabled as one of the slowest of the slow trains of Queensland, with its overall start to stop speed of 17.8 km/h and partly because Chillagoe was noted for its old copper smelter chimneys, monuments of industrial archaeology, and for its limestone caves.

But another special reason for taking this trip was to find out something about Almaden, where the weekly mixed train lingered for half an hour at teatime on its outward journey and a similar period at breakfast time on its return, where the line from Cairns branched into two and where, for just 15 minutes at 9.00 on a Thursday before the Wednesday train ex-Cairns left there for Forsayth, Almaden junction became a fully operational relay node in the network and a passenger could cross the platform to change from one connecting train to another.

What facilities, I wondered, did Almaden offer the weary traveller who might decide to make this harrowing journey? I had to find out, and the only reasonable way to do so was to go there.

I joined the train at Mareeba, where I had spent a pleasant night at Dunlop's Hotel ("Best tucker in town," the locals told me) after a railcar trip up into the Atherton Tablelands from Kuranda to Ravenshoe. Scheduled to take seven and a quarter hours for its 165 km run from Mareeba to Chillagoe the train arrived in Mareeba an hour late to begin with, but managed to complete its business there in record time and left for Chillagoe only half an hour behind schedule. It was allowed half an hour at each of three other 'major' stops; Dimbulah, Lappa and Almaden, and two minutes at a place called Verdure. In fact we made nine stops altogether, spending 199 minutes immobile. Travelling time totalled five hours and two minutes, making our mean point to point running speed a quite healthy 55.5 km/h – three times the overall start to finish speed.

Stops on such trains are always interesting. The train crew were veritable mines of information, and each place has its own story. At Tabacum the water gins were brought into action: the method of conveying water from these tank wagons to the 'roadside' storage containers being the crudest imaginable. A sort of flume is held up to the tap on the tank wagon, and almost as much water spills to the ground as finds its way to its proper destination.

At Dimbulah, a major centre for tobacco growing, there was shunting to be done. Shunting is never very popular with guard or driver on these mixed trains. They would naturally prefer to enjoy their rest periods in the cool verandah of the station (and Dimbulah was definitely in that category) and share a friendly cuppa and chat with the station master. But the working timetable decreed that train number 62 Up would shunt if so directed by 'Control' and I assumed that Control had so directed that day. Number 62 also "waters camps", said the rule book, and I must say it did so, very thoroughly, not only at Tabacum but later on at Petford.

The guard pointed out the 865 metre Boonmoo Pinnacle, a prominent landmark of the ranges west of Eureka Creek. The crew had their meal break at Verdure, the next station. So much for a two minute scheduled stop! After that the line begins its climb of the Featherbed Range, traversing the attractive glen of Emu Creek, up to the disused station of Cape Horn, nearly 500 metres above sea level. From here, 100 km inland as the crow flies, the sea off the coast north of Cairns can be seen on a favourable day through a gap in the Great Dividing Range 45 km to the east.

It might have been the sea I saw away beyond the ranges, or it might have been the sky. The distance haze did not permit precise identification.

The Emu Creek glen at Cape Horn boasted the smallest telegraph pole on the railway. It was about a metre high and stood on a rock at the far side of the gorge. It may still be there but, like the railway itself, is no longer in use.

The line then descends slightly to Petford, where there was 'roadside' to attend to, that is, goods to unload. Railway people always call the railway the 'road'. This is not derived from the US term 'railroad'. Even in conservative Britain, birthplace of modern railways, the track or 'permanent way' is referred to by railwaymen as 'the road'.

How Petford was named I do not know. Queensland's timetables used to contain several interesting snippets of history and geography, explaining aboriginal and other station names, but had nothing to say about Petford. The girl in electric blue shorts who was there to collect goods for the local shop (not, unfortunately, to join the train) was sure to be someone's pet. On the other hand there was the beast I nearly stepped on when leaving the shop counter where I had bought a can of bitter lemon – a large hound lying on the floor right behind me, making it necessary to tread like King Agag before Samuel – delicately. The appellation 'pet' could hardly have applied to the large and dangerous looking Santa Gertrudis bull grazing among the temporarily lush grass of the station yard, which advanced purposefully to investigate this stranger invading its domain. I hastily rejoined the train, and we were on our way to the next stop, Lappa.

Lappa consisted of two houses and a derelict pub. This was a refreshment stop in days gone by, and the lady who kept it was famous for her scones. Goats' milk was another speciality there. All that remained of the closed Mount Garnet branch, noted for its steep gradients and four chain (80 metre) radius curves, was a dead-end siding with a capacity of over a hundred wagons, still operational if required.

Koorboora and its surroundings seemed infested with particularly vicious March flies, and one had the choice between roasting with the windows closed or enjoying a biting-insect-laden breeze! It was a relief to get out of the train for a while when it reached Almaden.

Here was an excellent pub, the Railway Hotel (what else?), immediately opposite the station. The latter consists of an island platform, with sidings and an avoiding loop between the Chillagoe original main line and the Forsayth branch. East of the station-master's and booking offices is a huge old water tank, now used as the town supply. A friendly cow wandered along the platform to investigate goings on. Almaden is also known locally as Cowtown: opposite the station on the other side is Cowtown Store.

There are two different stories of how Almaden was named. One is that originally it was settled by Germans and the name Almaden, pronounced 'Almahden' was of German origin. Then in World War I, wanting to avoid all things German, they changed the accent to the last syllable and put a hyphen in it. Alma-den is still sometimes used. The railway timetable favoured it but the Post Office (and the station nameboard) does not. The licensee at the hotel said the name came from a Spanish tin mine, and that there was a place in California named the same from the same source. He had a flagon of Almaden wine from California on a shelf behind the bar. This at least was fact. I was served a half bottle of Californian Almaden Burgundy once on the *Ann Rutledge* train in America, but was there in fact a place in Spain of that name? – and what did the locals say anyway? The licensee might not have been a born and bred Almadener.

On a later journey I chanced to meet a lady who had spent her childhood there. Definitely Alma-den, she said. The German origin was all rubbish. After all, they did not change the names of other German-origin places in Australia, like Hahndorf in South Australia. And there is an Almadén in Spain near the Badajoz–Madrid railway north of the Sierra Morena. So where do you go? I went to Chillagoe.

From Almaden to Chillagoe the line passes through heavily timbered country with numerous termite mounds and a fair amount of wildlife. Near Chillagoe are jagged rock walls, but the country opens out at Chillagoe itself, which was green and pleasant and I found a delightful meal awaiting me at the hotel close to the station. From the station master I obtained an old book of ticket sale records, about to be discarded, and in which I found interesting clues to the line's use over the years from 1927 to 1968. Mareeba seemed to be the most popular destination for booking, with up to about 400 ticket sales a year. Almaden itself attracted a fair amount of travel. I could not find the records for Cairns but ordinary single tickets to Brisbane were being issued at an average of 20 a year from 1927 to 1949. Passenger numbers in the 1960s departing from Chillagoe appeared to vary from one or none up to about twenty on each train. There were four or five other passengers on the day I travelled in 1984.

Returning the next morning we reached Almaden on time. At the opposite platform was the Forsayth train, number 100 Up, with one passenger looking well set for the journey, armed with suitable supplies and bedding. The last verse of the Negro Spiritual said it all: "This train don't pull no extras, this train" (i.e. no dining car or sleepers). Train crews as well as passengers bound for Forsayth were not advised to venture beyond Almaden without a tucker box full of provisions as it was always possible to be held up for a day or more by floods, derailment or other minor disaster. Even at the best of times, the branch includes the longest 'section' on Australian railways in terms of time, three hours for the 66.4 km from Einasleigh to Forsayth.

I had not sufficient free time to join the Forsayth train that day as I would have liked. I learned that some people took this train to the end of the line at Forsayth, to go from there by road to Croydon to catch the *Gulflander* train to Normanton on the Gulf of Carpentaria. My friend Mike Kent travelled this way and has raved about the trip ever since. He hitched a lift with a truck driver from Forsayth to Croydon. But to make the journey by public transport it was necessary at that time to change to the bus at Mount Surprise. Not only that; it involved waiting four days at Mount Surprise and two at Croydon. The return trip was even less convenient, since the *Gulflander* railcar was based at Normanton and ran only once a week. The round trip would have taken 23 days from Cairns.

The Forsayth branch is noted for its lightweight rails and tight bends, some so severe that couplings could become locked and trains derailed. Crew had to slacken off the screws on the couplings to prevent this. When I finally made the trip near the end of 1986 the lightweight 36 ton diesel hydraulic DH class locomotives were still in use beyond Mount Surprise, the normal blue diesel-electrics being said to be too heavy and long in the wheelbase to safely negotiate the frequent reverse curves, yet a few years later the 61½ ton 1000 hp (746 kW) 1720 class Co-Co diesel-electrics were working the line all the way.

The occasion for my trip north this time was work-related. My friend and colleague Mario and I were to discuss a student project on Kuranda with the local Council in Mareeba. We therefore travelled north in style on the *Queenslander*. On the same train there was a large number of newly appointed school teachers travelling to government appointments in outback places. Naturally on the long journey, meeting in the lounge car, we soon became acquainted and exchanged personal information relevant to the occasion.

Stephanie was a teacher from Brisbane. Tall, dark, and very attractive, part Scot and part German in origin, she was easy to talk to. She liked jazz – this probably came out when I was having a turn on the lounge piano.

I was carrying some copies of *Great Rail Non-Journeys* with me to take to people who had asked for it and said I would be writing another book some time. "Will you write about me?" asked Stephanie. "If you'd like me to," I replied, "but what shall I say?"

"I met a very lovely smart girl on the train who wouldn't put up with any 'bull' from my friend Mario," Stephanie replied. Sorry, Mario, mate! And there you go, Stephanie, as they say in Queensland.

The *Queenslander* arrived at Cairns in just nice time for me to catch the Forsayth train. Stephanie was doing the rest of the trip next day by her own car, which was carried on the train. In this way she avoided a Dimbulah arrival at half past one in the morning – in fact it would have been nearly two o'clock as the train was late. Middle of night arrival and departure times are always a disincentive to potential passengers, but another was the fact that the trains on these lines were no longer advertised. The 1986 public timetable said "goods trains only on this line" yet the Working Timetable revealed that the trains stopped at various stations to take up or set down passengers as required. This was really the beginning of the subtle attrition process described in the previous chapter.

In 1983 the Forsayth and Chillagoe trains had been re-numbered. This Monday train was now train 7A98. I had checked that passengers were still allowed and had informed the then Commissioner of my intended travel. At that time the train started from the goods yard instead of the station platform and a railway car was waiting to take me there. There were two passenger coaches. Several people were already on the train and it was ready for the right away. The locals clearly knew the trains still ran.

Leaving Cairns with the dusk we had a marvellous view back down to the lights of Cairns as we climbed up the tortuous curves of the Kuranda Range, but we were first held quite a while at Redlynch, the foot of the range. We were supposed to cross the evening railmotor from the Tablelands at Stoney Creek but being late we had just reached Redlynch at the time the railcar was due at Stoney Creek, 11 tortuous kilometres, 15 tunnels and 200 metres above us in the ranges. The railcar turned out to be late. Thus we waited from 19.23 to 20.15 while it wound its way slowly down the single track and we arrived late in Mareeba, only just in time for me to persuade the licensee's lovely daughter to let me have a six-pack of XXXX to sustain me on my travels. She came to the train to see me off, but it was to be another hour and past midnight before shunting was finished and the train left Mareeba.

It was a beautiful moonlit night. Crossing the Great Dividing Range from Mareeba to Chewko I was fascinated by the cloud pattern in the clear sky. There is no pollution up in these ranges. I was still gazing at the sky, lying there just looking out of the window as we came into Dimbulah. I noted our arrival as 1.53 and for a while there was utter silence, broken only by the coughing of a bloke in the adjoining compartment. There was no shunting: I thought the engine and crew must have gone to sleep. Anyway, that was what I must have done, because the next note in my log was when we left Almaden at 6.50 in the morning.

There we had discarded the extra passenger carriage. The station-master was not happy about the extra weight and there was no need for it with only myself and I think one other passenger at this stage. A kind-hearted lady in the house near the station gave us a beaker of tea and some ham sandwiches. Taking the extra coach, the guard told me, would have meant leaving behind some 'roadside' because of its weight. These old wooden carriages were very heavy. He could not understand why an extra coach had been attached. He had heard it was because head office had said some writer bloke was expected on the train: why that merited an extra coach was not clear to him, nor to me either but I kept quiet.

It was going to be a hot day out along the track, they said. Forty Celsius was forecast for Forsayth and when we stopped at a fettlers' camp early in the afternoon near Gelaro it was certainly close to that. The workmen were all resting "under the shade of a Coolabah tree". I found the scenery extremely varied. Trees there were in abundance and of great variety. Some complain of the sameness of Australian bush country but it is rarely so when you have time to look, and on the Forsayth train, time is what you have plenty of. There were Ironbarks, Cottonwoods, Bloodwood, Ghost Gums, Ti-trees, Pandanus and bush lemon. In among the trees were glimpses of wildlife, and everywhere were 'ant-hills' (correctly called termite mounds, but don't try telling the locals that: they know better than the entomologists). The ant-hills were of every conceivable shape and size.

After Gelaro the track passes close to Hanging Rock, though not, I think, the one where the famous picnic took place, and twisting its way across Rocky Tate River, Double Barrell Creek and Bullock Creek, it enters an area between two ranges known locally as the Giants' Playground. Here boulders of fantastic shapes are balanced on rocky pinnacles as though put there by some huge cranes. It is utterly astonishing country. After this comes the Lynd River crossing and the small settlement of Lyndbrook, which boasts a landing strip. After another crossing, Fossilbrook Creek, the line becomes comparatively straight and level through what is called the 'dreamtime' country south to Mount Surprise. There is in fact an 11.7 km dead straight stretch through Frewhurst, by far the longest straight on the whole 423 km from Cairns along the coastal strip to Freshwater and up through the ranges all the way to Forsayth.

Mount Surprise is well supplied with food outlets and the trains in each direction conveniently arrive there around lunchtime. The pub specialities are their homemade pies: you are offered a choice – "cat or kangaroo", but in fact they are all just beef. The Forsayth Mixed would always have shunting to do at Mount Surprise, and then again at Einasleigh, where we stayed so long that the guard complained to me, "This isn't a job; it's an endurance test".

Poor old Bob. He was always grumbling but we became good friends even after I had admitted to indirect responsibility for the extra coach. There is a rock named 'Stack's Monument' after him and on the return trip when he knocked off duty at Almaden I joined him to Dimbulah by car.

THE LAST RIDE

But first to Forsayth. After leaving Mount Surprise the timeless country is with you all the way. There were still 121 km to go, for which 7A98 was allowed a generous five and half hours. The permitted maximum for all trains on this section is 30 km/h, with reductions to 20 km/h for tight curves and bridges. And bridges there are. Before Mount Surprise the Tate River bridge is the most spectacular but from Mount Surprise to Einasleigh there is Junction Creek, Camp Creek, Telegraph Creek, Ellendale Creek, Bowerbird Creek and the crossing of Einasleigh River before the tight curve and further dip down to cross the gorge into Einasleigh station yard. On the way there is endless rock-strewn bush, seemingly empty of habitation and untouched by human hand, while on the left is seen the Douglas Range, on the right Mount Nigger Range, The 'Lighthouse' mountain on the left, Mount Alder and the Caterpillar Mountains on the right.

The train waited long enough in Einasleigh for a few cool ones at the Central Hotel – the only one, though there may have been more in days gone by. Railway pictures adorn the walls. Next door is what some say is the former Town Hall, Australia's answer to Pisa's Leaning Tower. Whether it is the bougainvillea growing through it that has pulled it askew, or whether the cause was an earthquake or mining subsidence I did not find out. Folk in the outback are not always forthcoming about things they are not sure whether to be proud of or not.

Before reaching Einasleigh, the train had paused long enough for the crew to show me the bowerbird nest some way off in the bush. What is another 10 minute delay on such a leisurely schedule! Just over the road from the pub is the gorge of the Copperfield River. I had heard there were crocodiles in the deep pools, but the water looked very cool and inviting in the afternoon heat. Freshwater crocs are supposed to be harmless 'unless provoked', unlike 'salties' which are lethal at all times. I wondered what it took to 'provoke' a 'freshie' – disturb it when mating, perhaps?

I did not find out. Talking about the railway to 'mine host' over a stubbie of beer or two seemed a safer way to spend the time. Besides which, Einasleigh seemed well populated with attractive young females with time on their hands playing pool in the pub bar.

Between Einasleigh and Forsayth there are more ranges to cross; the Newcastle Range past Mount Misery, and then Wirra Range where, on a relatively straight and level bit of track 7 km before Wirra the line reaches its highest point at 727 metres. From Wirra the line wends its way down Delaney Creek Gorge. Rock wallabies hop among the rocks at the line-side, seeking morsels from passengers. Especially impressive is to stand by the line-side just east of Forsayth when the train is coming down the ranges as I did on a later occasion. Its mournful hooting and the occasional protesting shriek of the wheels on the tight curves herald its approach to this remote outpost. The Goldfields Hotel stands waiting with a warm welcome for customers. Traditionally, cold beer and home-cured silverside with mustard sauce would be typical fare. To my astonishment on my last visit the hotel had not only been enlarged with demountable units at the back, but champagne on ice was to be had over the bar counter.

At breakfast on the morning of that first trip I met a railway engineering inspector who invited me to join him on his motor trolley for part of the return trip. Leaving at the early hour of six-thirty I rode for the first few kilometres with the driver, then joined Pat on his trolley to experience the kind of close-to-the-rails travel the fettlers were familiar with in the days when they had to push the trolley along by manpower – a see-sawing kind of propulsion known as 'hard yakka'. The sun was barely up when we started: I would not have liked a long journey on an open trolley in the heat of the day and did not envy the groups of fettlers we kept passing. We stopped four or five times to unload new sleepers and caught up with the train somewhere near Wirra Wirra, after stopping to inspect a dead snake lying across the track. There I climbed back up into the carriage with assistance and some more minor grumbles from the guard.

At Einasleigh and again at Mount Surprise there was roadside and shunting to attend to and we were over two hours late by the time we

THE LAST RIDE

Swimming stop at Fossilbrook Creek on the Forsayth Mixed. (Neville Smith)

reached Frewhurst, 141 km from the start. There our scheduled stop of two minutes was extended to half an hour. It was clear we would not reach Dimbulah, my intended nightstop, much before midnight.

At Almaden it was revealed there would be a further delay, I think due to some engine fault. Bob was finished with his tour of duty and offered to take me by car to my hotel. In view of the time this seemed a good idea and I was grateful for his advice. Nothing seemed to have gone right for me that day, nor for him. I could now appreciate his comment about an endurance test.

I have no record of when train 7C99 Down finally reached Dimbulah: I think it was early the following morning. I forget whether I had a lift or caught the Chillagoe train for the last 43 km into Mareeba, but I do recall seeing the Wednesday train, 7A90 Up, coming into Dimbulah that day, and I really felt for old Bob Stack. He would have had a fit. There was not one passenger coach; not two, but three! Now they could hardly blame me for that, but I wondered. Someone, somewhere, had got the wires crossed.

TRAINCATCHER

In the first edition of *Australia by Rail,* published in 1988, I gave a timetable for an itinerary which included the Forsayth train. Journalists and others began to travel the line and write about it. In 1990 John and Grace Smith devised an excellent leaflet advertising the train. With the active support of the Far North Queensland Promotion Bureau, even Queensland Rail (QR) began to see this almost forgotten railway as an asset of tourist value and began again to advertise the service, even though it had been reduced by then to once weekly.

In September 1993 to celebrate my retirement, my wife and I made a tour of Australia which took in Ayers Rock, Arnhem Land and North Queensland, going by rail from Adelaide to Alice Springs and from Cairns back to Brisbane. Half way into the trip I had to fly back to Brisbane for a conference. My wife was to stay an extra week with family in Darwin and I was to meet her again in Cairns. This allowed time to undertake a trip I had long sought to make, on the *Gulflander* from Normanton to Croydon, and to take the Forsayth Mixed again back to Cairns. I had previously worked out that one way to cover both the Normanton and Etheridge railways was to take the train to Mount Isa, bus or 'plane from there to Normanton, and then buses again from Croydon to Forsayth. By this time, thanks largely to the efforts of people in North Queensland, bus and train timetables had been to some extent coordinated to make such an itinerary possible and be advertised in leaflets at railway and tourist information centres.

Inclusion of the Forsayth train was important to me because in July 1993 the possible complete closure of the line, along with 28 other branches, had been mooted. If this happened I would have little chance of ever travelling on the isolated Normanton to Croydon line.

My round trip began with the *Sunlander* to Townsville, connecting after a longish lunch break with the *Inlander* to Mount Isa. From there I would return to Cloncurry by train, stay the night and catch the Mount Isa to Normanton bus there the following midday. This would reduce the misery of six hours on a bus to a more tolerable four and a half and incidentally allow time for a quick lunch before the ordeal.

THE LAST RIDE

But these "best laid schemes" went the way Burns said – "agley". After leaving Cloncurry the westbound *Inlander* seemed to be having a rough time of it. Track work was in progress and it seemed the whole section from 'The Curry' onwards was being reconstructed and the rails were only loosely held in position. We crawled along, swaying from side to side, and it took 2½ hours to cover the next 51 km to Malbon junction. At km post 796 between Marimo and Mitakoodi the train seemed almost to keel over. No-one would have wanted it to go any faster with the track in such condition and I wondered why such a long stretch had to be worked on all at the same time.

The Mount Isa line takes a lot of heavy produce traffic and it seemed to me that if it needed so badly to be rebuilt there would have been merit in investigating another route. The Curry and the Isa are only 108 km apart as the crow flies and a shorter route leaving the present line a few kilometres north of Slaty Creek and thence via Mary Kathleen, coming into Mount Isa from the northeast might well be a sound long term investment.

It was still a great trip in spite of these hairy moments, but when the train became over three hours late I realised I could not get back to Cloncurry before midnight (not a good time to rouse up mine host at the local hotel). I spoke to the train supervisor. A quick radio call was made to 'Control' and they soon fixed up for me to change to an ore train at Duchess and thence back to 'The Curry'.

This was my first chance to visit the pub at Duchess I had heard about and seen from the track. There were no camels at the bar, but the licensee knew the Smiths who ran the Goldfields Hotel at Forsayth so we had something to talk about while I waited for the train.

The bus trip to Normanton next day was frightfully uncomfortable, enough to shake the brains loose, enlivened only by occasional glimpses of the abandoned Kajabbi branch of the railway paralleling the corrugated highway, and the stop at Burke and Wills Roadhouse where the tame emus came out to inspect the passengers. Normanton was a welcome relief and the Normanton hotel put on magnificent food at ridiculously cheap prices.

Next day the *Gulflander* left three minutes early and after we got going, the driver stood up, left the controls and wandered through the carriage handing out leaflets. The train just trundled on happily round the bend. There were all sorts of people on board, young, elderly and families. All or most would have been tourists but there was not the usual crop of Americans and Japanese that one finds in the more accessible parts of the continent.

We had a lunch stop at Blackbull and at the end of the trip all the passengers received a 'Certificate of Courage' signed by Len Taylor, the current driver/stationmaster/ticket collector/booking clerk/manager, which read:

Certificate of Courage

This is to certify that the undersigned plucked up the necessary courage to cross the Norman River, dine on homemade cake and cordial at Blackbull, view Bower Bird nests and wild banana trees, battle through the hostile scrub country near Golden Gate and, 152 kilometres later, discover the gold mining town of Croydon.

Colin J. Taylor

should be congratulated for following his/her sense of adventure to travel aboard the

GULFLANDER TRAVELTRAIN

on *Wednesday 29th* day of the month of *September*

in the year of *1993*

Signed *Len J. Taylor* Your host

Croydon is marked more for ruins than anything else. The passengers (those who were continuing on to the Forsayth train and those who were going the other way the next day) as well as the driver, all stayed at the one and only pub which had acquired demountable extensions in the last few years as tourist numbers had increased several-fold.

After the overnight stop we boarded the bus to Georgetown. This and the later trip in the postal van from Georgetown to Forsayth along twisting gravel roads were nearly as hair-raising as journeys by mammy-wagon in West Africa or in my son Keith's Ute through Arnhem Land but I survived and met more interesting people, both on the journey and at Forsayth. In the pub at Forsayth I tried to teach a young lad how to play '301 up' with 'arrows' on the pub dart board. We both had to give up after failing for ages to split '11' after not making the closing double '1'. He then showed his sister and they both did rather better. Champagne and a good meal rounded off that day.

That evening I watched the train come in. There were 80 passengers on board – more than it would have had in a year a few years before, such was the interest that had been generated as the route was 'discovered'. By this time, QR had found it necessary to require advance booking and seat reservations for the train, something I am sure must have never before happened with the Forsayth Mixed or any other Queensland "goods train with passenger accommodation attached, but liable to cancellation or alteration without notice".

The seat allocations were loosely observed. There were 62 booked on the return trip, and throughout the journey people wandered from carriage to carriage making new friends and re-discovering old ones. It was like an extended family on a holiday. The train crew, and all the people at places where we stopped, wanted to make it a memorable journey. I wondered if the politicians and some of their advisers 2000 km away in Brisbane had any real appreciation of what the railway meant to these people out there. Very little, I concluded. In the middle of the night the train stopped at Stoney Creek falls in the darkness to get its breath back (I think it was technically for a brake test before it trundled down the Kuranda ranges to Cairns) and only the sound of the swishing water of the falls disturbed the night air.

By this time many of the returning passengers had left the train, either at Almaden the previous evening or at Mareeba round about midnight. In the previous year or so the train had been re-timed to reach Cairns at four in the morning and I suspect this tended to discourage some people from staying on to the end, especially those with young children, but it was amazing how many did.

Arriving so early in Cairns I had to knock my wife up at the hotel at about five in the morning, but that was my usual rising time so it was no great hassle. To compensate I took her on a boat trip – she is a very bad sailor – to Green Island on the edge of the Barrier Reef. It was rather rough (a bit like the Normanton bus) but we both survived and even went on a semi-submersed cruise in a "yellow submarine", as they called it, to see the fish and corals at close quarters without getting wet.

The next day we took the train up to Kuranda and back, the 'village in the rainforest' and visited the local open air market. We had a nice light and tasty lunch at the 'bottom pub' opposite the railway station and I bought a bottle of special wine they called Kuranda Hotel Motel Claret. The label reads:

> "An unusual rough-as-guts wine that has the distinctive bouquet of being downwind of a native sewerage system. It is best drunk with the teeth clenched to prevent ingestion of seeds and skins. Connoisseurs will savour the slight tannin taste of burnt cockatoo feathers and soiled medical dressings. Possessors of a cultivated palate admire the initial assault on the senses which comes from the careful and loving blending of travelling circus cage floor hosings with perished jockstraps. The maturing Tableland slaughter yard hog's heads give it a very definite nose. In North Queensland this wine is becoming known as saviour brand (nine out of ten people who drink it for the first time exclaim "J-E-E-ESUS CHRI-I-IST") It won a bronze medal at the Atherton Homosexuals' Convention in 1973. CAUTION: Avoid contact with the eyes and open cuts. Keep away from naked flames (both old and new)".

THE LAST RIDE

Actually it's a good Barossa quaffing red. I remembered it from an earlier trip and soon had half the tourists in the bar buying bottles as souvenirs.

Returning from Kuranda, we were taken by coach to Gordonvale where Mike Kent, driver of the *Mulgrave Rambler* and friend from way back, took us on an unforgettable trip by steam train on the narrow gauge cane railway through the canefields and rainforest to Orchid Valley where we were entertained by a Polynesian music and dancing troupe.

I thought then that there was a good possibility that the Forsayth train would remain. Public indignation at the 29 branch line closure proposals had been intense. The Premier had gone round various rural centres to say the government didn't really mean it; it was just a recommended option; no decisions had been made (the usual political 'damage control' technique). A 'Task Force' chaired by the Deputy Premier and Minister for Rural Affairs was set up to review the proposals.

At no stage was it made public where or how the proposals originated. The Transport Minister, who only a couple of years earlier had been assuring Parliament that "the vision of this Government is ... not cutting off the arms of Queensland Railways but rather, playing to the strengths and re-investing and redeveloping the range of services that Queensland Railways can provide" and "this Government does not have a program to deny the people of Queensland passenger services" (Queensland *Hansard,* 18 April 1991), was strangely silent and so were the railway people. Clearly there was a political stuff-up, if not a snafu! No doubt, like any reasonably competent organisation, QR would have been constantly reviewing their operations and would know where the greatest profits and losses occurred. The government would have access to internal reports and be aware of options but for all this to happen so suddenly was unrehearsed.

There is no doubt that political pressure was being brought to bear by the Federal Government, always reluctant to hand money to the States. A 1993/4 Interim Budget Statement by the Queensland Treasurer outlined various proposed savings measures in response to a decline in General Revenue Grants from the Commonwealth. Apart from a decision to abolish first class air travel for public servants, the major savings were to be achieved by closing parts of the rail system, in line with what the Industry Commission had been urging. A convenient, ready-made 'quick fix' solution to a temporary cash shortfall, catching everyone, QR and the Minister included, on the wrong foot! All the branch lines alleged to be loss-making could of course have been supported by cross-subsidisation from the huge profits made on coal haulage. Yet ironically and illogically, the Australian government wanted QR to stop making these profits!

The hidden 'bottom drawer' plans, which might have remained that way indefinitely, were therefore gleefully seized upon by the economic gurus in the government and paraded before the public in July 1993. Yet less than a month later, the government published its *Adventure Atlas of Queensland: Reef, Range and Red Dust*, which included the following paragraph, vetted and accepted by the government's own appointed scrutineers over the year immediately preceding publication:

"The adventurous could try the three day round trip on the Etheridge Railway to Forsayth and back, described as the world's Last Great Train Journey. Up and down the line goes, here curving along the side of a gorge, there descending to the creek bed and meandering among boulders. For this journey a blanket, some mosquito repellent, and an Esky with supplies are needed. There is no dining car or sleeper, but room to lie down and plenty to see."

The atlas containing the passage quoted above was launched and endorsed by the Premier who, in his Foreword, wrote: "The Adventure Atlas of Queensland reflects our purposeful mood. The catch phrase 'Reef, Range and Red Dust' exemplifies the unique environment that is so characteristically Queensland."

Did that include the World's Last Great Train Ride?

The Task Force reported in November 1993. There was some doubt about whether the report accurately represented what the committee had decided, since it was penned by public servants on the basis of notes made at meetings, and in fact there was considerable anger, and claims and counter-claims by some of its members when the draft was first leaked.

The final published report did not please everybody. A general impression was given by the media and by government spokesmen that more than half the lines had been reprieved but this was not confirmed by the actual text. In fact, of the 29 branch lines, none were given a total reprieve. Fourteen were to "remain open with enhanced cost recovery targets" yet with reduced services and total withdrawal of passenger trains. Seven, which had been abandoned and left to rot for several years in any case, were to be officially closed from January 1994 except for part of one of them which was to be left as a private siding. Five were to be 'mothballed'; that is, left to rot like the preceding seven had been, and the other three were to be "subject to special arrangements".

One of these was the Cairns Railway from Mareeba to Mungana including the branch to Forsayth. Of the 1245 submissions made to the Task Force during its deliberations 139 referred specifically to this line, and more submissions were made on the issue of its future potential than were made on the future potential of any other of the lines proposed for closure.

The Task Force recommended that there should be a review over a six month period from 1st November 1993 of the potential use of either the Mareeba to Forsayth or the Mareeba to Chillagoe line for tourism. At the end of this period a decision would be made whether to operate one of them on this basis for a trial period of three years. Any decision to close the Forsayth line following the review implied, among other things, the operation of the Chillagoe line for tourists.

The recommendations, reported as being accepted by Cabinet, were not followed. As far as can be established, no consideration was given to the Chillagoe line on which the last scheduled trains had ceased in March that year and on which passenger vehicles had not been provided since the previous October. There were some discussions with some local people during 1994, following which it was announced that Cabinet had made a final decision – the whole system west of Dimbulah was to go except for the 121 km Mount Surprise to Forsayth section. This was to become a completely isolated dead-end line like the Normanton Railway. It would be worked by a refurbished railcar, while goods would be carried on road trucks. The Last Great Train Ride would be no more as soon as the railcar was ready for service (it had previously been asserted, when all the railcars in Queensland were withdrawn a few years previously, that they were all unserviceable.)

Around October that year the date for the final run was announced as 29 March 1995. Patronage had ranged from about 20 to 50 or so while uncertainty remained. Many people were still unaware of the train or of its proposed withdrawal but as the news spread, passenger bookings surged. They came from Cairns, they came from Brisbane, they came from interstate and they came from overseas.

In January I took the trip again as far as Einasleigh and back. On my way up to Cairns on the *Sunlander* I met two people who had never heard of the Forsayth train. When they did so they wanted to make bookings straight away, but they were probably too late. Most remaining runs from then until the end of March were fully booked. In fact the railways had to give up bothering about booking at the end, so great was the demand.

On my last trip there was a couple from Apollo Bay in Victoria who had come specially up to Queensland for it after they had heard me talking to Ian McNamara about the train on ABC Radio's *Australia All Over*: there was also an elderly couple from Nottingham, England, touring Australia, who had made a special diversion to include this journey. The man was a retired signalman from the LNER.

There were 63 passengers booked on the way out and 71 on the return. This was more than QR's proud flagship the *Queenslander* had been carrying for some months; certainly more than its average, and it represented over a thousand percent increase in patronage from the average of a few years previously. No train service anywhere else in

THE LAST RIDE

Australia could boast such figures. Demand exceeded supply, and left the Premier's injunction to "Use it or lose it" looking rather cynical in retrospect.

So incensed were local people that one of the trains was blockaded and held while a meeting was sought with the Transport Minister. He proved unavailable, being already away for Christmas holiday, and the blockaders were eventually persuaded to let the train go. After all, what real point was there in stopping something the government already wanted to take away? But it was a protest, and it gained media attention and probably even more community support. The passengers who were inconvenienced were not angry with the protesters, only with the political decision makers. They were not very impressed with the road coach which QR, dutifully being responsible to its passengers, provided to replace the train that day. A new bus, but it caught fire. Extinguishing the fire and checking the damage meant further delay.

A month later, the week before I was due to travel, the train was derailed. There had been very heavy rain and the loco heeled over on a curve as its weight pushed the rail out of alignment. The driver skilfully applied the brakes and no-one was hurt but once again a bus trip faced the unlucky passengers. Exceptional rain forced the cancellation of another service, when one of the bridges was under water. An added problem was that the road was under water too.

Such incidents were widely publicised by the media, serving to increase interest even further. The train on 15 March carried 123 passengers. The following week a coach load of old folk arrived while the train was in the station at Mareeba. It left there with 141 passengers on board. As many as eight passenger coaches were seen together on that train in its last months of travel. Carriages had to be taken from the popular Kuranda Scenic Railway down in Cairns. What would dear old Bob Stack have thought if still alive? And what did the authorities think? As far as we know, they ignored it. The decision, like the laws of the Medes and Persians, could not be altered – even if by then most people must have seen it to be a bad mistake.

TRAINCATCHER

My last trip was quite eventful. I decided to overnight at Einasleigh because it would be less crowded than Forsayth, the people there I knew to be friendly and the place looked interesting. Swimming in the gorge had been recommended and some people had done this on my last previous trip. In any case, the gorge would be worth exploring a little.

Friendly though the people were, the mosquitoes were not, and it was not until the following morning I found there was an electric repellent switch I should have turned on. When the train stopped there for the best part of an hour on the outward trip most passengers had flocked to the pub or down to the gorge for a swim. There is safety in numbers and I joined them. It was cool and refreshing. At one stage a large kangaroo suddenly appeared on the rocky side of the gorge, plunged in and swam across to the other side. There the poor beast had awful difficulty climbing up the steeply sloping rock. He would scratch away with his little front paws, but kept sliding back. "A bit to the left," people shouted, the slope there being slightly easier. Eventually he caught on, got a toe-hold (or maybe a tail-hold?) and made it to the top, to the accompaniment of a loud cheer from the spectators.

The following day before the train returned I ventured in again myself. Beautifully cool, but the river was still swollen with run-off from rains further upstream. A fair amount of debris was floating across the wide deep pool where people swam. Up on my right a rock wallaby hopped from rock to rock at great speed, sure-footed as any mountain goat; stopping once to look quizzically at the lone intruder before bounding away out of sight. He did not go for a swim like big brother the day before.

Then I noticed a curious sort of log slowly moving with the flow, coming in my direction. But was it a log? Suddenly I remembered about 'freshies'. The front end of the log was shaped just like the snout of a crocodile. I was out of the water so fast! They may well have been 'harmless unless provoked' but in which category was this one?

Oddly, none of the train passengers came in this time for a dip, although some turned up at the pub. Had they been warned? In the event, the train stopped further down the line, at Fossilbrook Creek, where most of the passengers went for a wallow in the pools under the bridge.

Before that we enjoyed the usual lunch stop at Mount Surprise. Mike had written a song to commemorate the train and some of us gathered at the pub piano to give it a try-out, just like when *Waltzing Matilda* was first performed at the North Gregory Hotel in Winton.

Here are some of the words. It has a rousing and easy to remember tune:

The Last Great Train Ride

It's Wednesday night in the City of Cairns/ And down at the platform side/ There's a train in the station ready to roll/ And they call it the Last Great Train Ride

CHORUS
Let's board the Last Great Train Ride/ Let's climb on that Last Great Train /We'll say goodbye to the lights of Cairns/ Through the tunnels on the Last Great Train Ride

They used to call it the Forsayth Goods/ With passenger van attached/ But passengers increased a thousand percent/ 'Tis a record that cannot be matched

It's sixty pound rail till through Cowtown we pass/ But then it's just forty-two pound/ Two wires through the sand and the stones and the grass/ By the train wheels will surely be found

CHORUS
Let's board the Last Great Train Ride/ Let's climb on that Last Great Train/ Two wires through the sand and the stones and the grass/ Are the rails of the Last Great Train Ride

Copyright by Mike Kent. Used with permission.

There must surely be nothing else quite like Train 7A90. Where else in the world would a train stop to let people study a bower bird's nest or take a dip in a freshwater pool? The leisurely schedule of the Forsayth train allowed time to relax at Fossilbrook Creek and Einasleigh Gorge. Part of its uniqueness, and an attraction to many – particularly rail buffs of course – was that it was a goods train. Passengers have rarely been allowed on goods trains, and there would be fewer on which they are allowed nowadays than ever before.

In the 1977 timetable, QR said of the Cairns Railway:

"The line is retained today as a most important connection with the outside world for the large grazing industry which the area now supports. One of the tourist attractions is the limestone caves at Chillagoe and nearby, at the site of the old Chillagoe copper smelters, remains one of the large brick chimneys a sentinel reminder of once prosperous days." At that time they had nothing special to say of the Forsayth line, but they do now.

The train passes through timeless country where you just let it all happen. It remains to be seen whether the railcar substitute has anything like the same appeal. It may attract a new, different market - but why abandon the market that has already been established? There is nothing wrong in principle with a Mount Surprise to Forsayth railcar, as long as it is additional to the Forsayth Mixed. But if a railcar is all that is offered, the long and harrowing road journey to reach it over dangerous roads frequented by massive road trains is certain to frighten some people away.

The 'Savannahlander', as the railcar has been called, has certainly been well publicised and promoted. But it is not easy to persuade people that something new is better than something they have been enjoying. The XPT as a substitute for the *Brisbane Limited* was not readily accepted. The current schedule for the railcar has it reaching Forsayth at 18.00 much as 7M90 did, and leaving again at 7.30 next day. In its first few runs the average number of passengers staying overnight in Forsayth was two but up to 25 have been since reported. Patronage may yet build up further, but the mid-1995 scene is a far cry from the figures over the preceding 18 months. It could it be that some government

THE LAST RIDE

accountant types are already rubbing their hands with glee as the prospect of declining patronage brings the ultimate complete closure of the line closer to reality.

After the evening meal in Almaden on our return trip there were few who attempted to sleep much before Mareeba. Parties developed spontaneously. There were singsongs, including *Train Whistle Blowing* and of course Mike's new *Last Great Train Ride*; there were exchanges of addresses and there were discussions on what if anything could still be done to keep the train running. People leaned out to look at the bush as we wound our way down the ranges, our train augmented by the addition of three carriages left at Almaden, and by extra goods wagons. The way the loco headlights lit up the bush away ahead was a marvellous sight.

One anxious moment was when it was reported that someone was on a carriage roof. The guard hurried through the train, quite properly concerned for the safety of his charges but it turned out to be a false alarm, or at least an exaggeration. Someone may have been leaning well out of the window and grasped the roof of the carriage, but roof-walking, no.

I was not able to travel on the very last train but my friend Mike took it as far as Mareeba. It was like an Irish wake. The previous Saturday there had been a street march in Cairns to protest about the closure, and all the locals were aware of what was happening. Groups on house verandahs were partying and waved as the train passed. Car horns hooted. They were not going to let the death of the Last Great Train Ride pass unhonoured. According to Mike, 136 people took that train but in some ways it was a sorry spectacle. Deprived of its usual rake of goods wagons it was shorter than usual. Already the Q-link road trucks were lined up to take away the freight business which had been an integral part of the former economic and social base of the line.

On the weekend before the last train there had been a special charter trip planned by a Victorian-based tourist group. This four-day tour, covering the Mareeba–Almaden section of the line in daylight and including hotel accommodation, meals, photo-stops and a coach trip to Chillagoe and back, failed to materialise. The reasons were unclear. It may have been over-priced or QR may in some way have failed to meet the promoters' requirements. The story varies according to the informer. One thing is clear. The Chillagoe trip could not be done by rail because QR demanded a very high price to cover necessary rehabilitation of the track, on which there had been no trains for some time. "Trains on this branch run only with the approval of the General Manager, Freight" meant they did not run at all. An earlier stage in service downgrading is marked by timetable expressions like "Runs only as required" and "Subject to cancellation or alteration without notice". According to the locals, freight had been actively discouraged on the Chillagoe line for the past year or more.

Train 7A90 and the whole line from Cairns to Forsayth is something unique, of world heritage status, and certainly a significant part of Queensland's history and future. Successive Queensland governments have been entrusted with this line since 1919. It has taken until the late 1980s for people to realise its potential with the growing world interest in outback and unusual tourism.

The decision to withdraw the Forsayth train 7A90 is a foolish mistake, a short-sighted decision. It was public pressure that forced the government of the day to reconstruct and reopen the line when it was closed after the 1927 floods. No government should underestimate the strength of public pressure, especially when something they treasure is taken from them. The present Queensland Government suffered a severe voter swing against it in July 1995 – rail closures being one among other factors where public perception was of a government not caring. One member – a government minister – in a nearby electorate lost his seat. The Premier has promised to review all recent decisions: the Government will have to live with its decision, to its shame, for a very long time if it fails to reverse this one. There is no reason why, actively promoted and efficiently operated, this line, including the Chillagoe branch should not continue indefinitely and bring an overall positive return to the Queensland economy, whether it achieves full cost recovery in isolation or not. And this could be done without requiring "a substantial capital upgrading" to Class 'A' standard at a cost of $30 million or more as the Task Force was told in its background briefing. This is like saying that every airstrip in outback Queensland should be capable of taking a Jumbo Jet.

As I asked in my own submission to that Review:

"Do the Italian authorities calculate whether they recoup all the tremendous cost of maintaining the Leaning Tower of Pisa so that tourists can gawp at it and photograph it? No, they regard it as a world attraction and they maintain it because it is one of the things tourists come to Italy to see and they spend their money all over the place."

If the government fails to restore the service to the whole of the line, even the *Gulflander* itself could be under threat, as one means of access to it has been truncated. But at least the worst scenario, of complete closure, has been averted so far. While there is life there is hope. It would be unforgivable if the government, following the now effected closure of the line between Dimbulah and Mount Surprise, were to pursue a scorched earth policy and rip up the rail line, making future replacement prohibitively expensive. This would be an act of vandalism which in my view would make the misguided efforts of some elements of modern youth who practice their ideas of contemporary art on vacant walls and other plain surfaces pale into insignificance by comparison.

But there may be hope yet from an unexpected source. A recent report on 'National Competition Policy' accepted by the Australian Government, while advocating measures which would generally produce the kind of chaos being experienced on British Railways through the application of similar theoretical concepts, does envisage the idea of a right of access to rail tracks. Thus a private organisation could take on what the Queensland Government have failed to do! Come on, all you entrepreneurial rail enthusiasts. Here's your chance!

Last Great Train Ride, RIP. We look to the Resurrection.

TRAINCATCHER

Talking of which, and of trains bound for glory, one might ask, will there be railways in Heaven? At Sunday school we sang a hymn: those who went to join the King of Kings in the glory up yonder would "follow in His train". In the innocence of youth I was quite clear about this — a train was a train! I surely wanted to "be there in that number" when those Saints went marching in! If Heaven means the fulfilment of human desires there is still hope. Good food and wine, yes; big friendly dogs and pussies too perhaps, but please God, let there be trains! Some would say that travelling so much on Australian trains — not to mention British Rail, I have already had my share of Hell.

Talking of which, place names are fascinating. There is definitely a railway station in Hell. It is on the Trondheim to Bodø line in northern Norway. The kind of place I would like to have visited just to send a card back to my best friend with a 'Wish you were here' message.

Meanwhile, *Bon Voyage*, *Gute Reise* or whatever. Yours till Hell freezes over (as up there in Scandinavia it probably does), but I can stay no longer. I have to catch a train.

Appendix I

"There are lies, damned lies and then there are statistics"

— Attributed to Benjamin Disraeli.

The quotation may well apply to some of the figures adduced by authorities wanting to close down railways and withdraw services but figures can also represent factual data, and for the statistically minded I offer the following.

Longest Journey by Rail (Ref. Chapter 17)

Note: The following shows the shortest route between the two places furthest apart by rail in the world, where the journey can be made without using any other form of transport except walking between platforms or between stations conveniently close together and able to be covered by no more than about 10 minutes walk. Ferry connections are not counted as rail connections unless they are genuine train ferries in which passengers can remain on the train, e.g. between Puttgarden and Rødby would be counted as a rail connection, whereas between Lisboa Santa Apolónia and Lisboa Barriero would not.

The timetable is given according to information available in October 1994 from *Thomas Cook European and Overseas Timetables* except for some minor local services which are taken from national timetables and may not be quite so up-to-date.

TRAINCATCHER

Timetable for the World's Longest Rail Journey (1994)

In this table, times are depicted by a five figure notation using international 24-hour clock and days of the week shown as 1 = Monday to 7 = Sunday, thus: 1:22.15 = 10.15 p.m on a Monday. A change of train is needed at all places shown

Station	km	Day	Time	Remarks
Ho Chi Minh City	0	0	5:19.40	See footnote
Hanoi arr	1726	2	7:12.10	
Hanoi dep		2	7.23.00	May not run –
Liuzhu arr	2374	3	1:23.07	Check Cook's TT
Liuzhu dep		4	2:04.17	
Guiyang arr	2981	4	2:18.31	
Guiyang dep		4	2:20.23	
Chongqing arr	3444	5	3:07.35	
Chongqing dep		5	3:07.48	
Baoji arr	4617	6	4:11.20	
Baoji dep		6	4:11.53	
Ürümqi arr	6012	8	6:18.43	
Ürümqi dep		8	6:23.00	*Genghis Khan*
Aktogay arr	7067	9	7:18.44	
Aktogay dep		9	7:23.19	
Barnaul arr	7960	10	1:18.20	
Barnaul dep		10	1:22.04	
Karasuk arr	8405	11	2:09.40	
Karasuk dep		11	2:12.56	
Tatarsk arr	8625	11	2:19.40	
Tatarsk dep		11	2:21.40	
Omsk arr	8794	12	3:00.03	
Omsk dep		12	3:01.06	
Yekaterinburg arr	9692	12	3:14.44	
Yekaterinburg dep		13	4:04.18	

APPENDICES

Moskva (Kaz) a.	11360	14	5:10.25	via Kazan
d.			***	Metro – frequent
Moskva (Smol) a.	11364		***	service
Moskva (Smol) d.		14	5:13.10	*Moskva Express*
Terespol arr	12471	15	6:06.50	
Terespol dep		15	6:08.00	
Luckow arr	12560	15	6:09.31	
Luckow dep		15	6:10.40	
Pilawa arr	12620	15	6:11.48	
Pilawa dep		15	6:12.43	
Skierneiwiçe arr	12720	15	6:14.36	
Skierneiwiçe dep		15	6:15.38	
Kutno arr	12787	15	6:16.45	
Kutno dep		15	6:18.12	*Varsovia* EC 40
Frankfurt (Oder)	13145	15	6:22.04	
Frankfurt dep		16	7:04.40	
Grunow arr	13169	16	7:05.24	
Grunow dep		16	7:05.53	
Beeskow arr	13178	16	7:06.09	
Beeskow dep		16	7:06.59	
Luckau arr	13234	16	7:08.36	
Luckau dep		16	7:10.07	
Falkenburg arr	13291	16	7:12.39	
Falkenburg dep		16	7:12.59	D 2754
Leipzig arr	13361	16	7:13.51	
Leipzig dep		16	7:14.04	IC 650
Frankfurt (Main)	13739	16	7:18.35	
Frankfurt dep		16	7:18.51	*Loreley* IC 726
Mainz arr	13777	16	7:19.24	
Mainz dep		16	7:19.35	train 3436
Saarbrücken arr	13943	–16	7:21.55	
Saarbrücken dep		17	1:06.38	
Metz arr	14025	17	1:07.38	

431

Metz dep		17	1:07.45	
Nancy arr	14080	17	1:08.24	
Nancy dep		17	1:08.56	train 1704
Toul arr	14113	17	1:09.15	
Toul dep		17	1:13.28	
Dijon arr	14309	17	1:15.23	
Dijon dep		17	1:16.58	
Moulins arr	14507	17	1:19.26	
Moulins dep		17	1:19.32	train 59330
Clermont Ferrand	14613	17	1:20.46	
Clermont Ferr. d.		18	2:06.57	
Périgueux arr	14884	18	2:11.21	
Périgueux dep		18	2:11.27	
Bordeaux arr	15020	18	2:12.43	
Bordeaux dep		18	2:12.59	TGV
Irun arr	15293	18	2:15.15	
Irun dep		18	2:22.00	*Sud Express*
Entroncamento a.	16217	19	3:11.57	
Entroncamento d.		19	3:12.04	IR 822
Setil arr	16267	19	3:13.32	
Setil dep		19	3:16.06	
Vendas Novas arr	16336	19	3:17.34	
Vendas Novas dep		20	4:00.42	Estimated time
Vila Real de SA	16677	20	4:07.44	

Note: An alternative by the same route is by leaving Ho Chi Minh City at 19.00 on Saturday, arriving Hanoi Monday 06.45, departing 23.00, losing a day at Ürümqi, arriving 7:18.43, departing 1:23.00, thus taking 21 days for the whole trip.

APPENDICES

Timetable for Fastest Route between the Same Places

Ho Chi Minh City	0	0	5:19.40	
Hanoi arr	1726	2	7:12.10	
Hanoi dep		2	7:23.00	May not run –
Beijing arr	4686	4	2:09.14	check Cook's TT
Beijing dep		5	3:07.40	Train 3
Moskva Yaroslav.	13687	10	1:17.25	
dep			***	Metro – frequent
Moskva (Smol) a.	13691		***	service
Moskva (Smol) d.		10	1:20.15	*Ost-West Express*
Aachen arr	16253	12	3:10.55	
Aachen dep		12	3:14.10	EC38 *Jacques Brel*
Paris Nord arr	16744	12	3:18.59	
dep			***	Metro – frequent
Notre Dame dep	16749		***	services
Paris Austerlitz	16753		***	
Paris Auster. dep		12	3:22.24	
Irun arr	17571	13	4:07.17	
Irun dep		13	4:08.15	IC 202
Madrid Chamartin	18210	13	4:14.58	
Madrid Cham. dep		13	4:23.20	*Lusitania Exp*
Entroncamento a.	18781	14	5:07.18	
Entroncamento d.		14	5:07.51	
Setil arr	18831	14	5:08.30	
Setil dep		14	5:12.45	
Vendas Novas arr	18900	14	5:14.12	
Vendas Novas dep		14	5:16.51	Estimated time
Beja arr	18997	14	5:18.12	
Beja dep		14	5:20.20	Estimated time
Funchiera arr	19061	14	5:21.50	
Funchiera dep		14	5:22.09	IR 873
Vila Real de SA	19241	15	6:01.06	

433

TRAINCATCHER

Statistical comparison of above journeys (facts not lies!)

Comparison item	Route: Shortest	Quickest
Rail distance (nearest km)	16677	19241
Total time in hours⊕	476.07	349.43
Travel time in hours*	363.42	288.51
Waiting time in hours	112.55	60.92
Number of train changes	40	15
Overall journey speed (km/h)	35.0	55.0
Mean train speed (km/h)	45.9	66.7
Longest wait for connection (hours)	13.57	22.43
Shortest connection (minutes)	6	19

Assuming of course the trains run on time!
⊕ allowing for 8 hour time difference
* including intermediate stops but not waiting time for connections. Metro journeys are nominally counted as two minutes travel time for each kilometre which is deducted from connection time where it occurs.

No doubt some zealous rail buff will question whether the selected places are in fact the furthest apart by rail by the shortest route. The author would welcome any correspondence. To avoid unnecessary checking, here are some of the runners up, all from Ho Chi Minh City via the 'shortest route' given above except as indicated below.

Lagos, Portugal	16627	Route as above to Tunes
Algeciras, Spain	16335	via Belfort & Barcelona
Lisboa S.A., Portugal	16324	Route as above to Setil
Cadiz, Spain	16316	via Belfort & Barcelona
Huelva, Spain	16273	via Belfort & Barcelona
Pontecesures, Spain	16252	via Medina

APPENDICES

Porto Campanha, Portugal	16238	Route as above to Guarda
Almeria, Spain	16156	via Belfort & Barcelona
La Corunna, Spain	16155	via FEVE Irun to Ferrol
Narvik, Norway	16002	via Berlin, Stockholm
Bodø, Norway	15727	via Berlin, Oslo
Thurso, Scotland	approx 15580	Köln, Fréthun, Motherwell
Murmansk, Russia	12992	Kirov, Vologda, Volchov
Kolari, Lapland	12988	Kirov, Vologda, Kuopio
Vorkuta, Russia	12013	Kirov, Kotlas
Archangelsk, Russia	11828	Kirov, Vologda

Appendix II

The Railway Roundabout

The model, at a scale of 1:100 was constructed of Peco N gauge rail track and operated electrically, mainly using Lima scale model trains. The original idea of having miniature car bodies on rail wheelbases was abandoned to avoid the cost of special manufacture.

The layout design was the reverse tangent entry type, which is the optimum layout for a roundabout, facilitating rapid exit and slower entry.

Each of the four 'highway entries' was of three lane width, represented by three parallel rail tracks. On the roundabout, weaving between lanes was achieved by the points system, to simulate the paths which should be followed by motor vehicles.

The three exit lanes, paralleling the entries, disappeared into tunnels to re-emerge at another entry after three successive right angle turns.

With smart control work, it was possible to have twelve different 'trains' negotiating the central roundabout feature at the one time, e.g. one from north to east on the north side, one north to south just leaving the 'weaving section' on the east, and one north to west just entering on the north entry curve, and similarly for each other entry.

Copyright Colin Taylor.

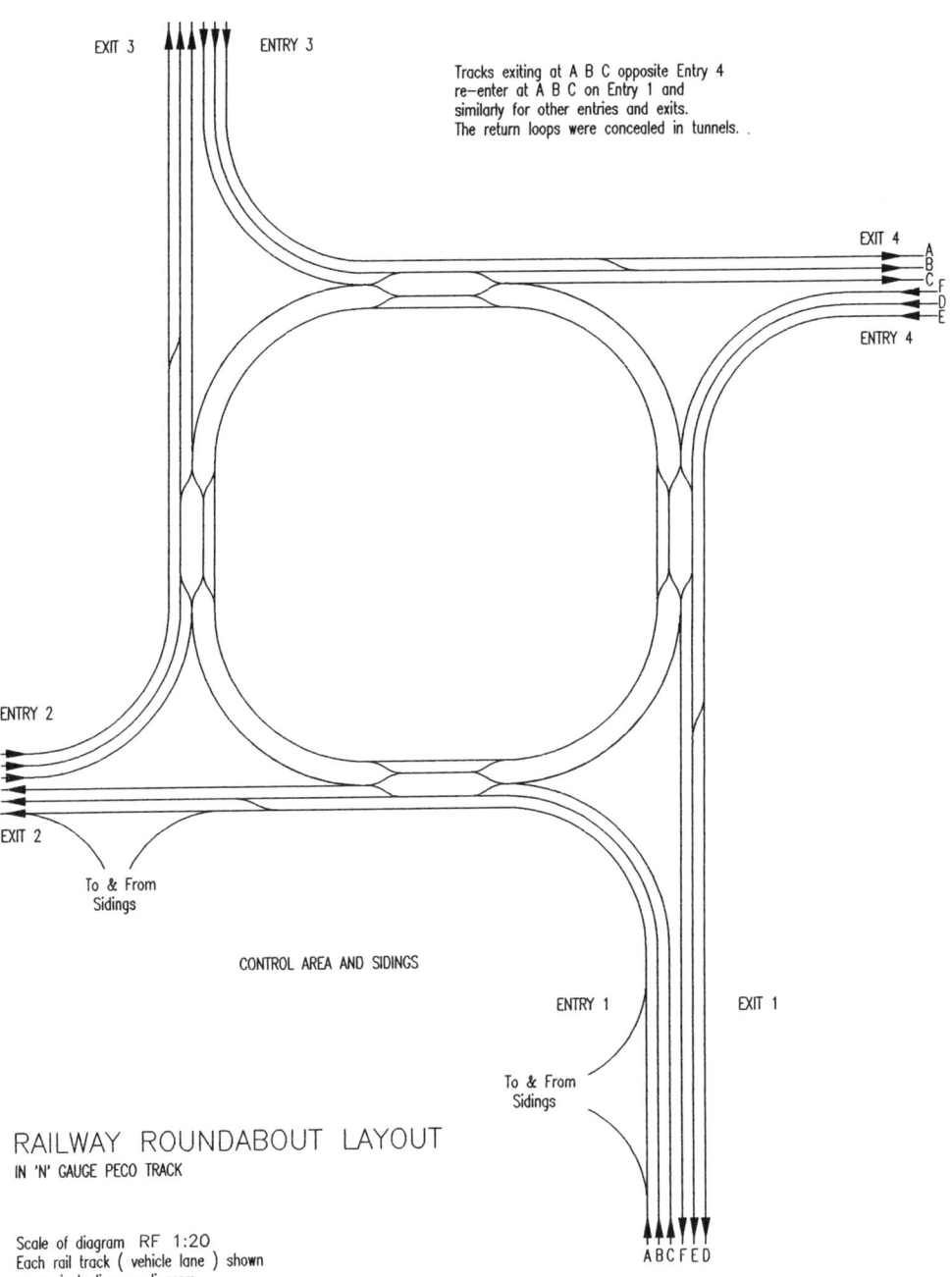

Maps

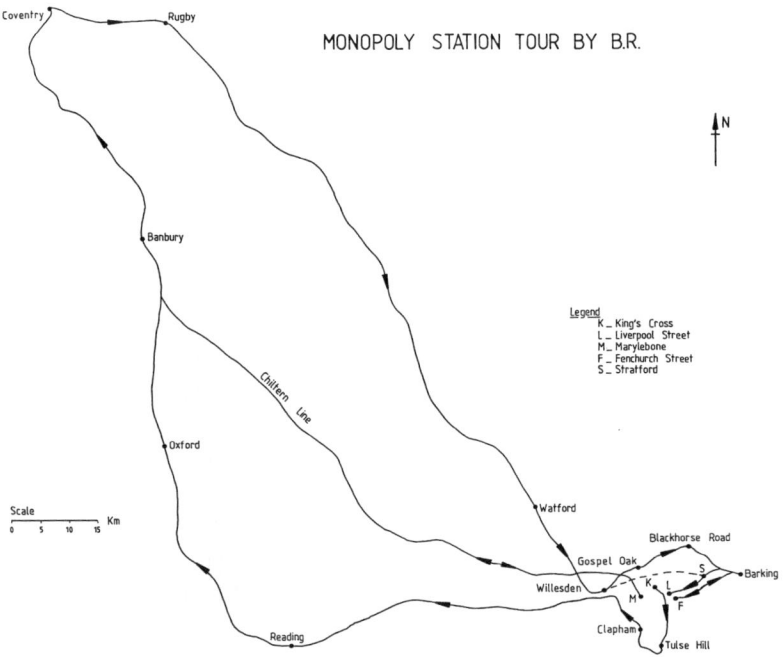

MAPS

MONOPOLY STATION TOUR
LONDON AREA ENLARGEMENT

TRAINCATCHER

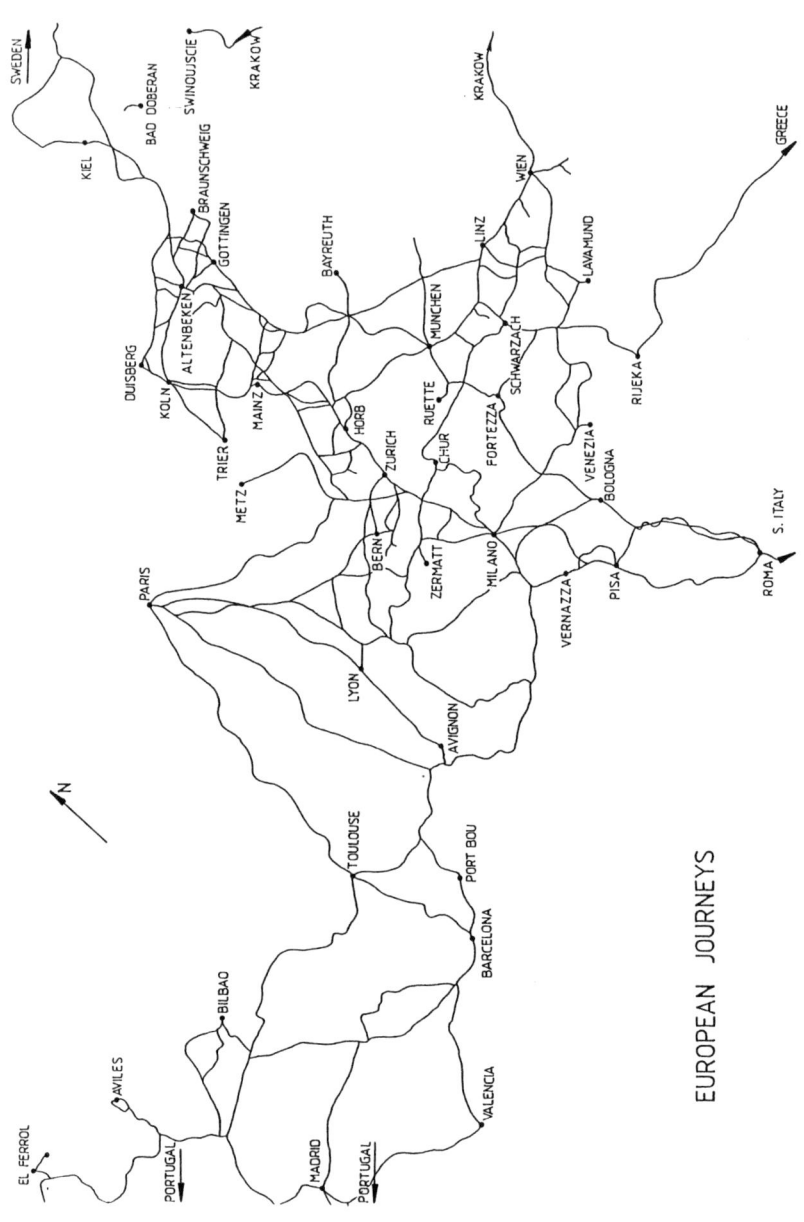

EUROPEAN JOURNEYS

MAPS

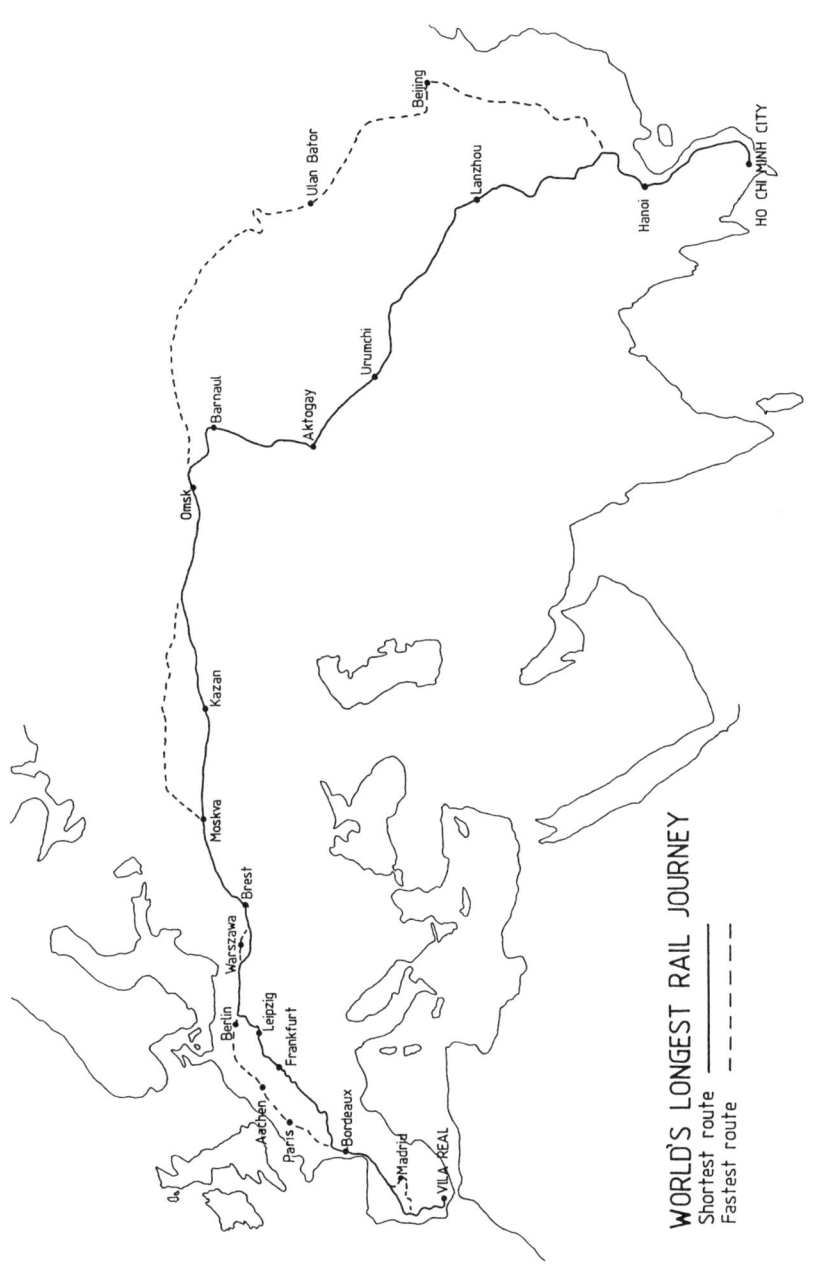

TRAINCATCHER

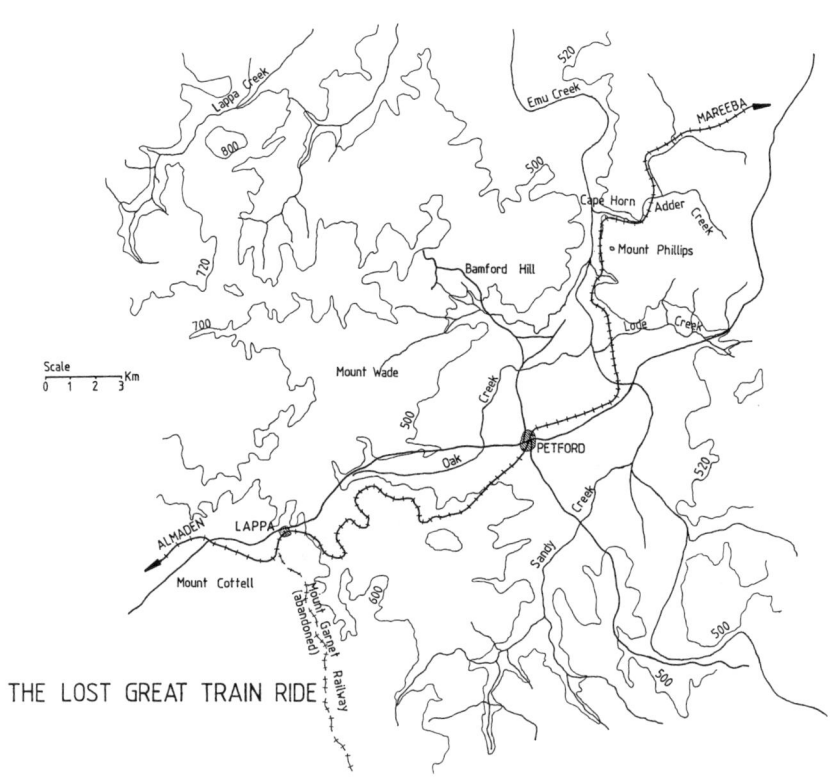

THE LOST GREAT TRAIN RIDE

Bibliography

As well as various railway public and working timetables, fare lists, leaflets and menus, the following books have been particularly useful. Many others have been consulted for small items of information or quotations and these are referred to in the text.

1929 Handy Rail Atlas of the United States (Kalmbach Publishing)
Bartholomew's Reference Atlas of Greater London 1948
British Railways Pre-Grouping Atlas and Gazetteer (Ian Allen)
Encyclopedia Brittanica
Encyclopedia of Railways (Ed. O.S. Nock, Octopus Books)
Guinness Book of Rail Facts and Feats
Guinness Book of Records
Mile by Mile (Ed. David Maxey, Peter Watts Publishing)
Rail Atlas of Great Britain and Ireland 4th Edn (S.K. Baker, Oxford Publishing
Railway Directory (Railway Gazette 1993 Yearbook)
Railway Electrification in Australia and New Zealand (G.B. Churchman, IPL Books, 1995)
Railways in Ireland 1834-1984 (Doyle & Hirsh, Signal Press, Dublin)
Railway Wonders of the World (Ed. Talbot, Cassell & Co. circa 1912
Titled Trains of Great Britain 6th Edn (Cecil J. Allen, Ian Allen)

Various dictionaries, especially the *Macquarie Dictionary*, the *Compact Oxford English Dictionary* and the *Concise Oxford Dictionary of Quotations*

Various issues of the journals *Railway Gazette International*, *Railway Magazine*, and *Modern Railways*.

Thomas Cook Rail Maps: Europe; Britain and Ireland; World Transportation Maps of U.S. Federal Railroad Administration.

Acknowledgements

I am indebted to the following for assistance during my travels and research related to this book: Mario Basile, Ken Crawford, Trevor Dundas, John Gransden, Mike Kent, Heatherbell Lambert, John Kerr, Peter King, Tom McRae, John Price, Robin Read, Paul Reynolds, Ralf Rossberg, Spencer Routh, Peter Semmens, Grace Smith, Phillip Smith, Roger Stanton, John P.A.Taylor and Jean-Marie Willigens.

Ewen Anderson of Thomas Cook, Brisbane, provided biographical details of Thomas Cook and the history of his first rail excursion.

The following provided information and/or travel assistance: Thomas Cook Timetable Publishing Office of Peterborough, British Rail, Iarnrod Eireann (then Coras Iompair Eirann), Deutsche Bundesbahn (German Federal Railways), Railways of the Jungfrau, Österreichische Bundesbahn (Austrian Federal Railways) especially Gerold Koherr, Statens Järnvägar (Swedish State Railways), FEVE, Lufthansa, Ravenglass & Eskdale Railway, British Columbia Rail, Amtrak, New Zealand Railways, Australian National especially John Morley, Queensland Rail especially Chief Executive Vince O'Rourke, State Rail Authority of NSW, Victorian Transport and Westrail.

Personal thanks are due to Austin Briggs who prepared the maps and to Lesley Briggs who checked the text for clarity and continuity and to ensure that extreme examples of sexist or politically incorrect language were avoided, lest some minority or disadvantaged (sorry, 'alternatively advantaged') group (like Poms, Poles, politicians, policemen) or persons of alternative sexual preference might conceivably be offended.

Also, special thanks are due to Janet, Nola, Jackie, Mira, Jean, Andrea, Kelli, Keryn, Merlene, Debbie, Roseanne, Suzanne, Kim, Deirdre, and the many other hostesses and buffet car attendants who have made my travels so pleasurable. So as not to be branded as sexist and have the book condemned by the political correctness mob I will also thank specifically by name, Charlie, Danny, Manuel, Greg, Don, Bob, Rick, Reg, Frank, Keith, 'Aspro' Lyons, and a host of other great blokes whose names are buried in my notes but would be restored to instant recognition at our next meeting.

Finally, without the indulgence of my wife and family, and the encouragement and help of Geoff Churchman of IPL Publishing, this record of my misdeeds would not have seen the light of day.

Index to Named Trains

AVE	35, 151	Central West XPT	136
Aberdonian	55, 145	Chillagoe Mixed	400-404, 406
Akropolis Express	19	Chopin	119, 160, 321
Al Andalus	152	City of New Orleans	84
Albury Express	126, 231	Cleveland Executive	119, 227
Alfred Nobel	160, 327	Coastal Pacific Express	361
Alice	see The Alice	Cooma Mail	146
Alpensee Express	157	Cork Express	181, 189
Andreas Hofer	160	Cornish Riviera	73, 128
Ann Rutledge	4, 403	Dachstein	165
Arlberg Express	31	Deep Duffryn Diddler	157
Aurora	161	Denver Zephyr	156
(see also Southern Aurora)		Desert Wind	352
Ausseerland	315	Direct Orient Express	144, 318
Australind	306-307	Dirranbandi Passenger	262
Ayrshire Trader	147	Down Limited	90, 92
Ballyhooley Express	296	E 740 (ÖBB)	313-314
Beethoven	160	ETR 450	156, 194, 232, 343
Beograd Express	27		
Bernina Express	342	Eastern Limited	90, 91
Blauer Enzian	165	Eastliner	236
Blue Train	150, 152, 232, 235	Endeavour (NZ)	228
		Etheridge (loco)	398
Bluebird	240	Euro-City	150
Brighton Belle	161	Eurostar	82, 210
Brisbane Express	133, 261	Fair Maid	55, 160
Brisbane Limited	121, 131-142, 162, 165, 390-391, 424	Fish and Chips	see The Fish & The Chips
		Flèche d'Or	160
Brisbane XPT	266, 385, 393	Flying Flea	272-276
California Zephyr	161, 351-352	Flying Scotsman (loco)	143, 162
Canberra Monaro Express	132-134	Flying Scotsman (train)	55, 143-144, 212, 217
Capitals United Express	130		
Capodimente	345	Forsayth Mixed (7A90)	120, 149, 397-427
Capricornian	150, 283		
Cariboo	149, 354-355	Franz Schubert	160
Carmelit	158	Freccia del Sud	160
Catalan Talgo	36, 212	Freccia della Laguna	215
Centenary Express	157	Gasteinertal	157
Central West Express	121	Gatwick Express	194

445

Genghis Khan	430	Jacques Brel	433
Ghan	113, 143-144,	Jimmy Shand (loco)	206
	161, 166-168,	Jos Limited	90-91
	211, 223, 271,	Jules Verne	160
	272, 297, 347	Kaduna Junction Limited	90-91
Glacier Express	149, 153, 335	Kano Limited	90, 91, 93
Glamorgan Growler	157	Karnten Express	165
Gold Coast Motorail Exp.	165, 390	Kingston Flyer	356
Golden Arrow	156, 160	Knock Special	187
Gondoliere	213	Koskiusko Express	146
Grafton Express	121	Kuranda Tourist Train	421
Gulflander	405, 412,	L'Arbalete	38, 152
	414, 427	Laguna Express	215
Gustave Eiffel	160	Leschenault Lady	308
Gutenberg	160	Ligure	156
Hans Holbein	160	Locomotion No. 1 (loco)	54
Heart of Midlothian	55-56, 144,	Loreley	431
	158, 160	Lufthansa Airport Exp.	149, 154, 231,
Hebridean	150		332
Heron	see The Heron	Lusitania Express	433
Highland Chieftain	145	Manchester Pullman	214-215
Hohensalzburg	315	Melbourne Express	257, 378
Holiday Coast XPT	141, 382, 385	Mid North Coast XPT	134, 165
Holland Italy Express	31	Midlander	278-281
ICE (DB InterCity Exp.)	151, 154, 156,	Mistral	160
	281	Molli	104, 327-328
Indian Pacific	64, 111, 114,	Moskva Express	431
	132, 141, 161,	Mount Gambier Bluebird	257
	223-227, 240-	Mozart	160
	253, 265-267,	Mule	see The Mule
	271, 369, 394	Mulgrave Rambler	296, 417
Inlander	278, 283,	Murwillumbah XPT	98, 385,
	412-413		390-393
InterCity (BR)	107, 116, 119,	Newcastle Express (NSW)	121, 165
	143, 192-194,	Night Aberdonian	145
	209, 215, 366,	Night Ferry	73
	381-382	North Briton	55, 146
InterCity (other rlwys)	107, 120, 230,	North Coast Daylight Express	136, 165
	259-260, 379	North Coast Overnight Express	136
Intercapital Daylight	121, 137, 139,	North Mail	137
	369, 378, 392	North Yorks Pullman	150, 152
Inter-Colonial Express	257	Northerner	228-229, 357
InterRegio (DB)	388	Number 1 Parcels	54
Irish Mail	144, 146, 193	Olympic Spirit	122

INDEX TO NAMED TRAINS

Oresundspilen	326	Royal Scot	156
Orient Express	143, 150-152, 223	Royal Scotsman	152
		Ruta de la Plata	38-39
Ost-West Express	311, 433	Savannahlander	424
Otscherland	161	Scottish Pullman	195
Otto Lilienthal	160	Settebello	36, 150, 156, 343
Overland	113, 121, 132, 161, 166, 257, 260	Sevilla Express	117
		Shinkansen	70, 156
Pacific International	354	Silver City Comet	240-241, 377, 396
Paddy	see The Paddy		
Panoramic Express	231, 335	Silver City Limited	240
Pickering Pullman	152	Silver Fern	228, 357, 370, 395
Pioneer	see The Pioneer		
Plateau Limited	90	Silver Jubilee	147
Pongau	161, 333	Silver Meteor	168
Puffing Billy (Vic)	104, 160	Silver Star	356
Pustertal	161, 221, 338	Sir Nigel Gresley (loco)	160
Queen of Scots	55, 152	Skunk	160
Queenslander	102, 111, 115, 149, 165-166, 212, 222-223, 229-232, 264, 286, 288, 296, 297, 347, 405, 406, 420	Skye train	150
		South Mail	378
		South XPT	378
		Southern Aurora	121, 129, 131, 132, 141, 156, 161-164, 232, 378
Ratty	159	Southerner	228, 361
Red Dragon	130	South West Chief	147, 224-225, 349, 352
Rembrandt	160		
Rheingold	13-14, 36, 150, 156	Southwest Limited	147
		Special Scotch Express	144
River Cities	83	Spirit of Capricorn	230, 248, 281
Riverina Express	132-133	Spirit of Progress	106, 121, 146, 162-163, 378
Riverina XPT	122, 165, 372, 379		
		Spirit of the Outback	279
Riviera Express	156	Spirit of the Tropics	113, 165
Roma Express	34, 161	Stachus	314
Rocket (loco)	321	State House	84
Romulus	16, 27, 119	Steiermark Express	165
Rossia	150, 243, 267	St Mungo	160
Royal Duchy	130	Sud Express	432
Royal Highlander	18, 145, 150, 203	Sunlander	121, 150, 212, 233, 264, 286-294, 412, 420
Royal Hudson	354		

TRAINCATCHER

Sunshine Daylight Rail Experience (or Sunshine Daylight Rail Tour)	288, 290	Up Limited	90
		Val Pusteria	338
		Vinelander	230
Sunshine Express	286	Walter Gropius	160
Super Chief	147	Welsh Collieries Rambler	158
Sussex Scot	76	Welshman	147
Sydney Express	378	West Wind	83
Sydney Limited	146	Westlander	223, 272-275, 277-278
TGV	43, 151, 154, 156, 220, 280, 281, 340	Westliner	236
		Whitsunday Queenslander	297
Tablelands Xplorer	121, 266	Wiener Walzer	340
Talgo	37, 43, 117, 118, 222	Wild Beaudesert Train	169
		Wulfenia	320
Talisman	160	X2000	155-156, 220, 232
Tauern Express	165, 333		
Tea and Sugar	248-251, 270-272	XPT	106, 121-123, 137-139, 141, 142, 224, 240, 266, 366-367, 375, 378, 381-386, 389-394, 424
Tees-Thames	56-57, 73		
Tejo	222, 347		
Tenterfield Mail	263		
Texas Eagle	83-84, 256, 350		
Thangool Rocket	169-175	Yaraka Mixed	281-282
The Alice	212, 270, 297	Y Cwmro	147
The Chips	146	Yenesei	161
The Fish	147	Yorkshire Pullman	161
The Ghan	see Ghan	Yorkshire Ranger	157
The Heron	146	Zephyr	156, 161, 240, 352
The Mule	84		
The Overland	see Overland		
The Paddy	256		
The Pioneer	351-353		
Train 7A90 (Qld)	see Forsayth Mixed		
Train Bleu	150		
Trans Australian	235, 237-238, 253, 270		
Trans Europ Express	13, 30, 38, 150, 343		
Trans Siberian Express	see Rossia		
Transalpin	165		
Transcantabrico	152		
TranzAlpine Express	360		